THE PIONEER HISTORIES
EDITED BY V. T. HARLOW, M.A., AND J. A. WILLIAMSON, D.LIT.

THE EXPLORERS OF NORTH AMERICA
1492–1806

THE PIONEER HISTORIES

Edited by V. T. Harlow, M.A., & J. A. Williamson, D.Lit.

First Titles

THE EUROPEAN NATIONS IN THE WEST INDIES

ARTHUR PERCIVAL NEWTON, D.LIT.

Rhodes Professor of Imperial History, University of London

ENGLAND'S QUEST OF EASTERN TRADE

SIR WILLIAM FOSTER, C.I.E.

Formerly Historiographer to the India Office

THE PORTUGUESE PIONEERS

EDGAR PRESTAGE, D.LITT.

Camoens Professor of Portuguese Language and History in the University of London

THE EXPLORERS OF NORTH AMERICA

J. BARTLET BREBNER, M.A., PH.D.

Assistant Professor, Department of History, Columbia University

In Preparation

THE GREAT TREK

ERIC A. WALKER, M.A.

Professor of History, University of Cape Town

THE EXPLORATION OF THE PACIFIC

J. C. BEAGLEHOLE, PH.D.

THE SPANISH CONQUISTADORES

F. A. KIRKPATRICK, M.A.

Reader in Spanish in the University of Cambridge

EDITORS' PREFACE
TO THE SERIES

THE Pioneer Histories are intended to provide broad surveys of the great migrations of European peoples—for purposes of trade, conquest and settlement—into the non-European continents. They aim at describing a racial expansion which has created the complex world of to-day, so nationalistic in its instincts, so internationalised in its relationships.

International affairs now claim the attention of every intelligent citizen, and problems of world-wide extent affect the security and livelihood of us all. He who would grasp their meaning and form sound judgements must look into the past for the foundations of the present, and, abandoning a local for a universal perspective, must take for his study the history of a world invaded by European ideas. It was less so in the days before the Great War. Then the emphasis was upon Europe itself: upon such questions as that of France's eastern frontier inherited from Richelieu and Louis XIV, the militarism of Germany derived from Frederick the Great, and the Balkan entanglement which originated with the medieval migrations of Slavonic peoples and with the Turkish conquests of the fourteenth century. Now the prospect is wider, for these ancient domestic difficulties in modern form cannot properly be estimated except by correlation with the problems of a Europeanised outer world.

The Orient is in ferment and Asiatic difficulties compel the attention of Geneva because long ago the Portuguese, followed by the Dutch and the English, rounded the Cape and came to India. For the same reason, Africa is no longer an unknown continent but a vast area in which civilised enterprise demands direction and control. Knowledge of the process by which North America was discovered and gradually filled with Europeans is the necessary basis for an understanding of the modern reactions upon each other of the new continent and the old. In South America the same process is to be seen at work, though incomplete while Nature is yet unsubdued. Similarly, it may be appreciated how the search for an unknown but credited continent lying about the South Pole has helped to shift the centre of gravity to the Pacific, and has created a white Australasia. The present series will show how the permanent factors in these great regions first presented themselves to European minds and how achievements were then effected which have governed all subsequent relationships.

But if the subject has this interest for students of affairs, it has also its appeal to those who dwell most on individual character, courage and ingenuity. Movements are made by men, and in these stories of European expansion are to be met men worth knowing, whose deeds carry inspiration for this generation as for all others.

Each volume takes for its subject the history of an important movement and, while related to others in the series, is thus complete in itself. The authors whose co-operation we have been fortunate to secure have all had experience of research in the original evidence pertaining to their subjects, and in their contributions to this series they give the results of that research in narratives which should appeal to the general reader. Each book is designed to embody the most recent information available, and some will be found to deal with subjects of which no full treatment has hitherto been accessible in English.

V. T. HARLOW
J. A. WILLIAMSON

CONTENTS

CONTENTS

MAPS

FOREWORD

THE editors of The Pioneer Histories have allowed me to try to draw together as a related whole the explorations which first revealed the general character of the North American continent. Hitherto the subject has usually been treated regionally or nationally, with some loss of intelligibility as a consequence. I hope that scholars who may happen to read this book will feel that the greater unity of a continental design which emerges from examining together Spanish, French, Dutch, English, American, Canadian and Russian explorations justifies its publication, for it has few other claims to originality. Throughout, I have been interested chiefly in shewing why men explored, where and when they went, and who promoted and supported the expeditions.

For the general reader, I have tried to write an introduction to some of the most interesting men in history. Our generation has been too hospitable to the fictionalised narratives of supposed pioneer adventurers. I venture to put forward what seems to me something better, by providing, as liberally as my space will allow, samples from the narratives of genuine pioneers and guidance to where the complete narratives can be obtained. Without wishing to be invidious, I suggest that Bernal Díaz and Samuel Hearne, for instance, have better stories to tell than all but the most remarkable explorers of recent times. I have tried to make the principal explorers tell their own stories, and all the quotations in my text are from original narratives contemporary with the events they describe.

The limitations of this series prevent the publication of a bibliographical guide to the enormous literature which has grown up around the subject. Fortunately most of the published narratives listed at the end of each of the following chapters are furnished with references to interpretative books. There are other bibliographical guides, notably F. J. Turner and F. Merk, *List of References on the History of the West* (Cambridge, Mass., 1922), and *The Review of Historical Publications relating to Canada* (Toronto, 1896–1919), continued since 1920 as part of *The Canadian Historical Review* (Toronto). In the cases of particular regions, it will be found that special reviews (*e.g.*, *The Mississippi Valley Historical Review*), or the publications of local learned societies will usually serve as a guide to the most recent scholarship.

This book could not have been written if scores of scholars had not already studied and written much on various parts of its subject. I have been permitted to indicate in footnotes the principal controversies still open among them. My own conclusions have been arrived at ultimately from the source materials which had led me to the belief that there was some unity in the pattern of North American exploration. I owe much to the great resources of my own university's library, and I enjoyed the hospitality of the Baker Library of Dartmouth College during the summer of 1931. The Public Archives of Canada kindly provided me with photographic copies of some unpublished materials. Dr. Williamson's scholarship, generously given, has helped me to fill some gaps and to avert errors and misinterpretations, and Mr. Harlow has eliminated nearly all the difficulties of publishing across the Atlantic. My colleague, Mr. Samuel McKee, Jr., has extended to me his own special knowledge, as he read and commented on my manuscript. My wife has not only had patience with my long preoccupation, but has helped greatly by suggestions for greater clarity. Finally, I wish to mention the names of some Columbia College students with whom I found it enlightening to work over part of the explorations. They are Messrs. E. I. L. Baker, R. L. Currie, J. M. Eagan, N. I. Laidhold, G. Lamprinos and J. N. Webb.

J. B. B.

Seth Low Library, Columbia University,
    New York, *March* 1933

THE EXPLORERS OF NORTH AMERICA

1492–1806

CHAPTER I

COLUMBUS AND THE LURES TO THE CONTINENT

(Map No. 1, page 104)

I'll have them fly to India for gold,
Ransack the ocean for orient pearl,
And search all corners of the new-found world
For pleasant fruits and princely delicates
.   .   .   .   .

From Venice shall they drag huge argosies,
And from America the golden fleece
That yearly stuffs old Philip's treasury.

MARLOWE: FAUSTUS. c. 1588

UNLESS mankind is to embark some day on inter-planetary exploration, there can never again be a geographical adventure like the discovery and explora-tion of the Americas. Until that work began, men had thought of their Earth as being a single land mass com-posed of Europe, Africa and Asia, set in a circum-ambient ocean. Now they discovered that west of the western and east of the eastern limits there lay two connected continents which stretched unbroken from an arctic block of land and ice to what seemed to be a mere storm-wracked narrow channel penetrating a similar barrier in the antarctic. It took them almost 300 years to plot the coastal outlines, and the arctic shores had to wait still longer. There were islands which for decades were thought to be mainland and

3

mainland which might turn out to be island. Until the middle years of the eighteenth century there seemed to be a chance that the whole might be an appendage of Asia. For two hundred years men tried to find a sea-passage through the Americas or round them to the north. Geographers were so sure that it was there that they gave it a name, the Strait of Anian.

We look at a neat modern map of the Americas and draw lines to shew where men coasted their shores or penetrated the interior. Our imaginations would serve us better, would enable us to apprehend the outlook of the discoverers and early geographers, if we started with a map which left empty the space between the fairly familiar eastern shores of the Atlantic and the almost entirely imaginary western shores of the Pacific. Then we might draw in, bit by bit, as the true slowly emerged from masses of error, first the shore lines of the Carib-bean islands, then fragments of the continental coastline south and west and north of the West Indies, and finally, from Cape Horn and from Panamá, the Pacific coast up to the point where the most resolute searchers were turned back by arctic ice. If we shared the hopes of the ocean explorers, each gap in the coastline on either Atlantic or Pacific might mean an entry into the Strait of Anian until it was explored, and even after hopes of a sea-passage had faded, we might still believe that North America had an inland sea with rivers running from it to both coasts.

If the known emerged from the unknown slowly and in fragments for the navigators, the process was just as slow and fragmentary for those on land. It was not until the last half of the eighteenth century that Spanish, English and Russian mariners completed their probing of the Pacific fiords from Panamá to the Arctic Ocean.

Until that time, what land pioneer entering from the Atlantic could be blamed for dreaming that a lucky, bold thrust might take him to a swift river down whose currents he might float to the Pacific? He did not even know how far it was from the Atlantic. As a matter of fact, the inland explorers first burst through the mountains to the northern Pacific at almost the same moment as the coastal survey was completed. That 'dead heat' occurred 300 years after Columbus reached the Antilles.

The race had begun for Europe on 11 October 1492, when Columbus' company saw lights on one of the Bahamas. If others from Europe and Asia had been to America before, they had failed to incorporate the fact in the main body of European geographical knowledge. The Iceland, Greenland, Markland and Vinland of the Norsemen and the fishermen were not associated in men's minds with the 'Indian' archipelago which Columbus and his studious companion and navigator, Martín Alonso Pinzón, thought they had reached. The north, men understood, held volcanoes, Judas on his annual day's holiday near the mouths of Hell, icebergs, and implacably hostile natives called Skraellings. The soft islands of the Caribbean were a far cry from this, and their gentle inhabitants seemed appropriate dwellers for the Spice Islands of the East. 'Always the land was of the same beauty,' wrote Columbus, 'and the fields very green and full of an infinity of fruits, as red as scarlet, and everywhere there was the perfume of flowers and the singing of birds, very sweet.' Even the pigeons 'had their crops full of flowers which smelt sweeter than orange blossom'.

Inasmuch as the whole train of North American events runs in a continuous line from the work of Columbus, it is unfortunate that modern scholarship and various kinds of animus and imagination have adorned him with all the confusions usually attendant on a myth. This has been possible because almost everything that he wrote or said has come down to us through partisan hands. As it now is, his birth, training, knowledge, ideas and motives have been the subjects for a huge library of controversial literature. Any account of him, therefore, even when based upon the best corroborated record of his life, must be to some degree a matter of historical taste and individual judgement. For our purposes a great deal of the controversy may be ignored. We are interested in seeing what Columbus and his associates did to initiate the exploration of North America, and while questions of his motives may be debatable, there is little room for doubt but that by his undisputed actions he set in motion a logical sequence of events which could only lead to penetration of the mainland.

Reading history backward, as we do, makes us quite likely to take it for granted that America was certain to be discovered about the end of the fifteenth century and, once discovered, would immediately be explored. Yet the Portuguese took three-quarters of the fifteenth century to work down and round Africa and explored it hardly at all, and England and France knew about North America for over a century before they found it worth while to colonise and explore it. Ships have always represented a large capital investment, and the manning and provisioning of them has always been costly. Kings and merchants have been willing occasionally to gamble on maritime expeditions to the unknown, but they have been slow to be convinced and unwilling to venture a second time when the first has not yielded

6

dividends. The crossing of the Atlantic near the equator was the longest continuous voyage yet known to man. Even after arrival at the other side, the sea which stretched from Trinidad to the mouth of the Río Grande was larger than the Mediterranean and had a confusing ocean barrier made up of the Florida peninsula and of hundreds of islands, two of which were 400 and 700 miles long respectively. The ocean was stormy and forbidding enough, but the Caribbean with its tornadoes and its coral reefs was worse. Its waters swarmed with the teredo-worm, which could riddle a ship's hull in a single voyage, and other marine life fouled the ships' unprotected bottoms so quickly as to impede navigation and to require frequent careening for cleansing. It is necessary, therefore, to see first how Columbus won his initial backing and then what made him and others return to the lands which he discovered.

In spite of having had to wait at least fifteen years to get financial support for his Atlantic venture, Columbus had so strong an inner conviction of his mission that he invited (and twice or more received) refusal of support because of the extravagance of his demands for authority and revenue in the event of success. Perhaps it was that stubborn fatalism which finally made the sovereigns of a united, Moor-purged Spain call him back after their earlier refusals and send him off on almost his own arrogant terms. He had deep in him the faith that, like some medieval knight chosen for a quest of high emprise, he was 'called' by God to explore the unknown Atlantic. 'God willed not that men should be able to sail over the whole world,' wrote Giovanni de' Marignolli, papal ambassador to Cathay in the fourteenth century, but in the expansive days of Portuguese African exploration, of the expulsion of Islam from the Iberian peninsula,

7

and of successes over the Moslems even in Africa, Columbus was assured. 'The Blessed Trinity moved your Highnesses to this enterprise of the Indies,' he wrote to Ferdinand and Isabella, 'and of His Infinite goodness has chosen me to proclaim it to you.'

His colossal, mystical self-confidence made him hard to deal with and a failure as administrator of the lands he discovered. It was confusingly mixed up with greed, lack of practical imagination and braggadocio. Yet it was so integral a part of him that he could believe on one occasion in his voyaging that God had led him to the New Heaven and New Earth of Revelation, and in his darkest hours he knew that God spoke to him in encouragement. On his third voyage, for instance, when faced by rebellion and injustice, he was about to give up, when 'our Lord comforted me miraculously, saying to me, "Take courage, be not dismayed nor fear, I will provide for all; the seven years, the term of gold, are not yet passed; and in this, as in the rest, I will redress thee" '. Again, on his fourth voyage, being sorely tried by illness, Indian attacks, terrific storms and almost. shattered ships, he fell into a trance and a voice spoke to him at length. 'O fool, and slow to believe and to serve thy God, the God of all! What did He do more for Moses, or for David His servant, than He has done for thee? . . . Fear not, but trust; all these tribulations are recorded on marble, and not without cause.' This was the language of the mystic in the mouth of one who was forced by circumstances to be a promoter and who wanted the status of a prince and the fame of a great discoverer and geographer. Indeed, in his letters one has the impression that he attached more importance to the writings of theologians than to those of the geographers. He himself was a good navigator and a devout Christian, but as a geographer was not remarkably impressive. Yet as a man under heavenly guidance he made a strong appeal to Catholic, crusading Spain.

It is by no means certain what he wanted or expected to find before he set out because he subsequently revealed himself to be a most complex person, and because our records of him were compiled after his success. If we grant him his sense of mission, and his desire for fame and a principality of his own under Spain, then the most probable of the other motives attributed to him was the discovery of the lands which many of his contemporaries believed lay out in the Atlantic beyond the comparatively recently discovered Azores and Canaries. There were many tales of shores seen and lost when storms drove men far to the West, and of objects and strange un-European bodies brought to Europe by western storms. The geographers had even named half-mythical islands and placed them on their maps of the Atlantic. There were also many ancient and medieval accounts of Asia, recorded by genuine travellers or by talented romancers like Sir John Mandeville. No one knew how much open sea lay between western Europe and eastern Asia, and no one knew for certain whether farthest East and nearest West consisted of continental Asia, the territory of the fabulously wealthy Grand Khan; or of Marco Polo's island of Cipangu (Japan) where palace roofs and windows were of gold; or of the thousands of Spice Islands reported to exist off the south-east coast of India beyond the Ganges.

These things Columbus sailed to find out. The fact that Ferdinand and Isabella so altered his final commission as to convey to him rule and rights only in *new* lands which he should discover and conquer, leads one to believe that they, if not he, half expected him to reach Cathay and the mighty empire of the Grand Khan. They also gave him a letter to that dignitary. There was talk of souls to win for Christ and there was no objection to territorial aggrandizement for a Spain recently so favoured by Providence, but unquestionably the discovery in 1492 of a short sea-route for the inexpensive transportation to Europe of Eastern goods and spices would be a glittering prize. There were too many middlemen on the route by the Levant, and Venice and Genoa, not Spain, controlled the Mediterranean and took the last profit. Besides, Europe was being drained of gold, and by all reports that coveted commodity was much more plentiful and much less valued in the East. Altogether, if Columbus was right and the Atlantic was not an insuperable barrier to reaching the East by sailing west, there were enough possible rewards to make it worth while to give him his chance. And even if Christopher, the bearer of Christ, went out purely as a missionary, none knew better than he that the good tidings of salvation could be carried only by men operating from an economically advantageous base. Look at the situation as you will, whatever Columbus discovered had to pay.

On his first voyage of 1492–93 he made his landfall in the Bahamas, turned south-west until he struck the northern coast of Cuba, and, on finding that it ran northwest, turned back and south to the north shore of Haiti, which he named Española. He thought Cuba to be either Cipangu or possibly the mainland of Asia, in spite of the natives' signs to the effect that it was an island; but he found no Asian ports swarming with commerce nor did his land parties with their samples of spices have any better luck. He shewed the natives some gold and they assured him that he would find quantities of it on an island to the south-east. Here we meet for the first time with a habit which narratives of explorers all over North America reveal to have been almost universal among the aboriginal peoples and one which had great consequences in exploration. However awed by the god-like strangers, and however avid of the strange and alluring goods which they possessed, the natives sooner or later were made apprehensive by their presence. There are some notable exceptions to this in the case of natives who aspired to be middlemen between the Europeans and as yet untouched tribes, but very often the embarrassed aborigines adopted the simple and to us transparent technique of finding out what the explorers wanted and telling them that it was farther on. The explorers, in their feverish anxiety to hear what they had come wanting to hear, were usually taken in. Columbus was no exception.

Owing to the temporary defection of Martín Pinzón with his ship and the wrecking of another, Columbus left a small group of his men on the north shore of Haiti and hurried for Spain in order to receive credit for his remarkable discovery. He spent the return journey in composing a prospectus for its exploitation made up of what he had actually seen, what he imagined he had seen, and what his backers wanted him to have seen.

The mere fact of having discovered lands indubitably new was a feat in itself and won for Columbus his title of 'admiral of the Ocean' and his office of viceroy and governor, but he knew that to profit or to fulfil his mission he must win further support. He therefore encouraged the belief that he had reached Cipangu and the Spice Islands and, if he could not report cities and ready wealth, he felt that he could promise almost everything else—amazingly fertile lands rich in natural resources, spices, cotton, mastic, gold, souls to save, and bodies to serve a Europe already awake to the possibilities of slave labour. Like a wise man he brought back samples—some natives impressively arrayed for show purposes, the gayest parrots he could capture, animals, reptiles and plants. Naturally he scored a complete success and went back for his real opportunity in September 1493, with seventeen ships, 1500 colonists and noble adventurers and twelve priests.

This time he took further advantage of the southern route and its eastern winds in crossing the Atlantic and entered the archipelago near Guadelupe. He touched Porto Rico, but on going to pick up his settlers on the north coast of Española, discovered that their greed and amorous extravagance had betrayed them to death at the hands of the infuriated natives. He chose a new site farther to the east therefore, and set his men to work to build a city as the capital of his new empire while he went off to explore it. Unfortunately for him, if decisive for the future of the Americas, gold was discovered in the stream-beds there, and it proved next to impossible to keep men planting and building when they thought they could wash fortunes from the sands. 'Now there is not a man, down to the very tailors, who does not beg to be allowed to become a discoverer.' In spite of increasing disciplinary difficulties and the steady revelation of his ineptness as a governor, Columbus went off to circumnavigate Española and Jamaica and then pressed along the lovely, if treacherous, south shore of Cuba to the point where it turned south-west and convinced him that it was mainland after all, doubtless the land of Mangi, or south Cathay, reported by Marco Polo and other medieval travellers. He went back to Spain in the spring of 1496, leaving Española in a ferment which was close to administrative chaos, but he now had *terra firma* to report and the King's fifth of the gold which had been mined to heighten his welcome. He needed commendation, for reports went back with him of affairs in Española, where disease and dissension wrought havoc among men who preferred gold to the fruits of the soil, and where the hitherto leisured natives were being forced to work for their new masters. Moreover he had discovered that his monopoly was being infringed by the opening up of his Indies to other traders and adventurers.

He still had a chance to regulate and hold his empire, however, for settlement and gold-washing had committed Spain quite deeply, and he set out in January 1498 to add to his knowledge and to try again for Asia on a third voyage. This time his landfall was the island of Trinidad, and here, at the mouth of the Orinoco, he thought he had found what God sent him out to see. The mighty outpourings of fresh water for miles into the sea convinced him that such a river could only flow from a continent, and presumably from the one withdrawn from the ken of man since Adam's sin and expulsion from the Garden of Eden, for there legend and theology agreed was the great terrestrial river-fountain. His thoughts swiftly wove themselves into a mystical and novel cosmogony to account for his newly discovered hemisphere. 'I have come to another conclusion respecting the earth, namely, that it is not round as they describe, but of the form of a pear, which is very round except where the stalk grows, at which part it is most prominent; or like a round ball, upon one part of which is a prominence like a woman's nipple, this protrusion being the highest and nearest the sky. . . . I believe it is impossible to ascend thither, because I am convinced that it is the spot of the terrestrial paradise, whither no one can go but by God's permission . . . for its site coincides with the opinion of the holy and wise theologians whom I have mentioned.'

He coasted westwards a little to just beyond the passage between Margarita and the continent, and to his delight the natives were noble in appearance, amiable, and festooned with pearl necklaces. He bade them collect some pearls for his return and went north to Española with his settlers and supplies. But affairs there had been rushing to a crisis while he was away, and Spain had responded to the complaints of the men whom he expected to build the economic base for his principality by sending out a governor to supplant him. In 1500 this man, Francisco de Bobadilla, made a bid for local popularity by sending Columbus and his two brothers back to Spain in chains.

Ferdinand and Isabella released him from durance, treated him generously in compensation, and gave the impression of reinstating him, but he found that his favour was really on the wane and that other men were establishing colonies and plantations in Española and were receiving grants of land and native labourers while he could not get ships in which to leave Spain. Moreover in 1499, Vasco da Gama, the Portuguese, came back to Lisbon from the first return voyage round Africa to India with a cargo of Eastern goods whose value made Spain's West Indian venture seem meagre. Another Portuguese, Pedro Álvarez Cabral, in 1500 touched at Brazil and claimed it for Portugal. It seemed urgent to Columbus to make good his claim that he had reached an Asian archipelago and to penetrate it to the mainland. Thus he might forestall the

Portuguese if they should travel still farther east beyond India.

In these circumstances he set out in 1502 with a small ill-found expedition of four ships and 150 men to re-make his reputation. The Indies were unfriendly, other men had his old authority, and more single-minded adventurers than he were supplanting him in royal confidence, but if he could sail straight west to Asia all would be well again. To this end he went through terrific trials by storm, hunger, thirst and deep despair in a year's exploration of one of the most inhospitable shores in the world. From the ill-disguised hatred and contempt of the colony at Española he sailed for his first 'mainland', the island of Cuba, which he thought was southern China. From near its western extremity he sailed south-west across what for him must be the Sea of China to strike Ciamba (the medieval name for Indo-China). He found himself in a gulf (of Honduras) the shores of which ran off to the west, but he turned back to the east until the land fell away again to the south.

To-day that coast is called the Mosquito Coast and its dunes and shifting shoals and lagoons are still dreaded by navigators. Columbus, however, risked everything in storm-racked ships, 'pierced with worm-holes, like a bee-hive', to follow the shores until they should open before him in the passage to India. A storm locked him in one river-mouth by closing it with sand-bars. A freshet, long awaited, swept him out. He and his men were starving and thirsty, sometimes attacked by natives, and sometimes tempted by their stories to go farther on. At any rate they kept going south and east until they reached the north-west ex-tremity of the Gulf of Darien. Then with unprobed waters still stretching away to the south, their ships were too frail to risk more and they had to run recklessly for the Spanish islands. Thence, after many tribulations, a few sailed home to a reception of misunderstanding, ingratitude and poverty, which culminated in Columbus' death in 1506.

Before he died, however, the contents of his glowing reports and despairing memorials were bound to have their effect in encouraging others. The natives whom he met along the isthmian coasts seemed to him to be more like the fringes of a settled, civilised people than any he had seen. They appeared to have proud chieftains whose courts contained professional magicians; they wore gold necklaces and collars 'delicately wrought' in animal designs, and Columbus had a glimpse of a formally built stone tomb containing a preserved body. 'In all these regions gold is found among the roots of trees, along the banks and amongst the rocks and stones left by torrents', and a native 'would willingly part' with his gold collar 'for three hawks' bells'. The natives took some of his men 'to a very lofty mountain, and thence showing them the country all around, as far as the eye could reach, told them there was gold in every part'. The 'Indians' would not permit the founding of a settlement, however, and their leaders were dignified men with large bodyguards. To Columbus it was certain that this district called Veragua was Ophir (King Solomon's Mines) or the Golden Chersonese (Malay Peninsula) of Ptolemy. The natives told him that nine days' journey overland to the south was the Kingdom of Ciguare, a richer and more civilised land than their own. He was sure, therefore, that close to him was Cathay and the territory of the Grand Khan, and that if his ships had lasted longer he could have sailed through the passage and back to Europe from the East. 'Ten days' journey' from Ciguare 'is the river Ganges'. It was tragic to have been checked on the brink of success after a solid year's defiance of fate and the elements, but Christopher Columbus was never able to go back to discover how wrong he had been at the last.

Thus he never found the rich cities or the crowded ports of Asia. He never saw his province teeming with contented colonists. He never explored even the outer confines of that continent where Eden lay. Great stretches of the Caribbean and the Gulf of Mexico were still unknown. Few souls had been won for Christ except by summary baptism on the threshold of death. Yet Columbus had introduced Spaniards to fertile new lands where they could live bountifully if they wished to. He had not found the well-known Eastern spices, but the many new plants and trees required only time and experiment for exploitation. The natives, as long as they lasted, were man-power for the plantations and the gold-mines which the Spaniards established, and it was convenient to discover such evil traits among those elsewhere than Española as to justify their capture and enslavement.

The chief lures for further adventure, however, which were discovered by Columbus were gold and pearls. The poor natives of the Caribbean were practically exterminated in less than a generation by the Spaniards, who came to loot them of their accumulated gold and then to work them to death in extracting more. Reform was to come ultimately, but 'Spanish relief arrives late' and the sad work was done so well that slave-raiding elsewhere became an established enterprise. When Columbus happened upon the wealth of the Pearl Coast, the news was allowed to leak out to a favoured few. Alonso de Ojeda, along with Columbus'

2

old pilot, Juan de la Cosa, and Amerigo Vespucci, made a slaving and pearling expedition in 1499 from what is now Guiana to a little west of the Gulf of Venezuela or Little Venice, so-called because they found there a village built on piles in the water. In the same year Pedro Alonso Niño, who had been with Columbus on the first two voyages, also went to the Pearl Coast and apparently had the luck to collect the hoards which Columbus had asked the natives to make. His expedition got 'ninety-six pounds of pearls at eight ounces to the pound which they had obtained at an average price of $2\frac{1}{2}$d'. In 1500 La Cosa and Roderigo de Bastidas pushed on from Ojeda's stopping-point and followed the shores west and north until they reached the site of the later Nombre de Dios.

All these men took what they could get, gold or pearls or slaves, so that by Columbus' retirement in 1503 the coasts of South America and of the Isthmus of Panamá had been seen and spoiled from the mouth of the Amazon to the Gulf of Honduras. Land exploration had not yet begun, because the coasts still paid well enough and untouched stretches still existed. The change, the transition from sea to land, however, was to be the logical consequence of these maritime coasting enterprises, for while Columbus fumed and fretted to his death with illness and disappointment, other men went dashing towards his Veragua, Castilla del Oro, Golden Castile, in order to make their fortunes or find the strait or both.

NARRATIVES

Practically all the contemporary materials relating to Columbus, together with much scholarly elucidation, are to be found in *Raccolta di Documenti e Studi pubblicati dalla Regia*

Commissione Colombiana, etc. (Rome, 1892–94). The more important and sequential of these have been made available in English in the Hakluyt Society Publications by R. H. Major (London, 1847; 2nd ed., 1870), C. R. Markham (London, 1893) and L. C. Jane (London, 1930). Another collection in English will be found, edited by E. G. Bourne, in *The Northmen, Columbus and Cabot* (New York, 1906). F. A. MacNutt has translated the best running account of Columbus and his contemporaries in Peter Martyr's *De Orbe Novo* (2 vols., New York, 1912). C. R. Markham's translation of *The Letters of Amerigo Vespucci* (London, 1894) should be supplemented by G. T. Northup's *Vespucci Reprints*, vol. iv (New York, 1916). The most convenient compendium of ancient and medieval geographical knowledge and legend is W. H. Babcock's *Legendary Islands of the Atlantic* (New York, 1922). Probably the most convenient sequence of maps, illustrating the growth in knowledge of North America, is *Atlas of the Historical Geography of the United States* by C. O. Paullin, edited by J. K. Wright (Washington, 1932), plates 8-32.

CHAPTER II

PRELUDES TO MEXICO

(Map No. 1, page 104)

He raised his hands to Heaven and saluted the South Sea.
BALBOA'S DISCOVERY OF THE PACIFIC IN 1513

THE excitement over the expanding world which prevailed in Spain after 1492 could not fail to provoke to action many historians and recorders. Andrés Bernáldez, for instance, took his father's advice and put down from day to day the mighty deeds which made so notable the reigns of Ferdinand and Isabella. Other chroniclers, like Bartolomé de Las Casas, were men who had actually been to the Indies and seen at least some of the wonders which they described. Yet in many ways it was an Italian, who conducted an academy for the Infante of Spain and his young companions, who compiled the most winning and typical narrative concerning the New World. This was Peter Martyr of Anghiera, a voluntary exile who retained the affection he had won at the Spanish Court during the crusade against the Moors by recording, at first for Italian dignitaries of Church and State, and finally for all Europe, the almost incredible achievements of his adopted Spain in the lands beyond the Atlantic.

He enjoyed several advantages. For one thing he was an Italian and therefore a congenial host to the Italian

20

navigators like Columbus who worked for Spain. Moreover, he was at Court and could tender his own invitation to dinner or conversation after some hero of the
Indies or learned geographer had made his formal
appearance before the sovereigns. Finally he could
write, if not in the marmoreal style so fashionable in
Renaissance Italy, yet in a lively colloquial way which
was really more attractive even in neo-classical Rome.
At any rate, express messengers for Italy waited in his
house for the completion of his letters, and Leo X, the
Medici pope, had them read to him and his household
at dinner.

The general reader will do well not to worry greatly
about his chronology or about the necessary corrections
of fact supplied by his modern commentators. The
reward will be to recapture the authentic savour which
made Martyr's letters and the 'Ocean Decades' of *De
Orbe Novo* rank with the most popular books of his day.
His stories run the gamut of the credible and the incredible from magnetic variation to mermaids, from the
Sargasso Sea to the Strait of Anian, from actual Caribs
to reputed Amazons, and from the deeds of missionaries
and *conquistadores* to the folk-ways of the Americans
whom they brought under their sway.

Martyr's outlook is neatly epitomised for us in the
opening words of *De Orbe Novo*: 'It was a gentle
custom of the ancients to number amongst the gods
those heroes by whose genius and greatness of soul
unknown lands were discovered. Since we, however,
only render homage to one God in Three Persons, and
consequently may not adore the discoverers of new
lands, it remains for us to offer them our admiration.
Likewise should we admire the sovereigns under whose
inspiration and auspices the intentions of the dis-

coverers were realised; let us praise the one and the other, and exalt them according to their merits.'

Such a man was quite naturally an inspiration and model for Richard Hakluyt, and it was most understandable and appropriate that the young Oxford geographer, made chaplain to the embassy at Paris so that he might learn for Elizabethan Englishmen what their European predecessors had accomplished overseas, republished there in 1587 and dedicated to Sir Walter Ralegh the first complete edition of the *De Orbe Novo* since the Imperial command edition of 1530. Moreover, on the map in his issue Hakluyt followed Martyr's precept of admiration for royal patronage by proclaiming to the world for the first time his great Elizabeth's fame in 'Virginia'.

In Martyr's pages can be found the exploits of the men who mapped the Caribbean and the Gulf of Mexico in their efforts to find a passage, to set up principalities, and to make their fortunes from slaves, gold and pearls. For ten or fifteen years after the departure of Columbus they trembled on the brink of the two discoveries which were to make the Americas the determinants of an epoch —the Mayan and Nahuan cities of Central America and Mexico that marked an established, opulent American civilisation, and the Pacific which led to the Incan civilisation of Peru and across to the Philippines and Far Eastern trade. This interlude was a trying time, but by process of elimination it brought out the qualities of endurance which, added to Spanish medieval pride, chivalry, religious devotion and romantic imagination, toughened men for the tasks at hand. The navigators had sailed in crazy, ill-found ships which had no copper sheathing to protect them against the tunnelling of the omnipresent teredo. The men who now ventured on the mainland had to cope with fever and jungle diseases, with thirst and hunger, and with the slowly roused combative spirit of the natives.

The first focus of their interest was on the Isthmus of Panamá. While successive Portuguese and Spanish navigators were skirting South America and, like the Portuguese on the west coast of Africa fifty years before, were probing for a passage to the East, a succession of Spaniards pushed on from the Pearl Coast in order to give their attention to Columbus' Castilla del Oro. Ruthless, greedy expeditions to South America had quickly exhausted the accumulated native stores of pearls, and that kind of contact with the Spaniards had disillusioned the Indians. The Ojeda-La Cosa-Vespucci expedition of 1499 carried off 200 slaves. An expedition by Vicente Yañez Pinzón in 1500 captured more. The natives, therefore, either fled the Europeans or, when cornered, did their best to resist them or encourage them to go away. The adventurers themselves, stimulated by da Gama's discovery of the African route to India, by reports of the La Cosa-Bastidas expedition of 1500, and by Columbus' faith that there was a passage near his Veragua, pressed westward towards the fever-ridden shores of that area.

In 1504 Columbus' intrepid Basque pilot La Cosa, again with Vespucci, explored the Gulf of Urabá (Darien) in order to make quite sure whether the passage was there. The shores closed in before him as had been his experience in 1500, but brought him to the delta built up by the substantial Atrato river. He made his way up the river for over 100 miles as it flowed straight from the south between two great mountain ranges, but the mountains, like the sea coasts, closed in and blocked his way.

That Gulf of Urabá, which we know as Darien, was to see the blighted hopes of many men. Its pall was yellow fever, and that disease exacted a heavy toll from those who dared it. But La Cosa, if he failed to find a passage, did find gold in the river sands, and gold would bring back Spaniards to the jaws of death. Indeed, in this case it lured men to settle. All Española dreamed of gold to be had for the taking in Veragua. The vigorous Ojeda, not content with settled life, along with an Andalusian planter, Diego Nicuesa de Baëcca, applied for rights to colonise Golden Castile. To Ojeda (his lieutenant was La Cosa) was granted the coast from the Gulf of Venezuela to the Atrato river, and to Nicuesa, Columbus' Veragua from the Atrato to Cape Gracias à Dios. King Ferdinand's growing greed, whetted by the royal fifth of the takings of coastal looters and Españolan miners, had at last led Spain to undertake mainland colonisation as a basis for control and exploitation of the Gold Coast.

The venture proved to be the most costly in men and materials that the Spaniards had undertaken. Ojeda sailed first for the continental coast and landed at what was later to be the site of Cartagena. He immediately attacked the natives, his royally assigned victims, but they yielded small spoils, and he followed the fugitives to a village twelve miles inland, where he massacred the women and children. The frantic native men thereupon made a wild attack on the Spaniards with poisoned arrows until they fled to their ships, leaving behind them, as a blood-sacrifice, La Cosa, Columbus' old pilot, and seventy other Spaniards. Ojeda waited until Nicuesa arrived with his 785 men and twelve ships, and before they departed for their respective principalities the two together destroyed the natives by penning them in their flaming village.

But the ill-fated Spaniards continued to wreak their own destruction. Ojeda built a small fort, named San Sebastián, on the east coast of the Gulf of Urabá twenty-four miles across from the mouth of the Atrato. His men were almost starving and the poisoned arrows of the natives kept them from securing food by raids. He had arranged with Martín Fernández de Enciso, a judge from Española, to meet him with further supplies, but Enciso was slow in arriving, and the little group, reduced from 300 to 60, would have perished but for the arrival of a freebooter in a stolen ship. Ojeda had been wounded and poisoned by a wronged husband, his companions said, who came with eight companions, dedicated to revenge and death, and attacked Ojeda instead of paying ransom for his wife. The dying leader induced the freebooter to take him to Española to get Enciso, and left Francisco Pizarro, the later conqueror of Peru, to command in his place.

Pizarro and his companions held on for fifty days and then started to follow. They met Enciso off the coast near Cartagena, however, and, encouraged by his supplies of armament, food, seed and domestic animals, went back to San Sebastián to settle, only to find it destroyed and the natives determined to obstruct their penetration inland. They suffered losses of men, supplies and ships in war and tempests. They therefore crossed the Gulf to the mouth of the Atrato, captured a native village, and began their settlement in the fever-marshes of the delta with the town of Santa María del Darien.

Meanwhile Nicuesa's much larger expedition, composed of the most privileged class in Española, was gradually going to pieces along the sands and rocky shallows of Castilla del Oro. Commanders fell out, boats were wrecked, no one knew where Veragua could be.

25

Nicuesa himself was marooned for months among blazing sand dunes. Finally he managed to gather together the starving and rebellious remnants, left one group in a small fort at Porto Bello, another detachment similarly at Nombre de Dios, and set out to follow the coast to find Ojeda. When he was picked up by an expedition sent out from Darien to find him, only sixty men of his company remained, half crazed by hardship and perils.

Out of this welter of misery, death and massacre there emerged a leader, described by Peter Martyr as 'a man of action rather than of judgement'—Vasco Núñez de Balboa. He had been with Bastidas in 1500, he had farmed in Española, and when Ojeda and Nicuesa were sifting the applicants for their venture he was poor and in debt. To him as to the others fortune seemed to beckon from the Isthmus and, having failed to embark with the leaders, he stowed away in a provision barrel which was loaded with Enciso's stores. Even before the settlement was founded at Darien the resolution and decision of this stowaway made him stand out among the waverers and those who had only birth and wealth and official favour to pit against the perils of that inhospitable coast. Without loss of time he set out to become a governor in his own right, the first of the *conquistadores*, the men who carved out kingdoms for themselves and won Spanish royal approval by virtue of the *fait accompli*.

After much plotting and counter-plotting over the gold which had been looted, and stupidly arrogant behaviour on the part of Nicuesa, Balboa and Roderigo de Colmenares, the captain of a relief expedition, succeeded in engineering the departures of Enciso and Nicuesa and in having the former accompanied by agents to protect their interests. Nicuesa, poor wretch, was put on a leaky brigantine with seventeen of his sixty survivors. 'He sailed in an evil hour and no news was ever again heard of that brigantine.'[1] The hardened little colony at Darien now looked for leadership to a man even harder than themselves.

He organised a supply force which induced neighbouring natives to yield up food and gold and began to enquire about the territory inland. 'Up to the present time [1513] we have valued the eatables more than the gold, for we have more gold than health, and often have I searched in various directions, desiring more to find a sack of corn than a bag of gold.' In this he was assisted, as was Cortés in Mexico and many another Spaniard, by his native mistress, the daughter of Careta, a neighbouring *cacique* or chief in the district of Coiba, on the western shore of the Gulf. For eighteen months Careta had been sheltering three deserters from Nicuesa, 'naked as the natives, but plump as the capons women fatten in dark places', and the language difficulty was thus overcome, but he found the alliance with Balboa both alarming and arduous. He therefore contrived to engage him in an attack on one of his enemies for the sake of the loot. This expedition took them sixty-five miles up the coast and over the coastal range, but its success opened up the prospect of still another attack on the *cacique* Comogre of Comogra, who was reputed rich and who lived inland from a point about forty miles

[1] Narváez in the autumn of 1513 rescued from captivity among the Indians in Cuba one man and two women who may have been survivors. Most of their company was massacred and this gave Matanzas Bay its name. Another possibility is that Aguilar and Guerrero, whom Cortés found in Yucatan, were survivors of Nicuesa's company. It seems impossible to determine whether these rescued castaways sailed with Nicuesa or whether they may have been with the later lost company of Valdivia. Peter Martyr's information connected Aguilar and Guerrero with Valdivia.

farther up the coast. This chieftain was a person of superior intelligence who lived in a stone and timber palace, 80 paces by 150, and had a mausoleum for his mummified ancestors in 'cotton' shrouds and golden face-masks. He treated with Balboa instead of fighting, and his eldest son, Panciaco, superintended the payment of a large tribute of gold and seventy slaves.

A dramatic incident now occurred which determined the immediate course of history. The Spaniards were preparing to melt down the gold objects presented to them, to set aside the royal fifth, and to share among themselves. Naturally they quarrelled, and to their surprise Panciaco 'struck the scales with his fist and scattered the gold in all directions', before bursting out in an impassioned tirade. 'Is it possible that you set a high value upon such a small quantity of gold? You nevertheless destroy the artistic beauty of these neck-laces, melting them into ingots. If your thirst for gold is such . . . if you exile yourselves from your country in search of gold, I will show you a country where it abounds. . . . We place no more value on rough gold than on a lump of clay, before it has been transformed by the workman's hand.' Six days' journey over another mountain range to the south were a sea, many gold-mines and civilised people whose utensils were of wrought gold and who could navigate with sail and oar. To prove his tale he offered to guide them thither. They would need 1000 armed Spaniards to reinforce Comogre's army and smash their way through the Kingdom of Tubanama to the sea.

It was the winter of 1511–12. No one had yet reached the southern limit of the South American coast. Even the Gulf of Mexico was not yet explored. No one knew yet whether the mainland was a vast unrecorded projection from Asia or a separate continental system. No one had any idea of what lay in the gap on the geographers' globes between Veragua and the India and Spice Islands which the Portuguese were at the moment exploiting. Now to the rebel and self-appointed governor of Darien there opened prospects which if true would enable him almost to make his own terms with authority —a sea, cities and untold, little-valued gold.

Balboa, however, appreciated Panciaco's estimate of the difficulty of fighting a way through, and after baptizing Comogre and his family he returned to Darien. He knew that his fate was in suspense both in Española and in Spain; but he had friends, as he thought, in both places, and he could now send off by Juan de Valdivia the best gilding for his reputation, the royal fifth of his huge hoard, a *douceur* of 300 eight-ounce pounds of smelted gold. While he waited for approval and formal appointment to command, he spent almost two years on short rations and in doubt as to his status, occupying himself in raids for gold near the coasts and up the rivers. Thanks to the loyalty of his native mistress he escaped the consequences of a native alliance against him, but of his emissaries for reinforcement Valdivia and his ship's company were wrecked with their gold and massacred by natives, and the others, 'yellow as though they suffered from liver complaint', were delayed on their way to Spain. As a result, their protests were too late to prevent the King from sending out in April 1514 Pedro Arias de Ávila with a large expedition to enquire into the venture that had cost the lives of Ojeda, Nicuesa and La Cosa, had brought about the expulsion of Enciso, a royal appointee, and had thrown up to leadership the hitherto obscure Vasco Núñez.

Balboa was lucky enough to get warning of Ferdinand's attitude and of Pedro Arias' appointment, and characteristically he decided that the time had come to gamble all on the trip to the sea. He gathered up 190 veterans and adventurers from Española, and many slave-porters, and set out from somewhere near Acla in September 1513. It was a wild journey, first over the Atlantic range and then down into the central valley. He made friends with Careta's old enemy, who furnished guides to lead him across the marshy Chuquunaque valley. They cut their way through tropical forests and swamps, and built bridges for the streams they could not ford. They were stopped near the crest of the Pacific range by the haughty ruler of Quareque and his men, with the command, 'Retrace your steps, if you do not wish to be killed to the last man'. The Spaniards routed his army with their muskets and cross-bows, and cut 600 of the naked warriors to pieces with their swords. Other villagers were torn to pieces by dogs. The survivors consented to collaborate.

Sixty-six Spaniards still remained fit for the last dash, a six days' march which required about twenty because of the forest barriers and other difficulties. On 26 September their Quareque guide led them to the last slope. 'Vasco looked longingly at it. He commanded a halt, and went alone to scale the peak, being the first to reach its top. Kneeling upon the ground, he raised his hands to Heaven and saluted the South Sea. . . . Prouder than Hannibal showing Italy and the Alps to his soldiers, Vasco Núñez promised great riches to his men.' With their small cannon and fighting dogs they cleared the last natives from their path, and four days later, on the Gulf of San Miguel, 'They took possession in the name of the King of Castile, of all that sea and the countries bordering on it'. Loaded with gold and with pearls, which they themselves saw taken from the ocean, and with working relations among the neighbouring chieftains established, they made their way back to Darien in January and despatched to Ferdinand his fifth of gold and 200 especially selected pearls.

This first land expedition, then, was no caprice. It lay in a direct chain of succession from the Discoverer himself and it found what he sought, cities and the sea which led to India. The isthmus was an obstacle, it is true, but within five years of Balboa's feat the delirious, fever-stricken adventurers who came out with Pedro Arias had ravaged it from the Atrato to Nombre de Dios; Balboa had been executed by his rival; and the governmental seat had been moved from the Atlantic to the southern end of the great road that led from Nombre de Dios to the Pacific port of Panamá. Balboa himself had built four ships on the Atlantic shore near Acla, and Indian slaves had carried them over his route to the Gulf of San Miguel, but he was killed on the eve of his new adventure. His successors were to build their ships on the Pacific and gradually fill in the unknown western shores as they ranged north and south for the straits which might afford a water route back to the Atlantic.

Meanwhile, however, other Spaniards had not been idle in the Caribbean, and they, too, were questing for loot and a strait to rival Portugal's route to India. One group of them devoted their attention to trying here and there along the North American coast for sea-leads to the West, sometimes slave-raiding, sometimes seeking cities and gold, but always adding, piece by piece, to the geographical outlines of the continent. In 1513 Juan Ponce de León, who had come out with Columbus in 1493, and later conquered Porto Rico, explored the

Bahamas and both shores of the Florida peninsula, meeting a bitter reception from the Indians. In 1519 Alonso de Pineda, on behalf of the governor of Jamaica, skirted the whole coast of the Gulf of Mexico from the southern tip of Florida to the Pánuco river. Between 1521 and 1525 a series of slave raids on behalf of Lucas Vázquez de Ayllón followed the Atlantic Coast still farther north and east. This revelation was completed in 1524–25 by the systematic survey conducted by the Portuguese, Estevan Gómez, from the Grand Banks south to Florida on behalf of the Council of the Indies in Spain 'to search whether amongst the multitudes of windings and the vast diversities of our ocean any passage can be found leading to the Kingdom of him whom we commonly call the Grand Khan'. He did a very thorough piece of work, even making his way up to the head of the Bay of Fundy, and came back with a ship-load of sample natives and with clear descriptions of the lands in the north temperate zone, 'agreeable and useful countries, corresponding exactly with our latitude and polar degrees'. 'But what need have we of what is found everywhere in Europe?' wrote Peter Martyr. 'It is towards the south, not towards the frozen north, that those who seek fortune should bend their way; for everything at the equator is rich.' It was for that reason, so commonly held in Europe, that activities leading to land exploration continued to be directed from the Caribbean, and, second in time to the Darien exploit, came the ruthless drive of the nest of *conquistadores* bred to their work in Cuba.

In 1508, after sixteen years of disagreement as to the true character of Cuba, Nicolás de Ovando, governor of Española, had sent out Sebastián de Ocampo to settle the matter. He did so by a successful circumnavigation, and King Ferdinand, as well as a number of the island magnates, began to develop an interest in Cuba's potentialities. In late 1510 or early 1511 Diego de Velásquez, the richest man in Española and a colonist since 1493, was sent out in command of an expedition which was to make friends with the natives and Christianise them, investigate the resources (particularly in gold) of the island, and establish settlements. Thirty crossbowmen under the command of young Pánfilo de Narváez were sent across from the just concluded conquest of Jamaica to join them.

Perhaps owing to the hostility of native refugees from Española there developed at once the appalling travesty of the original pacific intentions which kindled the wrath of the priest Bartolomé de Las Casas. Within four years Narváez and the other leaders systematically terrorised most of the island into submission by massacre, arson and torture. Las Casas accompanied Narváez and his soul sickened at the miseries which he was forced to witness. Devout churchman that he was, one capricious massacre of innocent native onlookers made him forget his cloth and commend Narváez and his men to the devil. Inhatuey, a native leader from Española, when burned at the stake, refused to let the priests baptize him lest he go to their heaven and find only Christians there. This massacre of the Cubeños was the price paid for the slow beginnings of a reformed native policy, for Las Casas went to Spain and so moved Charles V and his advisers by his eloquent recital of the depopulation of the Indies that in 1516 the responsibility for the welfare of the natives was handed over to a tribunal of three stern Jeronomite monks at Santo Domingo. By that time, however, the Cubeños were so few in number that slaving had begun on neighbouring coasts to find labourers for the great estates set up under the *repartimiento* and *encomienda* systems. Those systems had been the embodiment of Ferdinand's facile hope that, by granting the natives to the proprietors of the new lands, their spiritual and temporal welfare might be combined with Spanish profit from their energies. It was in Cuba that a brutal slave overseer, hearing that his charges were about to hang themselves, told them that 'he had come to hang himself with them, to the end that if he gave them a bad life in this world, a worse would he give them in that to come'.

By 1516 the supply of easily available gold in Cuba was almost exhausted and, while settlers began to develop the lands, the adventurers turned their thoughts to slaving and new coasts to loot. Velásquez' brood included his nephew, Juan de Grijalva, Pánfilo de Narváez, Francisco Fernández de Córdoba, Pedro de Alvarado, and his own humble secretary, Hernán Cortés, all of whom proved themselves to be of the same breed as Balboa. Slave raids began about 1516 to the islands off the coast of Honduras, and the business became the more alluring when the slavers collected very substantial amounts of gold and gilded copper from natives who seemed to them, as to Columbus, to be more cultivated than those in the archipelago. In fact, it was these natives' very enterprise in capturing a vessel in which they had been imprisoned and sailing it home from Cuba which first seems to have involved the interest of Governor Velásquez.

The record of the ensuing Cuban enterprise which was later to grow into the conquest of Mexico has come down to us from an eye-witness who took part in both of the preliminary expeditions and in nearly all the Mexican adventure. This was a blunt, likeable soldier,

34

Bernal Díaz del Castillo, who came out to Darien with Pedro Arias, but left that ravaged colony with a group of adventurers, when the conflict with Balboa developed, to try his fortune in Cuba. At seventy years of age, still poor and honest in spite of being the last survivor of the Mexican *conquistadores*, he was disgusted with the histories of the conquest which came to his hands and set himself the task of describing what he himself had seen 'quite simply, as a fair eye-witness, without twisting events one way or another'. He magnificently succeeded sometime about his seventy-sixth year (1568), and in his long narrative the events come alive even more convincingly than in the letters of Cortés. Corroboration from other sources proves his memory to have been extraordinarily accurate. It was great good fortune which preserved his manuscript in Guatemala to permit its accurate publication in our own times.

The first of the formally commissioned Cuban expeditions to the mainland set out in February 1517 under Córdoba, and it was linked to the adventures of the Discoverer by being composed chiefly of Bernal Díaz' company, men who had seen the mainland opportunities at Columbus' Veragua, and by taking as pilot the same Antón de Alaminos who had accompanied Columbus on his fourth voyage across the same waters. The last sad voyage of 1502–3 was bearing fruit. Adventurers hailing from the first mainland colony were now setting out to find the unspoiled equivalents of what they had already seen destroyed. Alaminos was to take them to northern Veragua, but the winds took command as soon as they had passed the shelter of Cuba and blew them west to the treacherous shallow northern coast of the Yucatan peninsula near Cape Catoche. The natives seemed friendly at

35

first and comparatively highly civilised, but they soon proved themselves to be most dangerously hostile. Moreover, the whole peninsula of Yucatan is very little more than a coral-limestone reef raised slightly above the ocean, and its coast is a maze of lagoons and sandbars. Navigation was very dangerous. Landing for the collection of drinking water was a problem in itself involving miles of separation from the ships, and, sorely tempted as the adventurers were by the substantial towns of stone buildings which they encountered, the natives were too numerous and too hostile for them. They managed to get as far west as the modern Champotón, beyond Campeche, but a pitched battle with a large army of resolute native soldiers there convinced them that they should run for home. They hated to go back empty-handed, and Alaminos, who had been with Ponce de León to Florida in 1513, took them there. Again natives attacked them and the few survivors reached Cuba with difficulty. Córdoba died of his wounds and the others dispersed to recuperate.

Their news was electrifying, however, and they wrote to Velásquez, 'telling him that we had discovered thickly peopled countries, with masonry houses, and people who covered their persons and went about clothed in cotton garments, and who possessed gold'. Moreover, they had captured two natives, 'old Melchior' and 'little Julian', and a few examples of highly skilled native handiwork in terracotta and gold alloyed with copper. Velásquez cross-questioned the natives by signs and became convinced that his adventurers had touched the fringe of an established empire. Without loss of time he got ready an expedition under Grijalva, his nephew, to go back to what blunt Bernal Díaz told him should be called 'the land where half the soldiers who went there were killed, and all those who escaped death were wounded'.

Grijalva's expedition of 1518 consisted of four vessels with Alonzo de Ávila, Pedro de Alvarado and Francisco de Montejo as assistant commanders of the ships and of the 240 adventurers. Melchior and Julian were taken as interpreters, and another was picked up in the person of a Jamaican castaway and slave on the island of Cozumel. After a short survey of the east coast, they rounded the cape and made directly west for Champotón in order to wipe out the defeat of Córdoba's men there. Once more the ranks of native warriors in their quilted cotton armour came down to meet their boats with clouds of arrows. Even the discharge of falconets did not frighten them, and they stood firm until the Spaniards got ashore and began their sword-work. The native sword was a broad, two-handed wooden blade with chips of obsidian set in the edge, and it proved no match for steel. 'I remember that this fight took place in some fields where there were many locusts, and while we were fighting they jumped up and came flying in our faces, and as the Indian archers were pouring a hail-storm of arrows on us we sometimes mistook the arrows for locusts.' The native losses were over 200 before they broke, and word of the defeat and of the might of Spain ran westward through the country.

The prestige of that victory paved the way to Mexico. As was afterwards learned, Motecuhzoma (Montezuma), the timorous, gentle war-lord of Tenochtitlan (the city of Mexico) and suzerain of most of the country, was put in a fever of apprehension and indecision by the letters which swift runners brought to him telling of the invincible foreigners and of their steady advance. Unable to get comfort from his gods or from his astrologers and magicians, he decided to temporise by ordering the natives to deal peaceably with the strangers and barter food and small quantities of their alloyed gold, especially for the blue and green beads which the Spaniards offered. Meanwhile the magicians were instructed either to effect the departure of the Spaniards by magic or the translation of Montezuma to the heaven of the kings and warriors of antiquity.

Under such favouring circumstances the expedition moved in leisurely fashion along the coast, exploring the great Laguna de Terminos, the mouths of Río de Tabasco (or Grijalva), of Río Papaloapan (or de Alvarado) and of Río Jamapa (or de Banderas) just south of what was to be Vera Cruz. They saw cities and temples (whose priests and human sacrifices horrified them), were much impressed by the dense population and the trained native armies, and became gradually aware that the vast empire whose fringes they were skirting was already rotten and yielding at the core. They complained to native chiefs of the small amounts of gold brought to them and of its poor quality, and they decided to settle at San Juan de Ulúa, the island harbour of Vera Cruz. Alvarado was sent off to Velásquez with their tidings and the gold and other native objects, but ultimately those left behind prevailed upon Grijalva to follow him. The autumn found them at Santiago de Cuba making their plans in the islands and at the Emperor's Court in Europe, to secure a monopoly of the ripe prize which seemed so ready to fall into their hands. The coast was empty of their embarrassing presence, and at Tenochtitlan Montezuma and his magicians congratulated themselves on the might of their spells!

NARRATIVES

For Peter Martyr see Chapter I. The best collection of narratives for this period is M. F. de Navarrete, *Colección de los Viajes y Descubrimientos, etc.* (5 vols., Madrid, 1825–37), and there are other huge Spanish collections and Spanish histories with almost the value of contemporary narrative, such as those of B. de Sahagun, T. de Motolinia, G. F. Oviedo y Valdez and F. L. Gómara. The violent tracts concerning the Indies from which Las Casas' histories were finally compiled were very popular among the Protestant enemies of Spain and were frequently translated, but a more judicial account, which although not narrative is based upon the rich Archive of the Indies at Seville, will be found in I. A. Wright, *The Early History of Cuba* (New York, 1916). Many English editions of Bernal Díaz del Castillo's *The True History of the Conquest of New Spain* are based on the garbled version published by Alonzo Remón in 1632. A most thorough English translation and commentary, with unique maps and other aids, was made from Genaro García's exact copy and Mexican edition of the original by A. P. Maudslay for the Hakluyt Society (4 vols., London, 1908–16). The most convenient narrative in English of early Central American affairs is C. R. Markham's translation for the Hakluyt Society of Pascual de Andagoya, *Narrative of the Proceedings of Pedrarias Dávila* (London, 1865). It contains an excellent map and a translation of Balboa's long despatch of 20 January 1513.

CHAPTER III

STOUT CORTÉS

(Map No. 1, page 104)

I stood looking at it and thought that never in the world would there be discovered other lands such as these.

BERNAL DÍAZ' COMMENT ON THE VALLEY OF MEXICO, 1519

THE first part of North America to be subjected to systematic European exploration can conveniently be divided into three areas: the northernmost, which for convenience may be called Mexico, bounded by the Gila river, the Río Grande, the Gulf of Mexico, the isthmus of Tehuantepec, the Pacific and the Gulf of California; the central Mayan land between the isthmuses of Tehuantepec and of Guatemala, with its north-easterly projection in the peninsula of Yucatan; and the south-eastern section, from Honduras to South America. Mexico is a great plateau above the sea resting on the broad oval of the two ranges of the Sierra Madre, with brief coastal plains on the Pacific and the Gulf of Mexico, and confused tangles of mountains at the arid north and well-watered south. The land of the Mayas slopes north-east to the lowlands of Yucatan from the high Sierras close to the Pacific which form the backbone of the isthmuses. Mountains fill most of the third section of the continental link except for the lowlands of the Mosquito Coast and two valleys (the Coco and San Juan river systems) which almost cross it from Atlantic to Pacific.

Altitude and humidity provide the determinants for all these tropical lands, although the Pacific slopes are in general more arid than the Atlantic. On the whole it is the height above sea-level and the capacity to retain moisture which graduate the progressions from blazing heat to bracing snows, from steaming swamps to airy forests or uninhabitable desert plateaus, and from palms to tropical hard-woods and mountain pine and oak. The abundant bird and animal and reptile life is distributed in the same way, and the degree of moisture has determined the agricultural wealth upon which corresponding human cultures could be raised. Widespread volcanic activity provided the mountainous areas with supplies of soft light stone for building. Long-past labours of coral-builders laid down easily cut limestone under the forests and jungles of Yucatan.

When the Europeans arrived in this part of North America the third of three recorded civilisations was just past its zenith. Generalisations concerning these cultures must be tentative for many years while the interpretation of the fruits of archaeological activity is gradually agreed upon, but one illuminating explanation by analogy seems to have much to support it. The American sequence of Mayan, Toltecan and Aztecan cultures has been set over against that of Greek, Etruscan and Roman. The Mayas were the first people to carry the highland agriculture down to the humid lowlands, in the neighbourhood of the northern half of the isthmus of Tehuantepec and thence east across Yucatan. The increased return set them going on a cumulative progression of wealth which corresponded in time with the first 600 years of the Christian era and which gave them the broad fertile territory in which their successors were seen by Columbus and the Cuban adventurers. They cleared the forests, built scores of stone cities, and with marvellous rapidity developed a high civilisation which was marked by an original and profoundly conventionalised aesthetic, remarkable mathematical and astronomical competence, and broad civilising influence in the neighbouring lands. When Cortés came, they still peopled Yucatan and Guatemala, but were disunited and no longer politically independent.

Meanwhile another and larger linguistic stock, the Nahuan, had also been coming down from the arid, irrigated slopes, and of them the Toltecs, stimulated by Mayan influences, began to build up their civilisation at the well-watered southern end of the Mexican plateau, in the gracious Valley of Mexico. They too built great walled cities, with pyramids and temples even higher (though architecturally feebler) than the Mayan ones, and they rose in power as the Mayas declined, that is, from the seventh to the thirteenth centuries. Their transmutation of Mayan civilisation had its influences by contact and can be traced over the wide areas which they dominated, even in Mayan Yucatan. Civil war or pestilence destroyed them.

When they disappeared there emerged the Romans of the American sequence, the brusque Aztec warriors who built up their power within the former Toltec lands. They began as vassals, but won a refuge and place for themselves on the marshy shores and islands of Lake Texcoco. About 1325 they started to rear their American Venice from the waters of the lake. Canals drained the marshes and the excavated soil made land on which to build. When Cortés arrived at Tenochtitlan (Mexico City) on 8 November 1519, it was a great walled fortress with its lighthouses and its twenty-five temple pyramids rising from the lake, and with three long causeways and an aqueduct leading from the shores. Moreover, the Aztecs had been mighty warriors and had set up a martial hegemony over all the surrounding country except for a few stubbornly independent cities like Tlaxcala or the unconquerable Tarascan mountaineers of Michoacan to the west. When Cortés came, they seem just to have passed the natural climax of their empire. Almost exclusive preoccupation with war and tribute had debauched their powers, degraded their religion into a frenzy of human sacrifice and cannibalism, and saddened their poets and philosophers. Their elective polity had become a privileged aristocracy, internal dissension was apparent, and any really serious shock from outside might crumble the edifice whose foundations were war, cruelty and terror. Had Cortés never come to raze the city and tumble its buildings into its own canals, the rot which was personified in vacillating Montezuma and his blood-stained priests would sooner or later have brought it to a similar end. Many Aztecs were longing for a more beneficent régime.

It is impossible within a few pages to recapture all of the qualities of the conquest of Mexico, and indeed many of its aspects are quite secondary to our theme. It is one of the great stories of mankind, and it should be read in the words of the four eye-witnesses who have left us their tales: Cortés himself, Bernal Díaz, the anonymous *conquistador*, and Andrés de Tápia. If these are read with disciplined imagination, the great *crescendo* of triumph will come convincingly to life. Perhaps the greatest advantage of our having these soldiers' accounts is that it becomes clear that the conquest was no ruthless massacre of almost helpless primitives, but a not unequal contest between a military genius with a few ambitious followers and a professionally trained military empire which was robbed at the crucial moment of the good leadership which was its only need at least temporarily to hold its own. Cortés won because he exploited not only every known and half-known element of the Spaniards' inherent prestige, but as well every fissure and weakness in his opponents and their position which his remarkable perception revealed to him.

The chief actors seem far from our day and kind. Cortés was like some lean, predatory Roman scenting the weaknesses which lay beneath the wealth and cruelty of Alexandria and the Nile delta in the days of Ptolemy IV. Montezuma, a very Hamlet for indecision, was bemused by strange legends and prophecies which might be applicable to the fair, bearded strangers who had come in water-castles to his coasts. Cortés had to school his clutch of desperadoes to his will and awe his Indian. allies to almost as implicit an obedience and co-operation, but the Spaniards' very inferiority in numbers helped to make them cohere the more closely. The Aztecs had to see Montezuma, the symbol of unity in their confederacy, lost to them by his own weakness before they could rally their powers under new leadership, too late to escape the consequences of their own arrogance to the tributary cities and states. It was a fateful, far-off struggle in which Cortés was in the position of having to win all or lose all. His will and his genius made him win.

One other factor always present in, and deeply affecting, the exploits of Cortés and his successors is also far from our ken, so far perhaps as to make our comprehension of it impossible. That was religion and the manifold actions which passed for it. In its various manifestations it was a tough and broad fibre in the complex personalities of Spaniards of the day, fresh from the conquest of Granada which concluded their seven centuries of domestic warfare with Islam, and already embarked on forcible conversions in Spain and war against the Turk on the Danube and in the Mediterranean. It ranged from the Christ-like poverty and self-denial of barefooted friars who ignored the protection of physical force in their passion to teach the Word of God, to what was held to be the honourable, soldierly decency of baptizing your enemy if possible before putting him to death. The theology and the practice of it had as their only common denominators a very simple original doctrine and a very complex Spanish character. Much of the animating force of Spanish achievement in North America will be missed if one forgets that Spaniards were crusaders for souls.

Wherever he went, Cortés made it his first duty to bid the native priests remove their images, cleanse their temples of the stains of human sacrifice, and set up Christian altars, and when they refused the Spaniards often did the work themselves with a confidence explainable only by a certainty of divine protection. They were to themselves a chosen people, the army of God to smite the heathen and win souls for Christ. At home the Holy Office dealt with Jews and Moors and other heretics. In America the soldiers must till a field grown up with weeds of ignorance. If they seem in many cases to have been somewhat easily satisfied with the formality of baptism, it was because there were so many of the lost and because a benign Providence would take into account that they and their missionaries had done what they could.

In Mexico this mighty religious strain was enormously heightened in importance by a curious reciprocal condition among the more devout and speculative Aztecs. Odd as it may seem, their blood-stained, polytheistic religion had a number of close analogies to Christianity, notably in baptism, in a sort of eucharistical communion, and in the use of the cross. Moreover, their religious mythology and their legend-history of Toltecan times had become blended in a fateful way. The fair, benign creator god of their pantheon was Quetzalcoatl, and in Toltec times this god was born of a virgin and came to earth to rule and guide the Toltecs in what history held to be their golden age. His brother god and fated opponent, Tezcatlipoca, fought hard against him and at last defeated him by causing him to lose his chastity while drunk. In shame he departed to the seashore and sailed away. He prophesied that he would return once more to lead his people and that the time would be in the first year of one of the fifty-two-year cycles of the Mexican calendar. The year 1519 was such a year, and the skies and other omens had already been searched before Cortés and his fair companions came over the waters from the sunrise. Their message was unconsciously like fulfilment of prophecy, for they said that they came at the bidding of one beyond the seas greater than Montezuma to bid the Aztecs give up their cruel gods and cruel practices and make way for the veneration of the gentle Virgin Mary and the kindly saints as the true path to the salvation promised by the Prince of Peace. Much of Montezuma's subsequent fatal vacillation arose from his alternate hopes and despairs of averting the prophecies of his people's gods.

Cortés reported that when they first met, Montezuma, the Aztec 'Chief of Men', spoke to him as follows: 'We have known for a long time, from the

46

chronicles of our forefathers, that neither I, nor those who inhabit this country, are descendants from the aborigines of it, but from strangers who came to it from very distant parts; and we also hold, that our race was brought to these parts by a lord, whose vassals they all were, and who returned to his native country. . . . And we have always held that those who descended from him would come to subjugate this country and us, as his vassals; and according to the direction from which you say you come, which is where the sun rises, and from what you tell us of your great lord, or king, who sent you here, we believe, and hold for certain, that he is our rightful sovereign, especially as you tell us that since many days he has had news of us.'

The chief greatness of Cortés lay in his uncanny ability to measure the growing dimensions of his own prestige and the increasing fatalistic resignation in the heart of Montezuma. When he left Cuba, chosen as leader by Velásquez in a compromise from among a welter of eager candidates, he had no conception of what he was to find. Velásquez' idea was that they should go out only to trade on a profit-sharing basis. Cortés was to follow old paths, but with greater power than his predecessors—more men, more guns, and most important of all, for mainland America knew no such animals, with horses. Time was to reveal, however, that he was like Balboa in being an artist in leading men, and, as his unexpected opportunity revealed itself, he resolved to forget his subordination to Velásquez and strike for himself. The Indians of this new region should be pacified, their cities conquered, the land colonised, and he should rule New Spain when the day came to parcel out its lands and inhabitants in great estates.

Even before he left Cuba he had begun to build up

his personal prestige and authority. He had standards made to be set up at his doorway, he 'began to adorn himself and be more careful of his appearance', and at Old Havana, his port of departure, he took pains to end the more serious rivalries among his captains and 'to organise a household and be treated as a Lord'. His armada consisted of eleven ships and a launch, 508 soldiers (including thirty-two crossbowmen and thirteen musketeers), about 100 sailors, sixteen horses, ten brass guns, and four falconets, and he had welded it almost into one instrument by the time he reached Cozumel in early February.

Here he began to work out what became his technique of conquest. He insisted on pacific and fair relations with the natives, established these with a small display of force, and by the time he left had destroyed the island shrine which revolted him and his followers, and had left a Christian altar in its place. Under Alaminos' piloting, he pushed on along the north coast past Champotón and Laguna de Terminos to Río Tabasco. He had had an extraordinary piece of luck in securing the services of Jerónimo de Aguilar, a Spanish castaway from Darien,[1] who had been living for seven or eight years among the Mayans and who knew their language well. His only surviving companion, Gonzalo Guerrero, would not come, for he had become a famous warrior and 'gone native'. 'I have my face tattooed and my ears pierced, what would the Spaniards say should they see me in this guise?' Another useful acquisition was Grijalva's fighting lurcher, which, when they found her on the coast, 'wagged her tail and showed other signs of delight and came at once to the soldiers'.

At Tabasco Cortés tried to repeat his pacific pro-

[1] See note, p. 27.

cedure, but in spite of gifts and appeals to common sense, the Tabascans insisted on war. The men of Champotón had sneered at them for their friendliness to Grijalva, and in a series of battles which culminated on 25 March 1519, in a fight to a finish in front of their city Cintla, they resisted to the limit of their ability. Indeed Cortés and his men were on the verge of exhaustion and willingness to give up when the Tabascan majority at last decided on peace. Artillery and cavalry had provided the supplement to fine infantry tactics which was necessary to offset overwhelming superiority in numbers. Cortés was not slow to realise this. 'Do you know, gentlemen, that it seems to me that the Indians are terrified at the horses and may think they and the cannon make war on them by themselves?' He thereupon devised some novel deceptions to heighten this impression and used his advantage to make an alliance, to deprecate their clinging to their impotent gods, and to urge the duty of submission to Charles V and the Christian Church.

He also took neat advantage of the native usage of presenting him with women by insisting on having them taught and baptized before he would consent to distribute them among his principal officers. The valuable objects which he received as gifts were not greatly esteemed, for they seem to have been gold plate on copper, and delicate rather than heavy, but his hopes were strengthened when he asked the Tabascans where they got gold and jewels and they told him in the West 'and said "Culua" and "Mexico"'. He had another remarkable bit of luck in being given among the twenty maidens an exiled Aztec princess, Marina, who knew both the Mayan and the Aztec languages and who, although at that time the mistress of Puertocarrero, was extremely useful to Cortés and devoted to his interests. Little Julian was dead, Old Melchior had fled after going over to the Tabascans, but now with Marina to translate from Aztec to Mayan and Aguilar from Mayan to Spanish, the most intricate negotiations were quite possible.

The Tabascan campaign left another people awed into submission behind him, and Cortés advanced a step farther towards independent action by ignoring his intermediate authority and taking possession of the land directly in the Emperor's name with a good deal of legal ceremony. When, therefore, on 18 April 1519, after celebrating Palm Sunday as an object lesson to the natives, he proceeded north towards San Juan, it was not with the idea of trading for himself and Velásquez, but to take formal possession of New Spain for himself and Charles V. They coasted along northwards during Holy Week, and the veterans like Bernal Díaz got a good deal of satisfaction out of airing their knowledge of the shores they had visited with Grijalva and thus endearing themselves to their increasingly impressive commander. It seemed particularly fitting and promising that they should arrive at San Juan on Holy Thursday and begin negotiations with emissaries from Montezuma under the happy auspices of their celebration of Easter.

To Montezuma the return to his coasts of the foreigners under Cortés had seemed to forebode the unhappy fulfilment of prophecy and the futility of all that he and the priests could do. The Spaniards' command of thunder and lightning, their invincibility when hopelessly outnumbered, the pacifications which they effected, and, particularly, the centaurs who accompanied them, seemed to spell the end of Aztec empire as it was. Montezuma embarked, therefore, on the policy which Cortés was quick to estimate, that of bribing men who might be Quetzalcoatl's emissaries to stay away from Tenochtitlan. The first Aztec messengers even went out in a canoe to meet Cortés and escort him to a camp-site where they made him comfortable and arranged for supply services. They brought gifts symbolical of the god whom he was presumed to represent, and listened patiently while Cortés urged on them the desirability of submission to Charles V and the Holy Catholic Church. They even brought artists with them to make pictures for Montezuma of all they saw, and Cortés made sure that this included the firing of his cannons and that the horses were never seen without men in the saddles and on firm ground where the man-horses could charge impressively.

He, too, made gifts of beads, an ornate chair and an embroidered cap with a medal of St. George and the dragon. One of the Aztec ambassadors had noticed a rather rusty half-gilt helmet on one of the soldiers and was unwise enough to remark that 'it was like one that they possessed which had been left to them by their ancestors of the race from which they had sprung, and that it had been placed on the head of their god, Huitzilopochtli'. Cortés gave it to him for Montezuma and asked him to bring it back full of the kind of gold they had in their country so that Charles V could see whether it was the same as they had in Spain. 'When the great Montezuma . . . examined the helmet and that which was on his Huitzilopochtli, he felt convinced that we belonged to the race which, as his forefathers had foretold, would come to rule over that land.'

During the next four months, while gasping runners and straining porters carried news to and fro and increasingly imposing gifts from Montezuma to Cortés, the new Balboa was consolidating his position, measuring the growth of his prestige against that of Montezuma's apprehensions, and building up the minimum of strength which he felt necessary for his great gamble with Fortune. Discovering that the neighbouring city of Cempoala hated its greedy Aztec overlords, he propelled it and a local confederacy of some thirty cities into rebellion against Mexico and acceptance of Spanish and Catholic alliance. Five lordly tax-gatherers had come to one of the cities demanding twenty sacrificial victims for the altars of Mexico. The arrogant Aztecs had affected not to be aware of the Spaniards. 'Their cloaks and loin-cloths were richly embroidered . . . and their shining hair was gathered up as though tied on their heads, and each one was smelling the roses that he carried.' Cortés effected their arrest. The coast-dwellers were as appalled by this overt act as by the Spaniards' destruction of their idols, but they were swept along in Cortés' irresistible train. He, in turn, made a double profit by secretly releasing the captives and sending them back to Montezuma.

He decided to colonise, and adroitly silenced the partisans of Velásquez while the majority of his followers professed to go through a complicated and somewhat farcical legal procedure of founding Villa Rica de la Vera Cruz (about thirty miles north of the modern city) and of setting up municipal institutions directly under the Crown. They then 'required' Cortés to give up trading and surrender the authority which he had from Velásquez, and, now that he was legally no rebel, immediately 'elected him, in the name of Your Royal Highnesses, to the office of Justice and Superior Alcalde', until permanent governmental arrangements should be made in Spain for the new lands. In order to be sure that these should confirm Cortés, they sent off a ship by the Bahama Channel to 'short-circuit' Velásquez and reach Court before him. They wisely sent on it all the tribute they had collected, quite the greatest and most exciting hoard that the Americas had produced. In it were two huge chased and sculptured discs like cart-wheels or mill-stones, one of gold representing the sun and one of silver for the moon; the helmet full of gold dust, which 'was worth more to us than if it had con-tained £5000, because it showed that there were good mines there'; numerous animal and bird figures of gold; gold necklaces, which were intricately fabricated with emeralds, pearls and other jewels; and great quantities of ceremonial clothing, armour, weapons, textiles and unique feather-work. Peter Martyr saw the whole col-lection and confessed that words failed him to do justice to the splendour and wonderful artistry. 'If ever artists of this kind of work have touched genius, then surely these natives are they. . . . I have never seen anything, which for beauty could more delight the human eye.' With this sure guarantee of success on its way, the adventurers dismantled and destroyed their ships. There never was a more thorough or decisive example of risking all on one throw. Like Napoleon years later with the ragged army of Italy, Cortés could intoxicate his men and bend them to his will by comparing them to the storied heroes of antiquity. 'One and all we answered him that we would obey his orders, that the die was cast for good fortune, as Caesar said when he crossed the Rubicon, and that we were all of us ready to serve God and the King.'

It was 16 August 1519, and the middle of the rainy season, when Cortés and his company set out 'to order

Montezuma not to rob or offer human sacrifices', and he was reinforced by forty allied chieftains as quasi-hostages for Vera Cruz and by 200 porters. He had decided to make for Tlaxcala, for the Tlaxcalans were 'mortal enemies of the Mexicans'. Uncertain of their reception along the easiest pass through the first range, they took a safer route in allied country which necessitated a climb over rough ground between Cofre de Perote (13,403 feet) and Orizaba (17,365 feet) by a pass over 10,000 feet high. They were ill-clothed for such a venture, and the snow, ice, winds and night frosts plagued them bitterly as they struck across the uninhabitable salt-marshes and sandy deserts of the first plateau, still 7000 or 8000 feet above the sea. They turned north to Xocatla, which was won over to them by the urgings of the Cempoalans, and Cortés was so elated that it was with difficulty that the Franciscan restrained him from the appalling tactical error of immediately cleansing the native temples. 'It seems to me, gentlemen, that there remains nothing for us to do but to set up a cross.' There were no ships to retreat to now, and others found the discretion which Cortés lacked.

The next objective was Tlaxcala and its integration in the growing offensive alliance against Mexico, but in spite of every possible effort through his native allies and clever interpreters, Cortés could not dissipate the Tlaxcalans' suspicions and make them understand his aims. His dealings with Montezuma were well known and very disconcerting, so that although he laid waste a good deal of their country, he had to defeat the hitherto invincible Tlaxcalans in several skirmishes and in two terrible pitched battles before they would treat. This was far more serious than Tabasco, bad as that had been. 'If those Tlaxcalans . . . could reduce us to these straits, what would happen when we found ourselves at war with the great forces of Montezuma?' They were so short of supplies that they melted the fat of the Indian dead to get ointment for wounds. All the ingenious eloquence of Cortés was needed to prevent the complete collapse of his men. One of their 'immortal' horses was killed and its body captured. At last, by working on their captives and always setting them free, a truce was established and Cortés set to work, tactfully and respectfully, by force and by wiles, to draw these mighty warriors into his train.

Montezuma was appalled and saddened by this victory of 400 over scores of thousands, and Cortés was quick to point the moral to the Tlaxcalans when embassy after embassy came laden with princely gifts and promising him anything if he would only give up his insistence on meeting the Aztec leader. It took from 31 August to 23 September to get into Tlaxcala, and it was not until 12 October that the march could be resumed. The three-week interval had been spent in the now usual exhortations to join Spain and the Church, and in neat playing-off of Mexico and Tlaxcala through Marina's eloquence and skill, but appetites had been whetted by authentic descriptions in words and pictures of the capital city and of its wealth and strength. Indeed when Diego de Ordás came down to the camp from his daring ascent of the great volcano Popocatepetl (17,887 feet), his description of the shining city which he saw shimmering in the distance over forty miles away on Lake Texcoco was the last stimulant necessary to overcome the very natural fears of the invincible Four Hundred. 'His opponents, seeing with what determination Cortés expressed himself, and knowing that many of us soldiers were ready to help him by crying, "Forward and good luck to us", dropped all further discussion.'

The whole train of events now came rapidly to its climax. Escorted by the whole Tlaxcalan army, the little force marched to the holy Aztec city of Cholula, which received them in friendly fashion once Cortés had sent most of the Tlaxcalans away. Just over the mighty volcanic ridge which ran north from Popo-catepetl lay the network of roads and causeways which knit together the white lake-cities of the Mexican basin. Montezuma was in a panic of vacillation and his servants hurried to and fro as he sought advice from his gods. He planned an overpowering ambuscade to take place when the Spaniards left Cholula with a supposedly friendly escort, but the redoubtable Marina, the devoted mistress of Cortés since Puertocarrero had gone to Spain, detected the plot. Cortés dramatically revealed his knowledge of all its ramifications, winning thereby the reputation of a seer, ruthlessly put the two or three thousand natives in his escort to the sword, and called in the Tlaxcalans for a field day of looting. Then he let the Cempoalans go home and, with only enough Tlaxcalans to serve as porters, he climbed the shoulder of Popocatepetl to enter Mexico.

Montezuma tried to stop him with excuses, bribes and the final promise of any annual tribute he might ask, but Cortés was not to be stopped. Before him stretched a basin of over 3000 square miles, a chain of five shallow lakes forty-five miles long and eighteen miles across, and on all sides, set among gardens and waters, the burnished white capitals of a rich empire. Not until he was less than a day's march from Tenoch-titlan did the Aztecs resign themselves to his coming, and then it was with the hope that, having got him and his men inside their island fortress, their war-god Huitzipochtli would deliver them into their hands. Then, at long last, these stubborn foreigners might be stretched on the sacrificial altars for the incision and the swift snatch by which the priests would offer up their still-beating hearts to the gods.

Neither Cortés nor his men were unaware of the risks they ran, but they were inflamed with a success which could only be evidence of divine approbation. They were gambling, too, with the prestige of the fatalist Montezuma, in the hope that it would offset the plans of the realistic military aristocracy. They had not failed to notice, either, that there were many cities eager to throw off the irksome Aztec yoke. If they could reach the centre they might disintegrate this empire and reintegrate it for Charles V and the Holy Catholic Church. They had their horses, their cannons and their record of invincibility, and they were hampered by no softness of heart or chivalrous scruples. The abhorrent religion of the Aztecs, the cannibalism which accompanied the human sacrifices, and the sodomy which they had denounced wherever they found it, had built up in them the conviction that they might employ any means to their ends.

They also had the comfort of legality. Ever since Tabasco they had been elaborating and equipping with procedural apparatus a most anomalous legal form of conquest. The Pope had granted the Western Hemisphere to Spain, and the authorities in Spain had drawn up a formal requirement of submission which was ceremoniously used in the cases of such cities as Cholula. Those of the natives who chose to be Spanish vassals were told that they might do so, but those who did not were henceforth, by canon and civil law, rebels against a pope and an emperor of whom they had never before heard. It is of course absurd to think that Cortés did not see how preposterous a performance this was, but for many reasons of his own he cherished the procedure. Rebels against Spain and heretics against Christianity were convenient descriptions for the Americans who stood in his path. He gave them a chance to ally themselves with the spiritual and temporal heads of his own world and granted them the boon of the only formula for entry into Heaven.

He and his men were almost overawed by the magnificence and wealth of what they found. Bernal Díaz tells the tale best. 'We were amazed and said that it was like the enchantments they tell of in the legend of Amadis, on account of the great towers and temples and buildings rising from the water, and all built of masonry. And some of our soldiers even asked whether the things that we saw were not a dream. . . . I say again that I stood looking at it and thought that never in the world would there be discovered other lands such as these. . . . We did not know what to say, or whether what appeared before us was real, for on one side on the land, there were great cities, and in the lake ever so many more, and the lake itself was crowded with canoes, and in the Causeway were many bridges at intervals, and in front of us stood the great City of Mexico, and we—we did not even number four hundred soldiers.'

After passing through several cities and being impressed by their beauty and amenities, on 8 November 1519 they started out with an escort of Montezuma's highest dignitaries along the seven-mile causeway which led due north to the lake capital. The lordly Montezuma himself, whom no Aztec dared look in the face, came to meet them and escort them to the palace of his father. For the moment all was friendly and as king meeting king. Yet within six days the Spaniards had poured contempt on the Aztec gods, had proposed to build a church at the top of the great pyramid, had bidden Montezuma yield himself to Spanish vassalage, and, when their fears began to overcome them, had snatched the Aztec emperor from his lovely palace and bound his fortunes with theirs in their cannon-guarded mansion. They had already discovered that in it, behind a freshly plastered doorway, lay the ancestral treasure hoard of the Aztecs, and they had the sublime arrogance to hope that they could loot the empire behind its discredited leader.

NARRATIVES

For Bernal Díaz del Castillo see Chapter II. F. A. MacNutt has translated *The Letters of Cortés to Charles V* (2 vols., New York, 1908). M. H. Saville has translated *The Narrative of the Anonymous Conqueror* (New York, 1917). The narrative of Andrés de Tápia is in J. G. Icazbalceta, *Colección de Documentos para la Historia de Mexico*, vol. ii (Mexico, 1866). H. J. Spinden's *The Ancient Civilizations of Mexico and Central America* (New York, 1922) is a very useful handbook which might well be supplemented by Paul Radin's *Sources and Authenticity of the History of the Ancient Mexicans* (Berkeley, Cal., 1920). Buckingham Smith's somewhat inaccessible translation of the standard Spanish requisition for native submission is available in W. H. Lowery, *The Spanish Settlements in the United States, 1513–1561* (New York, 1911), pp. 178-80. Some fine coloured photographs of Aztec feather-work are to be seen in *The Illustrated London News*, 2315, vol. 89, 5 September 1931.

CHAPTER IV

AFTERMATHS OF MEXICO

(Map No. 1, page 104)

THERE was a good deal of similarity between the Spanish conquest of Mexico and the examples set by the Normans and the Turks in Europe, if due allowance be made for the differences in religious policy. In each case an effective military organisation conquered lands occupied by sedentary agricultural peoples and used its authority to exact from them sustenance, taxation and man-power. In the course of time, miscegenation and the imposition of the conquerors' institutions produced an amalgam of victor and vanquished, least notably in the case of the Turk. Yet the actual conquests largely amounted to the displacing of one military rule by another and the rapid acquisition of the accumulated, quickly realisable wealth of the conquered country.

In Mexico Cortés at first shewed an amazing optimism as to the ease with which these ends could be effected. Once he had captured Montezuma and established a complete personal ascendancy over him, he set out to rule from behind his throne, not realising that the Aztec military leaders could easily elect another king. He did not overlook ordinary precautions for the safety of his little army, and he did effect the seizure of other princely Aztecs, but he shewed by his arrogant actions that he underestimated the spirit of the people whose administration he had captured. He forced Montezuma to bring from the coast a local native governor and some officials who had dared to fight with the Spanish garrison there and had them publicly burned at the stake. He cleansed the principal native temples, tumbled the images 'in which they have the most faith and belief' down the steps of the pyramids, substituted Christian images, and forbade human sacrifices. Under the aegis of Montezuma he sent out trusted Spaniards to collect information about the gold-mines and other resources of the Aztec confederacy and in particular to find a port. These men went to a number of placer mines in Oaxaca to the south-east, and there are reasons for believing that one of them may even have reached Zacatula on the Pacific. Another expedition went eastward across country to the valley of the Papaloapan (Alvarado) river, and an expedition under Diego de Ordás surveyed the Gulf coast from Vera Cruz to Coatzacoalcos, which seemed to hold some promise as a settlement and port. Finally Cortés bethought him of the Aztec tribute rolls. 'I spoke to Montezuma one day, and told him that Your Highness was in need of gold, on account of certain works ordered to be made.' Out came the tax-books and out went the Spaniards to collect, from Montezuma downwards, a tribute for Charles V to 'testify that they began to render service'.

This happy state of affairs lasted from November 1519 to May 1520, when suddenly Cortés was confronted by the necessity of defending his conquest successively against rivals from the Caribbean islands, the Aztecs themselves, and still other Spanish rivals operating from Darien and Panamá. The full story of the ensuing five years is perhaps a more thrilling one than that of what had already passed, but only parts of it contributed to the exploration of North America and much of it must be summarised here even at some risk of a confusion of names and places.

The immediate threat from the islands was the rage of Velásquez and the cupidity aroused by news of Montezuma's earliest gifts. Word had reached Velásquez of Cortés' success when the messenger ship of 1519 from Vera Cruz touched at Cuba to provision, and in April 1520 he sent out the redoubtable Pánfilo de Narváez with eighteen ships, eighty horses, over 800 men and twenty guns to supersede the Conqueror. As soon as he learned of this, Cortés shewed that his confidence in his diplomatic and military skill was not confined to dealings with American natives, for he left Pedro de Alvarado with a garrison in Mexico and himself set out for the coast with only seventy men. By bribes, negotiation and adroit use of the members of his own coast garrison and of the Coatzacoalcos expedition, he seduced from Narváez enough of his followers to render a night surprise possible. In less than a month Cortés had made his sally, captured his enemy, and secured the reinforcement of the men and supplies sent out by Velásquez against him!

Twelve days later he realised how much he needed that reinforcement, for word came that Alvarado in Mexico had overreached himself by an unwarranted attack on the unarmed Aztecs during one of their principal religious festivals and was now straitly besieged in his quarter of the island city. Provisions were short and his astute enemies had burnt the boats which the Conqueror had built to ensure a safe retreat. Cortés did not hesitate. Within two weeks he was back in Mexico. No one had opposed his return, but he had taken the precaution of striking for the west shore at

Texcoco and going round the northern end of the lakes so as to enter by the shortest causeway, that leading from Tacuba.

Once their enemy was in the city, however, the reorganised Aztecs struck, and between 25 June and 1 July they set to work to exterminate the 1250 Spaniards and their thousands of Tlaxcalan allies. The appeals of Montezuma for peace evoked a shower of stones which are said to have caused his death, and relentless attacks were pressed from all sides. The extrication of the Spaniards proved to be an extraordinary military feat. By means of their artillery and three movable wooden towers they broke down the enemy barricades, and managed to establish control of the approaches to the Tacuba causeway, filling in the canal gaps with rubble and timbers as they progressed. On the night of 30 June (*La Noche Triste*), they almost made a clean escape, but their portable bridge jammed at one of the openings, and from the irresistible attack on them which followed only a remnant of the rearguard escaped over a tangle of debris, canoes and bodies, having lost nearly all the treasure, all their artillery and all but a few horses. 'God alone knows the trouble and fatigue we sustained, for no horse of the twenty-four was left which could still run, nor any horseman who could raise his arms, nor a sound foot soldier who could move.' Cortés' own estimate of the losses was 155 Spaniards, forty-five horses and over 2000 Indian allies killed, but more disinterested recorders put the dead at 450 Spaniards and 400 Indians. Marina was one of the three women who got safe to shore.

It is the measure of Spanish prestige and of Cortés' genius as a leader that the battle-worn company, including as it did the disillusioned followers of Narváez, could survive harassing pursuit, fight one fierce pitched battle at Otumba on 7 July, and reach Tlaxcala by the northern route on 12 July. Cortés promptly settled down there with a nucleus now of only 400 Spaniards to build up by threats, war and wiles a native confederacy to smash the Aztecs in Mexico. On 28 December 1520 he set out to do so by subduing the Valley cities and then concentrating on a siege of Mexico by land and water which lasted for ninety-three days and resolved itself into the complete destruction of the city and the extermination of practically all of its inhabitants and their defenders. It was a *crescendo* of relentless warfare and slow starvation. While the war-god's snake-skin drum pulsed and roared from the pyramid top, the Aztecs tore out the hearts of their Spanish and Indian captives, and the altars reeked with the last awful offertory to gods whose day was ended. As they gradually mastered the island, the Spaniards pounded flat what must have been one of the most beautiful cities in the world, and from the site of razed Tenochtitlan began to set Spain's mark on New Spain. The Valley was theirs.

Another might have paused, sated, but Cortés 'wished in everything to copy Alexander of Macedon', and his subordinates were as greedy as Alexander's generals had been. These sturdy veterans, woefully disappointed by the amount of loot which fell to them, now received their rewards by being sent out from Mexico on wild expeditions in search of gold and treasure, which were at first local repetitions of the central Mexican adventure and which ultimately opened up the country for the hordes who deserted the Caribbean islands in favour of rich Mexico. Gonzalo de

Sandoval was sent south-east from Tlaxcala in the autumn of 1521 to conquer the territory as far as Coatzacoalcos and establish there the town and port of Espiritu Santo. In the same year Francisco de Orozco was sent to exploit the gold-mines discovered in Oaxaca and was made captain of that province. Next year Cristóbal de Olid began the almost impossible task of subduing the Tarascan mountaineers of Michoacan, and he and others spent years in opening the country up to the Pacific near Zacatula and thence north to Colima. Cortés himself assumed the burden of coping with a threat from Jamaica which had begun in 1519 when the governor there, Francisco de Garay, sent Alonso de Pineda to search the whole Gulf coast. He did so very thoroughly, discovering the mouth of the Mississippi in the process. When by accident he had encountered Cortés near Vera Cruz, he skilfully avoided falling into his traps. The result of Garay's efforts, stubbornly, but on the whole unsuccessfully, prosecuted and ultimately appropriated by Cortés in 1522, was the establishment of a port at Pánuco (modern Tampico) and the exploration of the river there. To Pedro de Alvarado, a violent and impulsive man, fell Guatemala and the territory beyond it as far as modern San Salvador, and from 1522 to 1524 he fought and looted his way through it.

Up to 1524 the task was relatively uncomplicated, but in that year Cortés became aware that the profitable south-easterly expansion was to be confronted by another Spanish advance, this time north from Nombre de Dios and Panamá. Pedro Arias' men and his local rivals had pushed west from the Isthmus along both coasts and had been particularly fortunate along the Pacific as far as the Gulf of Fonseca. Andrés Niño and

Gil Gonzalez de Ávila had taken up Balboa's maritime design, and in 1522 Niño at sea and Gonzalez on land worked through and round Costa Rica into rich Nicaragua. Their methods were pacific and the rewards thereof were great. They baptized 32,000 natives and carried away much gold and pearls.

Moreover, the combination of the San Juan river and Lake Nicaragua seemed to promise the long-sought passage between Atlantic and Pacific. Pedro Arias promptly scared Gonzalez off to Española and sent his own agents, Francisco Hernández de Córdoba and Hernando de Soto, in to exploit the country, and in 1524 Soto started north through Honduras. The same year Gonzalez sailed back again, this time through bad navigation to the western extremity of the Gulf of Honduras. He established a base there and set out southwards to cross Honduras overland and reach his Nicaragua again. He had barely left before Cristóbal de Olid arrived to conquer Honduras ostensibly for Cortés, but actually following a secret agreement for independent action with the implacable Diego Velásquez of Cuba. Hot on his heels in turn came Francisco de las Casas, sent round by sea to chastise the rebellious Olid on behalf of Cortés.

Then the restless, vigorous Conqueror decided to settle matters himself, and set out in October 1524 to march across country to Honduras rather than risk the difficult circumnavigation of Yucatan. His journey was a most amazing feat, surpassing in difficulty anything of the sort yet experienced in North America. Bernal Díaz was commandeered to go along, and he devoted five lurid chapters of his history to an account of their cutting and bridging their way through the tropical swamps and forests of the vast Tabasco Basin. Cortés gave almost the whole of his fifth letter to this journey through the eastern Tierra Caliente. He began it like a king with a court of native princes, Spanish musicians and other ministrants to his glory, and ended it like a castaway after a seven-month journey, the last part of which took place during an unusually heavy rainy season. No one knows the details of his route, and to this day the region is devoid of railways and has few roads which are more than mule-paths, even when they are cleared of the invading vegetation. In general, Cortés marched to Coatzacoalcos (Espiritu Santo), thence along the coast to the Tabasco delta, and then struck south-west across the basin, up the Usumacinto river and over the coastal Sierra to the Gulf of Honduras.

Quite naturally there ensued a grand mêlée in Honduras among the five leading actors, with Cortés emerging on top, and the Mayan natives of the interior got their first prolonged experience of Europeans from watching their civil wars. The Isthmian adventure and the Cuban had met, and between them had effected the exploration of Mexico and Central America. In Yucatan the surviving Mayas retained enough military skill and strength to hold out for another twenty years, and up in Michoacan the Tarascans proved unconquerable, but the main outlines were clear. As yet, however, there was no strait. In 1522 Juan Sebastián del Cano had returned from the first circumnavigation of the earth to tell Spain of the way to the Pacific discovered by Fernão Magalhaes (Magellan) three years before, but meanwhile the North American adventurers, in spite of the optimistic hopes that began with Columbus, had failed to find a salubrious substitute for that bleak wintry way through the Straits of Magellan.

The search for a strait from the Pacific, added to hopes for another group of cities to loot, explains the remaining immediate aftermath of the conquest of Mexico. During the nine years (1524–33) spent by the patient, stubborn Francisco Pizarro in forcing South America to reveal in Peru an empire whose wealth made Mexico dwindle in importance, other Spaniards were exploring the Pacific coast of northern Mexico. Nuño de Guzmán, after a bloody failure to rule at Pánuco in 1528, took advantage of Cortés' departure to Spain for the settlement of his affairs, to drive an army in murderous fashion through Michoacan and Jalisco up into Sinaloa. He got very little rich loot and turned the country into a shambles before founding Culiacan in 1531 as an outpost for his slaving raids. When Cortés came back in 1530, Guzmán was still master of these troubled regions and had recently been doing his best to prejudice Cortés' reputation with the new governmental authorities from Spain.

His enmity and his strategic position, however, were insufficient to prevent the Conqueror from attempting to satisfy his curiosity about the Pacific Slope. He set up a shipyard at Zacatula and sent a series of expeditions up the coast in the hopes of finding a way to the Far East or a strait leading back to the Atlantic. Three of his vessels under Saavedra had crossed the Pacific in 1527, but the Portuguese were too strong in the East. Stubborn efforts along the American Pacific coast yielded little, and the long Gulf of California was confusing. Indeed, when Cortés left for Spain in 1539, never to return, the idea that the southern tip of the California peninsula (which he had discovered in 1533) was an island, was just in process of being exploded by an expedition which he had sent out under Francisco de

Ulloa and which followed the coast of the Gulf all the way from Mexico until it swung north again on the ocean. In general, the efforts of Guzmán and Cortés had been very expensive and unprofitable. The north was an arid region, much broken up by mountains, thinly settled, and apparently containing no civilisation worth looting. Even the dreamers of another Mexico or Peru became apathetic about the possibilities of the northern adventure.

NARRATIVES

Peter Martyr, Bernal Díaz, Andagoya and Cortés as above.

CHAPTER V

EMPIRES OF DREAM

(*Map No. 1, page 104*)

He found him very sad . . . because this was the outcome of something about which he had felt so sure.

CORONADO'S RECEPTION BY VICEROY MENDOZA, 1542

THE lull which gradually descended on Spanish North America after 1525 was suddenly broken in 1536 by an event which, when interwoven with old tales and present desires, sent hundreds of Spaniards out across the southern mainland of North America. In April of that year, four of Guzmán's slave-raiding cavalry, scouting on behalf of their exhausted, starving company on the upper reaches of the Petatlan river in Sinaloa, saw coming towards them two strange figures, barely distinguishable from their eleven Indian companions. They were Álvar Núñez Cabeza de Vaca, royal treasurer of the River of the Palms, and Estevan, a Moorish negro slave, bringing the first word of the fate of a proud expedition which had set out from Florida eight years before. 'They stood staring at me a length of time,' wrote Vaca, 'so confounded that they neither hailed me nor drew near to make an enquiry.' It will be granted that it was surprising to see travel-worn Spaniards emerge from the unknown north.

These men and two companions, Andrés Dorantes de Carranca and Alonzo del Castillo Maldonado, were the last survivors but one of 400 colonists under Pánfilo de Narváez who had landed in Florida more than eight years before, and they had walked about two-thirds of the way across the continent. There can be few chronicles of the sheer will to live more impressive than Vaca's narrative. Narváez had proved himself to be a hopelessly inept commander. He had landed on the peninsula which forms the western side of Tampa Bay on 14 April 1528, and lost his ships while he and his men marched north through groups of really poor Indians in quest of Apalache, a modest agricultural centre in the lake district north of St. Mark's Bay, to which they had been urged on by Indian assurances that there was much gold there.

Disappointed in this expectation and on the verge of starvation, they marched south to the coast in order to build boats in which to coast along to Pánuco, their destination. This boat-building was the one bit of commendable co-operation in their expedition. They melted down all their metal-work for nails, used their clothing for sails, wove horse-hair into ropes, and used horse-hide for water-skins. The 242 who had thus far survived short rations and harassing conflicts with the Indians set sail on 22 September in five overloaded boats and pursued a thirst-ridden course to the west, raiding the coastal villages and being attacked in return. Wind and current separated the boats off the mouth of the Mississippi, and Narváez, in a frantic effort to save his own skin, ruined Vaca's effort at reunion. On 6 November Vaca's solitary boat was cast ashore on an island, apparently off Galveston or Matagorda Bay, where within a few days he was joined by the survivors of another wrecked craft. It was later learned that the other three barges were in turn cast ashore and their occupants exterminated.

It was the adventurers' misfortune to be thrown among destitute nomadic Indians who were always on the edge of starvation. They had no agriculture of their own, but lived on fish, oysters and the roots of water plants, except in the autumn when they went inland to gorge themselves on prickly pear, walnuts and pine-nuts. They got an occasional deer by infinite labour, but they were south of the buffalo ranges, and Vaca, who was probably the first European to see those animals, did so only three times in seven years. The Indians were inclined to be friendly towards considerate white men, but the helplessness of the whites and their own destitution meant that they could do little to help. By the spring there were only fifteen left of the eighty who had been cast on the island, these survivors being the men best able to help themselves. Some of the whites had even resorted to cannibalism and dried the flesh of their dead companions to have food in reserve.

The story of the next six and a half years cannot be repeated in full here. Vaca survived because he made a place for himself as an itinerant trader in coastal and inland commodities among the tribes of south-eastern Texas, and because he garnished his trading operations and won his safe-conduct by acting as a healer. He never gave up hope of working west from this 'country so remote and malign, so destitute of all resource' to Pánuco, and he took great pains and risks to facilitate the escape with him of all the Spaniards he could locate, now slaves among the Gulf tribes.

After heart-breaking defections and disappoint-ments, his little company of four broke away from the feast of the prickly pear somewhere between the Sabine and Trinity rivers in September 1534.[1] Their technique

[1] The narrative is so vague in chronology that almost as good a case can

of travel was to multiply Vaca's medical practice by four, gradually equipping themselves with the recognised apparatus of medicine men and learning systematically how to avail themselves of their repute. They were fortunate in effecting their cures marvellously easily because of the Indians' susceptibility to suggestion. After each group of successes they promptly made it clear that they must go on towards the west, healing each band as they came to it, and they won a reputation for disinterestedness by returning all the gifts offered them except what they needed for sustenance. Sometimes their hosts were very stubborn about letting them go, one tribe keeping them eight months, but eventually their progress became amusingly formalised in a novel variation of Indian barter. Their successive hosts would accompany them *en masse* to the next tribe, explain how beneficent and generous they were, and depart regretfully after helping themselves to whatever they coveted of their neighbours' possessions! In this manner they travelled all the way to Sonora. It was a curious echo of ancient Toltec tales of healing, guiding gods.

It is naturally impossible to be certain of Vaca's route, but a reasonably good approximation would be from the Sabine or Trinity to the Nueces river along a line about fifty miles from the poverty-stricken coastal lagoons, thence north and west to cross the Pecos above its junction with the Río Grande, on over the uplands to the mouth of the Conchos, thence up the Río Grande, west across the arid north Mexican plateau to a pass leading down to the Yaqui river and along the hospit-

be made for 1535. For a careful re-examination of Vaca problems see the editorial articles by H. Davenport in *Southwestern Historical Quarterly*, xxvii, 2, 3, 4, xxviii, 1, 2 (Austin, 1923–24).

able Pacific Slope to the exciting point where 'Castillo saw the buckle of a sword-belt on the neck of an Indian and stitched to it the nail of a horseshoe'. These unmistakably European articles had been obtained from Spanish slave-raiders who had driven the Yaquis in terror from their placid agricultural pursuits. 'In a manner of the utmost indifference we could feign, we asked what had become of those men. . . . We told the natives that we were going in search of that people, to order them not to kill nor make slaves of them.' Vaca kept his word and had the satisfaction of seeing his last friendly escorts peacefully settled on the Fuerte river in spite of their Spanish rescuers' efforts to enslave them all.

Inasmuch as Vaca told a perfectly straightforward story of the countries he had seen and the miseries which he had experienced in them, it might seem peculiar that his reports set in motion a series of expeditions into and beyond the country through which he had passed. He reported little agriculture save near Appalache and in the interior near the Río Grande. He had seen no cities and few permanent dwellings beyond an occasional small *pueblo* or group of one- and two-storied timber and mud houses in and about the Río Grande valley. He did have a few Indian tales of larger *pueblos* and of agricultural people to the north-east, and he mentioned turquoises and green jade from the same region, but his whole account was a very discouraging one. Why then did the Spaniards rush into the lands from which he had struggled so hard to escape?

The answer must be found in a medley of elements. To begin with, news of the incredible wealth of Peru in South America became public in 1533. After rich Mexico, richer Peru. After Peru, who could tell?

Pizarro had gone south, his successor might be one who went north. Perhaps Narváez had been mistaken about Appalache and it was farther inland. Perhaps the great *pueblos* to the north-east of Mexico were another Peru. After all, Mexico City had been merely a very grand *pueblo*, for all its stone facings and burnished plaster. Moreover there was an Aztec legend about the Seven Caves in the north from which their people had been led, and an Indian slave of Guzmán's said that his father 'had gone into the back country with fine feathers to trade for ornaments and that when he came back he brought a large amount of gold and silver, of which there is a good deal in that country'. The route was forty days' journey across the central desert plateau, and the Indian himself went with his father once or twice and 'saw some very large villages, which he compared to Mexico and its environs. He had seen seven very large towns which had streets of silver workers.'

In all probability it was the recurrent 'seven' which did the work, impossible as it is to decide whether the Indians implanted the idea in Spanish minds directly from their own or, as so often happened, gave back what the Spaniards wanted to hear. For they, too, had a legend of 'seven' cities. Their tale went that when the Moors overran Portugal in the early eighth century, seven bishops fled from Oporto by sea to the west and set up new episcopates in fabulously rich lands out in the Atlantic, often called the island of Antilia. This legend attached itself to another medieval tale of the island of Brasil, where there grew red dye-wood like that which was so costly an item in Levantine commerce. The island of Brasil and the island of the Seven Cities, either separately or blended, sometimes in the form of a disc and sometimes a ring enclosing seven islands, strayed about the Atlantic Ocean of medieval and early modern maps and globes in unconvincing if persistent fashion. Perhaps, after all, either or both really lay north of Mexico! Guzmán had thought something of the sort in 1530 when he made his expedition into Sinaloa, Cortés had played with similar ideas, and now Vaca's unemphasised Indian gossip grew in importance in the minds of the Spaniards until it dwarfed the verities of his great chronicle. If the Seven Cities were insular, there must be a sea. If there were a sea, there would probably be a strait. The strait would surely be that of Anian joining Atlantic and Pacific.

At any rate, there were three immediate efforts made to solve the mystery, one in the eastern and one in the western half of the continent, and one along the Pacific coast. They all began in 1539, and perhaps it will be most convenient to take them in order from east to west.

Hernando de Soto was in Spain when Vaca arrived there and had just secured from the Emperor the reversion of the grant to Narváez, for almost nine years had passed without word and Narváez must be dead. It is easy enough to understand Soto's motives before he saw Vaca. He had gone out with Pedro Arias to Darien, and having lived through the period of exploitation in Central America, had subsequently shared with Pizarro the patient, slow process which ended in the incredible looting of Peru. He had heard of what Pineda and Garay had done on the Gulf of Mexico and of what Narváez hoped for, and now that Mexico and Peru were past history, southern North America seemed their logical successor. He was a great figure at the Spanish Court, for his fortune was large enough to make it worth the Emperor's while to borrow from him. After his well-earned taste of fame and adulation, it was natural for him to think of confirming his reputation in a new adventure. 'It was his object to find another treasure like that of Atabalipa [Atahualpa], lord of Peru,' wrote the Gentleman of Elvas, chief chronicler of the North American adventure.

It is less easy to see why Vaca's arrival and narrative, three months after the imperial grant to Soto, did not end the adventure at once. To be sure it would have been a little humiliating to give up, and a little out of line with the flattering European conception of a true *conquistador*, and Soto had learned stubbornness as well as patience during the weary years which had preceded the conquest of Peru. He set himself, therefore, to pump Vaca for encouraging news and to get him to go out with him. Now Vaca was bent on capitalising his fame and his hardship, but he would not go back to the Gulf of Mexico. Instead he succeeded in obtaining a Brazilian concession for himself. His fault, meanwhile, was that he could not refrain from letting his imagination embroider the gossip about the North which he had picked up in the Río Grande *pueblos*. Not that he was definite. 'He and another', he said, 'were sworn not to divulge certain things which they had seen . . . nevertheless, he gave them to understand that it was the richest country in the world.' Two of his kinsmen asked his advice about going with Soto. 'He would advise them to sell their estates and go.' This criminal magnification of Indian gossip was enough for Soto, who remembered that Peru was found nearly twenty years after Panciaco first told Balboa about its being south of Central America, and from Spain and Portugal a proud company of adventurers swarmed to his standard with their hastily realised fortunes on their backs.

Soto had in the back of his mind the persistent hope

of finding a passage from the Atlantic to the Pacific. The geographical knowledge of the day was still very confused, and it took centuries to kill the optimistic belief that some river like Pineda's River of the Holy Spirit (Mississippi) ought to flow from, or from near, the Pacific. Sixteenth-century maps of a partly known, partly imagined interior shewed strange interlacings of waterways. Again and again in the course of his wanderings Soto gave evidence of his conviction that in the north-west he would find a water-passage which would somehow link up the Pacific with either the Gulf of Mexico or the Atlantic. In the old medieval stories the Seven Cities had always been located near the sea and Vaca had hinted that he had been near the Seven Cities. It would be a great *coup* for Soto to find the cluster of cities on the shores of the Strait of Anian.

After provisioning in Cuba, Soto's 600 soldiers, 213 horses, pack of fighting hounds and herd of swine landed on the Florida coast on 28 May 1539, probably at Tampa Bay, but possibly at Charlotte Harbour farther down the coast. The ships were sent back to Cuba to return next year with provisions to a rendezvous on the north Gulf coast. Why Soto landed in country whose courageous natives had implacably fought off the Europeans for over twenty-five years and which Narváez found barren of loot, it is impossible to say, except that it was near Cuba, of which he had just been made governor. With little delay he and his army set off on what was to be over four years of relentless, courageous and unprofitable march, hither and thither over some 350,000 square miles of unexplored North America.[1] They appear to have ranged from 28° N. to

[1] For a recent discussion of their route, see T. Maynard, *De Soto and the Conquistadores* (New York, 1930).

36° N. and from 82° W. to 100° W., but in all that land they found no Peru and no treasure save marred fresh-water pearls. They might better have been warned by Juan Ortiz, who had been captured eleven years before when he came over from Cuba to find Narváez and who came to Soto within a day or two of the landing. He knew of no gold or silver in the country, but only of a petty tribal overlord 100 miles away.

No one could have been more determined or systematic than Soto. He was ruthless when he felt or found it necessary to overawe the natives. As he travelled about the country he used them as carriers, either by capturing the local chief as a hostage for their services, or by chaining together the iron collars which he fastened on those whom he captured in war. He soon discovered that an Indian once conducted 100 miles from his home dared not escape anyway. Soto's peregrinations, vague and irrational as they seem when drawn on a map, were determined by the answers given to his invariable question as to where were the largest populations. As each destination proved to be a mere Indian village of a few thousand inhabitants, he took what he could get, and set out for the always greater, richer 'city' farther on. He soon found that he could not expect gold, but until he died he did not give up his two fixed ideas, the discoveries of a great imperial centre, which ought to exist by all previous American experience, and of the wonderful cities which Vaca had heard of in the inland north. One or both of them should be close to a northern sea or strait. Perhaps the best example of his strength of purpose occurred in the autumn of 1540 when he heard through Ortiz that the supply ships had kept their rendezvous and were near at hand. 'He feared that, hearing of him without seeing gold or silver or other thing of value from that land, it would come to have such reputation that no one would be found to go there when men should be wanted; so he determined to send no news of himself until he should have discovered a rich country.'

One ought to distrust any account of the Soto expedition which presumes to be specific as to where it went. Indian villages are transient things; there are hundreds of mounds and mound sites in the area, and huge rivers like the Mississippi, the Arkansas and the Red can alter the courses they dig in alluvial soil by tens of miles in hundreds of years. Burnt-over and cleared lands can change and be reconquered by forest. Old swamps can fill up and floods can make new ones. Even the coasts and the lagoon-like bays to-day are not what they were in 1540. The account given below, while the result of the studies of many men, can only be an approximation.

Between the time of landing and October 1539 they ranged the western half of Florida pretty thoroughly before settling down for the winter at Appalache, where Narváez had been, and not far from the beach which was still littered with his horses' skulls. The Indians had earned their genuine respect, for they were hard to hit with cross-bow or arquebus and their arrows could pierce mail. In March 1540 Soto's company broke camp and set out north-east to visit a province which by report 'was governed by a woman, the town she lived in being of an astonishing size, and many neighbouring lords her tributaries, some of whom gave her clothing, others gold in quantity'. They found the lady on the Savannah river about seventy-five miles from its mouth and she did enjoy a wide authority, but her village was a flimsy affair and she could give them only large quantities of spoiled fresh-water pearls in place of gold.

They stayed with her for a fortnight and then, taking her with them, made almost due north into the Blue Ridge Mountains near the headwaters of the Broad river. This country was rich in game but poor in agriculture, so that they turned south and south-west again, passing in succession a number of pretentious Indian chiefs. One of them, for instance, was 'borne in a litter on the shoulders of his principal men, seated on a cushion and covered with a mantle of marten-skins . . . he was surrounded by many attendants playing upon flutes and singing'. Yet since even these local princes possessed little to loot and were ready to defend that, the company marched on with short halts. They came ultimately close to the Gulf at Mavilla, somewhere near the head of the great river delta north of Mobile Bay (where Soto heard of his ships), but they had a serious battle and a disastrous fire there, and on 17 November they struck north-west again almost to the Mississippi. They wintered (1540–41) on the eastern edge of the river-bottom forest between the Yazoo river and the Mississippi, about 125 miles east of the mouth of the Arkansas river, in fruitful and fairly friendly country.

At the end of April 1541 they set off northwards, cutting their way through forest and river-swamps to reach 'the great river' in May, somewhere a few miles south of modern Memphis. The narratives betray no awe at the size of the river. It seemed merely a very awkward military obstacle requiring a month's hard foundry and shipwright work to make barges for the crossing under the hostile eyes of haughty and impressive Indians. Soto thought that he should be reaching either a strait leading to the Pacific or the borders of Vaca's mythical lands, but after he had tracked down some chiefs in the lake district to the immediate north-west, he took the natives' word for it that the lands still farther on were cold and 'that cattle [buffalo] were in such plenty, no maize-field could be protected from them'. 'To the south . . . were large towns.' Hearing of the Ozark mountains, Soto went west hoping for minerals, but they were disappointing, and he seems to have made a great circle before settling down for the winter at a pleasant, fertile settlement on the Arkansas river near its junction with the Canadian. Here they had the unusual experience of a month of snow, but they amused themselves with learning how to snare rabbits.

By spring of 1542 they were in desperate straits, and it was imperative to get supplies from Cuba if Soto was to pursue his plan of driving west until he came to Vaca's cities. Ortiz had died, they had almost no European clothes or horse equipment left, and while they were confident that they could go on with their technique of travel, it was three years since they had left and their men and horses had dwindled in number. They made their way, therefore, down the Arkansas valley to the Mississippi during March and early April, expecting to come out near the sea, instead of 300 miles from it in a direct line and hundreds more by water. The local chief was almost contemptuous of them and said he knew nothing of the sea. A cavalry expedition tried to go down the river, but came back, having been checked by the bogs. Soto was fever-stricken and despondent over the present disappointment and the impossibility of maintaining his dwindling force without aid. He dared not settle down to build boats for

the river journey or a crossing until he had tamed his
Indian neighbours. He therefore selected a neighbouring Indian town and subjected it to systematic attack
and casual massacre. That done, 'he took to his pallet'
and died.

The successor to 'the magnanimous, the virtuous,
the intrepid captain' was Luis Moscoso de Alvarado,
whom the others thought 'preferred to see himself at
ease in a land of Christians, rather than continue the
toils of war', but that doughty *conquistador* had other
ideas. Having shrouded Soto's body in Indian buffalo-
hair blankets weighted with sand, he had it 'taken out
in a canoe and committed to the middle of the stream',
and he did his best to convince the Indians that Soto
'had ascended into the skies, as he had done on many
other occasions', leaving Moscoso in temporary command. He then called the captains together and convinced that amazing company that 'it appeared well
to march westwardly, because in that direction was New
Spain, the voyage by sea being held more hazardous'.
And west they marched that blazing summer, beyond
the Red river valley through the sandy pine-belt to the
black-soil prairie and on to the pine forest on the upper
waters of the Brazos river. So far as wealth was concerned, these lands bore out so truly Vaca's experience
in Texas that the discomfited men trailed back to their
wintering place at the mouth of the Arkansas at the
end of the year.

It was obviously time to strike for Spanish territory.
With great toil and resourcefulness they built seven
barges, melting down slave chains and collars and any
other iron for nails and shewing their customary inventiveness for other materials. They were lucky in
finding a Genoese cooper among them who, although

on the point of death, managed to make two water-barrels for each boat. A timely June flood spared them the risk of dragging their flimsy craft to the water and they sailed on 2 July 1543. They had constantly to fight off Indians in canoes as the Mississippi carried them 700 miles to the Gulf. They lost their last horses and some of their bravest men before they could turn west past the keys of the sandy coast, but the sturdy survivors retained enough courage to laugh at the sight of each other's mosquito-bitten faces. They prayed and pulled at the oars, took refuge behind the sand-bars during storms, and dug on the shores for fresh water. On 10 September 1543 they entered a river mouth and 'saw Indians of both sexes in the apparel of Spain . . . it was the Río de Pánuco . . . the town of the Christians was fifteen leagues inland. . . . Many, leaping on shore, kissed the ground; and all, on bended knees, with hands raised above them, and their eyes to heaven, remained untiring in giving thanks to God.'

It was a tribute to Spanish stamina that of the 600 who landed in Florida in 1539, 311 survived over four years of incredible hardship with enough innate arrogance left to be scornful of the poverty of Pánuco. After a kindly welcome there, they went on to Mexico with their tale. Added to Vaca's relation, it must have seemed to them harrowing enough to keep Spaniards away from the north Gulf coast for generations. They were to find that Mexico too had had its disappointments.

There had, of course, been a flurry of excitement in the Americas when news of Vaca and wish-embroidered versions of his reports began to go the rounds. Many a captain was anxious to discover and conquer the Mexico or Peru which might be in the north-east. Cortés and Guzmán were interested. Soto, as we have seen, got his chance. Pedro de Alvarado, who had just been ejected after an attempted invasion of Pizarro's Peru, hurried off to Spain for permission to approach it by sea from the Pacific. The man who ultimately arranged for the work to be done under his own auspices was Don Antonio de Mendoza, since 1535 the highest official in America, 'the good viceroy' of New Spain. He had been host to the Vaca party for several months, had failed to get any of them to undertake a return trip, but had taken the wise precaution of buying the negro Estevan from his master Dorantes and of training some of Vaca's Indian escorts as interpreters. In 1539 he heard of Ulloa's expedition by sea on behalf of Cortés, and he began his own careful preparations by sending off on a land reconnaissance a geographically minded Franciscan from Peru, Friar Marcos of Nice, with Estevan and the interpreters.

Friar Marcos, 'French by nation', has been much abused as a gaudy liar, but modern archaeological and ethnological scholarship has repaired his reputation as a keen observer who did his best to see things for himself and to corroborate what he was careful to make clear was hearsay. The complications arose in the first place because he and others read European, Mexican and Peruvian equivalents into what he saw and what he thought he saw of an American civilisation of a type as yet unknown to Spaniards, and in the second place, because of the remarkable behaviour of Estevan. That bearded black yielded to his dramatic instincts and cast himself for the rôle of the four Vaca medicine men rolled into one. He fitted himself up with plumes, and rattles and bells on his arms and legs, and arranged with Marcos that he should go ahead with a pair of greyhounds and an Indian escort, clad in an even richer regalia than that which had been such a wonderful key to success five years before in Texas. It must be admitted that for weeks he succeeded gloriously, gathering up rich gifts of turquoise and numerous women as he went. At his very destination, perhaps because his emblems of office identified him with the enemies of the *pueblo* Indians, the puzzled, greedy demi-god was toppled from his pinnacle by being put to death. There is a cluster of historical ironies in this picture of a negro slave captured in 1513 by Christian zealots from Moslem masters in Morocco, surviving the Narváez disaster by an unconscious echo of the legendary days when American gods came to earth as healers, enjoying two months of a similar but greater triumph quite alone in New Mexico, and then dying suddenly at the height of his success without at all knowing why. It is some consolation that his memory persisted in Zuñi folk-lore until fifty years ago.

Friar Marcos was one of a number of his order who had recently been pursuing missionary enterprise among the disunited tribes on the northern frontier. We have no very exact knowledge of their wanderings, but there are good reasons for believing that they had reached the vicinity of the lower Gila river or the mouth of the Colorado. At any rate, Marcos, although his extensive experience in Peru had given him some unfortunate prepossessions, knew a good deal about the mountainous north and was fortunate in having had the revered Vaca and humble Franciscans as his predecessors. He set out from Culiacan on 7 March and almost immediately became the object of kindly attentions from the Indians, who found him an appropriate successor to the beneficent Vaca and an agreeable contrast to the slave raiders. They put up garlanded huts for his resting-place throughout his whole northward journey and came for miles to touch his garments and receive his blessing, calling him 'Hayota, which in their language signified a man come from heaven'. Marcos had had to leave his Franciscan companion, Honoratus, behind on the Petatlan, but he himself moved along near the coast to the Yaqui river and then inland until he met the strikingly beautiful valley of the Sonora. It was from a village high up in that valley, where he rested for a fortnight while his Indians made enquiries on the coast, that Estevan set off (on 23 March) as his forerunner and herald. It was agreed that he should send back white crosses varying in size with the importance of his news, 'if more important than New Spain, he should send me a large cross'.

Four days later Indians came back 'with a very large cross, as tall as a man' and with startling news. Estevan had met Indians who had actually been in the settled cities of the north and was off at full speed to see them himself. 'It was thirty days' march to the first city of the country, which was called Cibola . . . in this first province there are seven very large cities, all under one lord, with houses of stone and lime, large, the smallest ones of two stories and with a flat roof, and others of three and four stories, and that of the lord with five, all placed together in order; and on the door-sills and lintels of the principal houses many figures of turquoise stones.'

It was to this *pueblo* centre, Cibola (Shi-uo-na), the range of territory of the Zuñis, on the high plateau between the Little Colorado and the Río Grande, that Estevan and Marcos after him now proceeded, finding vivid, even graphic, confirmation of the news at every village at which they stopped. The Indians pressed gifts of turquoise and leather garments upon them and joined their trains. Their route was up the Sonora and over the pass from its headwaters to those of the San Pedro, down that valley for five days and then northeast through an uninhabited wilderness of mountain, forest and valley to the cluster of adobe towns on the mountain plateau. On 21 May Marcos was only three days' journey from Cibola when he learned of Estevan's death and the maltreatment of his Indian escort, but with remarkable determination he insisted on going ahead until he could see the place for himself. His Indians were terrified, but he managed to keep them from killing him forthwith, even shaming two or three into accompanying him towards Cibola. From a mountain knoll he looked across the shimmering distance to his discovery. 'Its appearance is very good for a settlement—the handsomest I have seen in these parts. The houses are, as the Indians had told me, all of stone, with their stories and flat roofs. As far as I could see from a height where I placed myself to observe, the settlement is larger than the city of Mexico.' Regretfully he turned away and 'with far more fright than food' made his way back to Mexico, where he arrived late in August.

Although his report was interpreted optimistically and badly, his information was fairly correct. There had been seven cities in the Zuñi confederacy, and it was only one of the groups of *pueblos* which were scattered about the great mountainous oval formed by the Colorado, the Little Colorado, the Río Grande and the San Juan. They were not made of stone, but like Mexico they seemed to be, being built up of a pounded rubble of mud and stones (adobe), cemented with ashes, and smoothed off to a surface which reflected the blazing sun like dressed stone. The door-ways (which were in the flat roofs and reached by ladders) were ornamented with turquoise matrix, which was mined not far off to the north-east, and the buildings were often of more than one story. The village which he saw (Hawikùh) undoubtedly did look bigger than the Mexico City which the Spaniards had rebuilt, for it contained about 200 rambling houses for its 1000 or so inhabitants. The trouble as usual lay in what imagination, reinforced by European, Mexican and Peruvian analogies, did with the Friar's observations. His own imagination was not guiltless when it came to retrospect in conversation.

Next year (1540) the expeditions prepared by the deliberate, careful Mendoza set out to add this jewel to the Spanish crown and to augment the viceroy's reputation. It was a very different matter from the informal sally of Marcos and Estevan, for the Franciscans had turned their pulpits into recruiting platforms with great effect. It is true that the volunteers were not always of the best calibre, for one witness described them as 'for the most part vicious young gentlemen who did not have anything to do', and another suggested that 'their departure was a benefit rather than a disadvantage', but Mendoza selected about 300 of them under the command of Francisco Vásquez de Coronado, equipped them extremely well, and sent them off from Campostela on 23 February 1540 as the core of a huge force of Indians. They had pack-horses and mules by the hundreds, and herds of cattle, sheep, goats and swine were taken along for food. Hernando de Alarcón, in command of two vessels, kept a parallel course along the Pacific coast, hoping that he might find a waterway leading to the

Seven Cities which might also be pursued eastwards to the Gulf of Mexico or the Atlantic.

This cumbrous military force had none of the dash and romance about it such as single adventurers possessed, or even the company of Soto, which at that moment was about to break up its camp near the Yazoo river. There was a sort of blight of disappointment on it from start to finish. For one thing, the scattered little groups of Indians were frightened, hostile, and quite unable to provide useful amounts of food for such a horde, and it did not occur to Spanish soldiers to employ the gentle address which had been the protection of Vaca and Marcos. For another, the immediate country was not promising, and quite early in the expedition they met Melchior Díaz, who had been trying in vain to corroborate Marcos' tale for Mendoza. Cibola itself (Hawikuh *pueblo*) was a terrific disappointment, 'a little, crowded village' whose warriors insisted on putting up a fight, futile as that was. It was true that there were many other *pueblos* near by, but Friar Marcos found it wise to go home at the first opportunity, 'seeing that his report had turned out to be entirely false, because the kingdoms that he had told about had not been found, nor the populous cities, nor the wealth of gold, nor the precious stones . . . nor other things that had been proclaimed from the pulpits'.

The only thing to do was to discover whether there were greener pastures farther on, so that while the main army gradually came up and made its way to winter quarters at Bernalillo on the Río Grande, Coronado sent out small bands to investigate the sixty or seventy villages of the *pueblo* region and come to terms of sufferance with the scattered 20,000 or 25,000 inhabitants. It was too much to expect that this could be achieved without friction, but there was no justification for one captain's burning 200 Indians at the stake. The villages yielded abundant food and quantities of turquoise matrix, but from the Grand Canyon of the Colorado on the west to the Pecos river on the east there was neither gold nor silver. There was much that was strange and new, seven-story houses and beautiful pottery and textiles, mountain sheep with portentous horns and the huge hides of the plains buffalo, but a man could not fill his pockets with these. The Grand Canyon was a marvel, 'three or four leagues in an air line across' and 'impossible to descend', but it was only a barrier if it was true that India and China lay beyond. In fact, gloom settled on the adventurers until a plains Indian whom they called 'The Turk' told them about his country, Quivira.[1]

A year later they found him out as a liar, and before they garrotted him he told them that he had been put up to it by the Indians of the Pecos river 'to lead them off on to the plains and lose them, so that the horses would die when their provisions gave out, and they would be so weak if they ever returned that they could be killed without any trouble'. Yet his story had been an alluring one. 'In his country there was a river in the level country which was two leagues wide, in which there were fishes as big as horses, and large numbers of very big canoes, with more than twenty rowers on a side, and that they carried sails, and that their lords sat on the poop under awnings, and on the prow they had a great golden eagle. He said also that the lord of

[1] There can be no finality about Coronado's routes on the plains. For contrasted views compare M. A. Shine, 'The Lost Province of Quivira', *Catholic Historical Review*, ii, 1 (Washington, 1916), and D. Donoghue, 'The Route of the Coronado Expedition in Texas', *Southwestern Historical Quarterly*, xxxii, 3 (Austin, 1929).

that country took his afternoon nap under a great tree on which were hung a great number of little gold bells, which put him to sleep as they swung in the air. He said also that everyone had their ordinary dishes of wrought plate, and the jugs and bowls were of gold.'

Coronado spent the open season of 1541 exploding that lovely tale and in doing so covered a great deal of country, from settlements in the south which had seen Vaca to straw lodges in the north, 500 miles north-west of Soto's wanderings to the north of his Mississippi crossing. Indeed one of his captives broke away, to be picked up next year by Moscoso's men on their westward essay for Vaca's cities. Coronado and his company were as continuously amazed at the grassy prairie with its deep, tree-clad river bottoms and at the ever-present herds of buffalo, as they were disappointed at the absence of worldly wealth among the hunting Indians. 'The country is like a bowl, so that when a man sits down, the horizon surrounds him all around at the distance of a musket shot.' As for the buffalo, 'The country they travelled over was so level and smooth that if one looked at them the sky could be seen between their legs, so that if some of them were at a distance they looked like smooth-trunked pines whose tops were joined'. The nomadic Indians shewed little interest or curiosity, but being as yet unacquainted with horses and wheels, would pack up their meagre belongings on wooden frames (*travois*) pulled by dogs, and get away from the Spaniards as fast as they could.

It is believed that Coronado made a circle east and south from the Pecos river to the fork of the Brazos river about 100° W., then rode due north 'following the compass needle' across the Canadian river, turned north-east until he reached the Arkansas river at its southern bend, followed it north-east to the Great Bend and pushed on to some Wichita encampments near the Kansas river. Like Soto he learned there that the north was cold and thinly populated, and like Soto he turned back.

The journey home to Mexico in 1542 was a retreat from defeat which was relieved only by the heroism of two friars who stayed behind to minister and who quickly suffered martyrdom. Everywhere the Indians were rebelling in despair against the intolerable demands which had been placed on their modest productive economies. The Spaniards were bad-tempered, worn out and suspicious, and as soon as they reached their own settlements they deserted their leader in scores. 'With less than 100 men', Coronado 'came to kiss the hand of the viceroy and did not receive so good a reception as he would have liked, for he found him very sad . . . because this was the outcome of something about which he had felt so sure.'

When Soto's men came in a year later, the curtain fell for over forty years on the disappointing inland north. Alarcón had entered the Colorado from the Gulf of California and worked up its valley for fifteen days by making Indians drag his boats. Satisfied that it provided no passage or entry to the Seven Cities, he shot back down the river in two days. While Coronado was exploring, Melchior Díaz made a land expedition north-west from Sonora, on which he crossed the Colorado by raft and learned of the arid desolation of Lower California. Finally, in 1542 and 1543, two ships of the fleet which Alvarado had built on the Pacific but died before he could use, were sent out by Mendoza to explore the Pacific coast for a strait. In 1542 Juan Rodríguez Cabrillo, the Portuguese commander, struck

93

across to the outer side of the Californian peninsula and coasted north inquisitively to a point just north of San Francisco Bay, but died after being driven south again by the winter storms. His chief pilot, Bartolomé Ferrelo, took up the task in 1543, and by 1 March had reached a point about latitude 42° or 43° before he felt that his ships would not take him farther. It had been an extraordinary feat of navigation for two jerry-built vessels with inept crews on an inhospitable, unknown coast, but it settled for sixty years Spain's hopes for that elusive water-way which geographers felt sure should unite Atlantic and Pacific.

Mendoza's saddened resignation in 1543 became Spain's. North America held only one Mexico, and the seven medieval Portuguese bishops were still alive only in the fertile brains of map-makers. The Strait of Anian had eluded Gómez on the Atlantic and Ferrelo on the Pacific. The thing to do was to settle down and develop what was known to be fertile and productive, to teach the Gospel, and people the land in peace. Yet here and there old soldiers felt their wounds stiffening, and as they warmed themselves in the sun or by the fire, kept wondering whether perhaps after all their leaders had just missed the way. They wrote narratives to encourage others 'to discover that better land which we did not see', for 'their hearts weep for having lost so favourable an opportunity . . . to go on further from there'. In his old age, Pedro de Castañeda, who was Coronado's best chronicler, could still argue that if his leader had only ascended the Río Grande and crossed the mountains to the west he 'would have reached the lands . . . on the edge of Greater India'.

NARRATIVES

Babcock as above. The principal narratives of Vaca, Soto and Coronado are translated in F. W. Hodge and T. H. Lewis, *Spanish Explorers in the Southern United States, 1528–1543* (New York, 1907). That of Friar Marcos of Nice is translated in F. R. and A. F. A. Bandelier, *The Journey of Álvar Núñez Cabeza de Vaca* (New York, 1905). A number of parallel narratives are translated in G. P. Winship, *The Journey of Coronado* (New York, 1904), and another important collection of documents and translations is the Bandelier papers, edited by C. W. Hackett as *Historical Documents relating to New Mexico, etc.* (2 vols., Washington, 1923, 1926). The only English version of Alarcón's voyage is a paraphrase in R. Hakluyt, *The Principal Navigations, etc.*, vol. ix (Glasgow, 1904). A translation of the Cabrillo-Ferrelo narratives is in H. E. Bolton, *Spanish Exploration in the Southwest, 1542–1706* (New York, 1916).

CHAPTER VI

FACING REALITIES

(Map No. 1, page 104)

IN the fifty years after the discovery of America by Columbus, the Spaniards had put forth astounding efforts in investigation of what they had found, but during the next two centuries it became very obvious that the days of mere cream-skimming were ended. Up to 1542 there had been enough immediately available loot or keen enough hopes for more to justify the extensive exploration of North America from the Isthmus of Panamá to several points across the continent north of 35° N., but the immediate rewards at any point north of the Valley of Mexico had been so small that backing could not be found either for prompt occupation or for further exploration. For the moment there was a definite shrinkage of the Spanish sphere of influence to the islands and to the lands near Mexico and south of it. There were simply not enough Spaniards available nor attractions strong enough to ensure the occupation of what had been surveyed. There was nothing to prevent a military expedition like Soto's or Coronado's from marching up through North America to the Great Lakes, for the success of such an enterprise depended only on organisation and sufficient capital investment, but consolidation and occupation were enormously more difficult and must be slow. From 1542 on, there was a lag between Spanish knowledge of North America and occupation of it which was never eliminated.

With almost negligible exceptions, Spanish exploratory effort in North America from 1543 to 1769 consisted in re-exploration and in filling some of the gaps on the map between the lines of former discoveries. These efforts were not less noteworthy than the pioneering adventures, indeed some of them were distinctly more difficult because of the character of the country and native resistance. The earliest explorers had chosen the best lines of march in terms of water and sustenance which they could find, and they had come upon the natives with the full impact of the prestige which their horses, arms and use of steel had given them. Their successors often had to devise ways of getting from water-hole to water-hole in arid, unfruitful deserts, and increasingly they were confronted by hostile Indians who were losing their awe and equipping themselves with the white man's techniques and instruments. The coming of the horse meant a revolutionary change in ways of living in North America, particularly among the buffalo-hunters of the plains. When Cortés left behind a wounded horse on his march to Honduras, the natives fed it with flowers until it died, and worshipped it in effigy, but within twenty-five years there were many ranges where horses ran almost wild and rapidly increased in numbers. Here it must be sufficient to say that Spanish expansion after 1542 was cramped by paucity in numbers, by difficulties of *terrain*, by the necessity for protected roads and large quantities of native labour, by recurrent bloody revolts on the part of negro or Indian labourers, and by attacks from the avaricious, embittered, nomadic tribes on the frontiers.

Where agriculture and cattle ranches were possible and native or negro labour available, the expansion was conducted by colonising missionaries or by *encomenderos*, but the regions in the north which were appropriate for this were not only rare between Mexico and the inland plains, but in widely separated river valleys. From time to time a jump would be made from the occupied *tierra de paz* to some fertile, well-watered spot far in advance, but difficulties of communication and protection again and again brought about bloody and expensive failures. Keener lures had to be found, for there never was the kind of agricultural expansion which is caused by pressure of population.

Most powerful of all these lures were the mines, predominantly of silver, with much slighter enterprises for tin, antimony, copper and gold. About 1546 attention was drawn to the extreme richness of ores in Zacatecas, and, with the discovery of the San Barnabé lode on 11 June 1548, there began that wresting of treasure from the western mountains of North America which was to carry men ever farther north until they passed the Arctic Circle at the end of the nineteenth century. For New Spain it meant the extraordinary wealth which is often epitomised in San Luis Potosí or Bonanza. It also meant that the millionaires, who were the products of this large-scale enterprise, were ever alert for new lodes and able to find the capital for their development. The total result was the intense exploitation of one of the richest silver deposits the world has known. Mining was pre-eminently responsible for the occupation of the northern central plateau between the ranges of the Sierras, and even attracted the operators and their gangs of labourers beyond the Gila and the Colorado into what is now western Arizona.

Here was an instance where an abundantly productive enterprise carried the Spaniards through otherwise repellent territory to Coronado's *pueblo* country and even a little beyond.

Second only to the miners as effective occupiers of the land were the missionaries, Franciscan, Jesuit and Dominican. We have seen that they had been numbered among the pioneers, but their subsequent rôle was a good deal more complex. The Counter-Reformation, in full swing during the last half of the sixteenth and the seventeenth centuries, produced many types of the most zealous piety and missionary spirit. For hundreds of friars and monks the world was well lost for Christ, among them the dozens of martyrs who preached and taught on the frontiers and paid with their lives for their failures really to win the natives to Christian allegiance. There were others, notably the Jesuits, who believed in a more practical winning of the world for Christ. Their most remarkable success was the segregated native empire which they established in Paraguay in South America, but the same idea of setting apart a North American region where they and their native charges would be uncontaminated by worldly influences was apparent from time to time, notably in the case of the Californian peninsula. Among the many obstacles to successful missionary work, first place should probably be given to the difficulty of communicating the essence of Christianity to the American natives, but a fertile source of misunderstanding was the fact that the orders were almost as greedy for the support and services of native labour as were the other agricultural colonists and the miners. The clashes over this kind of suzerainty were frequent and certainly did much to obscure the otherwise altruistic aims of the churchmen.

99

This quest for man-power, especially for the killing work in the deep silver-mines, was responsible for much of the Spanish re-exploration of North America. Captives in war were legitimately enslaved, and if one could get permission for a 'punitive' campaign, one could make almost as much by selling men as earlier adventurers had done by commandeering stores of bullion. Men were used up faster than they were bred in the early days and unsettled conditions militated against the normal increase of sedentary populations. Moreover, when the Spaniards had so much that the frontier natives wanted (notably iron, steel, mules and horses) and represented so much that they hated, friction was continuous and life on the borders tended to alternate between a grim accumulation of hates under superficially peaceful conditions and still grimmer revolts and their suppression. Where neighbours are basically unequal, the frontier will always recede in front of the stronger.

Then again, the old lures to exploration did not altogether lose their potency with the failures of Narváez, Soto and Coronado. As Portugal dwindled in strength, Spain found herself strong enough to maintain a foothold in the Far East in the Philippine Islands, and in spite of the difficulties of Pacific navigation, found it best to maintain communications by way of America. The Manila galleon found its first haven on the western American coast and its goods were transhipped overland to the Atlantic carriers. The regrettable expense of that operation kept alive until the end of the eighteenth century a hope so deep as almost to be a conviction, that a water-way through North America, the Strait of Anian, might yet reward the devotion of an explorer.[1]

[1] See pp. 4-5.

It was admitted that there might not be a continuous ocean strait, but somehow, the least to be expected of Providence was that inland America contained a large sea, a Mediterranean, with navigable rivers flowing from it to the Atlantic and Pacific coasts. The will to believe in the strait goes far towards explaining the occasional unprofitable expeditions which went out from the known into the unknown at the head of the Gulf of California, north and north-west from the *pueblo* country, and north and north-west from the rivers of what are now Alabama and the Carolinas.

There were also those who believed that Vaca, Soto and Coronado had either barely failed to find the rich inland kingdoms or concealed their knowledge of them. Both Cosa (on the upper Alabama river) and Quivira (on the Kansas river) were alluring enough to attract adventurers who were not checked by the disillusionment which corroboration of past exploration brought them, but pushed on farther to the same disappointments as their predecessors. In that way Tristán de Luna y Arrelano, one of Coronado's captains, made his way up the Alabama river and westward towards the Mississippi in 1559–60; Juan Pardo explored the eastern slope of the Blue Ridge in 1566, and his lieutenant, Boyano, crossed the mountains next year to the Alabama valley; Fray Agustín Rodríguez in 1581 established the route by the Conchos and Río Grande valleys to long-deserted Zuñi, and in 1582–83 Fray Bernardino Beltrán and Antonio de Espejo linked the whole Pecos valley with this new approach to the *pueblo* country and the buffalo-plains; Juan de Oñate revisited the frontiers from the Gulf of California on the west to Quivira in the north and east between 1598 and 1605; and a freebooting murderer, Antonio Gutiérrez de

Humaña, actually rode north from Quivira to the Platte river in 1594.

Finally, there was the novel note of European competition in the exploitation of North America. In the beginning, the Papal bulls of demarcation had been the international law by which Spain enjoyed monopoly in North America, but the Reformation provided one basis for contempt of that ordinance and the growing strengths of France, Holland and England provided many more. No longer was Spanish occupation of the continent merely to await Spanish competence. Now frontiers threatened to become international in a European sense and enterprise to be dictated by strategic considerations.

Before turning to these rival European enterprises in America, however, it seems desirable to summarise the threats they embodied, as they were seen through Spanish eyes, in order to understand the response which was made. The first spectacular warning that Spain was not to have everything her own way in North America came in 1522. Cortés, having just reconquered Mexico and being anxious to ensure for himself the most favourable possible relations with his Emperor, gathered up from among his company as generous and representative a collection of treasure as he could and despatched it to Spain. Unfortunately for his hopes, his emissary was captured off Cape St. Vincent by a French corsair, and the store of mosaic masks, gold and silver objects, and fascinating feather-work went to delight the renaissance court of Francis I. This was only the beginning of the enthusiastic piracy by which French, Irish, English and Dutch seamen secured compensation for their exclusion from the Americas. Indeed some of them were quite willing to let the Spaniards extract

American wealth if they might have the chance to snatch at it on its way to Europe. What agitated the Spaniards most, however, was that they began going to America to do their work and, in particular, that they infested the neglected Caribbean islands and the Bahama Channel between Florida and the islands. It was realised that if any enemy country could establish a base on the North American mainland or master an island near the Channel, the Spanish galleons would suffer sadly.

Exciting as the hostile forays of the sixteenth century were, and as disastrous to prestige as were the Dutch revolt and the English defeat of the Armada, Spain's actual territorial sovereignty in America was little threatened at that time by French, English and Dutch efforts at securing permanent footholds. The change came in the seventeenth century. Then failing Spain had to see Caribbean islands snatched from under her nose by all three of her rivals and had to substitute a naval convoy system for the protection which territorial monopoly had once afforded. More serious still was the tardy success of England and Holland in actually finding ways in which to support permanent settlements on the mainland. It was under these circumstances that it became highly important to occupy south-eastern North America (Florida) and win its native inhabitants to religious and political allegiance. It seems very doubtful whether Spain would have attempted the costly and on the whole vain enterprise of occupying that territory had it not been for protection of the Bahama Channel.

Even these Atlantic outer-works seemed to have failed to protect when about 1675 it was discovered that the Indians of the interior who provided the frontier problem in both east and west were equipping themselves with fire-arms and other instrumental aids through trade with the French in the north. In 1673 a French expedition paddled down to the mouth of the Arkansas on the Mississippi. In 1682 a Frenchman actually reached the Gulf by the same route, and between 1678 and 1684 an exiled, discredited Spanish governor of New Mexico proposed to Louis XIV, in succession, the conquest of Quivira, the establishment of a French colony at the mouth of the Río Grande and the conquest of Pánuco as a base for capture of the richest mining area of New Spain. With the English working inland from the Atlantic coast and the French occupying the Mississippi valley, Spain rallied her failing energies in a vain effort to establish a frontier from Atlantic to Pacific and effectively to occupy the North American lands which her sons had explored. But before turning to this European congress and conflict in the Mississippi valley, it is necessary to see how and when the new rivals had come to North America, what they found which enabled them to exploit what Spain had disdained, and, in particular, to trace the steps by which they had found their way across an unknown continent to trouble Spanish frontiers.

NARRATIVES

Hackett (vol. ii) and Bolton as above. G. P. Hammond and A. Rey have translated and edited Baltasar de Obregón's contemporary account of the northward expansion of Mexico up to 1584 under the title of *Obregón's History* (Los Angeles, 1928). For the south-east, the Florida State Historical Society at Deland has published much illustrative material under the editorship of J. T. Connor; H. E. Bolton has edited *Arredondo's Historical Proof of Spain's title to Georgia* (Berkeley, 1925); and

H. I. Priestley has edited *The Luna Papers* (2 vols., Deland, Fla., 1928). Clark Wissler's 'The Influence of the Horse in the Development of Plains Culture', *American Anthropologist*, N.S., xvi, 1 (1914), and chap. iii, sections 2 and 3, of W. P. Webb, *The Great Plains* (New York, 1931), discuss the effects of the introduction of horses to North America.

CHAPTER VII

THE ENIGMA OF THE NORTH ATLANTIC

(Map No. 2, page 258)

This See is called the great Occyan
So great it is that never man
Coude tell it sith the worlde began
Tyll nowe within this xx. yere
Westwarde be founde new landes.

RASTELL: A NEW INTERLUDE. C. 1519

EUROPEANS knew north-eastern North America 500 years before Columbus and had visited it regularly for a century after him before they made it yield a permanent foothold. Spain found it profitable to occupy the Caribbean as soon as possible after its discovery, but the Norsemen of Iceland, after colonising Greenland about 960 and failing in several similar efforts along the North American coast in the early eleventh century, were forced to abandon even the Greenland venture to lonely extinction. The medieval Papacy had to resign itself to the disappearance of its outpost in the arctic seas, and gradually memory of that venture faded from men's minds. The north had failed to provide an insistent incentive to European acquisitiveness, and neglect was its reward.

Yet for one group of Europeans the northern seas provided a continuous lure. The fishermen of the Atlantic coast, who provided a Catholic Europe with a basic article of diet and with its principal fast-day food, followed the banks fisheries from the North Sea and the Irish coast to the very Iceland from which the first Europeans had gone to America. Fishermen, however, are seldom public-spirited geographers or over-communicative about the best fishing-grounds they know, and there have come down to us only indirect inferences which lead us to believe that before Columbus roused Europe with his southern discoveries, close-mouthed men from the northern and western limits of what was still a Mediterranean world had furled their sails and dropped their boats to take in the rich harvest awaiting them off the north-eastern coast of North America. What knowledge they had was no part of the general body of European geographical lore. It was the gossip and tale-telling which an alert man or an initiate could pick up in the taverns of northern and western ports. It could whet the appetites of men like the Italian and Portuguese navigators of the fifteenth century, it could lead sound business men of Bristol to fit out expeditions to essay the seas west and south of Iceland, and it could even win the attention of that mercantile-minded, treasure-hoarding Tudor, Henry VII of England.

It must be admitted that this knowledge would probably have had little effect had it not coincided with that passion in outer Europe to find the East by sailing west, to which the career of Columbus provided such a striking response. It is well to remember that the Atlantic states of Europe were the last stations on the long line of middlemen who delivered preservative Eastern spices to Western kitchens and luxuries like precious stones and radiant textiles to the courts of kings. The Venetian or the Genoese citizen or the burgher of a Hansa town respected middlemen's profits, if only because he took some of the last of them, but Portuguese, Spaniards, Frenchmen and Englishmen longed for the chance to secure Eastern commodities at the risk of a single voyage devoid of customs barriers, brigands, pirates and go-betweens. There is a high irony in the fact that Italians shewed them the way. Be that as it may, before Columbus sailed, England and France were the homes of ocean-going fishermen and traders in fish, who traded by sea not only with Portugal and Spain, but with Iceland and the Azores, and who shared in the excitement which prevailed over the unknown islands and lands of the Atlantic.

The English effort began, so far as we know, on 15 July 1480, when John Lloyd, 'the most expert shipmaster of all England', on behalf of John Jay and other merchants, set out from Bristol 'to the island of Brasylle in the western part of Ireland, to traverse the seas'. He was out nine weeks before storms and shortage of supplies forced him back to an Irish port, but he found no 'Brasylle'. Apparently, however, this idea of discovering Atlantic islands retained its attractions among the Bristol merchants, for in 1498 Pedro de Ayala, writing to his Spanish sovereigns from London, where he was acting as ambassador, said that 'for the last seven years the people of Bristol have equipped two, three, and four caravels in search of the island of Brazil and the Seven Cities'. Indeed there is a remote possibility that Robert Thorne and Hugh Elyot reached Newfoundland in 1494. What was needed for sustained endeavour was the infection of England with the idea which was fermenting in men's minds all over Europe that Asia, not mere islands, could be reached by sailing west.

Columbus may, as Bartholomew Columbus reports,

have tried to sell that idea to Henry VII, but if he did, his arrogant terms were too high and the actual agent was a humbler man, Giovanni Caboto, 'another Genoese like Columbus', who had been admitted to Venetian citizenship in 1476. He had been to Mecca in the spice trade, and 'when he asked those who brought them what was the place of origin of these spices, they answered that they did not know, but that other caravans came with this merchandise to their homes from distant countries, and these again said that the goods had been brought to them from other remote regions. He therefore reasons that if the easterners declare to the southerners that these things come from places far away from them, and so on from one to the other . . . it follows as a matter of course that the last of all must take them in the north towards the west.' He came to England, burning with this idea, some time between 1484 and 1490 and settled, not, as might be expected, among the Italians of Southampton or London, but at Bristol among the merchants adventurers who were already interested in the west. Columbus chose to sail a little south of west from Spain. Cabot preferred what he believed would be a shorter northern route. Henry VII gave him his chance by granting him letters patent on 5 March 1496, 'to sail to all parts, regions, and coasts of the eastern, western and northern sea . . . to find, discover and investigate whatsoever islands . . . which before this time were unknown to all Christians'. The Bristol merchants bore the costs.

John Cabot, and possibly his subsequently famous son Sebastian, set out from Bristol in a company of eighteen on board the bark *Matthew* on 2 May 1497. They made their American landfall on 24 June, probably near the western end of the south shore of Newfoundland, but possibly at Cape Breton Island, or less possibly on the Labrador coast. They coasted south and west an undetermined distance (in any case, as far as Cape Breton Island), and were back home by 6 August. Like Columbus five years before in the West Indies, the reconnaissance had been made and now the problem was one of exploitation.

Cabot and his backers hurried to London to report to the King. Their arrival and news caused a tremendous sensation. 'He is called the Great Admiral and vast honour is paid to him and he goes dressed in silk, and these English run after him like mad.' He was confident that he had reached the north-eastern projection of Asia and that by coasting south and west from there he could swiftly reach Marco Polo's Cipangu (Japan), whose gilded description he knew by heart. Henry VII, 'who is wise and not prodigal', gave him £10 from his Privy Purse and an annuity of £20 from the customs receipts of Bristol'.[1] He promised his favour for a large expedition in 1498.

At this point even our relative certainties come to an end, except for the preparations and start in 1498. The trouble is that Sebastian Cabot made his living during the first half of the sixteenth century by trading on his father's as well as on his own exploits, and succeeded so well in blending them that for centuries the son received most of the credit for his father's achievements. In the process, the 1498 voyage seems to have had added to it elements which belong properly to an attempt made by Sebastian to find the North-West Passage years later.[2] If it has not, the voyagers

[1] The pound was worth twelve or fifteen times as much in 1500 as to-day.
[2] Those interested will find the various interpretations in G. P. Winship, *Cabot Bibliography* (New York, 1900), in H. P. Biggar, *Voyages of the Cabots*

reached the main American coast only after a trip up the eastern coast of Greenland and back along Labrador and Newfoundland. If it has, their six ships loaded with trading merchandise set out on a more direct course early in May, and we have only hints on which to base the conclusion that some of them reached America and returned, and contemporary maps to convey the impression that they made a lengthy coasting voyage so far south as to excite the apprehensions of the Spaniards in the Caribbean.

As far as the exploration of North America was concerned, however he may have travelled, Cabot's efforts for years seemed to have effected nothing. He had not found Cipangu, nor did his Asia bear any resemblance to that described by the medieval travellers. He had seen Indians here and there, but the evidences of their culture which he brought back promised no wealth beyond the doubtful prospects of a slave trade. Briefly, he had little with which to win more royal favour or mercantile support. Moreover, the sixteenth century opened, as we have seen, with the dawning apprehension in Europe that the Americas might be a separate continental system and lie between Europe and Asia. Finally, Henry VII had decided that friendship with Spain must be a cardinal tenet of his foreign policy and Spain had happened on the only American regions where satisfying amounts of treasure could be found.

Of course, curiosity as to the northern regions did not die away at once. The empty spaces on the maps had to be filled in and hope provided incentives until experience proved that there was but slight reward for per-

and of the Corte-Reals (Paris, 1903), and in J. A. Williamson, *The Voyages of the Cabots* (London, 1929), or in Biggar's criticism of Williamson's thesis, *Canadian Historical Review*, June 1930.

sistence. One João Fernandez, a Portuguese of the Azores, who seems to have been searching the northern seas as early as 1492, got a patent from the King of Portugal in 1499. Reasonably reinforced tradition makes him the *llabrador* (small squire) whose name was given in succession to Greenland and Labrador. Another Azorean, Gaspar Corte-Real, after receiving a patent in 1500, in June of that year visited Greenland. He went back again in 1501 and worked south to the south-eastern extremity of Newfoundland, whence he sent two ships home with sixty Indian slaves and himself sailed off south and west to disappear for ever. In 1502 his brother Miguel went out directly to Newfoundland to look for him and had the bad luck to be aboard the one ship of his group of three which also disappeared. Another of his vessels appears to have entered the Gulf of St. Lawrence and followed the western coast of Newfoundland. In 1501 Fernandez turned up in London and, along with two other Azoreans and three Bristol merchants, secured a patent for discoveries from Henry VII. They probably made voyages in 1501 and 1502 to the north-west. Still another Bristol-Azores group received a patent in December 1502, and there are traces of their voyaging to America during the three subsequent years, but by now the barrier presented by thinly populated North America had shifted men's thoughts from its meagre exploitation to the possibilities of finding a passage through it or of getting around it by the north.

It is almost certain that Sebastian Cabot made the first of these attempts for England in 1509. Peter Martyr, who knew him well after his entry into the Spanish service in 1512, heard the story from his own lips and wrote two convincing accounts of how 'even in the month of July he found great icebergs floating in the sea and almost continuous daylight'. He made an intelligent and critical voyage down the coast past the Banks to a point opposite the Straits of Gibraltar (Cape Hatteras). He noted that he had reached the longitude of Cuba. About 1550 he wrote concerning the early part of the voyage to the geographer Ramusio, claiming that he had 'gone on for a long time towards the west and a quarter north . . . at the latitude of 67½ degrees . . . and finding the sea open and without any obstacle, he firmly believed that by that way he could pass towards Eastern Cathay, and he would have done it if the ill-will of the masters and sailors, who were mutinous, had not compelled him to turn back'. Ramusio corrected the latitude to 67° N. and reported that he was turned back 'owing to the cold'. Nothing was to come of this adventure until over fifty years later, when Sir Humphrey Gilbert began his great agitation for an English discovery of the North-West Passage.

Henry VII was dead when Sebastian got back. Sebastian himself in 1512 went over to Spain and tried to secure the command of an expedition to find the mid-continental strait which his study of currents like the Gulf Stream had convinced him must exist. When he came back to England in 1548 his place was in the tavern chimney-corner or at the company directors' table, arranging ventures for younger men than he. The geographers and promoters, however, studied his narratives and his maps and made therefrom a convincing argument that he had entered the North-West Passage and seen the Pacific, or as we would put it, had sailed through Hudson Strait and seen Hudson Bay.

In 1517, Sir Thomas More's brother-in-law, John Rastell, with some encouragement from Cabot, and a naval officer named Thomas Spert, prepared a costly expedition for the north-west, but dissensions among the partners halted it before it left England. In 1521 Sebastian Cabot, discomfited by Spanish obsession with Mexico, angled in England and Venice for a chance to reveal the North-West Passage, but failed. In 1527, while Cabot was off on a Spanish venture in South America, John Rut went north-west with two ships, one of which appears to have turned up in the Caribbean near Santo Domingo, where its calm arrogance worried the Spaniards. Another English expedition of 1536 under 'Master Hore' of London degenerated into cannibalism on the Newfoundland or Labrador coast before a lucky chance delivered a French fishing-vessel into its hands and permitted a return home.

Englishmen were not alone in the field. Sometime about 1520 João Alvarez Fagundes, under Portuguese patent, conducted extensive explorations south and west of Cape Race (Newfoundland), it may be even into the St. Lawrence river and the Bay of Fundy, and apparently attempted settlement on Cape Breton. Francis I of France, perhaps stimulated by the loot stolen from Cortés' messengers in 1522 and perhaps by the news that Magellan's expedition had circumnavigated the globe, sent out Giovanni da Verrazano, a Florentine, late in 1523, to see whether he could find a northern passage to Asia for France. Verrazano appears to have reached land along the coast of what is now New Jersey, to have mistaken Delaware or Chesapeake Bay for the Pacific when he saw it across the narrow sandy peninsula between it and the Atlantic, and then to have turned north. His careful probings of the shore line took him into what is now New York harbour, Narragansett Bay, and up to the coast of Maine. Then,

as we have seen,[1] in 1524–25, Estevan Gómez re-
surveyed the whole coast from Nova Scotia to the
Caribbean and submitted the report on those temperate
shores which produced such complacent scorn of them
as that expressed by Peter Martyr. His investigations
almost disposed of Verrazano's Pacific, although the
idea persisted until the English tried to colonise Virginia. Even yet it was not known whether the Americas
were separate or attached to north-eastern Asia.

Thus for about thirty years the agents of four European nations had been searching the North American
coast from Labrador to Florida and even questing
among the fogs and ice of Davis Strait, without adding
to general knowledge any of the three great water-
entries into the continent, the Hudson river, the St.
Lawrence and Hudson Bay. It is not difficult to understand why, if one remembers that Europeans were
merely in the process of developing ships that would
sail at all well into the wind, so that coasting was a
matter of almost continuous dilemma as to when to
take advantage of a favourable wind and when to proceed more slowly so as thoroughly to explore the coast.
And the uncharted coasts with their reefs and shallows
and enshrouding mists were exceedingly difficult to
survey. From Greenland to Cape Race icebergs complicated the summer season and two great ocean currents
upset reckonings. Fogs were frequent, some shores
were more ice than land, and a profusion of islands gave
the impression held even by Sebastian Cabot about the
middle of the century that all northern North America
consisted of islands. Conditions bettered a little as men
worked south-west down the coasts, but endless confusion was caused by the fact that every great river from

[1] See p. 32.

Narragansett Bay southwards had its entrance and estuary masked either by islands, or by miles of sand-dunes and keys, or by overhanging peninsulas like those of New Jersey and Maryland. Every voyage, therefore, had to be a compromise between extent and thoroughness.

Thus the annals of the thirty years are doubtful and meagre. Sebastian Cabot may have reached Hudson Bay. The brothers Corte Real almost certainly entered the Gulf of St. Lawrence. There are evidences that Fagundes even entered the St. Lawrence river. Verrazano had been at the mouth of the Hudson. Either Fagundes or Gómez had sounded the Bay of Fundy to its head. Yet none of these leads had as yet really tempted men inland. Of course their meetings with the poverty-stricken Eskimos and Indians had discouraged them from expecting Mexicos or Perus, but the prospects of finding a passage to Asia or of getting around in front of Spanish exploitation of the interior were still powerful lures to imaginative men.

NARRATIVES

The records of the coastal explorations before 1534 will be found in original and translation (except from the French), edited by H. P. Biggar, in *The Precursors of Jacques Cartier* (Ottawa, 1911), and in translation, edited by J. A. Williamson, in *The Voyages of the Cabots, etc.* (London, 1929). An illuminating example of what can be done to complement such narratives with their contemporary cartography is to be found in the work of W. F. Ganong, notably his 'Crucial maps, etc., of the Atlantic Coast of Canada,' in *Royal Society of Canada Transactions*, Third Series, vols. xxiii and xxiv, section ii. Verrazano's personally annotated report is in the *Fifteenth Annual Proceedings* of the American Scenic and Historic Preservation Society of New York (Albany, 1910).

CHAPTER VIII

KINGDOMS IN THE NORTH

(Map No. 2, page 258)

Voilà un Diamant de Canada.

A FRENCH GIBE

THE stalemate was broken in 1534 on behalf of France by Jacques Cartier, an experienced navigator and substantial citizen of St. Malo, then in his forty-third or forty-fourth year. It is impossible to say definitely what he went out to seek, although the narrative of his first voyage contains many references to his disappointment over not finding 'the passage'. Magellan had revealed the separation of the southern part of the American continents from Asia, and Saavedra had crossed the Pacific from Mexico, but Cabrillo, Ferrelo and Francis Drake had still to make their explorations of the northern Pacific coast and the geographers still portrayed North America as north-eastern Asia. Thus Cartier may have thought in terms either of a passage to the Pacific or a route into the interior of Asia. In either case there might be revealed to him a way through or a way round the northern mass of the Americas. There was also the possibility that he might forestall the Spaniards somewhere in the interior of America in what up to 1534 had seemed to Frenchmen to be a continuous orgy of incredibly profitable conquest. His voyage was officially described as 'to

117

the New lands [the supposed archipelago which time revealed to be Newfoundland] to discover certain islands and countries where it is said that he should find great quantity of gold and other valuable things', and it was undertaken with financial support from Francis I. He sailed on 20 April 1534 from St. Malo with two ships of about sixty tons each, manned in all with sixty-one men.

The journey began with all the confidence of knowledge. They sailed quickly to Cape Bonavista on the east coast of Newfoundland, where they repaired their ships, went on to Funk Island, where they did their share in causing the extinction of the great auk by killing large quantities for food, and on 27 May entered the Strait of Belle Isle to explore what they and the French fishermen knew as the Great Bay. They were held up by ice for two weeks, assisted another French vessel engaged in fishing near Cumberland Harbour, and then cut across to the western shore of Newfoundland. Labrador disgusted Cartier—'I am rather inclined to believe that this is the land God gave to Cain'. They had seen some Beothuck Indians, who were sealing from canoes, but their possessions were so scanty as to be negligible. It was with surprise, therefore, that after following the west coast of Newfoundland almost to its southern extremity, a change of course to the south-west brought them to the fertile Magdalen Islands group. Brion Island proved 'the best land we have seen; for two acres of it are worth more than the whole of Newfoundland'. Wild grains and fruits indicated what cultivation might effect. Moreover in the first week of July Prince Edward Island (which along with the Magdalens Cartier believed to be mainland) was even more seductive and fruitful.

'It is the best-tempered region one can possibly see and the heat is considerable.'

Hopes ran high during the second week of July; for it was discovered that open sea lay before them to the west and they pressed on. At daybreak of 10 July the wind served, and they 'sailed on until about ten o'clock in the morning, at which hour we caught sight of the head of the bay, whereat we were grieved and displeased'. Chaleur Bay had closed in before them. They worked back and northwards along the Gaspé peninsula and were deceived by fog or mirage into believing that land stretched north-east from Cape Gaspé. As a result, they crossed the St. Lawrence to low-lying Anticosti, rounded it at its eastern end, and continued westward between it and the mountainous north shore until the river-gulf opened again at its westward end. Progress was extremely difficult because of adverse currents. It was now 1 August and they had been out over three months. At a council they decided to turn home with their news and this they did by the north shore and the Strait of Belle Isle.

Measured by immediate rewards at current American expectations, they had little enough to report. They had found extraordinarily rich fisheries, abundance of sea-fowl to furnish meat, herds of seals and walruses, and tempting fertile lands. The shores were usually covered with excellent timber for masts and spars. But kings were not yet awake to the need of such staples as these. Mercantilism was young. The fever of the day was for bullion, jewels and Eastern goods. Cartier had met many Algonkian and Huron-Iroquois Indians in Miramichi and Chaleur bays. They were demonstratively friendly, quite naturally avid for European goods such as knives and axes, and they literally stripped themselves naked in order to barter in return. 'They offered us everything they owned, which was, all told, of little value. . . . This people may well be called savage; for they are the sorriest folk there can be in the world, and the whole lot of them had not anything above the value of five sous, their canoes and fishing nets excepted.' They did offer an opportunity for Christian missionaries, for their friendliness convinced Cartier 'that these people would be easy to convert to our holy faith'. He took back to France with him, by permission, two sons of one of the chiefs to become interpreters.

Such being the case, the real attraction of this new region for Cartier and Francis I must have been the discovery of waters still open to the west. Unfortunately the evidence is so scanty and indirect that certainty is impossible. Yet it does seem clear that Cartier did not assume that the open passage was a sea-strait to the Pacific. The two Indians whom he took to France with him had been engaged in a summer expedition to the Gulf, but belonged to the Huron-Iroquois group who lived on and about the island of Montreal, or as they and Cartier called it, the Kingdom of Hochelaga. They promised to guide him there. Moreover they knew of two other kingdoms: Saguenay, which had its centre on the river of that name, and Canada, the region on the St. Lawrence around Stadacona (modern Quebec) and the island of Orleans. They were under no illusions about the St. Lawrence river, for they described it very accurately in advance as 'the great river of Hochelaga and the route towards Canada'. 'The river grew narrower as one approached Canada; and also that farther up, the water became fresh . . . furthermore that one could only proceed along it in small boats.'

This information Cartier could readily harmonise with his own experience. He had seen the gulf narrow in width from over 300 miles to about 20. At that point lay Anticosti, which might be a peninsula, but which bore every resemblance to a river-mouth island. The ebb tides through the northern channel had been so swift 'that it was impossible to make a stone's throw of headway with thirteen oars' in a long-boat. Even their large vessels 'only lost way' and drifted to the east. It would be strange, indeed, if Cartier, instructed by the Indians, did not realise that they had been contending with river current as well as with tide. He was a very competent, thorough and matter-of-fact navigator and explorer. It seems probable, therefore, that, with the King's support, he set sail again on 19 May 1535, with his mind open to at least three possibilities beyond the mere investigation of a fruitful land populated by receptive Indians. He might find a sea-strait to the Pacific somewhere in the gulf before it narrowed to a river. He might ascend a river which led into the interior of North America. He might find that his river flowed from north-eastern Asia. In any case there were at least three 'kingdoms' known to his Indian guides. They might be like Mexico and Peru or they might be tributary outposts to American empires or to the territories of the Grand Khan in Cathay. The rather staid Cartier and the mercurial Francis I needed only a tithe of the imaginations of their contemporaries, Narváez, Soto and Coronado, to urge them on to explore their new world.

At this point a short geographical digression is perhaps in order because certain widely prevalent and erroneous mental images of northern America are otherwise likely to distort the course of events. Possibly it is recollection of the appearance on modern political maps of the 1400 miles along the forty-ninth parallel which form the western boundary between Canada and the United States which makes most casual observers think that the St. Lawrence and Great Lakes basin lie on a line with, or even north of that emphatic stroke across the map, instead of far to the south. Perhaps it is forgetfulness that the Atlantic coast swings north-east, not north, in a great bow from Florida to Cape Race. Whatever it may be, readers of these annals are advised to erase modern political boundaries from their minds, to notice that the northernmost point of the Gaspé peninsula and of Lake Superior are in the same forty-ninth parallel, and to remark that the St. Lawrence river and its first two tributary lakes run sharply south-west from that northern limit to a point almost due west of New York. The St. Lawrence does not run east and west, nor do the Ottawa and the Saguenay run north and south. Remembrance of these things will make more credible the explorers' universal testimony to the fruitful lands and salubrious summer climate of the St. Lawrence basin. After all, the mouth of the St. Lawrence, its farthest north, lies opposite Cherbourg.

During the last half of July and the first three weeks of August 1535 Cartier convinced himself that no sea-strait led away from the north shore of the gulf nor from anywhere in the river-mouth west of Anticosti. He thus completed his circumnavigation of the gulf. That done with his usual thoroughness, he let his Indians guide him past the black chasm through the mountains of the north shore which was the water-route to Saguenay, on past the lovely river islands and their rich September harvest of grapes and fruit and nuts, to the noble cliff and natural fortress which had been chosen by a group of Montagnais as the site of their town of Stadacona (modern Quebec). The rich harvest of the waters and the soil was a constant delight to the travellers. They saw for themselves that this unexploited country yielded everything in abundance. There were innumerable varieties of fish. There were right whales, white whales (*beluga*), seals, walruses and those strange mammals, the sea-cows (*sirenia*), whose habit of rising above the surface with their young tucked under a flipper made belief in mermaids an article of faith. These mammals could yield hides, oil, whalebone and ivory. The hosts of birds ranged from nightingales (doubtless thrushes) to the most tempting land and water game. The Indians hunted the deer. They also cultivated maize, melons, beans, squash, pumpkins and tobacco. The land was clothed with timber of all the familiar sorts, and wild nuts and fruits were in profusion. The festoons of grapes on the island of Orleans earned it the name of Bacchus' Island. September on the St. Lawrence is a rich month, and Cartier and his companions saw it in all its glory from the gulf to the rapids at Montreal.

They had had some difficulty in getting away from Stadacona to the promised Hochelaga. The Montagnais had welcomed these benefactors with their precious articles of iron, brass and steel, and were loath to see another tribe reap the benefits. The two Indian guides added their discouragements, for they doubtless began to conjure up the discrepancies between the Hochelaga which Cartier wanted to see and Hochelaga as it was. Cartier was offered bribes of a girl of thirteen and two small boys not to go on. When that failed, they tried terror. 'They dressed up three Indians as devils, arraying them in black and white dog-skins, with horns as long as one's arm and their faces coloured black as coal.' 'Their god, Cudouagny by name, had made an announcement at Hochelaga, and the three Indians had come in his name to tell them the tidings, which were that there would be so much ice and snow that all would perish.' The French laughed and said 'that Jesus would keep them safe from the cold if they would trust in Him'.

These incidents formed an interesting commentary on the differences between European contacts with the native Americans in the north and in the south. The Spaniards despoiled and enslaved the Indians, because they had gold and pearls or could be compelled to secure them. If these Europeans seemed like gods to the natives, they quickly proved to be terrible deities. The French found nothing to spoil and no mines or pearl-beds to tempt them to enslave the natives. Life and shelter were easy to maintain in the south, but hard in the north. European tools were therefore infinitely more desirable to the northern tribes. Thus the French were in a position to retain the beneficent aspects of their inevitable deification.

Cartier and his men set out with the bark *Emérillon* and two long-boats on 19 September, and on 2 October arrived at the impressive Huron-Iroquois village of Hochelaga (Montreal). It was triple-palisaded, lay among cultivated fields, and was composed of about fifty characteristic Iroquois communal huts, 'each about fifty or more paces in length, and twelve or fifteen in width'. The inhabitants gave them the warmest possible welcome and, like Vaca's hosts that same year far away in the south-west, brought their sick to be healed. Cartier laid his hands on them and read aloud in French the opening of the gospel of St. John and its chapters dealing with the Passion, 'praying God to give them knowledge of our holy faith . . . and grace to obtain baptism and redemption'. He distributed gifts and finally succeeded in escaping from these ceremonies in order to climb the neighbouring 'Mont Royal'.

'On reaching the summit we had a view of the land for more than thirty leagues round about. . . . Between these ranges [the Laurentians and the northern Adirondacks] lies the finest land it is possible to see, being arable, level and flat . . . in the midst . . . the river [St. Lawrence].' Just below them to the south-west were the impassable Lachine rapids. 'And as far as the eye can reach, one sees that river, large, wide and broad . . . and it was told us . . . that there were three more such rapids . . . that after passing these rapids, one could navigate along that river for more than three moons. And they showed us furthermore that along the mountains to the north, there is a large river [Ottawa] which comes from the west.'

Thus Cartier had travelled about 1000 miles from the Atlantic to the head of navigation only to find that his river still led into the interior a whole summer's journey by Indian calendar. There was no 'passage to the other southern ocean'. Neither Stadacona nor Hochelaga had revealed any immediately realisable wealth. Only in the kingdom of Saguenay remained the chance of emulating Spain, and now his solicitous Indian friends set to work to paint it in the hues and habiliments which it possessed in Cartier's own mind's eye. The two guides of 1534 had already informed him that copper was found there, and when Cartier shewed them some as they stood on Mount Royal they and the Hochelaga Indians stuck to that story. More perplexing and exciting was a sudden action which just preceded Cartier's question. 'Without our asking any questions or making any sign, they seized the chain of the Captain's whistle, which was made of silver, and a dagger-handle of yellow copper-gilt like gold, that hung at the side of one of the sailors, and gave us to understand that these came from up that river [Ottawa].' It was too late in the year to go on. Crisp nights and the flaming warning of the autumn leaves taught Cartier that he must return to his ships and winter quarters across the little St. Charles river from Stadacona. The regretful Iroquois carried them on their shoulders to the boats.

The Indians of Stadacona continued to embroider their tales of the interior at intervals during the slow passage of the winter. They loved tale-telling and they wanted desperately to keep in touch with these richly equipped Europeans. Relations were often strained because of their greed, which now discriminated between a trinket, like a pewter Agnus Dei or a tin ring, and such an invaluable substitute for their own fragile clay, wooden or bark vessels and bone or stone tools as was provided by a brass kettle, a steel knife or a sharp steel axe. Of course scurvy set in among the Europeans when the men gave up exercise and ceased to obtain fresh meats, fruits and vegetables, but Cartier was shrewd enough to learn the Indian remedy of infusing conifer buds and bark before the Indians had learned how helpless the Frenchmen would be before an attack. The winter and spring slowly developed into a contest as to whether the chief Donnacona could capture Cartier and his much-coveted goods or Cartier kidnap Donnacona to make him recite to Francis I his marvellous yarns of the interior. The European won, but softened his victory by assurances of speedy return after Donnacona and his companions had seen the wonders of France. On 6 May 1536 the ships sailed, and by taking the southern short cut which Cartier suspected in 1534 was an alternative to the Strait of Belle Isle, they reached St. Malo on 16 July.

Because of the existing financial embarrassment of France, we can ignore as an incentive to further adventure the undoubted appeal of the St. Lawrence valley as a place to live in. It is important also to remember that Cartier never shewed any inclination to open a trade in furs. Francis I, who had come to the throne in 1515, had spent his whole reign in an uneasy position between the pincers of Charles V, monarch of northern Italy, Central Europe, the Low Countries and Spain. Although he had been very generous to Cartier in expectation of rich returns, he had no money to spare for ordinary colonisation, for he was at war with Charles for all but nine or ten years of his reign. North America must hold promise of treasure to win his further support. North America, in the person of Donnacona (doubtless encouraged by Cartier), proceeded to do so. In the process, Saguenay betrayed a regrettable tendency to stray from its geographical moorings, or perhaps to extend its boundaries in order to include the gold and silver up the Ottawa. It became a sort of island bounded (if one guesses at modern equivalents for the vague Indian descriptions) by the St. Lawrence, the Saguenay, the lakes of the height of land between the St. Lawrence and Hudson Bay, and with western boundaries that varied from Lake Superior eastward, sometimes Lake Huron, sometimes Georgian Bay and the Nipissing link to the Ottawa, and sometimes the long northern reach of the Gatineau from the Ottawa valley.

'And they gave us to understand, that in that country

the natives go clothed and dressed in woollens like ourselves; that there are many towns and tribes of honest
folk who possess great store of gold and copper.'
Donnacona 'assured us that he had been to the land of
the Saguenay where there are immense quantities of
gold, rubies and other rich things, and that the men
there are white as in France'. He also said he had been
'to a country distant from Canada by canoe one moon,
in which land grow much cinnamon and cloves'. This
was to be reached by going south up the Richelieu river
from the St. Lawrence, and oranges were growing
there. Of course, Donnacona knew no gold or silver or
spices or oranges until he was shewn them by Europeans, but it is not hard to understand the pride which
compelled him to say that they existed in his homeland.
For one thing he wanted to go back there and only
these Europeans could effect that. When he added
lands where the people 'never eat nor digest', lands
peopled by pigmies and 'men who fly', and others 'whose
inhabitants have only one leg', he had provided the
sixteenth-century map-makers with the richest sort of
illustrative materials for their decorative charts and
globes. The great Rabelais himself found in these tales
butts for his shafts against credulity. 'This chief is an
old man who has never ceased travelling about the
country by river, stream and trail since his earliest
recollection,' wrote Cartier's chronicler. He might have
added imagination to that list of highways.

There is no doubt whatever but that Francis I was
greatly excited, although wars, truces and diplomatic
negotiations prevented him from sending Cartier out
again until 1541.[1] The poor Indian story-teller had died

[1] There exists a memoir of September 1538, probably drawn up by
Cartier, printed in Biggar's *Collection*, pp. 70-74 (see below, p. 135), in which

after having done his best to please with the tall tales which were all he had to offer in compensation for the wonders of Paris, but Francis pored over charts with Cartier and a Portuguese pilot (spying for Spain), and the news of his knowledge and hopes put the Emperor Charles V and his chancelleries into considerable agitation. Francis and Cartier were agreed that the passage was not now in question, but colonisation and conquest of this 'outer limit of Asia' (*bout de l'Asie*) and indoctrination of its peoples in the Christian faith. The Portuguese reported that: 'He has in this matter a great desire and longing . . . and what he says and wishes to do would make men marvel. . . . He wishes to send two brigantines with the ships, and when the falls [Lachine] are reached, the brigantines can be taken overland; and beyond the falls the King of France says the Indian King told him there is a large city called Sagana, where there are many mines of gold and silver in great abundance, and men who dress and wear shoes as we do; and that there is abundance of cloves, nutmeg and pepper.'

One interesting consequence of the excitement in Spain was that Christoval de Haro, Charles V's confidant and servant in Burgos, tried to persuade poor Cabeza de Vaca, just back from his walk from Texas to Mexico, to lead an expedition to forestall the French on the St. Lawrence. Cortés, too, was considered by the Council of the Indies and the Emperor, and Pizarro was consulted. Vaca refused, 'it being a very doubtful business', and went off to South America instead.

it is said that in spite of his expenses and huge debts, and the fact that he knows there is neither gold nor silver in Canada, Francis has determined to send out Cartier merely in order to Christianise the natives. In the light of abundant other evidence this need not be taken seriously. It was intended for public consumption, and the list of men required, including two goldsmiths and lapidaries, is in itself enough to invalidate the avowed purpose.

Secret service reports and elaborate discussions of the potentialities of the newly discovered region and of the threats it held for New Spain went back and forth between the Emperor and his servants, reaching their climax when in spite of protests, in May 1541, Cartier set out thoroughly equipped to colonise, and Jean François de la Rocque, Sieur de Roberval, as military commander, prepared to follow him. The prisons were opened to supply them with men. They had ten ships between them provided at the King's expense and provisioned for two years, 400 liveried sailors, 300 soldiers, materials for eighteen or twenty small boats to be fitted with light artillery, a group of pilots, masons, carpenters and ploughmen, some women of doubtful character, and a considerable herd of varied livestock. They were to colonise Canada and, from it as a base, proceed to the conquest of Saguenay. Cartier took five of the ships, but Roberval, who was delayed until the spring of 1542 by some adventures in Channel piracy at the expense of Portugal and England, took only three.

Charles V was sure that, in spite of the truce agreed upon at Nice in 1538, the perfidious Francis was planning war. The Bulls of Demarcation were brought out, pressure was vainly brought to bear on João III of Portugal to close the Azorean ports, and the Spanish Council of the Indies met in earnest sessions. The prevailing assumption among the Spaniards was that since this rich Canada lay 600 leagues beyond New-foundland and the northern regions were notoriously worthless, it must be in Ayllón's Florida, whither Soto had just gone. Therefore the real threat was to the Bahama Channel through which the gold and silver of Peru were pouring into Spain. Charles would have

combined the fleets of Spain and Portugal, sought out
the French and destroyed them and their ships. 'Let all
the men taken from the ships be thrown into the sea
. . . as a warning against the undertaking of similar
expeditions.' João III was coolly sceptical and refused
to co-operate. 'Make marriages with Castile, and preserve friendship with France' was his motto. The
Council of the Indies could not afford a naval expedition alone, and merely sent out two scouting ships to
Newfoundland. The Peru bullion was held at Panamá
and the Indies were put in a state of defence. Francis I
mocked the Emperor's ambassadors and held his
ground. He planned no war, 'but the sun gave warmth
to him as well as to others'. For him and France the
Pope had no jurisdiction whatever in temporal affairs,
'and he much desired to see Adam's will to learn how he
had partitioned the world'.

All parties concerned would have done well to remember Vaca's caution and João's scepticism. The
latter had a better intelligence service in the Newfoundland fisheries than did Spain, and by November
1541 he knew that Cartier had gone up the St. Lawrence. João told the Spanish ambassador that he and
his royal father had each lost two fleets there (probably
the Corte-Reals and Fagundes), 'and that the French
could not have gone to any place where they could do
less damage to his Majesty or to himself'. Indeed one
of Charles' own servants, García de Loaysa, Cardinal
of Seville, had dissented vigorously from the Council's
and the Emperor's fears immediately after Cartier's
departure. 'It seems to me that this is nonsense. Their
motive is that they think, from what they learn, that
these provinces are rich in gold and silver, and they
hope to do as we have done. They are making a mistake,

for . . . this whole coast as far as Florida is utterly un-productive. In consequence of which they would be lost, or at best would make a short excursion, after losing a few men and the greater part of all they took from France.'

The second of these shrewd, if doleful, predictions proved to be uncannily correct. In the autumn of 1541 Cartier set up a substantial base at Cap Rouge about nine miles beyond Quebec, but when he went on to reconnoitre at Hochelaga he found that the village he had known had disappeared and had been replaced, in Indian fashion, by another near by. We have no evidence that he did more than investigate the immediate rapids and the mouth of the Ottawa. The winter at Cap Rouge was an uneasy one because of Indian threats, and in the spring he set out for home. We are probably safe in assuming that he had lost his illusions about Saguenay, but doubt is cast upon this by actions on his part somewhat out of keeping with his rather sober character. Three Newfoundland sailors, when examined on oath by a Spanish agent at Fuenterrabia in September 1542, said that he carried back with him what were variously described as 'eleven barrels of gold ore and close on a bushel of precious stones, rubies and diamonds'; 'ten barrels of gold ore and seven of silver, and 700 pounds of pearls and precious stones'; or 'nine barrels of gold ore and seven barrels of silver, and a certain quantity of pearls and precious stones of great value'.

It was this exploit which enriched the French language with a synonym for the fraudulent and meretricious—'*Voilà un Diamant de Canada!*' What had actually happened is revealed in the scanty narrative of the expedition which has been preserved for us only

in the sixteenth-century English paraphrase made by
Hakluyt from the lost French original. Near the Cap
Rouge camp the men noticed some of the elements of
that geological salad, the Laurentian Shield, in all probability white and crystal quartz, iron pyrites, mica-
bearing rock, and the crystals of the corundum (native
alumina) group which in their finer manifestation are
ruby and sapphire. Their imaginations did the rest.
They list their discoveries: 'a goodly Myne of the best
yron in the world'; 'certaine leaves of fine gold as thick
as a mans nayle'; 'veines of mynerall matter, which
shewe like gold and silver'; and 'stones like Diamants,
the most faire, pollished and excellently cut that it is
possible for a man to see'.

Loaded with this rubbish (for the ores of the Laurentian shield yield themselves only to modern chemical
reductions), Cartier met Roberval in June 1542 at
St. John's, Newfoundland. They exchanged news and
examined the 'Golde ore', 'which ore the Sunday next
ensuing was tryed in a Furnace, and found to be good'.
The will to believe thus easily corrupted the judgement
of amateur metallurgists. Cartier told Roberval that
he was going back because of the Indian menace. 'But
when our Generall being furnished with sufficient
forces, commanded him to goe backe againe with him,
hee and his company, mooved as it seemeth with
ambition, because they would have all the glory of the
discoverie of these partes themselves, stole privily away
the next night from us, and without taking their leaves,
departed home for Bretaigne [Brittany].'

Roberval went on to Cap Rouge in the autumn and
wintered there. In the succeeding spring he planned
to go past the Lachine rapids (not up the Saguenay as
has been said) in order to winter at the Kingdom of

133

Saguenay. The Saguenay river, which it was thought might lead either to the Pacific or the China Sea, was investigated for eight or ten miles, but swift currents and tides seemed to prohibit its use. At that point the narrative fails us, and although Roberval may have pushed up the Ottawa, there is no trace of any journey beyond its mouth in the description of the country made by Jean Fonteneau, called Alfonse de Saintonge, his chief pilot. Probably the wooden huts on Montreal Island completed his disillusion. At any rate he was back in France in the autumn, ready to resume a martial career in the new war with Spain.

It is not entirely an accidental coincidence that in 1543 a lull in exploration descended simultaneously on the Spanish territories of southern North America and on the French lands in the St. Lawrence. War in Europe was one deterrent. France and Spain were at odds until 1558. France spent the rest of the century in a turmoil of religious and dynastic civil wars. Spain meanwhile faced revolt in the Netherlands, Islam in the Danube valley and the Mediterranean, and the defiant English and Dutch everywhere on the high seas. Overseas enterprise must yield profits without new investments of European capital. Another Mexico or Peru, or a strait, or even revelation that northern North America was really a part of Asia, would have meant expansion for New Spain or New France, but we know now that none of these things could be. North America had to await the development of more sober economic incentives, and in this Spain enjoyed the advantage of proximity to the fabulously rich mines of Mexico and beyond. So far as royal or official backing was concerned, for France the curtain had fallen on North America for almost sixty years during which a new individual enterprise was to grow to proportions which were finally to earn governmental attention once more.

The episode of 1497–1543 at the mouth of the St. Lawrence closes with the sturdy but unheeded words of Jean Alfonse, Roberval's chief pilot, who wove what he knew into the same fabric with Friar Marcos' tales of the *pueblo* country. 'The lands running towards Hochelaga are much better and warmer than those of Canada [Quebec]; and this land of Hochelaga extends to Figuier [Yucatan] and to Peru, where gold and silver abound. Mark, too, that the inhabitants say that in the city called Cebola . . . the houses are all covered with gold and silver, and equipped with vessels of gold and silver. These lands are attached to Tartary, and I think that they form the outer limit of Asia, reckoning from the roundness of the earth.' Yet mere assurance was not enough. Almost a century and a half were to elapse before Frenchmen from Canada made their disturbing reconnaissances up the Río Grande. For the moment the 'northern mystery' of New Spain and the 'southern mystery' of New France had descended into the same limbo of hopes deferred.

NARRATIVES

The records of Cartier and Roberval, in original and translation, have been edited by H. P. Biggar, as *The Voyages of Jacques Cartier* (Ottawa, 1924) and *A Collection of Documents relating to Jacques Cartier and the Sieur de Roberval* (Ottawa, 1930). French texts are untranslated in the *Collection*. The Cartier portrait frontispiece to the *Voyages* should be disregarded in favour of what is probably the nearest approach to a portrait extant, that is, the central figure of the Harleian Mappemonde opposite p. 129 of the same volume. Two gifted successors of

Cartier throw a good deal of light on his work. H. P. Biggar and others have now almost completed for the Champlain Society their notable illustrated edition and translation of *The Works of Samuel de Champlain* (4 of 6 vols., Toronto, 1922, 1925, 1929, 1932). W. L. Grant, for the same society, has edited and translated (except the poetry, *Les Muses de la Nouvelle France*) *The History of New France*, by Marc Lescarbot (2 vols., Toronto, 1907–14).

CHAPTER IX

FROM FISH TO FUR

(Map No. 2, page 258)

Nowe Frenchemen and other have founde the trade
That yerely of fyshe there they lade
Above an C. sayle

[Concerning the Indians]
Buyldynge nor house they have not at all
But wodes cotes and cavys small
No merveyle though it be so
For they use no maner of yron
Nother in tole nor other wepin
That shulde helpe them therto.

RASTELL: A NEW INTERLUDE. C. 1519

IN the preceding chapters mention has been made in passing of the European fishermen on the New-foundland Banks. These nameless men, Portuguese, Basques, Bretons and Englishmen, were the really consistent maintainers of European contact with north-eastern North America, rather than the explorers who from time to time got their names recorded in documents of state. John Cabot in 1497 had brought back one bit of what may, or may not, have been news to the fishermen of western Europe. At any rate his momentary fame gave it broad publicity. He said that when he reached the new land the sea was 'swarming with fish, which can be taken not only with the net, but in baskets let down with a stone'. 'These same English, his com-

137

panions, say that they could bring so many fish that this Kingdom would have no further need of Iceland.' Sebastian Cabot's version to Peter Martyr was that 'he found so great a quantity of a certain kind of great fish like tunnies . . . that at times they even stayed the passage of his ships'. No other invitation was needed. Each spring thereafter the ships went out for the harvest, at first in ones and twos, and finally, in scores. So far as we know, they have been doing so ever since and their sailors have been partially responsible for the racially blended populations which one finds to-day in the ports of Newfoundland and New England.

Yet fishermen would not normally be explorers. It seems probable that until Cartier shewed the way and told of the fisheries inside the Gulf, they had only accidentally, if at all, gone beyond the Strait of Belle Isle. They came out to America to fill their holds and hurry back to Europe to be first in the market. Oddly enough, however, it was their loyalty to the North American grounds which gradually produced, as a by-product, an incentive for invading the continent.

To understand how, one need only remember the backwardness of the Indians and Eskimos. All of their tools and utensils were the products of wood, bone, skin and stone, occasionally supplemented by fragile, primitive pottery. Some copper was mined in the Lake Superior district, but it was a valuable rarity on the coast. Suddenly they were confronted with men whose least-valued possessions were of a utility far beyond anything they had dreamed of. Axes, knives, mere nails, being of tempered iron, made stone hatchets and bone needles and awls antediluvian. An unbreakable, unburnable iron or brass kettle wiped out at a stroke all the labour and care incidental to a whole series of wooden, bark or even pottery vessels. As Father Sagard-Théodat remarked early in the seventeenth century, 'The Hurons think that the greatest rulers of France are endowed with the greatest powers and having such great powers they can make the most difficult things such as hatchets, knives and kettles. They infer from this that the King makes the largest kettles.' One need only set fire-arms over against bows and arrows to make the more obvious list of superiorities complete. And once these tools had supplemented their predecessors, a truly vital dependence of Indian on European had been created because the European remained the manufacturer and the Indian forgot his old skills.

Thus the mere arrival of the Europeans had created an insatiable appetite among the Indians. In the first encounters the exchange was the haphazard sort of barter which European sailors practised everywhere they went, an exchange of exotics which frequently had only curiosity for their value on either side. The moment the Indian motive became specific, it had to be backed by the discovery of some staple which the sailors would always take. Presumably labour services and the provision of fresh foods played their part, but very gradually fur emerged as the North American commodity which could buy European goods. It was not a sudden development, for it took a full century for the fur trade in North America to become important enough to be an end in itself, and even after that it alternated between princely profits and terrific losses. Between 1500 and 1600 the trade slowly grew from being the casual and capricious by-product of fishermen's days in harbour to possess an economic focus of its own.

Probably the greatest stimulus to the trade from the side of the Europeans came when they sought out harbours and beaches where they might salt and dry their catch before packing it away for transport to Europe. This shift from the 'green' to the 'dry' fishery involved more prolonged contacts with the natives and even some certainty of return to a specific spot. During the winter, while the Europeans were absent, the Indian could replenish his depleted stock of garments and build up a trading surplus of peltries against the coming summer. He and his family could also make up and wear robes of beaver-pelts with the fur against their skins, and thus impart to them the oily qualities which made them the greatly desired *castor gras* of the European hat-makers.

The narratives of the sixteenth century which have come down to us often refer to this fishermen's barter. Cartier himself entered the picture at a time when trade as well as fisheries came to men's minds when they talked or wrote about the St. Lawrence. In 1534 near Chaleur Bay the Indians fairly besieged Cartier's company in their anxiety to trade. 'The savages showed a marvelously great pleasure in possessing and obtaining these iron wares and other commodities . . . they bartered all they had to such an extent that all went back naked without anything on them.' Cartier himself distinctly disdained the fur trade. He shewed none of the keen commercial instinct which in another might have made the fur trade an end in itself. Even on his return in 1541 he did not come to trade; but used his European goods to obtain food, friendship and guidance to the kingdoms. In 1542 two men from the Banks were questioned in Spain about Cartier and the country he was exploring. Both had been inside the Gulf to fish and trade, and one reported that 'the people trade in marten skins and other skins and those who go there take all kinds of ironware'. It was the other who added to similar testimony that the French sailors believed 'that from the port of Canada one could reach the land of Peru'. To Cartier these romantic dreams of a northern Peru obliterated the homely profit in hand afforded by the fur trade. His shipmasters and sailors were more realistic.

After 1543 the fishermen who resorted to Newfoundland and the Gulf saw the fur trade gradually develop. In the courts of Europe there was an eager demand for the princely marten-skins. Other furs and the hides of elk, deer and bears satisfied a less discriminating taste. Specifically, however, it was the hatmakers who became the stimulators in Europe of a demand for beaver-skins which for the first time came at all near to reciprocating the Indian demand for European goods. The precise requirements of the hat manufacture were somewhat technical, but the basic consideration was that the downy hairs of beaver fur possessed in unrivalled fashion the gift of natural coherence into an extremely durable felt. So durable was it that in the late seventeenth century beaver hats made at La Rochelle were returned there after their French wearing to be re-made for sale in Spain, whence they were again returned to be prepared for Brazil and for the last time to be used for trade purposes by the Portuguese in Africa.

Had the beaver been a fugitive, elusive animal like the fox or rabbit, the *tempo* of North American history would have been slower. As it was, the beaver laid itself open to easy local extermination because of its domiciliary habits. This moderately prolific animal advertised its presence by the dams it made, the trees it cut for food and the lodges which it built. It had been a relatively serious labour for the Indians with their primitive tools to break into a beaver lodge fast enough to secure its inhabitants. It was much more practicable with steel axes. The beaver meadows nearest the coast suffered first, but northern North America with its wealth of water-ways provided relatively untouched areas farther on. Thus the hat-makers of Europe were transformed into the prime movers of an exchange in America which sucked into the interior the men who followed the ever-retreating 'beaver frontier' across the continent.

The men who fished and whaled and slew walruses in the Gulf during the sixteenth century were a mixed lot of exploiters with little thought of exploration. For almost a century they fished, quarrelled over harbours and beaches, and did some trading on the side, with little interference from or supervision by their governments at home. When individual enterprise gave way to combined action, it was usually under such an association of local adventurers as that at St. Malo, or in groups of suppliants to kings for monopolistic privileges. France was so seriously harassed by foreign wars and domestic differences over government and religion that her affairs in America underwent their natural development almost exclusively in private hands. Neither Holland nor England was as yet capable of serious adventure in North America. Spain and Portugal were busy exploiting their first discoveries and thought they had reason to be scornful of the profits to be made in the north.

Yet out of this transitional period comes one of the most remarkable stories of North American travel, the supposed overland journey of three Englishmen from near the Río Pánuco in Mexico to a river near Cape

Breton Island. The men were David Ingram of Barking, Richard Browne and Richard Twide. Their story was told by Ingram in 1582 (the other two had died), when he was very specifically examined by Sir Francis Walsingham, Sir Humphrey Gilbert, Sir George Peckham and Richard Hakluyt the younger at the time when they were planning a colonial venture in North America. His tale made a great impression, for it fitted in well with contemporary knowledge of North America in England, and Hakluyt printed it in 1589. By 1598 increased knowledge made him leave it out of his great three-volume edition of narratives because of what he called its incredibilities. Yet there exists well-corroborated evidence that these three men did set off on foot westward and later northward from the Río Pánuco in October 1568, and Ingram told his examiners in 1582 that there were still living in Honfleur 'diverse of the said Frenchmen which were in the said ship called the Gargarine', whose captain, 'Monsr. Champaigne', 'had a trade with the people of diverse sorts of fine furres', and had picked him up and brought him back to France and England in 1569.

The story deserves attention because, although probably untrue, it almost certainly played its part in tempting the English to the exploration of North America. Ingram in 1582 was an old sailor anxious to please and probably mightily flattered to be interviewed by Walsingham, the Queen's Secretary and the spearhead of aggressive policy in the Council. Almost everything credible in his story could have been derived from a mixture of his corroborated experiences and of such hearsay as was current among the better-informed English mariners. At any rate he wove an alluring narrative of what he saw on his walk. Sir John Hawkins, after the loss of several ships and a narrow escape from Vera Cruz (San Juan de Ulua) in late September 1568, had not been able to carry and feed all the survivors in his ship and had landed over 100 of them north of Río Pánuco. After this group had divided twice, Ingram and about twenty-five men went 'Northword', while the remainder suffered at the hands of the Indians or were ultimately enslaved by Spaniards in Mexico. One of the narrators from among the captives said he had reason to believe that some of Ingram's group 'marryed in the sayd countrey, at Sibola'. Ingram made no mention of this, but spoke only of himself and his two companions.

His story contained very little geographical description. He related a great deal of nonsense about Indian kings who 'weare great precious stones which commonly are rubies being VI ynches long & 2 ynches broad', about the abundance of gold, silver, pearls and crystal, and about the incidence of cities at short intervals all across the continent. That part of his narrative contained echoes of the narratives of Friar Marcos, Vaca, Soto and Coronado. The geography which he volunteered was confused and fantastic, but his mention of 'Ochala' and 'Sagonas' among the cities he visited tempted Hakluyt to translation into Hochelaga and Saguenay. In the same way an eager modern reader could apply to the Great Lakes or the bays of the Atlantic coast his statement that 'ther passe over manie great rivers in those Cuntries in Canoe or boats some 4 some 8 some 10 myles over, wherof one was so large that they cold scarse cross the same in 24 howers'.

This questionable story was told to a semi-official colonising group in England at a time when the experts still clung to the idea (derived from Verrazano's map) that the Pacific or an inland sea stretched east from the back of the Spanish settlements in Mexico to within sight of the Atlantic where we would place either Chesapeake or Delaware Bay. Ingram had a share, therefore, in drawing to Virginia the luckless settlers who made England's first colonial adventure there.

More valid and enduring than that largely political adventure, however, were the matter-of-fact activities in the Gulf and river St. Lawrence. The Basques made Tadoussac and the mouth of the Saguenay river a base for their whaling. Others, chiefly French, went there for the fur trade. Geography had already made it a centre for bartering among the natives of the north and south shores of the river and the gulf, even a place where native commodities crossed in their long, laborious transmission from Labrador and Newfoundland towards the west and south, from the Great Lakes and the St. Lawrence towards the east, and from the lower part of the Atlantic coast towards the north and east. We know very little about the details of inter-tribal and inter-regional trade in North America before the Europeans upset it, but we have enough information to be sure that the Gulf of St. Lawrence in the summertime was one of its great centres. When the Europeans also began to congregate there, they sent out towards the interior, in more and more rapid succession, waves of economic and cultural revolution, whose effects we can see in the meagre accounts of Indian wars and migrations of the sixteenth and subsequent centuries which archaeology and history have preserved for us.

It might reasonably be argued that the initiative in the exchange of Old and New World commodities passed from the Indians to the Europeans at the time when, instead of allowing the Indians to seek them out at various points around the Gulf of St. Lawrence, the fur traders began to seek out the Indians and thus begin the exploration of the northern half of the continent. The date seems to have been about 1581, when a group of merchants of St. Malo began to send their vessels up the river either to tap virgin sources of furs or to intercept the flow of them from the interior which the Gulf barter had already brought into being.

The truth was that the profits of the fur trade had now made it an end in itself for European adventurers, and competition among them very rapidly became keen. As early as 1588, two nephews of Jacques Cartier sought and obtained from Henry III of France a monopoly of the trade as compensation for the unpaid accounts of their uncle. This grant provoked such an outcry among French competitors that it had to be withdrawn. The last decade of the sixteenth century revealed to France that the summer fur trade of the St. Lawrence had become so valuable as to make desirable both regulation of it among Frenchmen and protection of it from encroachments by men of other nations. It was from this situation that there emerged Samuel Champlain of Brouage, the man who in his own person and in the activities which he initiated marked the abrupt change from mere sailors' visits along the shores of tide-water to such active exploration of the interior as necessitated the adoption of Indian methods of travel, and, as well, actual residence in North America.

NARRATIVES

There are no outstanding narratives of the activities referred to in this chapter, but fragments concerning them were industriously collected and published by Richard Hakluyt the younger. See the Glasgow edition of his *The Principal Naviga-*

tions, etc., as under Chapter V. David Ingram's narrative appears in the 1589 (one-volume) edition only and is to-day difficult of access. It was edited by P. C. G. Weston and privately printed in London in 1856 and by B. F. De Costa in *The Magazine of American History*, vol. ix (New York, 1883). It is invidious to select two secondary works from among many, but H. P. Biggar in *The Early Trading Companies of New France* (Toronto, 1901) first demonstrated from the source materials the relation between fisheries and fur trade, and H. A. Innis in *The Fur Trade in Canada* (New Haven, 1930) has made in the same way the demonstration of how peculiarities of the fur trade led Europeans into the continent.

CHAPTER X

CHAMPLAIN AND THE YOUNG MEN

(*Map No. 2, page 258*)

Que desires tu voir encore
Curieuse Témérité:
Tu cognois l'un et l'autre More,
En Ton cours est-il limité?

MOTIN: A MONSIEUR DE CHAMPLAIN, 1613

NORTH AMERICAN history knows few, if any, more sustained careers of original enterprise than that of Champlain. That is not to say that he was a mere dogged plodder who persisted in one aim through the deficiency of his imagination to provide him with another. A man of thirty-one years of age, he came to his life-work in 1598 when the end of the civil wars in France closed his non-combatant military career. He turned at once to active interest in the American enterprises which had made Spain the envy of Europe and particularly of France. He decided 'to make inquiries into particulars of which no Frenchmen have succeeded in obtaining cognizance, because they have no free access there, in order to make true report of them to his Majesty'. A series of happy coincidences, which hinged upon his uncle's being high in the pilot service of the Spanish navy, satisfied his desires almost at once, and in January 1599 he set out for the West Indies with the annual fleet and managed to remain there for over two years.

148

He used his opportunities to visit many of the settlements, even Mexico City, and came back to France crammed with information and ideas which ranged from tales (and pictures) of birds without feet and dragons with 'only two rather large feet', to descriptions and plans of the principal ports and a project for a Panama canal. His *Brief Narrative of the Most Remarkable Things that Samuel Champlain of Brouage observed in the West Indies* and the sixty-two illustrations which accompanied it seem swiftly to have provided the desired pathway to royal favour, for in 1602 Henry IV gave him a pension, attached him to the Court as a royal geographer, and in the succeeding year raised him from simple Samuel Champlain of Brouage to the lesser nobility as Sieur de Champlain of Saintonge. By 1603, also, Champlain had become involved in what was to be his lifelong effort to make New France, 'by means of Trade', a Venice, a Genoa or a Marseilles.

A relatively simple and straightforward narrative can be made of Champlain's doings after his return to France in 1601, but an explanation of them must be more complex. He happened to be in high repute as a geographer and colonial expert just at the time when domestic peace had at last descended upon France and when the growth of the fur trade in the Gulf of St. Lawrence was attracting official attention. It was quite natural that his services at once came into demand, for the additional reason that Henry IV and his advisers were smitten with the territorial ambitions of their day and had just begun to demand colonisation as the price of the monopoly of trade in North America for which individuals and companies were clamouring. Champlain had just written a report on the only existing North American colonies.

It seems probable that Champlain's position as royal geographer provides the main clue to his earliest motives in the matter of Canada. He was bent upon increasing his own fame, his country's possessions, and the sum of human knowledge. He had no private fortune beyond his capacities and his brief repute. His geographical ambitions, therefore, could only be satisfied if he became useful to business men made colonisers by force of circumstance. As we shall see, Champlain himself came ultimately to be a coloniser by conviction, but in his early American years he yielded to his geographical curiosity so fully that it must have been at some cost to his usefulness in trade.

Champlain seems never to have been afflicted with dreams of looting some northern Peru, but he laboured hard to discover what ways there might be of getting through what he and his contemporaries had come to accept as a large continent. He did not know how large it was. In suggesting a canal at Panamá, he had noted that, after its construction, 'from Panama to the strait of Magellan would be an island, and from Panama to the Newfound-lands would be another island', but he did not hazard a guess as to the length of the North American 'island'. The wanderings of Soto and Coronado precluded a water-way across the southern region, but there ought to be a sea-strait or open sea running diagonally north-east from the Pacific to the Atlantic, or there might be a great inland sea to which rivers from Pacific and Atlantic provided approaches.

The great difficulty in visualising the thickness of North America came from the extreme faultiness of the methods of making observations of longitude. It was hard, also, to bear in mind at the same time the north-eastern trend of the Atlantic coast and the southwestern trend of the St. Lawrence river. Champlain gave a great deal of energy and thought between 1603 and 1608 to working out a geographical hypothesis about the relations of the St. Lawrence, the Saguenay, the Ottawa and the Richelieu rivers, and even to the possibility that some one of the rivers which flowed into the Atlantic south of Cape Breton might flow from the inland sea. The St. Lawrence and Ottawa river Indians, in describing the Great Lakes, gave his imagination plenty to work on.

It was in 1603 that Champlain went out to the St. Lawrence on a voyage of reconnaissance and trade on behalf of the monopolist of the day. He went first to Tadoussac and then, acting upon the unrealised intentions of his recent predecessors, went on up the river in a small craft to the rapids beyond Hochelaga which had checked Cartier and Roberval two generations before. His companion, François Gravé, sieur du Pont (called Pontgravé), had already made at least one trip to Three Rivers at the mouth of the St. Maurice, and the expedition was a clear demonstration of what the future of the expanding fur trade must be—a greedy penetration of the continent in pursuit of the beaver.

Champlain found no Stadacona and no Hochelaga, and the disappearance of these semi-agricultural communities was probably another evidence of what the fur trade involved. North of the St. Lawrence and roughly parallel with it, there had grown up across the head-waters of the tributary rivers a difficult but busy trade route between the white men's ships at Tadoussac and the hunters of the interior. South-west of the St. Lawrence were the Iroquois tribes, as yet untouched by the Dutch traders who were later to reach them by way of the Hudson, but warlike and greedy for the magical goods which the northern Indians now possessed. The Montagnais of the northern head-waters and their customers and intermittent allies, the Algonquins of the Ottawa valley and the Hurons of the region between the Ottawa and Great Lakes, formed one group, loosely associated by their European contacts. The Iroquois tribes, in their remarkable confederacy which stretched from Lake Champlain to Lake Erie, were another, anxious to use the St. Lawrence to establish the same contacts. Between them they probably obliterated the Indians who had in Cartier's day been cultivating the fertile lands of the river-side above Quebec, and when Champlain went up to Lachine, the Indians of the north shore were, in their spasmodic way, fighting those of the south for control of the river. 'A settlement at Three Rivers would be a boon for the freedom of some tribes [from the interior] who dare not come that way [to Tadoussac] for fear of their enemies, the said Iroquois,' recorded Champlain.

His voyage was admirably systematic. The fiord-like mouth of the Saguenay was explored and information collected concerning its upper waters. The same procedure was followed at the St. Maurice, but the really engaging problem was as to what could be reached south of Montreal by the Richelieu, south-west by the St. Lawrence and west by the Ottawa. It is impossible to be precise about ideas which Champlain revealed in the course of reports which began in 1603 and ended in 1632, but one can approximate the conclusions which he drew from his own experience and from the reports of the several groups of travelling Indians whom he consulted in 1603.

The Saguenay, he learned, was the beginning of a canoe-route which led far into the north, and somewhere near where it crossed the height of land Indians from still farther north brought furs for trade with the Montagnais middlemen. 'These said savages from the north say that they are in sight of a sea which is salt. I hold that, if this be so, it is some gulf of this our sea which overflows in the north into the midst of the continent.' Thus the Saguenay-Mistassini traverse from the St. Lawrence to James Bay was recorded seventy years before any European followed it, and Hudson Bay was correctly imagined seven years before Henry Hudson found it. Other enquiries gave indication of the well-established trade-route west from the Saguenay to the St. Maurice and thence to the northern tributaries of the Ottawa. The Richelieu route to Lake Champlain was the next bit of knowledge, and again Hudson's discovery was anticipated by Indian description of the portage from Lake George to the Hudson River, 'which leads down to the coast of Florida'. Florida was the name given to the whole Atlantic coast south of the Bay of Fundy.

The St. Lawrence, the Ottawa and the Great Lakes, however, provided at once a geographical puzzle and a lively temptation to the geographer-merchant who could not go beyond the Lachine rapids in 1603. 'He who would pass them must provide himself with the canoes of the savages, which a man can easily carry,' he reported. 'With the canoes of the savages one may travel freely and quickly throughout the country . . . so that . . . a man may see all that is to be seen, good and bad, within the space of a year or two.' This wistful inspiration of 1603 was later to be the seed of the French successes in exploring North America. Lachine and the retreating beaver induced them to adopt the Indian mode of travel, to go with the Indians, to live like the

Indians, indeed to become better than the Indians as rangers over the vast territories of the interior.

Indian reports made the interior fascinating to Champlain in 1603. He collected information about it at every opportunity during his short visit and tried to make a consistent synthesis in his imagination. In general, he learned of three water-ways to the west, although it was assuredly not his fault that he never in his life was able to put them together in the design which comes out so clearly on the maps of to-day.[1] First of all, there was the St. Lawrence, whose rapids awed Champlain. 'I never saw any torrent of water pour over with such force as this does.' He learned from three separate groups of natives that it had ten or twelve rapids before it opened up into the large lake which we know as Ontario. The accounts of what lay beyond Lake Ontario were vague, and, although Niagara Falls was twice rather casually indicated, 'somewhat high, and where little water flows over', only the least impressive witness told of its being about 'a league broad'. Lake Erie was recognisable, and Lake Huron was shrouded in tall tales of hearsay. 'They say that in summer the sun sets to the north of this lake, and in winter it sets as it were in the middle of it; and that the water there is very salt, like that of our sea.' Champlain was cautious, but came finally to believe that what we know as Lake Huron 'can be nothing else than the South Sea'. He guessed that it was about 400 leagues away by water.

[1] The reader interested in the pioneer Champlain should certainly consult the map which he made for the 1632 summary of his voyagings. The Saguenay-James Bay and Saguenay-Ottawa-Lake Huron traverses, among others, are indicated, as are the routes of Champlain and Brulé for the attack on the Iroquois in 1615. An excellent reproduction of it accompanies vol. iii of the Champlain Society edition.

In such circumstances he gave little attention to reports of the other two water-ways. One of these led from the Bay of Quinté on the north shore of Lake Ontario, by the Trent river towards Lake Simcoe and thence by the Severn river to Georgian Bay. The other, which was to be for three centuries the main-travelled route to the west, was that up the Ottawa, across to Lake Nipissing, and down the French river to Georgian Bay. Champlain himself was later to make both of these journeys, but it is evidence of the difficulties of the St. Lawrence and of the fear of the Iroquois that he never followed the swift St. Lawrence along the route which so engaged his interest in 1603.

As a matter of fact, the enquirer is faced by the apparent anomaly that although Champlain spent most of the next five years in North America, he spent them in Acadia and in exploring the Atlantic coast. Inasmuch as in 1613 his retrospective picture of himself was as one member of the European host who sought 'to find a route to China by the north', indeed as one who had made a report to Henry IV upon how to do it 'without the inconvenience of the northern icebergs, or the heat of the torrid zone', this interlude of 1603–8 demands explanation.

No doubt part of the answer lies in the fact that he was not his own master, but more significant, considering the weight which his advice undoubtedly carried with his backers, was the effect of certain information about the Bay of Fundy and the Atlantic coast which he collected in the course of a short voyage along the south shore of the Gulf after his return to Tadoussac in 1603. He met there Jean Sarcel, Sieur de Prévert, an old hand in the Gulf trade from St. Malo, and from him and the Indians learned some exciting things about the Bay of Fundy. Prévert was not the first-hand witness he purported to be, but he gave a circumstantial account (with samples) of copper outcroppings at the head of the Bay and of 'mines' of other metals which seemed to be silver or iron. True, the region was said to be guarded by 'a dreadful monster, which the savages call Gougou', who stood twice mast-high and had a pocket-larder for his human victims 'so large that he could have put our vessel into it', but mines were a magic lure in 1603. In addition, Champlain got word of the St. John river as a route of access from the Bay of Fundy to Lake Champlain, and his thoughts ran again to the possibility of a river leading from the Atlantic coast to the South Sea. 'It is most certain that on the coast of Florida there are rivers not yet discovered, which reach the interior', he wrote.

His activities from 1604 to 1607, interesting and fruitful as they were in another sense, did not contribute, except negatively, to the exploration of North America. He searched for mines on the Bay of Fundy and found various outcrops. He helped to establish the first permanent French colonists in North America. More importantly, he systematically explored and charted the coast from Cape Breton Island to southern Massachusetts, and in doing so he looked for 'a passage which should lead near to the great lake . . . where the water is salt; [a boon] as well for the navigation of ships . . . as for the shortening of the way more than three hundred leagues'. He found the Kennebec and learned of the short portage from its head-waters to Dead river, the Chaudière, and thence to Quebec. For various reasons, however, he never reached either the Connecticut or the Hudson. Had he done so and learned of their long courses into the interior, it is reasonable to believe that the history of North America would have been very different.

As it was, he went back to the St. Lawrence in 1608 on behalf of his patron, Sieur de Monts, the holder of a one-year monopoly of the fur trade, with the intention of making a settlement to serve as a base, both for a more profitably conducted trade and for discovery of the passage to China, 'since the voyage would begin in this land beyond the ocean, along which the search for the desired passage is to be made'. Quebec commanded the St. Lawrence and from Quebec Monts and Champlain believed that they might 'penetrate inland as far as the Western Sea, and thence at some future day to reach even to China'.

In 1608 the St. Lawrence was the site of two conflicts, one between the Indians north and south, and one among the French fur traders. It was inevitable that Champlain should become involved in both. He had to make a choice in alliance between the Montagnais-Algonquin-Huron group with whom contact in some sort had existed for almost a century and the aggressive Iroquois who came out of their lands south of the Great Lakes by way of the St. Lawrence and the Richelieu. Naturally he chose the northern group, who were not only on the ground which he chose to occupy, but were in many senses permanently affected by their use of European commodities. He set out to cultivate their friendship and ensure their regular recourse to him at Lachine and Quebec for trade. He even assisted them in their wars with the Iroquois, and an attack during 1609 was the occasion for his ascent of the Richelieu and acquaintance with the lake which now bears his name.

Yet with the passing of the fur monopoly in 1609

Champlain had to give his chief energies to winning support for himself and the little colony at Quebec by surpassing his competitors in the fur trade. After 1608 they crowded in his wake up to Lachine, where, with such primitive customers as the Indians, the whole trade fell into unprofitable competitive confusion. It was Tadoussac all over again. From 1608 to 1613, therefore, Champlain was kept so busy consolidating his influence with the Indians and trying to earn dividends for his backers that he could not prosecute his search for a way to China. Only in 1612 was he able, under princely patronage, to have the fur monopoly revived. He had meanwhile built up a precarious reputation for dependability among the Indians, which meant that they slowly lost faith in more opportunistic traders ('women, who wish to make war only upon our beavers') and turned towards him. They were fickle, and they were learning to bargain. Moreover, their own trading activities were sending out, in fan-like formation along the inland water-ways, strands in the silken net of the coming economic dependence upon Europe.

Since Champlain himself could not go beyond Lachine, he determined to send others. Nothing is more notable in the conduct of the French in North America than their success in getting along with the Indians and in living among them. It was Champlain who invented, as it were, the *coureurs de bois* and the *voyageurs*[1] who carried French influence from the St. Lawrence to the Rockies and from Hudson Bay to the Gulf of Mexico. In 1610 he and Pontgravé found among the settlers at

[1] I use the first term for the traders who operated chiefly in the forested regions, and the second more generally or for those who journeyed beyond the forests into the plains. I do not, as has sometimes been done, mean only unauthorised traders by the term *coureurs de bois,* because that usage of opprobrium was a late and special development, often irregularly applied.

Quebec a youth, almost certainly Etienne Brulé, 'who wished to go with the Algonquins to learn their language'. They thought it an excellent idea for him 'to learn what their country was like, see the great lake [Huron], observe the rivers . . . explore the mines . . . so that on his return we might be informed of the truth thereof'. Brulé 'accepted the journey with great willingness'.

Champlain sent out other young men in the years that followed, as did at least one other trader. We have the names of some of them, but of others there are mere chance echoes. In fact, for over two centuries the student of North American exploration is often forced to admit that the great names belong to 'path-finders', whereas the 'trail-makers' are unknown. Usually, of course, the natives made the trails and established the routes, but wherever these avenues were integrated in some white man's design, there is the chance that lurking in a background of anonymity was some *voyageur* who was almost one with the natives.

One of Champlain's 'young men', Nicolas Vignau, turned up in Paris in the autumn of 1612, anxious to make capital out of having passed the winter of 1611–1612 with the Algonquins near Allumette Lake on the Ottawa river. Champlain had just ended a year's successful effort in France to set up a new monopolistic company under the powerful patronage of the Prince de Condé. The future seemed bright and its brightness gained lustre from the tale which Vignau had to tell. 'He had seen the northern sea' and reported that the Ottawa river 'came from a lake which emptied into it'. 'In seventeen days one could go from the St. Louis rapids [Lachine] to this sea and back again. He said also that he had seen pieces of the wreck of an English ship which had been lost on that coast.' The Indians had shewn him the scalps of the eighty survivors and were keeping an English boy for Champlain. Inasmuch as the ports of Europe were just then reverberating with echoes of Hudson's discovery of his Bay in 1610, Champlain found himself the possessor of news which was bound to interest the Court and win him support, but which seemed to him to be suspiciously out of line with what he himself had been told about seas far distant beyond the head-waters of the Saguenay, the St. Maurice and the Ottawa.

Yet it was to investigate this tale that in 1613 Champlain at last made real his dream of 1603 and took to the canoe to journey past Lachine. He still suspected Vignau, in spite of the youth's attestations before notaries, but anyway he felt that he had to go up the Ottawa to find his customers. Illness and business had kept him in France during 1612, and the Algonquins and Hurons, having decided that he had abandoned them, did not assemble at the Rapids in 1613. In the unexpected absence of the Indians, Champlain could not simply attach himself as an honoured passenger to an Indian brigade of canoes and be carried on his exploration. In fact, he was able to secure the assistance of only one Indian as a guide. In these circumstances, Champlain and four Frenchmen decided to become canoe-men themselves. They set out for the West on 27 May in two canoes 'laden with provisions, with our arms, and with goods with which to make presents to the Indians'.

There was a grand audacity about this venture which was the omen of what France would achieve in North America. The Indian canoe was a highly specialised craft, constructed as lightly as possible from a framework of some resilient wood like white cedar or spruce, and covered by thick sheets of birch-bark sewed to each other and to the ribs, and made water-tight by gum from the conifers. It was propelled by single-blade paddles and its steering was something of an art, for it had no keel to diminish drifting in a wind. Nowadays its equivalent, the sleek product of modern manufacturing resources, impresses the beginner (usually by spilling him) as a very cranky craft. Yet Champlain and his companions boldly embarked on the hardest kind of canoe travel up the Ottawa, against its swift current and past its rapids, 'partly by portage, partly by tracking' [towing]. 'We were forced to carry our canoes, clothes, provisions, and arms on our shoulders, which is no small labour for those who are not used to it.'

They spent a week at this arduous labour, during which the leader almost lost his life while tracking his indispensable canoe through the 'white foam' and rocks of the Long Sault rapids. They kept good guard against the Iroquois and drove stubbornly on, but it was with great pleasure and relief that on 2 June they met fifteen canoe-loads of Algonquins coming down to Lachine to find out whether the reports were true that Champlain had come back. 'They were astonished to see me in that country with so few Frenchmen, and with only one Indian. . . . When I informed them that I wished to go on farther to warn the other tribes [of a confederacy against the Iroquois] they tried to dissuade me, declaring that the way was bad and that we had hitherto seen nothing like it.' An exchange was effected, however, whereby the least useful Frenchman accompanied the Indians down to the trading vessels at Lachine, and an Indian was secured to steer Champlain's second canoe.

Henceforth professionals could at least keep the two canoes on their most efficient course.

The river journey continued without untoward incident. Champlain was much impressed by the natural beauties of the region now occupied by the cities of Ottawa and Hull, where the Ottawa plunged with a roar into a rock basin, the Gatineau waters swirled in from the unknown north, and the Rideau 'falls from a height of twenty or twenty-five fathoms with such impetuosity that it forms an archway nearly four hundred yards in width. The Indians, for the fun of it, pass underneath this without getting wet, except for the spray made by the falling water.'

After they passed Lac des Chats, Vignau began to grow uneasy and to try to end the expedition through discouragement over its difficulty. Champlain had long suspected his story and, before leaving Lachine, had explicitly given him a chance to withdraw it, but 'he reasserted, on peril of his life, all he had previously stated'. Now as the travellers were approaching the region of the Algonquin encampment where he had wintered, he tried to divert them from the Indian portage route to Allumette Lake and to have them fight their way up the impassable rapids. 'Our Indians said to him, "You are tired of living" . . . and I followed the advice of the Indians.'

Subsequently Champlain must have wondered just how bad the rapids could be, for the portage route was long and arduous in spite of their having left behind their maize supplies and other dispensable goods. The pertinacity of the mosquitoes in the woods was 'so great that it is impossible to give any description of it'. They subsisted on a few broiled fish. The trails were very bad and in one region which had probably been burnt over by one of the carelessly controlled clearing fires of the Indians, the tall pines had fallen against each other to form that bane of the overland pioneer, the tangle of a *bois brûlé*. 'One must go now over, and now under, these trees.' Champlain struggled along, 'being laden for my part alone with three arquebuses, an equal number of paddles, my cloak, and some small articles'. It was almost certainly he who dropped or abandoned the little *cache*, consisting of silver cups, copper kettles and a brass astrolabe dated 1603, which a Canadian farm-boy turned up with his plough in August 1867.

Towards the end of their two-day portage, they met an Indian chief who 'was astonished that we had been able to pass the rapids and bad trails on the way to their country . . . saying that we must have fallen from the clouds . . . for those who live in the country had great difficulty in coming along such difficult trails'. The chief gave his tribesmen to understand that Champlain was a person who carried out all he set his mind upon, as well he might, for the Algonquins had deliberately chosen an inaccessible region for their settlements. The Iroquois had already begun to plague them, not only on the lower Ottawa, but also by ambushes at the good hunting ground near the mouth of the Rideau.

On 7 June Champlain was conducted to the strong settlement of Chief Tessouat, Vignau's host, on an island in Allumette Lake,[1] and the next two days were crowded with the drama of Vignau's exposure as a liar

---

[1] This site is still inevitably in dispute. It has been fairly persuasively assigned to Morrison Island by S. L. Morris and H. P. Biggar, but serious discrepancies with Champlain's narrative and map remain. In this connection see C. H. Laverdière, *Œuvres de Champlain* (Quebec, 1870), iii, 307, and H. P. Biggar, *The Works of Champlain* (Toronto, 1925), ii, 277-9 + plates xi-xiv. See also Champlain's map of 1632 in either of these editions.

and with Champlain's regretful conclusion that he could not get assistance in exploring farther that year. There was a great clash and tangle of wills and circumstances. The Algonquins were glad to have Champlain back again and wanted him to build a fort and trading post at Lachine, but they clung tenaciously to their monopoly of the middleman position and effectively dissuaded him from trying to reach the Nipissings in the immediate west or the Hurons still farther west among whom Etienne Brulé had lived.

Champlain did not feel like pressing the issue, for he felt that he and all Frenchmen had lost prestige through Vignau, and he wanted to cover up the whole incident. He himself had at first pretended that he had been sent by the King to help the Indians (including the Nipissings) in their war against the Iroquois. Only when the Algonquins said the way was too difficult did he accuse them of being liars because Vignau had visited the Nipissings. Then the storm broke. Tessouat made Vignau repeat his assertion and then excoriated him. 'You are a brazen liar; you know well that every night you slept alongside of me and my children . . . if you visited those tribes, it was in your sleep.' Vignau still held out and Champlain then volunteered to the Indians his real quest, the northern sea where the English had been wrecked. Another storm of abuse broke over Vignau and a little later he confessed to Champlain, who in turn 'very sorrowfully' revealed his duplicity to the Indians. They would have killed him forthwith and only care for French prestige seems to have prevented Champlain from agreeing with them. He raised a great cross of white cedar bearing the arms of France, and in the midst of a fleet of Algonquin canoes went back to Lachine to trade.

Vignau's hopes of repute and reward had been defeated because Champlain had unexpectedly undertaken a journey which the youth had thought so difficult that no white man could manage it. Champlain himself was thrown back upon his old conceptions of the interior and somewhat disillusioned as to the ease of travel by canoe. He had not reached the Northern Sea. The great western lake on which the Hurons lived and which in 1603 he had taken to be the Pacific he now knew to be a true lake, the Sweetwater Sea. To reach it he must travel far beyond the Algonquins' encampments. But he had explored the first stages of the route which the Indians themselves had selected as the best way from the fur regions of the interior to the ships at Lachine, and he and they had begun the communication which was to pound the portage paths flat and clear away the obstructions to a flow of traffic which was to last until the nineteenth century.

NARRATIVES

Champlain and Lescarbot as above. There are two Indian accounts of the genesis of the wars between the Iroquois and the northern Indians. See *Radisson's Voyages*, edited by G. D. Scull (Boston, 1885), pp. 87-95, and E. H. Blair, *Indian Tribes of the Upper Mississippi and the Great Lakes Regions* (2 vols., Cleveland, 1911), vol. i, pp. 42-7.

CHAPTER XI

MISSIONS AND WARS AT THE SWEETWATER SEA

(*Map No. 2, page 258*)

Or les Pères Religieux . . . brusloient de faire le voyage, moyennant la grace de Dieu, affin de voir s'ils pourroient faire quelque bon fruit, & planter en ces lieux l'estendart de Iesus-Christ, auec une deliberation de viure & mourir pour son sainct Nom, s'il estoit necessaire, & que l'occasion s'en presentast.

CHAMPLAIN: VOYAGES . . . 1615–1618, ff. 7-7ᵛ

THE seventeenth century, especially during its first fifty or sixty years, was remarkable for one of those widespread outbursts of piety and of the missionary spirit which have occurred at intervals throughout the Christian era. Their quality can only be recaptured either by those who have actually been in the midst of such a broad popular emotion or who have individually been transported by the religious experience. Any objective description of the triumphant blend of faith, self-denial and devotion which provided so much of the motive force for Spanish and French missionary efforts in the seventeenth century must fail, because its quality was so overwhelmingly subjective. We can read the words of Father Gabriel Sagard-Théodat—'*la perfection des hommes ne consiste point à voir beaucoup, ny à scavoir beaucoup; mais en accomplissant le vouloir & bon plaisir de Dieu*'—but even when we read of the deeds by which such men lived up to their professions, we have only a partial understanding of what those words meant.

There are certain theological obstacles to assuming that some of the missionaries who went out to Canada deliberately courted the martyr's crown at the hands of the savages whose souls they devoted their lives to win. Yet the simple record of their acts, uncoloured by any speculations about motives, is the proof that not one, but several, of the early Canadian missionaries literally counted no cost too high to be paid for the mere chance to tell the tidings of salvation. They risked the Atlantic crossing; they circumvented the hostility of the trading interpreters and feverishly crammed up glossaries of native words; they disregarded civilian warnings as to seasons and places for their missions, and they tried at fearful cost to prove that where Indians could go they could go. The Indians did not understand them, and their ideas and behaviour often made them nuisances and embarrassments in the highly conventionalised Indian ways of living. The Hurons, for instance, said: 'You say things that pass our understanding and that we cannot comprehend by words, as something beyond our intelligence; but if you would do well, you should dwell in our country and bring women and children, and when they come to these regions we shall see how you serve this God whom you worship.' Champlain thought that this was 'natural good sense'. Yet it is notable that some of these martyrs received the Indians' highest tribute to an adversary, that is, the most devilish and prolonged torture that their fertile imaginations could devise.

The days of martyrdoms still lay in the uncharted future in 1615. Quebec had seen no missionary priests during its first six years of existence because no one had offered to subscribe to their support. From the first Champlain had hoped that they might come, but had been bound down by business considerations. Although his given name and the region of his birth make it very likely that he was born a Huguenot, yet during the recorded period of his life he appeared as a simply devout Roman Catholic, anxious from the beginning of his adventuring to bring Christianity to the Indians. When he came back to Canada in 1615 after spending a year in France, he brought with him at last four members of the ascetic branch of the Franciscans, known as the Récollets, from a community in his own town of Brouage.[1] They had left France feeling somewhat apprehensive of the difficulties and dangers of the new land, but when they entered the St. Lawrence in late May, 'they were greatly encouraged at seeing the place quite different from what they had imagined, and this increased their zeal' to such an extent that two of them determined to go off among the Indians at once. Two days after the vessels had reached Tadoussac, Father Joseph Le Caron was off with the first long-boats for Quebec and thence to Lachine. Father Denis Jamet accompanied Champlain a little later, while Father Jean Dolbeau and the lay brother Pacifique du Plessis set up the headquarters of their mission at Quebec. Within

[1] Religious differences, not only of Roman Catholic and Protestant, but even among Roman Catholic orders and among the supporters and opponents of the Jesuits or the Ultramontanes, have seriously coloured the original narratives of missionary history and more modern accounts as well. Small weight can be given to these complications here, but readers farther afield should always look into the predilections of the authors whom they consult. A striking example is afforded by the summary editions of Champlain's *Voyages* which appeared in 1632 and later years. Some editorial hand, friendly to the Jesuits, studiously cut out the enthusiastic references to the Récollets which Champlain had made in his 1619 edition, and awkwardly substituted matter about the Jesuits, who did not go to Canada until 1625.

six months of their arrival, one friar (Le Caron) was among the Hurons south of Georgian Bay and another (Jamet) was off on the winter hunt of the Montagnais in the hinterland of the north shore of the St. Lawrence. Only the 'young men', the *coureurs de bois*, could rival such enthusiasm and dare such novel adventures.

Champlain himself had not planned to do any exploring until the next year, but the Indians gathered at Lachine urged him to help them form a war-party against the Iroquois, 'representing to us that only with difficulty could they come to us if we did not help them, because the Iroquois, their ancient foes, were continually along the route and prevented them from passing'. Champlain and the Sieur du Pont decided that the long-promised assistance must be given and the former went back to Quebec to prepare for the journey. He had earlier met Father Le Caron on his way down the river from Lachine to Quebec to get ecclesiastical furniture preparatory to wintering with the Hurons and had tried to dissuade him from the enterprise. 'Nevertheless, in spite of everything I could make him understand or say or represent to him, he would not alter his plan, being urged by zeal for God and affection towards these people, and promising himself to make known to them their salvation.'

In spite of the presence of French merchants at Lachine, the Indians were nervous about Iroquois raids on the St. Lawrence and excited over the prospect of crushing their enemies once for all. It took Champlain about sixteen or seventeen days to make the trip to Quebec and back, and when he reached the rapids again on 9 July, he discovered 'that the savages had taken their departure much aggrieved because I had not gone with them, and that many of their number accounted us dead or captured by the Iroquois'. Father Le Caron and twelve Frenchmen had gone off with them, whereas Champlain would have liked to plan the military expedition more carefully. 'All this, however, did not make me lose courage for proceeding with the expedition, by reason of my strong desire to pursue my explorations.' The Sweetwater Sea and the Northern Sea still excited his curiosity.

Father Sagard-Théodat, a Récollet who spent 1623–1624 in Canada, was the recorder of the pioneer missionary enterprise, and Father Le Caron confided to him his memories of his trip to Georgian Bay. 'He suffered on the way to the limits of his physical capacity.' He had to do his part as canoe-man, with the paddle, wading through rapids, and plodding across the portages. He and his French companions had to keep up with the professional Indian canoe-men over a difficult route or be left to find the way alone. With the possible exception of Etienne Brulé or some other *coureur de bois*, they were the first Europeans to make the journey from the Ottawa to Georgian Bay. One can imagine that night after night their canoes came trailing in to the camping-place long after the others had landed and eaten and that their hours for sleep were short.

Champlain, accompanied by his personal servant, by Etienne Brulé and by ten Indians, followed them, and it seems likely that he did so with mixed motives. Primarily, his task was to help *his* Indians to deliver such a crushing blow against the Iroquois that Hurons and Algonquins and remoter tribes might come peacefully down to trade at Lachine. Already the Iroquois had driven the tribes out of the Trent river valley north of Lake Ontario and had made the route of the modern Rideau Canal their thoroughfare from the St. Lawrence to ambush the Algonquins far up the Ottawa river. They had been in commercial contact with the Dutch on the Hudson river since 1609. Really, when the Hurons fought the Iroquois in North America, France fought Holland, or Quebec and the St. Lawrence fought New Amsterdam and the Hudson. Both the Iroquois confederacy and the Huron tribes had by 1615 become middlemen, each with a European wholesaler, and each struggling for control of the Great Lakes and Ottawa river routes to the furs and the unsophisticated tribesmen of the western interior. Eight years later, Father Sagard-Théodat was naïve enough to suggest that peace between Hurons and Iroquois would be better for trade and for the spread of Christianity. 'Some members of the Company told me that it would not be expedient because if the Hurons were at peace with the Iroquois, the same Iroquois would lead the Hurons to trade with the Dutch and divert them from the more distant Quebec.'

With Indians as canoe-men, Champlain and Brulé were able to make rapid, rather uneventful progress in the wake of Father Le Caron. They left Montreal Island on 9 July and paddled up the Ottawa. Beyond Allumette Lake the travelling became difficult. 'We went some thirty-five leagues past a great number of rapids, either by portage or by tracking, through an ill-favoured region full of pines, birches and a few oaks, very rocky, and in many places rather hilly.' Their route by the Ottawa and the Mattawa rivers to Lake Nipissing was an entry into the great Laurentian Shield which extends its rocks and shallow soil and lace of water-ways from the Arctic, Hudson Bay and the North Atlantic to the northern fringe of the Great Lakes basin and the borders of the central plain. 'It is quite a wilderness, being barren and uninhabited except for a few Algonquin savages who . . . live by hunting and by the fish they catch. . . . God appears to have been pleased to give this frightful and abandoned region some things in their season . . . for I can assure you that along the streams there are such a great quantity of blueberries . . . and many raspberries and other small fruits, and in such plenty that it is marvelous.' Champlain had caught the summer flavour of the land where his countrymen were to become 'Americanised' and to surpass the aboriginal inhabitants in ranging the streams and lakes and forests.

They reached Lake Nipissing on 26 July and greatly enjoyed two days of rest and hospitality among the Nipissings. The run down the French river to Georgian Bay was easy, but it took them to that strange region now called the Thirty Thousand Islands, a maze of islands and channels which fills the eastern shore of the Bay until at its southern end the Laurentian Shield ends abruptly on the margin of fertile, if sandy, wooded hills and valleys. 'This district seemed to me very pleasant in contrast to such a bad country as that through which we had just come.' They had reached the northern settlements of the kindly country—a triangle bounded by Lakes Ontario, Erie and Huron on the south and west and with the Shield between it and the Ottawa river—which was occupied by the relatively sedentary, agricultural Hurons and their related tribes. The stability of the Huron settlements as compared with the conditions under which the other Indians were living in the seventeenth century led Father Sagard-Théodat to call the Hurons the nobility, the Algonquins the burghers and the Montagnais the rabble of the tribes. After a few days of search among the villages they came to one named Carhagouha about 4 August, and found Father Joseph. 'We were very glad to see him in good health, he on his side being no less delighted; for he expected nothing less than to see me in that country.'[1]

The month of August was spent in travelling about among the villages and in waiting on the shores of Lake Simcoe for the excited Indians to assemble the war parties which they had already, in their unstable way, postponed for a year. Their plans were most ambitious, for they had been in communication concerning an offensive alliance with the Andastes, a tribe which was hostile to the Iroquois and which lived south of Lake Ontario near the western head-waters of the Susquehanna river. Champlain was much 'satisfied', as he said, 'at having found this opportunity, by reason of my desire to gain intelligence of that country, which is only about seven days' journey from where the Dutch go to trade on the 40th degree'. The Dutch and the Iroquois had molested the Andastes, but in 1614 the latter 'captured three of the said Dutch who were assisting the enemy as we assist the Hurons'. In their innocence, 'having never seen a Christian and supposing them to be our men', they sent them home unharmed. Champlain was anxious to prevent that from happening again, and Brulé asked to be allowed to go with a dozen chosen Hurons who were to lead the Andastes from the west to the Iroquois fortress south-east of Lake Oneida so that when Champlain's party came from the north a really smashing victory might ensue. Champlain was

[1] The villages of Huronia were short-lived because sanitary and other considerations led to frequent changes of site. The most comprehensive archaeological research in the region has been assembled and mapped by A. E. Jones in the *Fifth Report of the Bureau of Archives for the Province of Ontario* (Toronto, 1908).

glad to agree, for Brulé could report on the country and its tribes.

Etienne Brulé, by his many daring single enterprises, commended himself to be the prototype and model for the scores of *coureurs de bois* and *voyageurs* who, in the next 250 years, played the major part in the revelation of North America. Like them, however, he was almost ignored in the records which have come down to us. Champlain and Fathers Sagard-Théodat and Le Caron all mentioned him and his doings, usually casually and often without giving his name, so that the historian of to-day must carefully piece together the journeys attributed to him with due regard to what others of Champlain's 'young men' were doing of the same sort about the same time.

Since his arrival in Canada as a sixteen- or seventeen-year-old boy in 1608, he had, as we have seen, spent the first two winters at Quebec and in 1610 had gone off with the Algonquins at his own request to learn what he could about the upper country and its resources. He and the Algonquin boy, Savignon, who went to France with Champlain, were re-exchanged in 1611. Brulé had by that time probably not been out of the Ottawa valley, the Algonquin country, but for 1611–12 he went home with the Hurons, so that he probably reached Georgian Bay and was the first European to see that portion of Champlain's 'Sweetwater Sea' (Lake Huron). He was the born adventurer, infected with the same curiosity as that which made Champlain drop trading in favour of arduous journeys through unknown regions, and possessed of that distinct courage and self-confidence which enables its possessor to try the untried without the company of his own kind. In 1618 Champlain spoke casually of him as having lived with the Indians 'for the last eight years, both as a pastime and to see the country and learn their language and mode of life'. It may be that his accomplishments increased his remuneration, but that consideration could not be sufficient to explain the explorations he undertook on his own initiative. By 1615 he had become an accomplished interpreter capable of dealing with the Montagnais, the Algonquins, the Nipissings and the Hurons, and Champlain naturally chose him to accompany him when he went to Georgian Bay.

Champlain was the first to get away from the rendez-vous at the village of Cahiagué on the western shore of Lake Simcoe, but his departure was delayed until 1 September. He and his exasperating allies set off in a fleet of canoes to follow the chain of lakes and rivers which led east and south to the Bay of Quinté on Lake Ontario. They then paddled around the eastern end of the lake to the south shore, concealed their canoes, and set off overland to attack the chief fortress of the Onondagas (the central clan of the Five Nations or Iroquois).[1] This moated, sturdily built stronghold, advantageously located not far from the outlet of Oneida Lake, could probably have been captured had Champlain and his little group of armed Frenchmen been able intelligently to direct the siege, but the Indians got out of hand and suffered such dispiriting losses in their spasmodic attacks that even when Champlain shewed them how to use a movable tower and portable parapets they bungled things badly. Futile attacks were made on 10 October and 11 October. Brulé and his 500 Andastes had been pledged to arrive on the 11th, but they did

[1] In order westward from Lake Champlain to south of Lake Erie were Mohawks, Oneidas, Onondagas, Cayugas and Senecas. The Tuscaroras later raised the number to six.

not appear, and the discouraged Hurons set out for their canoes some days after the 16th, carrying Champlain and the other wounded, and warding off occasional attacks from the victorious but respectful Onondagas.

A glance at the map immediately raises the question why Champlain did not simply go down the St. Lawrence from the eastern end of Lake Ontario to Lachine and on to winter at Quebec. The necessity of recruiting Algonquins, Nipissings and Hurons for the war party makes credible the round-about, thousand-mile journey from Lachine to Lake Simcoe and thence to Lake Ontario, but it is surprising to find the geographer Champlain, who knew the course of the St. Lawrence by description, making his way back to the Huron country for the winter and following the Lake Nipissing-Ottawa river route back next year. The truth was that although four men volunteered to take him, the leaders of his allies would not provide him with a canoe for the short route. They themselves were timorous about using that way because of the Oneidas and Mohawks, and anyway all of them wanted to do some fall hunting and get back to their villages before winter set in in earnest. 'And not being able to do anything, I had to resign myself to be patient', wrote Champlain, 'but some days later, I perceived that their plan was to detain me with my comrades in their country, both for their own safety and out of fear of their enemies.'

Naturally Champlain did not waste his time. He studied the country and its resources. He observed the manner of the autumn hunts and assisted in them. He even managed to get thoroughly lost without his compass for four days and three nights, when he pursued an unidentifiable bird 'with a beak almost like that of a parrot, as big as a hen, yellow all over, except for its red head and blue wings'. His chief preoccupation, however, after the difficult winter journey back to Lake Simcoe, was to obtain more explicit information about the Huron country and about the two 'seas' which were still unfixed in his mental picture of North America. In February, he and Father Le Caron visited the Petuns or Tobacco nation, who lived to the west of the Hurons, and the *Cheveux-relevés* (Tufted-hairs) who lived south-west of Georgian Bay. He learned about the Neutrals, who lived north of Lake Erie between Lake Ontario and Lake St. Clair and whose great resources in flints protected them from attack either by Iroquois to the south or Hurons to the north. Even the Fire-people (Mascoutens) west of the Detroit river were described to him. Yet, as is corroborated by his map of 1632, he failed to learn of Lake Erie and his ideas of the Sweetwater Sea were very confused. In fact, for many years the triple system of Lake Huron, Georgian Bay and Lake Michigan was imperfectly understood and Indian reports of grim, vast Lake Superior and its copper-mines were for ever being mixed up both with the Huron-Michigan waters and with European knowledge of Hudson Bay.

The great disappointment of his stay came from his being refused a chance to explore the north with the Nipissings so as to reach the Northern Sea. 'If anyone was sorry it was I; for I had quite expected to see that year what in many other preceding years I had sought for with great solicitude and effort amid much toil and risk of my life.' He had also been told that west of the Sweetwater Sea, 1000 miles away, 'there were people white like us and similar to us in other respects'. 'Only time and the courage of some persons of means, who can or will undertake to assist this project, can decide'.

Cathay and the Great Khan were still in Champlain's mind, but he was still the servant of the fur trade. The complicated structure of obstructions and excuses which the Indians of the Huron group built up by bribes and other devices to keep him from leaving them either for south-west or north is impossible to untangle to-day, but the plain inference is that, like the Algonquins before them, they were loath to lose their enviable middleman position. Algonquins, Nipissings and Hurons could co-operate in trading with Lachine, but the tribes beyond (whose trade buffalo skins Champlain had seen) must continue to depend on the eastern Indians' bounty rather than on direct trade with the French. Champlain went down with the trading party in the spring with a fairly clear idea of the 'island' made by the Ottawa route, the upper St. Lawrence and the Lakes, but instead of a map of Lake Huron and the waters beyond he had to be content with the materials for his very interesting treatise on the life and customs of the Hurons.

Just before Champlain left the Huron country, he learned that Brulé had been seen on the trail back to the Andastes village. It was not until 1618, however, that he met him again, this time at Three Rivers, and heard the story of his wanderings in 1615 and the succeeding years. They formed an extraordinary tale. He had left the rendezvous a week after Champlain, accompanied by twelve picked Hurons. Brulé did not describe their route, but from the nature of the country and from the time which elapsed, they probably went to the south-west corner of Lake Simcoe, paddled up the Holland river which empties there, portaged over to the Humber or the Credit, and so came to Lake Ontario some time before Champlain saw it at its eastern end.

Having skirted the western end of the lake to some point near the Niagara river (Brulé did not mention the Falls), their difficulties began, for the Senecas who lived there were at war both with the Hurons and with the Andastes. 'They sought a more secure path by traversing woods, forests and dense and difficult thickets, and by marshy swamps, frightful and unfrequented places and wastes, all to avoid the danger of an encounter with their enemies.' In spite of their precautions, they had one skirmish with a party of Senecas before they reached the Andastes' villages.

Brulé could not get his 500 Andastes to set out quickly, and although the Onondaga village was only three days' march away, he and his companions arrived two days after Champlain and the Hurons had left. Not daring to attack alone, they went back to their villages near the head-waters of the west branch of the Susquehanna. 'Brulé was forced to remain and to pass the remainder of the autumn and all the winter, waiting for company and escort to return. And while awaiting this opportunity he employed himself in exploring the country.'

His chief exploration that winter was a realisation of Champlain's efforts of ten years before when he had searched the Atlantic coast for a shorter route to the interior than the St. Lawrence afforded. Brulé 'made his way along a river [the Susquehanna] which discharges on the coast of Florida . . . and he continued his route along the said river to the sea, past islands, and the coasts near them'. It is not necessary to believe that he methodically made his way down through modern Pennsylvania, Maryland and Virginia until Chesapeake Bay opened out into the veritable Atlantic. The waters of the Bay are salt enough to declare its character. But from his comments on the mildness of the winter and the difficulties of the route and from the reports he received of hostility to the Dutch (possibly the Indians confused Dutch and English), it is clear that the youngster who adopted Indian clothing during his first winter with the Indians had developed into the most enterprising European pioneer of his day. First up the Ottawa, first at Lake Huron, first at Lake Ontario, he was the first to find the Susquehanna route from the Great Lakes to the sea.

He had a trying trip back from the Andastes to Huronia. He and five or six Indians who accompanied him were attacked and dispersed by a large band of Senecas. Brulé, lost and almost starving, finally found and entered a Seneca village. His enemies were not awed by his self-confidence, but 'rushed upon him, and tore out his nails with their teeth, burned him with red-hot firebrands, and plucked out his beard hair by hair'. They were preparing to torture him slowly before putting him to death, when a violent thunder-storm occurred, apparently at his bidding. The awe-struck savages released him, healed his wounds and conducted him to the borders of the Huron country.

Before going down to Three Rivers with his Indian allies, Brulé also tried his fortunes in the north. He proceeded up the eastern shore of Georgian Bay to the mouth of the French river and then paddled along the north shore of Lake Huron for ten days. 'The said Brulé would have proceeded farther to explore the lie of these regions as I had given him instructions, had it not been for a rumour of war preparations. . . . And he promised me to pursue and carry it out in a short time, with God's aid, and to guide me thither in order to get more ample and detailed knowledge of it.' Champlain, past his fiftieth year and mightily harassed by his responsibilities to the King and to his commercial backers, could still think of pressing westward beyond the Freshwater Sea. Yet he was to make no more explorations. His future rôle was to await on the banks of the St. Lawrence the reports of irrepressible adventurers like Brulé, and their rivals in endurance, the missionary priests.

NARRATIVES

Champlain as above. G. Sagard-Théodat, *Le Grand Voyage du Pays des Hurons* (2 vols., Paris, 1865), and *Histoire du Canada, etc.* (4 vols., Paris, 1866).

CHAPTER XII

THE STRUGGLE FOR THE INLAND SEAS

(Map No. 2, page 258)

They approach like foxes, fight like lions, and fly away like birds.
A JESUIT DESCRIPTION OF THE IROQUOIS

THE years between 1618 and 1650 seemed to spell the doom of all that Champlain had achieved, for a series of conflicts in and about New France prevented the concentration and singleness of effort by which alone the frail new colony could prosper. The very business side of the trade was in confusion as one arrangement of promoters after another failed to make the millions it had anticipated. In Europe the merchant adventurers of the French coastal towns fell out with the struggling government at Paris. Many of them were Huguenots, privileged under Henry IV's Edict of Nantes, but suffering under Richelieu's outright war against their cities and aware that the King's chief advisers regarded their Protestantism as a serious handicap to the attainment of national unity. Some of them had friendly feelings towards, or business understandings with, the Protestant English. Even within orthodox Catholicism there was dissension, as the Jesuits began to dominate the Court and to secure for themselves the monopolistic concessions of spiritual authority which seemed to them to offer the best way of winning the new worlds for Christ. A pious lady of the Court

182

secured Acadia for them in 1607, and the unassuming Récollets, vowed to poverty, welcomed the popular, well-supported Order to Quebec in 1625, unaware that within seven years the Jesuits would have excluded them from the colony.

More serious was the threat of international war. Ever since the days of Queen Elizabeth and of the mercantile councils which Richard Hakluyt had advised, the Gulf of St. Lawrence had attracted the English. Its fish and whales and furs were tempting. Its walruses held the promise of a great industry. 'With the bellies of five of the saide fishes they made a hogsheade of Traine [oil]', wrote Thomas James of Bristol to Lord Burghley on 14 September 1591, 'which Traine is very sweet, which if it will make sope, the King of Spaine may burne some of his Olive trees.' In a period notable for its ivory-carving, walrus tusks were also eagerly sought. During the great outburst of company promotion at the beginning of the seventeenth century the English formed a company for Canada. More romantically, the Earl of Stirling, a Scottish nobleman, used some halting efforts to colonise Acadia as the excuse for filling King James' coffers and his own by selling baronetcies of Nova Scotia.

The threat of the English and Scots materialised in 1628 and 1629. Some London merchants equipped three semi-piratical brothers, David, Lewis and Thomas Kirke, to capture Quebec and the St. Lawrence trade. The Earl of Stirling allied himself with them, and in 1628 and 1629 Acadia and Canada fell into British hands, for France utterly failed to support her feeble colonies, and the mercantile groups which were supposed to maintain them had thought more of immediate dividends than of the insurance afforded by adequate

183

defence. The whole French adventure in North America might well have ended had not Charles I of England decided to avoid the criticism of his parliaments by dispensing with their aid in securing taxation. Badly in need of money, he remembered that the French king had never paid the full dowry promised him when he married Henrietta Maria. In effect, Charles I gave Acadia and Quebec back to France in 1632 in return for the dowry. France thus received another chance in North America, a chance of which she took advantage in an only moderately aggressive way during the next generation.

Meanwhile the Dutch on the Hudson and they and their English competitors on such near-by rivers as the Connecticut and the Delaware, were living up to their reputations as the most aggressive traders in Europe.[1] Both groups could provide Indian trade goods at prices considerably lower than the French. That meant that the Iroquois, who lived between them and the Great Lakes, were being stimulated to the most vigorous efforts to divert the flow of western furs from the Ottawa and the St. Lawrence to the shorter routes by the rivers which flowed south to the Atlantic. It meant almost continuous ruthless war by the Iroquois against Hurons, Algonquins, Montagnais and ultimately against the French. New France had to contend with the adverse economic influences of geography in the seventeenth century just as the Dominion of Canada contends with them to-day.

It was against such a background of precarious politics, unfavourable geography and economic conditions, and interrupted, unconcerted effort, that the

---

[1] The inconvenient digression to deal with exploration from the coastal colonies is deferred until Chapter XVI.

next stage of French exploration in North America had to take place. Champlain himself did not set out again during the remaining years of his life. His 'young men', the pioneer *coureurs de bois*, had already begun to establish the characteristics of their breed by flouting authority, going off on unauthorised expeditions, and using their technical skill to fill their own pockets. One group of them, including Brulé, went over to the English in 1629, much to Champlain's disgust. Yet by efforts only part of which seem to have been recorded, the *coureurs* continued to lay down the main lines of the further exploration of the interior.

Their chief rivals in exploration were the missionaries, notably the Jesuits. Champlain approved of them, assisted them to the utmost of his ability and bequeathed to them a share of his estate. Their resolute, militant order hit upon the idea of making Huronia its own exclusive care, where the Indians might be Christianised and at the same time protected from the worst effects of sudden contact with Europeans. This policy, which was later to have a considerable success in Paraguay in South America, had little success in Canada. In fact, one cannot read the annual reports of the Canadian missions before 1650 without being struck by the pathos of the contrast between hopes or noble self-sacrifices and actual achievements. Neither group understood the other, and after twenty years of work little lasting impression had been made upon the Hurons. Yet in spite of that failure on ground chosen by themselves, the Jesuits could not resist being drawn to other fields, either in the magnificent gesture of visiting the enemy Iroquois or in ventures towards other unknown lands.

Naturally the explorations between 1618 and 1650

were concerned with the Great Lakes sytem, notably
with the relation between Lake Ontario and Lake
Huron and with the character of the waters west of
Georgian Bay. In 1618 Champlain had laid upon Brulé
the task of exploring the north and west, and doubtless
Brulé himself saw the advantages of breaking away
from the middleman group around the Bay and dealing
directly with the unspoiled natives farther on. Both he
and Champlain were also interested in tracking to its
source the copper which made its way in small quantities,
even as far east as the Montagnais and the Indian
traders at Tadoussac. Tales of mines and outcrops in
the west had been circulating ever since Cartier's time.
We now know of the Indian mine-workings around
Lake Superior, but in 1618 north-western copper was
merely another element in the lure of the unknown
country.

It is not known when Brulé made his journey or
journeys to the west, for Father Sagard-Théodat seems
to have extracted the story in fragments when he was
travelling with him between Georgian Bay and the
St. Lawrence. But, sometime between 1618 and 1628
(probably in 1623), Brulé and a companion named
Grenolle made their way, almost certainly in the lee of
the Manitoulin Islands, along the north shore of Lake
Huron towards the Sault Ste. Marie which leads to
Lake Superior. They brought back an ingot of copper,
whether, as they claimed, from an active mine or from
trade with Indians near Lake Superior it is impossible
to say. Brulé's own recorded account might have been
that of an eye-witness or hearsay. 'Beyond the Sweetwater Sea there is another very large lake which empties
into it by a waterfall which has been named the Saut de
Gascon and is nearly two leagues wide. The said lake

and the Sweetwater Sea together extend for thirty days' journey by canoe according to the Indians' account and for four hundred leagues according to the interpeter [Brulé].' The immensity and awe-inspiring character of Lake Superior, however, would be likely to make a much deeper impression on Brulé than is reflected in the rather matter-of-fact reports of what he said. It is possible that he saw the lake and travelled on it and the possibility should be credited to him, but even Champlain's map of 1632, in which he assembled all the knowledge he could collect, does not clearly corroborate that view. Brulé's information about Lake Superior happened to be correct. Other men could go there, if he did not. The really important consideration for Champlain was that Lake Superior, like Lake Huron in his experience before it, was fresh water, not salt. Neither the Northern Sea nor the South Sea (Pacific) were yet to be reached from the water-ways known to the French.

It was Brulé's ultimate and spectacular fate (probably in 1632) to be killed and eaten by the Hurons, among whom he had worked for so many years and who had come to hate him very bitterly, but before he passed from the scene he seems to have conducted one other pioneer exploration. In the summer of 1626 the Récollet Father Daillon reached the Huron country and was urged by Father Le Caron to visit the unexplored lands of the Neutrals, north of Lake Erie. He took with him two *coureurs*, Brulé's companion Grenolle and Lavalée. As well as Father Le Caron's encouragement, he mentioned that Brulé had given a 'grand account' and 'told wonders' of the Neutrals. The known present fertility of the region corroborates the enthusiastic account which Daillon gave of it, but he did not get far before being seriously maltreated, so that one wonders whether Brulé was repeating hearsay or whether some previous rascality of his own was responsible for the hostile reception of 1626. The importance of the visit was that fourteen years later two Jesuits (Brébeuf and Chaumonot) tried again, and at last established the character of the water-way between Lake Ontario and Lake Huron by visiting Lake Erie. Moreover, their reference to the 'so celebrated' Niagara river makes it likely that Niagara Falls was at least known, if not visited, seven years before it was explicitly mentioned ('a waterfall of a dreadful height') by another Jesuit (Ragueneau) in 1647. Brulé's visits to the Andastes and the Neutrals had borne some late geographical fruit. In the report for 1642 the Jesuits were quick to comment on the advantages of the continuous St. Lawrence and Great Lakes route to Lake Huron and to see that its use by the French must be conditional upon the attitude of the Iroquois.

Meanwhile Jean Nicolet, another of Champlain's 'young men', had been making discoveries which were to be of the greatest significance. Whether he set out in 1634 or 1638, and the second date seems the more probable,[1] it is clear that he was carrying out the wishes of Champlain, who died in 1635. Moreover, his conduct bore witness that the tales of white men in the west which Champlain heard in 1616 were still alive in his mind and connected with visions of the outskirts of China or other civilised parts of Asia. When Nicolet travelled to the West he packed away in his canoe a ceremonial robe made 'of China damask, all strewn

[1] The controversy can be examined in C. W. Butterfield, *History of the Discovery of the North-West, by John Nicolet, in 1634* (Cincinnati, 1881): B. Sulte, 'Notes on Jean Nicolet', *Wisconsin Historical Collections*, viii, 189-94; and S. S. Hebberd, *History of Wisconsin under the Dominion of France* (Madison, 1890).

with flowers and birds of many colours'. No *coureur* would give canoe-room to such gaudy raiment or carry it across the portages merely to impress the Indians.

It now seems almost certain, from our knowledge of the place-names and Indian habitats associated with later explorations, that Nicolet followed Brulé's route along the North Channel of Lake Huron to Sault Ste. Marie, continued due west to the Straits of Mackinac leading into Lake Michigan, followed the north and west shores of that lake to Green Bay, entered the bay, discovered the Fox river, and made his way up it to a point from which the upper reaches of the Wisconsin river (a tributary of the Mississippi) were only three days' journey distant. The slight element of uncertainty is caused by the vagueness of his chroniclers (the Jesuits Le Jeune and Vimont) about the separate identities of Lakes Michigan and Superior, and by Le Jeune's loose language in describing, from Nicolet's description, the route from the Sault to the 'second sweet-water sea'. This uncertainty is increased by the fact that Champlain's mistake (or his editor's) in making Green Bay an inlet from the north shore of Lake Huron on his map of 1632 was imitated as late as 1643 by Jean Boisseau, who, like Champlain, did not shew Lake Michigan as it is at all. Both cartographers seemed to shew, by the rapids at the entry, the lake (Superior) that was known by hearsay or perhaps by Brulé's ex-plorations, but the relation to it of Green Bay was roughly that of Green Bay to Lake Michigan. Lake Michigan had therefore found a place on the map, but unfortunately it was the place of Lake Superior!

Nicolet, after having lived among the Algonquins and Nipissings and having distinguished himself by a successful peace mission to the Iroquois, had become an official agent and interpreter for Richelieu's Company of New France before his journey to the West. As such, 'he was delegated to make a journey to the nation called the People of the Sea and arrange peace between them and the Hurons'. As he neared their home, he sent out heralds of his coming, an arrival which he made as impressive as possible by wearing his damask robe and clutching a pistol in each hand. These people were the Winnebagoes at Green Bay, 'a sedentary people who are very numerous, whom some of the French call the Nation of Stinkers, because the Algonquin word *ouinipeg* signifies stinking water and they give this name to the water of the salt sea, so that these people are called *Ouinipigou* because they come from the shores of a sea of which we have no knowledge'. 'We have been told this year [1640] that an Algonquin, journeying beyond these peoples, encountered nations extremely populous . . . he conveyed the impression of the cities of Europe. I do not know what there is in this,' wrote Le Jeune.

A somewhat startling occurrence at Quebec that summer furnished him with what might be a clue. An Englishman from the settlement on the Kennebec river on the Atlantic coast was brought in on 24 June by a group of Abenakis who lived south and east of the lower St. Lawrence. He had come 'to search for some route through these countries to the Sea of the North'. The governor sent him away under guard to be escorted towards his home, but, failing to make his way, he returned and had to be sent to Tadoussac to be shipped to England. Father Le Jeune had some talks with him before he left. 'I have learned', the Englishman said, 'that one can sail to New Mexico by the seas which are to the north of it. For two years I have ranged the whole southern [Atlantic] coast from Virginia to the Kennebec, to discover whether I could not find some great river or great lake which would lead me to peoples who had knowledge of that sea which is to the north of Mexico. Not having found any, I have come to this country to enter the Saguenay in order to penetrate, if I could with the aid of the savages of the country, to the Northern Sea.'

'This poor man would have lost fifty lives, if he had so many,' observed Le Jeune, 'before reaching this Northern Sea by the route which he contemplated, and when he had found this sea, he would have discovered nothing new, nor found any passage to New Mexico.' 'But I will say, in passing, that it seems highly probable to us that one can go down through the second great lake of the Hurons [Michigan] . . . into this sea that he was seeking. Sieur Nicolet, who has penetrated farthest into these very distant countries, has assured me that, if he had voyaged three days farther on a great river [Fox] which issues from that lake, he would have found the sea.[1] Now it is my strong conjecture that this is the sea which corresponds to that north of New Mexico, and that from this sea there would be passage towards Japan and China.' A century before, Roberval's pilot, Jean Alfonse, had dreamed the same dream of the St. Lawrence system leading to the gold and silver of New Spain and the trade of Asia. Now a daring Englishman and a French missionary at Quebec played with the same idea, while far to the south in the Spanish colonies restless men still wondered whether their predecessors by land and sea had not missed those Straits of Anian

---

[1] It is now generally held that Nicolet, who made no effort to struggle up the Fox river to the Wisconsin portage, was told by the Indians of the 'great water' or Mississippi system, to which the Wisconsin is tributary.

which led back to the Atlantic. There could be no better illustration of one of the active forces which were ultimately to bring Spaniards, Frenchmen and Englishmen into rivalry and conflict in as yet unknown parts of the North American continent.

One great name in the early period of French exploration still remains to be mentioned, not so much for the extent of his discoveries as for the devotion to Christian missionary enterprise which he displayed. This was the Jesuit father, Isaac Jogues. In late September 1641 he and Father Charles Raymbault set out from Georgian Bay to accept the invitation of the Indians at Sault Ste. Marie to visit them. Although urged by the Indians to do so, they felt that they could not set up a mission at the Sault, but before they left they learned more about Lake Superior through their enquiries as to nations farther west. The Sioux, they heard, lived eighteen days' journey away. 'The first nine days are spent in crossing another great lake, which begins above the Sault, and for the remaining nine days one must ascend a river which crosses those lands.' Now, without doubt, Lakes Michigan and Superior had been differentiated.

Father Jogues' companion went off to winter with the Nipissings on his return, but the season was so late that the attempt had to be abandoned, not, however, before Father Raymbault had been made mortally ill. In June 1642 Jogues took him down to Quebec to die, and was on his return journey in August when he, three Frenchmen and some Hurons were captured by the Iroquois. The ensuing twelve months were as hideous and abominable as only Indian cruelty could make them, and when one reads Jogues' description of the first three weeks of alternate torture and travel, it seems impossible that the human frame could stand so much. He was beaten and bitten and burned, lost the use of several fingers and had one thumb cut off—'I picked it up and offered it to you, O my God'. Shattered in physique, he became an abused family slave and, in the summer of 1643, was taken on a fishing expedition down the Hudson, where he was seen by the Dutch. They rescued him, sent him to Manhattan and thence to England and France.

He returned to New France in 1644 to attempt the most daring exploit in Canadian missionary annals— the conversion of the Iroquois tribes who were then threatening to cut off the French on the St. Lawrence from the flow of western furs which was the life-blood of their colony. The Jesuits were attempting to carry out the idea formed by Brébeuf and Chaumonot in 1642 by making the upper St. Lawrence and Lake Ontario safe for the French. If that route to the west were safe, the Ottawa route would be still safer. The governor saw their argument and the choice fell upon Jogues as agent, both from his own wish and because his experience had taught him the route by the Richelieu river to Lake Champlain, thence to Lake George, by portage to the Hudson, down it to its junction with the Mohawk and up that river to the Iroquois villages. He made a successful beginning in his religious and diplomatic tasks in May and June of 1645 and returned to Quebec to report. Late in September he 'could not endure to be so long absent from his spouse of blood' and started back to the 'Mission of the Martyrs' for the winter. He had barely arrived when a call to the evening meal led him to a lodge where an Indian who was hiding behind the door cleft his head with a tomahawk, cut it off and set it up on the palings.

His martyrdom was but typical of the fate which was

now descending upon the Jesuit enterprise in Huronia and threatening to exterminate New France. In spite of the foundation in 1642 of a military and religious outpost at Montreal which contributed some of the most heroic pages to the history of French effort in Canada, the Iroquois began in 1643 an almost uninterrupted twenty years' war against the French and their Indian allies. They closed the Ottawa for years at a time. They crossed to the northern banks of the St. Lawrence, of Lake Ontario and of Lake Erie, and began what was, for Indian warfare, a systematic extermination of the tribes within the triangle formed by the Ottawa and the Great Lakes. Terror grew in a *crescendo* among the Hurons, and in 1648 and 1649 the long-awaited final storm broke. The Iroquois stormed their villages, tortured and killed them and their Jesuit pastors and pursued the survivors even out to the islands of Georgian Bay. In 1650 a tiny remnant of about 300 sought refuge at Quebec.

From Michigan to Tadoussac the Iroquois were triumphant. Their Indian enemies and competitors were scattered westward as far as Lake Superior, northward to the rivers leading to James Bay and eastward to the shelter of French stockades. At ever shorter intervals from 1643 to 1663, the boldest Iroquois took delight in ambushing and scalping French colonists or chasing them from their fields to their forts. Still keener to the Indian mind was the exquisite pleasure of approaching by canoe or on land near enough to the French fortifications for chanted taunts and pointed scorn to reach the ears of the frightened inmates.

If French enterprise seemed to be almost at an end in 1650, yet it had contributed quite extensive knowledge of a part of North America very different from that explored by Spain. There had been no gold and no cities. The sea, that roadway for the Spaniards, had been left behind at Tadoussac, and the forests and waterways of *terra firma* in New France were effective barriers to the use of the horse. To learn what they had learned, Frenchmen had had to convert themselves from fishermen to fur traders and from fur traders to canoe-men and *coureurs de bois*. In spite of being opposed by the most effective Indian polity in North America, and that armed and equipped by the Dutch, the French had learned of the main character of the St. Lawrence and Great Lakes system; they knew the Ottawa, the Trent valley and the Humber river-Lake Simcoe short-cuts to Georgian Bay; and they knew the Hudson river and Susquehanna river routes south to the Atlantic. It was true that they were uncertain about the extremities of Lakes Michigan and Superior, that they did not know the distances to James Bay, the Pacific and the Gulf of Mexico, but they had heard of a sea or great water just beyond Green Bay which they hoped would lead to the richer lands which Spain was exploiting and to the Asia which was now yielding its coveted commodities to mariners who sailed the long ways around the southern Capes.

Actually New France was later revived, but before considering that revival and the remarkable enterprises which accompanied and followed it, we must turn back to discover what other Europeans, neither Spanish nor French, had been contributing to the revelation of North America. Three Protestant nations, the English, the Dutch and the Danes, had delivered a series of assaults from the arctic seas, which were to be woven into the continental design by a fusion with the labours of the French.

NARRATIVES

Champlain and Sagard-Théodat as above. The chronicles of French Jesuit enterprise have been collected with English translation and supplementary notes and documents by R. G. Thwaites, *The Jesuit Relations* (73 vols., Cleveland, 1894–1907). The arrangement is practically chronological and material used in this chapter is drawn chiefly from vols. xviii, xxi, xxiii, xxxi and xxxiii.

CHAPTER XIII

THE NORTHERN ENTRY

(*Map No. 2, page 258*)

. . . and a sea to the westwards.

HUDSON'S LAST ENTRY IN HIS JOURNAL

IT would almost seem that the mists and floating ice of Hudson Strait and Hudson Bay have combined to shroud from attention the importance of the enterprises which found the northern entry into North America. Hudson Bay bites into the mainland almost as greedily as does the Gulf of Mexico, and yet the names of the southern explorers are household words while the men of the north are almost forgotten. It is true that the northern entry was followed by only one successful colonisation, that of Lord Selkirk at Red river in Manitoba, and that it is associated in memory with quixotic, but 'impractical' arctic exploration and search for the North-West Passage, but it also led ultimately to extraordinarily widespread exploration in mainland North America and upset the economic activities, white and native, of more than half the continent. Moreover, it is a mistake to regard exploration of the arctic archipelago as having been wholly unjustified. Four hundred years of costly investigation have, to a considerable degree, separated land from water and ice from both, so that a reasonably accurate map is now a possibility. But to the pioneer explorers, what is now revealed to be an archi-

197

pelago was North America (or Asia) just as much as was the St. Lawrence valley or Mexico and Central America. Ice-locked straits, snow-covered mainland or islands and bays rendered menacing by icebergs made the task most difficult, but until it was done, one portion of the American barrier to Asia would continue to exist as a challenge to the explorer, with a possible mighty reward to the navigator who should discover a passage-way through it to the Pacific. For a century and a quarter (1497–1632) it was 'practical', as is evidenced by the subscriptions of hard-headed merchants, to support costly enterprises which would bring back certain information about arctic America.

The adventure of Hudson Bay began in the search for a North-West Passage. In the latter half of the sixteenth century Portugal monopolised the Spice Islands and riches of the East, and Spain was exploiting her rich new empire in the West. Meanwhile the hungry Dutch and French and English were growing ill-content with the crumbs that fell or that could be piratically snatched from the rich men's tables. The Turk occupied the Levant, Portugal monopolised the route by the Cape, and Spain claimed the Straits of Magellan and the Isthmus of Panamá. Europe and Africa were one barrier, and English, Portuguese, French, Spanish and Dutch expeditions in the course of the century gradually revealed that the Americas were another. What more natural than that men turned their thoughts to passing either or both by the north, and thereby winning for themselves and their nations the monopoly of what must be for Europeans a shorter route to the Spice Islands?

It was a pity that they could not have saved themselves toil and disaster by studying the exploits of the medieval Norsemen who had already ranged the edges of the arctic ice from Novaya Zemlya to Baffin Bay and on to the American mainland hunting the seal, walrus and whale. The only relics of their navigations which seem to have been used were the guide from Europe to Greenland, known as the instructions of Boty or Bartsen, and Alfred the Great's record of the voyage of Ohthere to the North Cape and White Sea about 870. The men of the sixteenth century, therefore, started all over again to learn painfully that even for men as willing as they to pit their wits and frail vessels against storms and crushing ice, there was no way by the north to the East. They did not fail for lack of confidence or trying. In fact they marvellously lived up to the implications of Robert Thorne's remark in his memorial of 1527 to Edward Lee: 'There is no land unhabitable, nor sea unnavigable. . . . If I had faculty to my will, it should be the first thing that I would understand, even to attempt, if our seas northward be navigable to the Pole, or no. '

John Cabot in his journeys of 1497 and 1498 may possibly have noticed the entries to Hudson and Davis Straits. The same may be said of the Portuguese brothers Corte-Real in 1500–1502. As has been seen,[1] there is a plausible case for John Cabot's son, Sebastian, having sailed through Hudson Strait to Hudson Bay in 1509. Several English writers saw maps and discourses of Sebastian (now lost) which apparently most confidently indicated a North-West Passage to the Pacific. Some Portuguese maps of the early sixteenth century also seem to indicate knowledge of the Strait and Bay. Yet, on the whole, it was Sir Humphrey Gilbert who popularised the doctrine of the North-West Passage for Europe. His interest began when he was

[1] See pp. 112-113.

a shareholder of the English Muscovy Company. Then, perhaps influenced by the seafaring Huguenots for whom he fought in France, about 1566 he turned his attention to the West. In an interval of his adventurous military and voyaging career, he studied everything geographical he could lay his hands on and wove the whole (from Plato to Jacques Cartier and Friar Marcos) into his *Discourse . . . to prove a passage by the north-west to Cathaia, and the East Indies*. 'Atlantis now called America, was ever knowen to be an island', and 'insomuch as the Sea runneth by nature circularly from the East to the West, following the diurnal motion of Primum Mobile', and as the Straits of Magellan are too narrow to permit the flow, therefore the current strikes up the shores of America to find its way to the West by a northern passage. 'It were the onely way for our princes to possess the wealth of all the East parts (as they terme them) of the world, which is infinite.' 'This discovery hath bene reserved for some noble prince or worthie man, thereby to make himselfe rich, and the world happie.' One of his most seductive arguments and one which reveals rather vividly how accounts of European explorations in America could be embroidered, was his statement that 'Coronado passing from Mexico, through the country Quivira, to Siera Nevada, found there a great sea, where were certain ships . . . who signified by signes, that they were thirty days comming thither: which likewise proveth America by experience to be disjoyned from Cataia'. It was the old Spanish dream of a strait from Pacific to Atlantic, it was the lively hope of Jean Alfonse at Lachine, but in voicing it Gilbert erred no more than Henry Briggs, Savilian professor of astronomy at Oxford, who wrote as late as 1622 that 'the straits of Anian, where are seated the large Kingdoms of Cebola and Quivira, have great and populous cities of civil people; whose houses are said to bee five stories high, and to have within them pillars of Turquesses'. Friar Marcos' tales thus lived for eighty years because men wanted so much to believe them true.[1]

Gilbert's enthusiasm happened to be matched by that of Michael Lok, a London merchant prince, who had been studying the subject of the Passage for years and who had accumulated 'a ream of notes'. Their faith infected the Queen and her advisers, who in 1575 forced the Muscovy Company to break its monopoly so as to allow Lok's sea-captain, Martin Frobisher, to go forth and seek the Passage.

In three voyages (1576, 1577, 1578), which were marked by a reckless refusal to be cowed by the hazards of arctic exploration, Frobisher began the penetration of the northern channels. It is true that he missed Hudson Strait and that the heavy black ore which he mined on the shores of Frobisher Bay (Baffin Island) turned out to be iron pyrites instead of gold, but he shewed that men could sail those seas in craft of as little as twenty tons, and he left behind him the alluring news of currents from the north and west. The financial needs of Michael Lok had kept him at mining and held him from exploring towards the west, but by 1578 a considerable group of men under his leadership had dared the icebergs of the seas between Greenland and Labrador and their tales were known in England. The grand processions of 'ice-islands' which came down from Baffin Bay and from the west seemed like adver-

---

[1] A map embodying Briggs' ideas accompanied the 1625 edition of *Purchas, His Pilgrimes*, and is reproduced in H. R. Wagner, *Spanish Voyages to the Northwest Coast* (San Francisco, 1929).

tisements of the sea-ways past North America. To-day, however, we read imperative warnings in the stories of ships smashed like egg-shells, of men standing for days at a time along the low bulwarks fending off bergs with pikes, of others standing on the floes and using them as fenders against still more, and of 'knees and timbers within board both bowed and broken' while timber, ropes and bedding, hung over the sides, failed to protect them.

Frobisher's three expeditions formed the prelude to a long series of attempts on the North-West Passage. Spain and Portugal took no share in these adventures because they were busy exploiting their own monopolies and because their own earlier explorations had convinced them that voyages to the north were costly and unprofitable. As we have seen in the case of Cartier and Roberval in 1541, they finally decided not to be disquieted by their rival's efforts. The northern effort was carried out almost entirely by Englishmen, sometimes for English backers, but also for Holland and Denmark. Anglo-Dutch relations were close between 1575 and 1625, and Christian IV, the beloved if politically inept renaissance King of Denmark, was brother-in-law to James I of England.

Yet the northern enterprises yielded paltry dividends. Sometimes the adventurers gambled on strange, heavy ores from which they hoped to smelt gold or silver. Often they traded trinkets with the Eskimos and Indians for furs. They themselves hunted when they could, especially the walrus for his ivory and oil. And always on those desolate beaches they searched in the flotsam for the sea-unicorn's twisted ivory horn. More credulous land-folk would still believe (and pay for the belief) that it came from the veritable unicorn and had great medicinal and magic qualities, but even the knowing who had seen the narwhal would pay high prices. Niels Slange, the Danish historian, tells of a skull which still held a six-foot horn and which was worth between 30,000 and 40,000 dollars. Moreover, the great arctic whale-fisheries accompanied these explorations. Biscayans (Europe's earliest whalemen) were sent out from Hull and Amsterdam and Copenhagen because they could take Leviathan with harpoons and lances, and reduce him to whalebone and train-oil for a Europe which was corseted, where soap was becoming fashionable, and where petroleum and its wax candles were as yet unknown.

The real quest, however, was for the Passage. After Frobisher, John Davis made three voyages (1585–87) which added greatly to the revelation of the unknown patterns of land, ice and water. He explored what are now Davis Strait and Baffin Bay between Greenland and the Arctic Archipelago, but he found no passage westward. Before the threat of the Spanish Armada and his own failure caused his backers to give him up, he noted the entrance to Hudson Strait and named it the 'Furious Overfall'. As John Janes, his recorder, reported it, they 'passed by a very great gulf, the water whirling and roring, as it were the meeting of tides'. That clash of currents won the attention of the newly formed English East India Company. They fitted up 'the good and luckie ship called the *Discovery*' and sent her out in 1602 under Captain George Waymouth to sail through the strait. He did sail into it for about 100 leagues, but his men grew frightened and turned the ship back one day while he was in his cabin. They were led by 'Master John Cartwright, our preacher', who had been to Persia and was now travelling with a brand-new clerical gown to impress the natives of Cathay. It seemed incredible that icebergs and polar bears could mark the way to the Spice Islands. Yet even Waymouth's failure served a purpose. 'These two, *Davis* and he, did (I conceive) light *Hudson* into his *Straights*', wrote Luke Foxe in 1635 as he compiled the arctic record from King Arthur to Thomas James.

Before Hudson made his mark, however, another group of English mariners added their explorations to the charts. Christian IV of Denmark determined to seek out the Danish colonists of Greenland who had been lost to knowledge in the fifteenth century. The English knew the way, and it was James Hall of Hull whom he retained as chief pilot in three voyages (1605–1607) which were intended to reunite the lost colonies under his crown. We know little of Hall before this, but there are reasons for believing that he had either served with Davis or been made acquainted with his discoveries. The colonists were never found, nor were their lands replanted. Much time and effort were wasted in mining supposed silver ore, and there was some trading with the Skraellings who had supplanted the medieval Danes. Hall was killed in 1612 when he went back on a commercial or mining voyage in his own interest and that of some English adventurers, but his voyages have their own importance. For one thing Hall thoroughly explored the west coast of Greenland and much of the ice-filled waters of Baffin Bay. He also trained other English navigators. Among them, Josias Hubert or Hubbart of Hull seems to have sailed with him in 1607 and to have begun to frame his theories of the Passage. Hubbart's friend William Baffin sailed with Hall in 1612, and the chief mate on that expedition was the William Gordon who was to serve the Danes again in northern waters in 1619.

All in all, however, the geographers have been right in their ultimate naming of the northern strait and bay which lead into the heart of the continent. Whatever the achievements of Portuguese, Spanish and English pioneer seamen, the world learned of those promising waters for certain when Henry Hudson proclaimed them with his tragic death in 1611.

Henry Hudson made an abiding place for himself in history by the achievements of the last four years of his life. He surmounted failings which were almost sufficient to disqualify him as a pioneer navigator, failings which finally brought him to his death. It is true that he was driven by a great curiosity and by a passion to find a northern passage to the East, which carried him on four voyages, to the arctic seas north of Europe, to the middle Atlantic coast of North America, and finally to his death in Hudson Bay. Yet he was vacillating, at times easily discouraged, and occasionally bemused into complete inability to make a decision. Moreover, he never seems to have known either how to fan his sailors' emotions into a flame of loyalty or to hold them in awe by the natural authority of professional competence and firmness of purpose. He was a good navigator and, in an age feverish to explore by sea, he made exploration his profession. He owed his employments by English and Dutch capitalists to the excitement in Europe over the explorations along the north coast of Russia, which seemed to spell out the promise to Holland or England of a short route to Cathay.

His first recorded expedition was in 1607 when, with a ship's company of ten men and a boy, he set out on behalf of the English Muscovy Company to sail, if possible, across the Pole, but if not, easterly to reach China and the 'warm sea'. No one then knew for certain what manner of place the Pole was, and learned geographers like Peter Plancius and Samuel Purchas held out the hope that warm weather prevailed there in the summer, and demonstrated, as do aerial navigators to-day, how short a way it must provide to the East. Thus encouraged, Hudson and his meagre company skirted eastern Greenland north until they reached the ice barrier and then turned east to Spitzbergen. The full record of their movements in the icy seas thereafter has never been convincingly established. The imaginative charts of the day and the confusion of storms, fogs, icebergs and snowy mountains left Hudson and his recorder, John Pleyce, in a maze in which Greenland and Davis Strait and Spitzbergen assumed geographical relations far out of line with the actual. They were back in London by mid-September without having found a North-East Passage.

The voyage satisfied the Muscovy Company that Greenland and the ice barred the way to Asia by the north-west. They sent Hudson out again in April of 1608 to try to find a good way along the northern coast of Russia to the Kara Sea and so to the East. This voyage of four months proved to be an inglorious one and contained in it the seeds of Hudson's final failure. They made good progress to Novaya Zemlya, sighting a 'mermaid' as well as the usual bears, walrus, whales and sea-birds on the way, spent ten laborious days trying to find a way through the long barrier island, and when they failed, turned west for home instead of trying to pass it by north or south. Perhaps owing to the presence as mate of Robert Juet, later to play so sinister a part in Hudson's career, there was something like a mutiny on board in early August, and Hudson weakly gave his men a certificate that he was returning of his own initiative and under no compulsion from them.

In spite of Hudson's two failures, tall tales of his arctic wanderings went the rounds of western European ports and company offices, and when the Muscovy Company felt him to be an expensive luxury, the Dutch East India Company called him to Amsterdam. During the winter of 1608–9 he divided his time there between the preliminaries to entering the Dutch or French service and eager talks with the geographers, Peter Plancius and Jodocus Hondius, about the northern passages. It would not do for one whose expertness in the ways towards the North-East Passage was his recommendation for employment to confess his disillusion with that route, and when the Dutch on 8 January 1609 signed a contract for his services, it was his assigned task to pass Novaya Zemlya for the East. Nevertheless, in his journal of the second voyage and in his talks with Plancius and Hondius, he had betrayed his interest in the alternative West. Captain John Smith of Virginia wrote to him to say that he thought that there must be a passage there and Plancius lent him Waymouth's journals. It seems clear that before he left Holland he was inclined to disobey instructions and ignore his contract by trying his fortunes in the West.

His first trial there had little enough to do with the true North-West Passage. In its place he discovered the river which now bears his name and which provided the second great entry to North America.[1] It is well to remember, also, that Robert Juet was one of the *Half Moon's* company, that mutiny twice raised its head, and that Hudson twice bowed to it. But the third voyage

[1] See Chapter XVI.

also made the English government determine to put a stop to Holland's profit from the prowess of an English navigator. His ship and the Dutch members of his crew went back to Amsterdam in the summer of 1610, but Hudson stayed in England, where a new merchant syndicate retained his services expressly 'to try if, through any of these inlets which Davis saw, but durst not enter, any passage might be found to the other ocean called the South Sea'. Its patron was Prince Henry, the promising heir to the throne whose premature death so warped the course of English history.

When Hudson sailed from the Thames in Waymouth's tough craft, the *Discovery*, on 17 April 1610, he had a fair idea of where he was going and his backers were convinced that there was a northern way through to the West. He made his North American landfall after ten suspiciously long weeks at precisely the right point and entered Hudson Strait on 25 June. His crew had been giving him trouble, notably his incubus Robert Juet, the mate, who jested 'at our master's hope to see Bantam [Java] by Candlemasse', and Henry Greene, a thorough young wastrel from Kent, whom Hudson had taken under his protection. The end of June was rather early in the year to pass through the Strait because of the prevailing early summer fog, and the flotillas of ice and bergs which came growling down from the west and north forced them to alter their course again and again. The southward trend of Ungava Bay was tempting, too, and they sailed to and fro between its southern shore and Baffin Island. The crew were frightened by the scoured, bleak rock forelands as they loomed up suddenly from the fog. The sense of unknown terrors kept them on edge, and when they openly refused to go farther, Hudson saw fit to hold a consultation with them about his knowledge and his plans before he sailed westwards through the Strait.

It must have been an eerie as well as a triumphant passage for Hudson. Those shores came down in great bare folds to the sea. There is a majesty and imperturbability about the slow curves of a Laurentian sky-line and an obduracy about its cliffs and precipices. Ice and snow instead of trees cling to the northern slopes, and the brief, opulent vegetation of July and August merely carpets some patches of the ground. As they tacked to and fro across the channel, the land sometimes rose through fogs and mists almost imperceptibly from the tidal shores and sometimes climbed in bleak cliffs which were alive with screaming sea-birds on and near their nests. Sounding their way cautiously, they seldom dared the rocks near the shore, but pushed on against the current and ice which flowed from the West and seemed to promise proximity to the Pacific.

Their reward was the discovery of an inland sea whose western waters might, for all they knew, stretch unbroken to Cathay. Hudson's surviving journal breaks off on 3 August 1610 with the words: 'Then I observed and found the ship at noone in 61 degrees, 20 minutes, and a sea to the westwards'. The gateway to Hudson Bay from the east is a channel about five miles wide between two headlands, Cape Wolstenholme at the north-west tip of Ungava and Cape Digges on what is now called Inner Digges Island. Ahead to the south-west and south lay the invitation of open water. Pausing only for a brief and dangerous landing on Digges Island, where the sailors found some Eskimo larders of sea-fowl, Hudson turned confidently south past the islands along the east shore of the Bay, sailing swiftly on until gradually there closed in before him the marshy, desolate deltas of the south shore of James Bay. The shock and bitterness of that landfall must have been profound. Four years of dangerous roving, of pressing diffident seamen on to novel exploits, a new sea discovered and at its southern end a continent! No one knows what went on in Hudson's mind and heart. His men grew puzzled as week after week he tacked east and west, north and south, between the low, forbidding shores of James Bay. Finally they could stand it no longer and spoke out their criticism. Hudson's answer was the public trial of the mate, Robert Juet, and his deposition in favour of the untested Robert Bylot. Then he resumed his futile wanderings in the Bay until frost closed in on him and he beached the old *Discovery* near the south-eastern limit of the waters.

They passed a dreadful winter racked by cold and scurvy. They killed some ptarmigan and, as spring preceded the general break-up of the ice, shot a few migratory water-fowl and caught some fish. Conifer buds dispelled their scurvy, but they were usually wet and always cold and hungry. Sheer want drove them to eat frogs and lichens. Their hopes rose when a lone Indian came to trade, but Hudson's greed frightened him so that he did not return, and when the commander went off in a boat to find encampments the Indians fled from him. There was nothing for it but to wait until ice conditions permitted them to sail. They left their prison on 12 June 1611. Now Bylot was estranged from Hudson, and the ignorant quartermaster, John King, took his place as mate.

It is hard, indeed, to understand why, after Hudson had spent two months in the late autumn of 1610 in vague wanderings about James Bay, he wanted to continue his exploration next spring. His journal for that period was destroyed and Prickett, who composed the only narrative, knew nothing of his motives. It seems likely, however, that, after the failure of 1610, a winter's soliloquies had built up in him a determination to sail west in the untried sea of Hudson Bay in the spring, with the desperate hope of living off the country for a short time at least. They had already looted Eskimo store-houses in the north, and they knew that there were Indians on the shores of the Bay. Unfortunately, Hudson's relations with his men were clouded with misunderstandings and favouritism. In that tiny ship and amidst men in literal terror of starvation he (according to Prickett's naturally biased account) took the colossal risk of hiding some reserves of food and of issuing the remainder as rations. He had an opening from his cabin to the hold, and his actions aroused suspicions that he and his favourites were better off than the rest of the crew. The smouldering fears and hates broke into open mutiny, apparently on 22 or 23 June, just after the *Discovery* had reached open water in James Bay.

The leaders of revolt were Henry Greene, who 'would rather be hanged at home than starved abroad' and who provided the brains and remorseless determination; Robert Juet, whose malign animus was mixed with fear of the ignorance of King; and William Wilson, the boatswain, who contributed his brawn. They concealed their ulterior design by affecting that they meant only to imprison Hudson, his son, John King, and two sick and two hale sailors in the shallop under tow until they had searched the ship for food. Under cover of the inevitable confusion, Greene seems to have wanted to get rid of as many hungry mouths as he could. Once the seven were in the small boat, it was realised that Greene planned to cut them adrift. Out of that horror there emerged one hero. A carpenter, Philip Staffe (or possibly John King), withered the mutineers with his simple commentary on their design. They wanted him and his tools and his services. He had a loyalty to satisfy and he would not stay in the ship unless they forced him. Moreover, 'there was not one in all the ship that could tell how to carry her home'. He knew upon which side God stood and he went down with tools, musket, cooking-pot and meal to join it rather than abide with God-forsaken mutineers. The tow was cut as the *Discovery* sailed away from the ice-field near which it had lain, and while it steered for the north and home, Hudson and his company rocked in the little shallop on the great inhospitable bay.

Philip Staffe spoke prophetically. Of the mutineers, Henry Greene was first wounded, and then killed by an Eskimo arrow while attempting to collect food near Cape Digges, William Wilson had his belly slit in the same fight and died 'cursing and swearing in a most fearful manner', and Robert Juet, after a vain if shrewd attempt to get the nine survivors to sail for succour from the fishermen at Newfoundland, died 'for meere want' on the way to Ireland. As worthy Samuel Purchas said, 'Everywhere can Divine Justice find executioners'. It was the pietistic, Scripture-quoting Abacuk Prickett, custodian (and presumably censor) of Hudson's papers, who was rescued with seven companions by a fishing-boat off Ireland. He had salved his conscience by evasions during the mutiny. Luke Foxe's comment on him was pungent, as he recorded the Hudson voyage —'Well, *Prickett*, I am in great doubt of thy fidelity to Master *Hudson*'. His life had been spared for his learning's usefulness in saving the mutineers from justice. His is our only sustained account of what happened after August 1610, and some instinct bade him preserve Hudson's chart and Hudson's journal up to the discovery of the Bay.

Justice demanded the hanging of the survivors, but mercantile cupidity conquered justice. They were examined and, when seven years later four of them were haled to court for the murder of Hudson, they were acquitted. The truth was that these starved mutineers were too valuable to hang, as parasites are sometimes valuable, because they had seen the shores and waters found by Hudson and recorded on his chart. They had killed their captain, but they alone knew the lands he had discovered. London and the Court were greatly excited over the apparent certainty that an English navigator had won for England proprietorship of the North-West Passage. Bylot and Prickett were particularly esteemed, at least by the merchants, and by May they were not only members of the company chartered to exploit the discovery, but present in Thomas Button's expedition which was off for the Indies by 'Hudson, his bay', China and Japan.

For another twenty years men tried to develop Hudson's discovery into what they felt must be its logical conclusion. The curious will find most of the story in the annals prepared by that literary mariner, Luke 'North West' Foxe. Foxe was not only a great student, but he was so careful in his preparations as a commander that he could boast after his own courageous journey to the Bay in 1631: 'I came into the Downes, with all my men recovered and sound, not having lost one man nor boy, nor any manner of tackling'. Moreover he was a confirmed euphuist, and it must be admitted that even persistent euphuism is an entertaining contrast to most sea-captains' narratives. Hear him at his most ambitious. 'This evening sun kist Thetis in our sight . . . and at the same instant the rainbowe was in apperance, I thinke to canopy them abed.' 'This morning Aurora blusht, as though she had usher'd her master from some unchaste lodging, and the ayre so silent, as though all those handmaides had promised secresy.'

Button and the 160 merchant adventurers who accompanied him in 1612 went out sure that they had only to sail to Asia. Prince Henry's letter of instruction on behalf of 'The Company of Merchants of London Discoverers of the North-West Passage' commanded Button to choose a spot 'on the back of America, or some island in the South Sea, for a haven or stacion for our Shippes and Marchaundizes'. King James gave him a Letter of Credence to the Emperor of Japan or other Oriental potentate. Button sailed due west from the Strait, was confronted by the west shore of the Bay and sailed south to Port Nelson, where he lost the *Resolution* and wintered, with the old *Discovery* to take him north next spring to seek a westward passage. Not finding one, he went home to London, where his backers had interpreted his long absence to mean that he had reached Asia.

Captain Gibbons, a relative of Button and member of the 1612 expedition, tried again in the *Discovery* in 1614, but never got inside the Bay. Robert Bylot and William Baffin took out the same veteran vessel in 1615 and in 1616. On the strength of their first voyage they decided that there was no tide from the west at Digges Island and on their second, when they pushed up western Greenland to discover Baffin Bay, they concluded like Davis before them that that part of the north was too ice-bound to provide a way. Captain William Hawkridge, another veteran of 1612, made another voyage, probably in 1617, of which we know nothing save its failure.

In 1619 Denmark provided another group of actors for the northern stage under the leadership of a distinguished navigator and trader, Jens Munck, who knew the seas from Novaya Zemlya to Brazil, who had distinguished himself in naval warfare, and who had recently founded a whaling company in the arctic seas. In 1618 he refused command of the first Indian voyage of the Danish East Indian Company, for out of his northern whaling and his study of Hall's achievements he had reached the determination to try his hand in 1619 at the North-West Passage, or failing that, to set up a fur-trading post in Hudson Bay. Like Hall, he took with him English navigators, William Gordon and John Watson. His expedition of sixty-five men in two ships was admirably equipped, even a surgeon being taken along with complete medical kit. Unfortunately, the English mates proved to be inefficient and kept him sailing about Ungava Bay from 9 July to 14 August, thinking they were already in Hudson Bay. With his men weary and ill, he finally sailed west to reach the mouth of the Churchill on 7 September, only to be overtaken by wintry weather and snow a week later. When boat trips north and south revealed no better harbour, they went into winter quarters.

Matters went reasonably well until Christmas in spite of cold which surprised the explorer who had known the arctic coast of Russia. The men were cheerful, there was some hunting and they had plentiful food and drink. For the offertory at the Christmas service, 'there was not much money among the men, but they gave what they had; some of them gave white fox-skins, so that the priest got enough wherewith to line a coat'. Then the cold struck and scurvy began to do its dreadful work on men who had eaten and drunk too much and who had had neither enough fresh food nor exercise. The surgeon was helpless. His glass bottles burst on 27 November. Munck suggested tin, but a tin vessel burst on 28 January. Men began to die almost daily, and on 8 June Munck struggled ashore from the boat which had become a charnel-house. He thought himself the only survivor, but he found two others on shore. The three ate everything green which they could find and caught a few fish. When the fresh food had cured them, they painfully warped the smaller of their vessels (the *Lamprey*) out from its moorings, sailed on 18 July, and succeeded in reaching home by September.

That tragedy and what had gone before might have been expected to ring the curtain down for a long time on European questings in Hudson Bay, but the enthusiasm of Luke Foxe took him out in 1631, for he had 'beene itching after it ever since 1606'. He had read all the records he could reach, had consulted the men who had been out, and he thought three possibilities were worth investigating. Two of them he derived from that Josias Hubert who served with Hall in 1607, was friend to Baffin, and acted as adviser to Button in 1612. Hubert urged going north through the passage west of Southampton Island, later named 'Sir Thomas Roe's Welcome' by Foxe, and he also thought it worth while to try the mouths of the Churchill and Nelson rivers. The Churchill bay was called 'Hubbart's Hope', 'the very place', wrote Foxe, 'where the Passage should be'.

In addition, the coast from the Nelson to James Bay was still unknown.

Foxe and his rather inept competitor from Bristol, Captain Thomas James, explored those last possibilities in 1631 and 1632. They met in August 1631, not far from Cape Henrietta Maria, and Foxe dined on James' ship. He poked fun at his host for flying his flag in such remote parts, to which James replied that he could not strike his flag when he was carrying a letter from Charles I to the Emperor of Japan. 'Keepe it up, then,' the disillusioned Foxe reported himself to have said, 'but you are out of the way to Japon, for this is not it.' Foxe went home in 1631 after what is still one of the northernmost penetrations of Fox Channel and Fox Basin. James wintered miserably on Charlton Island in James Bay, where he found relics which may have been of the marooned Hudson. Foxe and James covered about the same territory from the northern ice-barrier of the west coast down to the bottom of the Bay. Between them they temporarily ended the hopes of a North-West Passage. Coleridge was later to use James' sorrowful narrative as the raw material for his *Rime of an Ancient Mariner*. Occasional whalers may subsequently have followed where the explorers had led the way into the Bay, but as far as recorded history goes, it was to remain lonely and empty for another twenty-five years until a new twist in European enterprise awoke it again to life and stern conflict.

NARRATIVES

The Hakluyt Society of London has published most of the accounts of these explorations. The voyages of Frobisher, edited by R. Collinson, are in vol. 38 (1867); those of Davis, edited by

A. H. Markham, in vol. 59 (1880); those of Hudson, edited by G. M. Asher, in vol. 27 (1860); those of Button, Gibbons, Hawkridge, Foxe and James, edited by M. Christy, in vols. 88 and 89 (1894); those of Bylot and Baffin, edited by C. R. Markham, in vol. 63 (1881); and those of Hall and Munck, edited by C. C. A. Gosch and M. Christy, in vols. 96 and 97 (1896, 1897). Waymouth's narrative can be found in S. Purchas, *Hakluytus posthumus or Purchas His Pilgrimes*, pt. iii, lib. iiii, or in Henry Stevens, *The Dawn of British Trade, etc.* (London, 1886).

CHAPTER XIV

A USE FOR THE NORTHERN ENTRY

(Map No. 2, page 258)

We weare Cesars, being nobody to contradict us.
RADISSON'S NARRATIVE

Friend, once 'twas Fame that led thee forth
To brave the Tropic Heat, the Frozen North,
Late it was Gold, then Beauty was the Spur;
But now our Gallants venture but for Furs.

RESTORATION QUATRAIN, AUTHOR UNKNOWN

THE desertion of Hudson Bay by Europeans from 1635 to 1668, after so many expeditions to it and even after many Europeans had wintered there, provides an almost perfect analogy to the treatment of the St. Lawrence river between 1542 and 1603. In the case of the St. Lawrence, when the beliefs in a passage and in northern kingdoms had died away, it required sixty years for the fur trade to develop from being a by-product of the fisheries to become in itself a sufficient attraction to draw Europeans into the continent. In the case of Hudson Bay, the difficulties of navigating the Strait and the rigours of the winters were serious deterrents, but with the St. Lawrence as an example, it is surprising to find that no one save Munck thought of the Bay fur trade as being an end in itself. Denmark's share in the Thirty Years' War prevented him from returning to set

219

up a trading-post as he had planned, and without him the Bay trade had to wait until a French *coureur de bois* was inspired to see its extraordinary advantages.

That revelation was a round-about affair and was stimulated by a variety of coincident influences, but it is probably correct enough to see its origins in the dispersion by the Iroquois of the Indian tribes with whom the French had traded. The warriors from the south of Lake Ontario found vent for a time in Champlain's 'island', as formed by the Ottawa, the Great Lakes and the St. Lawrence. They looted and burned, tortured and enslaved, and even recruited their numbers by enrolling some of their recent enemies as warriors. Once the Huron-Algonquin group and the Neutrals were dispersed, the Iroquois discovered that they were almost irresistible because no other Indians were so thoroughly equipped with European goods and firearms. Naturally, then, they swept on. Some of them raided the island refuges of Georgian Bay. Others worked across the broad peninsula between Lake Huron and Lake Michigan, driving the resident tribes before them. By 1652 they had reached the eastern shore of the Strait of Mackinac (the entry to Lake Michigan) and were greedily contemplating attacks on the frightened refugees across the lake at Nicolet's former destination—Green Bay.

In 1653 they did cross to the western shore of Lake Michigan and in so doing overreached themselves. Green Bay had become a sort of asylum where remnants of the more eastern Indians, still modestly supplied with European equipment, mixed with the original Winnebago (Siouan) inhabitants. When the Iroquois approached, their intended victims withdrew to a fort too strong to be taken by storm, and the Iroquois decided to look for easier prey. Remarkable as their strategy and tactics had been by comparative Indian standards, they were hardly adequate for warfare on so extended a scale as that into which their successive triumphs had now tempted them. At this crucial moment, instead of concentrating their power, they divided into two groups, one to attack the Saulteurs to the northward near Sault Ste. Marie, and the other to march south against the Illinois near the southern end of Lake Michigan. The effort was too great. Both bands suffered ultimate defeat and the humbled remnants carried at least temporary humility back to the 'long houses' of the Iroquois country.

New France felt the effects of that humility almost at once, but in what proved to be precarious and confusing ways. In June 1653 the Onondagas (central Iroquois) saluted the watchers on the walls of Montreal with a request for peace negotiations. All summer, delegations from the several Iroquois tribes moved between Montreal and Quebec to the end that by September a general peace was concluded. Profiting by the interlude, a little party of the fugitive Indians set out from Lake Michigan in the same year to carry furs to the French and to replenish their European equipment. Not daring to use the Ottawa, they reverted to the old sixteenth-century route from the upper Ottawa to the head-waters of the St. Maurice, so that they surprised as well as delighted a harassed settlement by emerging from the hinterland at Three Rivers. The *coureurs de bois*, encouraged by that success, prepared to go out again themselves. The courageous Jesuits, believing that the blood of martyrs is the seed of the faith, decided that they must cultivate that seed even among Iroquois murderers. As token of the peace, Father Poncet of their order was brought back from captivity on the Mohawk in October 1653. His hurrying escort indirectly added to French geographical knowledge by using the short-cut by Lake Oneida and the Oswego river to Lake Ontario and thence by the St. Lawrence to Montreal. The Jesuits thereupon successfully reminded the civil administration that friendly Iroquois meant freedom to use the route of the St. Lawrence and the Great Lakes to the interior. The remarkable conciliatory talents of Father Le Moyne were at once brought into play, so eloquently that the general truce was reaffirmed in 1654. Next year Fathers Chaumonot and Dablon visited the Onondagas by the new route, and in 1656 a semi-military Jesuit mission was enthusiastically received by them.

Outward appearance and inward reality, however, failed to coincide. The truth was that the Onondagas, who lived on the Oswego river route to Lake Ontario, were inclining towards assuming the middleman rôle for the French, while the Mohawks, who lived near the Hudson, saw no reason for breaking with the Dutch. A general peace with the Iroquois, in these circumstances, did not always include the Mohawks. Moreover all the Iroquois tribes were so reduced in strength and so deeply committed to war with their Indian neighbours that it was of the utmost importance to them to get hold of the Huron refugees at Quebec to serve either as objects for torture, as slaves or as warriors. Indeed, their chief activities during the truce were directed to that end, often successfully and greatly to the mystification and distress of the Jesuits who had risked their lives to bring the Hurons to safety. To be brief, the period of truce from the summer of 1653 to the early spring of 1658 could be called a time of peace only in contrast to the days of the assault on Huronia. French lives continued to be lost, French settlements were terrorised, and the daring mission to the Onondagas escaped destruction only by secret flight in 1658 after its Onondaga neighbours had been systematically stupefied at a feast.

Yet those uneasy years provided a sufficient breathing-space temporarily to save New France and to open a new phase in the exploration of the interior. The agents of the new enterprise were two French emigrants, become brothers-in-law and inhabitants of much-tried Three Rivers, Pierre Esprit Radisson and Médard Chouart, Sieur des Groseilliers. Radisson had early in his Canadian career been captured and adopted by the Iroquois, had escaped and been recaptured and finally was rescued by the Dutch on the Hudson. Both men were exceedingly courageous and resourceful *coureurs de bois*, shrewd and imaginative students of the natives and of the interior, and independent enough to make Holland, France and England compete for their services. They had experienced so much and had so much information at their disposal that they could tell the truth, be secretive, or embroider the facts as best suited their purpose.

The Jesuits reported some of their activities, but in an important instance which seems to refer to them did not mention names. Radisson himself wrote eloquently, but confusingly, of their travels, and of his narratives which have survived, those in French make a fairly clear story. Unfortunately a desire to impress Charles II of England made him try to compose his most important narratives in unfamiliar English, with results which are interesting and vigorous, but inexact and exasperating to the student. He wrote years after the events, and his *pot-pourri* of places and happenings cannot be reconciled with the calendar or with the Jesuit accounts. In these circumstances, insoluble controversies have arisen, unimportant in the light of an unquestionable, remarkable inspiration, but making it necessary for the modern recorder to admit that he is stating merely his choice among alternatives.[1]

The governor of New France, Jean de Lauzon, a timid man, was much elated in 1654 by the arrival of a large fleet of canoes from the West, whose occupants told of the thousands of fugitives in the Wisconsin country beyond Lake Michigan, bereft of European commodities and anxious to scour rich territories for the fur with which they might purchase them, if the French could renew the trade. Lauzon, who had seen the company monopoly system of fur-trading fail, decided to relax it in favour of individual traders under licence, *coureurs de bois*, who should run the risks of the interior and bring the furs for sale on the St. Lawrence. In 1654 he permitted two young men to go back with the Indians, 'to bring backe, if possible, those wildmen the next yeare, or others, being that it [fur] is the best manna of the countrey'. It is almost certain that Groseilliers was one of them and Radisson may have been the other. The two Frenchmen returned in 1656 escorting fifty canoes 'laden with goods which the French come to this end of the world to procure'. Their success excited over thirty Frenchmen to the point of deciding to go back that year. Radisson, who with Groseilliers, forced a passage up the Ottawa in spite of Iroquois attacks and desertion by the western Indians, was

[1] The main outlines of the controversies may be found summarised in L. P. Kellogg, *The French Régime in Wisconsin*, chap. vii (Madison, 1925), L. J. Burpee, *The Search for the Western Sea*, part ii, chap. ii (Toronto, 1908), and A. M. Goodrich and G. L. Nute, 'The Radisson Problem', *Minnesota History*, xiii, 3 (September 1932).

rightly contemptuous of these men when they speedily grew faint-hearted and turned back. His strangely worded, pungent comment is worth recording as a passionate expression of the true *coureur's* attitude towards the braggarts and stay-at-homes: 'What fairer bastion [of self-confidence] then a good tongue, especially when one sees his owne chimney smoak, or when we can kiss our owne wives or kisse our neighbour's wife with ease and delight? It is a strange [different] thing when victualls are wanting, worke whole nights & dayes, lye downe on the bare ground, & not allwayes that hap, the breech in the water, the feare in the buttocks, to have the belly empty, the wearinesse in the bones, and drowsinesse of the body by the bad weather that you are to suffer, having nothing to keepe you from such calamity.'

Radisson jumbled together the journeyings of 1654–1657 into one story of considerable interest but of no certainty. It is relatively clear, however, that he and Groseilliers followed the old Ottawa route to Georgian Bay, skirted its southern and western shores, and then cut across Lake Huron to Mackinac Strait and the islands which mask the entrance to Green Bay. They were thus introduced to the great triangle of the Laurentian Shield whose corners were Sault Ste. Marie, the western end of Lake Superior and the southern end of Lake Michigan. Its south-western face shaded off into the prairie and its rivers flowed south or west to swell the 'great water' which Nicolet had heard of, the Mississippi river. The region was rich in furs and its water-ways made progress about it fairly easy.

Within the triangle there was an extraordinary flux of Indian tribes. The eastern refugees were too well equipped to be resisted by the Siouan primitives whom they found there, with the result that the coherent groups of Sioux were driven to the western extremities, while bands of all sorts of invaders either wandered about the new country or settled down in uneasy coalitions with fragments of the earlier inhabitants, near Lake Michigan or the Sault. 'Our wildmen out of feare must consent to their ennemy to live in their land . . . [they] had not for the most part the conveniency of our french merchandise . . . so that they joyned with them & forgett what was past for their owne preservation.' 'They [the Sioux] entreated the strangers [Ottawas] to have pity on them and to share with them that iron, which they regarded as a divinity.'

The two French adventurers set themselves the task of encouraging the Indians once more to come down to the St. Lawrence. Their methods were shrewd and dramatic. On the final occasion, for instance, they harangued about eight hundred Indians on their folly in not preserving the knives, hatchets and guns they had obtained from the French. 'How will you defend villages? With castors' [beaver] skins?' Radisson even beat one of the braves with a beaver robe, saying, 'We are used to fight with armes & not with robes. . . . Doe you think that the French will come up here when the greatest part of you is slained by your own fault? You know that they cannot come up with out you.' The Indians were at last shamed into risking the Iroquois ambushes and prepared to go down again to the St. Lawrence. The trip proved to be a most exciting one, particularly along the Ottawa and the St. Lawrence near Montreal, but the leaders finally won through with all their furs after subjecting the Indians to military organisation and even by building up in their canoes bulwarks of beaver-skins behind which they were safe from arrows and bullets. 'We came to Quebecq, where we are saluted with the thundring of the guns & batteryes of the fort, and of the 3 shipps that weare then att anchor; which had gone back to France without castors if we had not come.'

The actual extent of the wanderings of these pioneers between 1654 and 1657 cannot be ascertained. One or other or both seem to have penetrated the land triangle for considerable distances, it seems likely even to the upper Mississippi. Probably they coasted the western, southern and part of the eastern shores of Lake Michigan and the shores of Lake Superior nearest the Sault. Yet their new explorations were on the whole less important than two new factors which were gradually borne in on them. One was the question of food. Now that the Indians had to be followed as far as the Sault, or beyond it, or beyond the Strait of Mackinac, it was impossible to carry in canoes sufficient supplies to serve both in and out. In the old days it had been possible to secure the mainstays of canoe travel, Indian corn and animal fat, from the Huron villages. Now it was necessary to travel farther, and at the new destinations the Indians were so disturbed that most of them had relapsed into nomadic ways and there were no dependable permanent agricultural settlements. In order to be certain of food, Groseilliers spent one whole summer collecting Indian corn. Henceforth either expeditions in the interior would require two years, or the French themselves must establish permanent farm depôts at appropriate points in the interior to which the fur convoys might repair. In any case, the cost of getting furs out was bound to be almost doubled.

The second new factor was a new commercial relationship, most clearly demonstrated at the Sault, which, allied to the food and transportation problems, was soon to send Europeans from the Great Lakes north to Hudson Bay and south to the Gulf of Mexico. At the Sault and at Green Bay, the fugitive Indians from the east were consciously and unconsciously doing their best to exploit their more primitive hosts and neighbours, who did not use the canoe, by bartering with them bits of iron and steel and worn-out European articles for extravagant quantities of furs. The Crees gave the Ottawas 'all their beaver robes for old knives, blunted awls, wretched nets and kettles used until they were past service'. One group of these middlemen claimed 'that the great river [Ottawa] belongs to them, and that no nations can launch a boat on it without their consent. Therefore all who go to trade with the French, although of widely different nations, bear the general name of Ottawas.' Radisson and Groseilliers wanted very much to break through the sophisticated fringe and themselves get at the eager primitives. They earnestly collected all the information about them which they could, but had very slight success in establishing contacts with them in their first two voyages.

They learned that there were two chief groups: 'a nation called Nadoueceronon [Sioux], which is very strong . . . & another wandering nation [Christinos or Crees], living onely uppon what they could come by'. The former, armed as they were only with weapons of wood, stone and bone, had retreated westwards until they lived south of western Lake Superior along the short rivers flowing into the Lake or tributary to the upper Mississippi. The Crees, similarly ousted from the vicinity of the Sault, 'retired themselves to the height of the lake', that is, north and west. The tribes at the Sault 'make the barre of the Christinos from whence they have the Castors that they bring to the french'. In the journeyings of 1654–57, Radisson explained, 'we desired not to goe to the North till we had made a discovery in the South'. Yet his narrative of that period ends with a comment which may have been an after-thought drawn from his later career, but which in that place seemed to anticipate the great inspiration by which he and Groseilliers were to solve the problems of the fur trade in their day. 'My brother and I considered whether we should discover what we have seene or no; and because we had not a full and whole discovery, which was that we have not ben in the bay of the north [James Bay], not knowing anything but by report of the wild Christinos, we would make no mention of it for feare that those wild men should tell [should have told] us a fibbe.'

Thrilling as were Radisson's adventures during the next nine or ten months (1657–58), while he assisted the Jesuit mission to the Onondagas, they must be passed over in favour of the expedition of 1658 or 1659 to 1660, during which he and Groseilliers hit upon what Hudson Bay might mean to the fur trade in the way of solving the transportation problem and of circumventing the Indian middlemen. Once again it must be admitted that it is uncertain where they went and that Radisson may have woven hearsay into the tale which he composed to win the support of amuse-ment-loving Charles II in 1665, but even if he made some of his journey in imagination, it was an imagina-tion which changed the course of history for half the North American continent.

'Now during the winter,' wrote Radisson, 'whether it was that my brother revealed to his wife what we had seene in our voyage and what we further intended, or

229

how [ever] it came to passe, it was knowne.' The Jesuits, thwarted by the Iroquois wars, had hit upon Radisson's idea with a variation, being 'desirous to find out a way how they might gett downe the castors from the bay of the north by the Sacques [Indians of the Saguenay], and so make themselves masters of that trade'. Father Dreuillettes had been busy putting together what he could learn from Radisson and Groseilliers and from the stories of their wanderings brought to him by the dispersed Nipissings who were ranging the north from the Saguenay to the Sault just as the Hurons and Algonquins were ranging the west. His report filled a substantial portion of the *Relation* of 1657–58, and in it he described six routes from the St. Lawrence basin to the Bay of the Crees (James Bay), none of them requiring more than a month and several of them now known to us as practicable, if difficult, journeys. Radisson was friendly, but he was not to be diverted from returning with his brother to the West in order to head an expedition up the Saguenay for the Jesuits, for his Indian friends had told him that the Sacques 'would have hindred them, because they make a livelyhood of that trade'. He was willing to run the Iroquois gauntlet on the Ottawa again if he and Groseilliers could induce the Governor to let them go.

The negotiations were exasperating, for the new governor (Argenson) wanted them to take two of his men along and divide the profit equally. 'We made the governor a slight answer, and tould him for our part we knewed what we weare, Discoverers before governors.' They were forbidden to leave, nor could the friendly Jesuits make the governor change his mind. Then, in August 1658 or 1659, there arrived seven canoes of their Indian friends from the Sault, anxious to trade and get back quickly, and willing to take with them from Three Rivers Radisson and Groseilliers, but not the governor's servants. Their two French friends regretfully let them go, and then abruptly decided to defy the ban. 'That very night, my brother having the keys of the Brough [borough] as being Captayne of the place, we embarqued ourselves.' They caught up with the Indians before Montreal and, after a harrowing few days of successive battles with the Iroquois near Montreal and on the lower Ottawa, were once more clear on their way to the West. 'We left the Iroquoits in his fort and the feare in our breeches, for without apprehension we rowed from friday to tuesday without intermission.' They went from Montreal to Georgian Bay in twenty-two days, and pushed on by the Northern Channel to the Sault.

In brilliant autumn weather they paddled along the south shore of Lake Superior past Grand Island to Keweenaw Point, where they portaged rather than make the long circuit on the autumn lake. The vastness of the lake awed them and they hurried apprehensively along stretches of inhospitable cliffs where no haven existed to save them from the great waves of the occasional storms. Before winter set in, they had built an ingenious log fortress for their trade goods on the shore of Chequamegon Bay. They had had a most triumphant progress, welcomed eagerly for the 'hattchetts and knives and other utensils very commodious, rare, precious, and necessary in those countreys'. Longing savages accompanied them 'in hopes to gett knives from us, which they love better then we serve God'.

At Chequamegon they found themselves in the midst of a competition for their goods among the fugitive Ottawas, with some of whom they had come from Quebec; the Ottawas' incipient enemies, the Sioux;

and Crees from the western end of the lake and its northern shore. They made a visit inland to the Ottawas on Lac Courte Oreille and suffered mightily with them in the throes of a winter famine. Later, the haughty Sioux persuaded them to visit their village farther west. Before the winter was over, the Crees brought on toboggans great quantities of rich northern furs which especially excited their admiration 'We weare Cesars, being nobody to contradict us. We went away free from any burden, whilst those poore miserable thought themselves happy to carry our Equipage, for the hope that they had that we should give them a brasse ring, or an awle, or an needle.' With great imagination and considerable dramatic skill, they ceremoniously proceeded to exploit their prestige for the benefit of the Sioux, who had particularly aroused their interest with their elaborate costumes, their wooden and stone weapons, their horn-tipped arrows, their copper ornaments and their swiftly erected skin wigwams. These mighty warriors were glad to accept the Frenchmen's efforts to protect them from the guns and the hatchets of the Ottawas and Crees.

During the late winter Radisson and Groseilliers held a great feast, similar to the Indian Feast of the Dead, to ensure peace between Crees and Sioux, before they themselves went off into the interior 'seaven small Journeys' to visit 'the nation of the beefe [buffalo]'. Before they left, they 'promised in like manner to the Christinos ye next spring we should come to their side of the upper lake [Superior], and there they should meete us, to come into their countrey'. On their return, still before the ice and snow had melted, they 'resolved to know what we heard before'. After some inexplicable journeying and the building of a new fort, they sent off a party of Crees and, on a pretext of hunting, followed them during the night, much vexed by the ice-floes of Lake Superior. After a dangerous crossing, they found the Cree village and were warmly welcomed. 'They suffered not that we trod on ground; they leade us into the midle of their cottages in our own boats like a couple of cocks in a Basquett.'

Then the narrative says: 'We went away with all hast possible to arrive the sooner att the great river. We came to the seaside, where we finde an old howse all demollished and battered with boullets. . . . They tell us particularities of the Europians. We know ourselves, and what Europ is, therefore in vaine they tell us as for that.' Those words and some rambling remarks which follow are the basis for the claim that Radisson and Groseilliers reached either Hudson or James Bay. As we know, there were old houses on the bays and the Crees could have taken the Frenchmen to Lake Winnipeg or to Lake Nipigon and thence down the Nelson or the Hayes or the Albany river to the sea. The description Radisson subsequently gives of the sea is applicable to conditions there. Yet any reader of his story must have some doubt of it, partly by reason of its brevity and partly from the difficulty of fitting the journey into the time which we know remained available for it in 1660. There is even the possibility that they were taken only to Lake Winnipeg.

The inclination to believe him comes from such sentences as these. 'We went from Isle to Isle all that summer. . . . We weare well beloved, and [they] weare overjoyed that we promised them to come with such shipps as we invented. . . . That river [of the Cree summer camp, probably at the mouth of Rupert river] comes from the lake and empties itselfe in the river of

Saques, called Tadousack, which is a hundred leagues in the great river of Canada, as [= equal distance from?] where we weare in the Bay of the north. . . . It is an ordinary thing to see five six hundred swans together.' There is no way of settling the question, but the adventurers went down to Quebec in the summer of 1660 with an argosy of furs, with a distinct preference for the northern furs brought them by the Crees, and with a determination to end the risks and labours of the traditional route by carrying their trade-goods henceforth in capacious ocean vessels into Hudson Bay itself. We can date their return from their having passed the site of Adam Dollard's great fight with the Iroquois, 'which saved us without doubt', shortly after it occurred in June 1660. The Jesuit Journal dated the arrival at Montreal as 19 August and reported that Groseilliers had wintered among the sedentary Sioux.

Radisson and Groseilliers quite reasonably expected to be received as heroes when the Montrealers looked out to see 'so great a number of boats that did almost cover the whole River', but their unlicensed departure was still unforgiven and they were speedily embroiled with 'a Governor that would grow rich by the labours and hazards of others'. His difficult term (1658–61) was about to expire, and he proceeded to make his victims disgorge their profits 'that he might the better maintain his coach & horses at Paris'. Thoroughly disgusted, Groseilliers went to France for redress and, failing, made a rendezvous with Radisson in a small vessel at Isle Percée in the southern Gulf of St. Lawrence. After touching at St. Peter's on Cape Breton and at Canso on the Nova Scotian peninsula, the resourceful pair decided to seek trading affiliations in New England. Port Royal (modern Annapolis Royal), on the Fundy shore of Nova Scotia, happened at that time to be 'inhabited by the French under the English Government', following the Cromwellian conquest of 1654, and the French *coureurs* found there 'some English shipps that brought about our designes'.

The chronology of the succeeding years is in doubt until 1668, but during them Radisson and Groseilliers displayed extraordinary devotion to their brilliant idea concerning Hudson Bay. It seems to have been in 1663 that they secured a New England ship (captained by Zachariah Gillam) in Nova Scotia or Boston, and in it got as far as the entry to Hudson Strait. They failed to go farther because of the timidity of 'our master, that onely were accustomed to see some Barbadoes Sugers, and not mountains of suger candy [ice floes], which did frighten him'. A second effort next year with two ships failed really to get started and culminated in an acrimonious New England law-suit. Then luck put them in the path of Charles II's commissioners for colonial reorganisation following the Restoration. In 1665 one of the commissioners, Sir George Carteret, managed to get them to plague-stricken England and out to Charles II's retreat at Oxford, after an adventurous sea voyage which involved capture by the Dutch. Their stories and proposals fitted into English experience and desires so neatly as to be sure of English attention, even a generation after Foxe and James had abandoned Hudson Bay. A group of merchants, who enjoyed the patronage of adventurous Prince Rupert, prepared to equip an expedition, and King Charles himself, in spite of the Plague, the Fire of London and the Dutch War, maintained the two Frenchmen and placed a naval vessel, the *Eaglet*, at their disposal. Meanwhile the Dutch were trying in vain to win them to their service.

Finally, after many discouraging delays, Radisson in the *Eaglet* (Captain Stannard) and Groseilliers in the *Nonsuch* (Captain Gillam) set sail from Gravesend on 3 June 1668. Radisson's ship was driven back by storms, as indeed he was again driven back next year, but Groseilliers won through, and by 25 August had reached the Cree summering place in Rupert Bay, the first vessel to be there since Henry Hudson in 1610 or 1611. While a fort was being built for the winter, he brought his skill to bear on the natives, so that they gathered furs for him, to be bartered in the ceremonious primitive pretence of interchange of gifts. The scale was absurdly profitable among these remote aborigines, the skins, especially the beaver, were the prime of North America, and the *Nonsuch* carried a fair-sized cargo of cheap-won peltries back to the fortunate merchants of London in 1669.

Out of that success grew the lusty trading enterprise known to this day as 'The Governor and Company of Adventurers of England trading into Hudson's Bay'. Its immediate problems were those of getting the natives accustomed to bringing their furs down the rivers to the Bay, of meeting and anticipating the rivalry of the indignant French in Europe and Canada, and of actually fighting on land and sea to hold their priceless monopoly. For the moment their servants did nothing to further the exploration of the continent, but it is well to remember that the existence of the Hudson's Bay Company and the inception of the exploring enterprises it was later to foster grew out of the actual or imaginary journey of Radisson and Groseilliers from Lake Superior to the Bay. By it the work of two great pioneers, Champlain and Hudson, was welded into a living design.

NARRATIVES

Radisson's Voyages, edited by G. D. Scull, were published by the Prince Society (Boston, 1885). His MSS. fell into the hands of his neighbour in London, Samuel Pepys, and were dramatically rescued from serving London tradesmen as wrapping paper by Richard Rawlinson in 1750. Corroboratory material is to be found in *Jesuit Relations*, vols. xlii, xliv, xlv. The Indian narratives of the dispersion collected by Perrot about 1667–70 will be found in his *Mémoire*, partly translated in vol. i of E. H. Blair, *Indian Tribes of the Upper Mississippi and the Great Lakes Regions* (2 vols., Cleveland, 1912). The material on Hudson Bay in John Oldmixon, *The British Empire in America* (2 vols., London, 1708), was drawn directly from seventeenth-century reports made to the Hudson's Bay Company and from conversations with men who had been active there. Gillam's journal of 1668–69 is to be found in J. Robson, *An Account of Six Years' Residence in Hudson's Bay* (London, 1752).

CHAPTER XV

PAST THE IROQUOIS TO THE SOUTH

(*Map No. 2, page 258*)

Here we are, then, on this so renowned river.
THE JOLLIET-MARQUETTE NARRATIVE, 17 JUNE 1673

FROM 1624 to 1661, two cardinals in succession, Richelieu and Mazarin, ruled sorely troubled France and nursed its feeble monarchy. On the morning after Mazarin died, Louis XIV, a young king of whom no very high hopes had been held, announced to his startled ministers that henceforth he would rule in person. He would be glad of their information and advice, but he forbade them to act without his order. Very soon afterwards he selected one of Mazarin's assistants, Jean Baptiste Colbert, to be his principal collaborator. The two men, by sheer hard work and by selecting a brilliant hierarchy of subordinates, speedily converted French potentiality into the political hegemony and cultural leadership of Europe. The magnitude of their European achievement, ornamented as it was with vast dynastic schemes, intricate political alignments, and wars in which the fates of several nations hung in the balance, has tended largely to overshadow one of their most remarkable accomplishments—the transformation of a feeble, even dying, colony into the parent community of millions of the North Americans of to-day.

New France was again on the verge of extinction from 1658 to 1663. The Iroquois, backed by the Dutch, drove the French and their neighbouring Indian allies behind their stockades or attacked them in their fields. The annual death-roll of between fifty and a hundred French inhabitants cut sadly into a population of about 3000. The arrogance of the Iroquois knew no bounds. In 1659, for instance, they murdered the Montreal Sulpician, Father Le Maitre, and then horrified the Montrealers by using his garments to enliven a mock Christian funeral procession around the walls. Appeal after appeal by lay and spiritual emissaries went to the young king of France, until during the winter of 1662–1663 he decided to act.

This is not the place to tell of how men and women, soldiers and munitions, money and equipment were poured into New France, or of how, in the person of the intendant Jean Talon, King Louis sent out the civil administrator whose vigorous actions set the colony firmly upon its feet in an economic way. It is perhaps worth noting that, when Baron Dubois d'Avaugour retired as governor in 1663, he drew up a military and naval plan for his sovereign whereby he guaranteed to end all the colony's troubles by capturing Boston, Manhattan and Fort Orange, and thus controlling North America south to the Hudson. Doubtless this could have been achieved in 1663, but France had many colonial problems, and Quebec had to wait until her military saviour, the Marquis de Tracy, had first dealt with the more valuable Guiana and the French islands of the West Indies. He arrived in Quebec in June 1665. He had no orders to besiege the southern towns. His task was to deal directly with the direct menace by smashing the Iroquois. Meanwhile, however, the English had captured for themselves the Dutch posts on the Hudson.

Tracy promptly blocked the main avenue of Iroquois attack by putting three forts and 800 troops of the Carignan-Salières regiment along the Richelieu river. The eager new governor, Daniel de Rémy, Sieur de Courcelles, rushed off into the Mohawk territory in the middle of winter with a volunteer force, but got lost and came home, having effected nothing. Tracy bided his time until September 1666, when he and his veterans of the Turkish wars set out in full panoply to find the warriors of the Mohawk valley and destroy them. Inevitably the savages fled before this great European engine of war, leaving to Tracy their wooden villages, their stores of food and the crops standing in the fields. The French burned them all and in less than two months were back in Quebec, for the first time in fifty years completely rid of the chief menace to their existence. Next year the Iroquois not only asked for final peace, but for French emissaries of all sorts to cement the understanding between them.

The curbing of the Iroquois broke down the barrier behind which all sorts of energies and ambitions, religious and secular, had been pent up for years. The Jesuits had been greatly excited over the reports made by Radisson and Groseilliers and by the far-wandering Indian middlemen of the north and west. They now had explicit information about 'the lake which we call Superior, from its position above that of the Hurons', about the refugees there and the lead- and copper-mines, and they had heard fascinating tales of turquoise (amethyst) and gold. Still more exciting was 'entirely new light . . . touching the route to Japan and China'. 'For we learn from these peoples [at the western end of

Lake Superior] that they find the Sea on three sides, toward the South, toward the West, and toward the North; so that, if this be so, it is a strong argument and a very certain indication that these three Seas, being thus contiguous, form in reality but one Sea, which is that of China.'

Indeed, Father Lalemant, who composed the *Relation* of 1659–60, pictured the western end of Lake Superior as the sort of central crossroads for North America, which it subsequently proved to be. 'Proceeding Southward for about three hundred leagues . . . we come to the bay of St. Esprit . . . in the Gulf of Mexico.' 'In a Southwesterly direction . . . it is about two hundred leagues to another lake, which empties into the Vermillion Sea [Gulf of California] on the coast of New Granada.' 'Following a River toward the North, we arrive, after eight or ten days' journey, at Hudson Bay.' 'Ten days' journey westward lies the Sea.' The news which Radisson and Groseilliers gave them of the great congress of tribes in the Michigan-Superior triangle called strongly for a mission, particularly when it included word of a Petun group six days' journey south-west of Lake Superior, who lived on 'a beautiful River, large, wide, deep, and worthy of comparison, they say, with our great river St. Lawrence'. This was the upper Mississippi. Between 1658 and 1663 the Jesuits had thought, as Radisson did, of developing the north as an alternative to the Iroquois-ridden Great Lakes district. Fathers Dablon and Dreuillettes even made an unsuccessful attempt to reach Hudson Bay by the Saguenay. Yet as soon as Tracy had cleared the way, the south and west reclaimed their attention.

Nor were the Jesuits the only missionary workers in that field. The Sulpicians of Montreal, the spiritual core of the colony's most exposed outpost, were eager to go west along the Lakes. They had been sorely tried and tested. They now wished to try their own kind of missionary enterprise, in which, as in other things, they differed from the Jesuits. A perceptible rivalry whetted the missionaries' appetites for souls.

The missionaries were the first recorded beneficiaries of the curbing of the Iroquois, for we know very little about the many *coureurs* who swarmed out to the West. Radisson and Groseilliers met some of them on their first journeys to the West; indeed, most of the records of the day tell of nameless individuals or groups of traders who either dared the Iroquois menace or hurried forth once it was removed. After 1666 it was like plenty after famine. As Perrot said, 'it was a Peru for them'. The old routes were travelled again and tales of the dispersion and of new homes for old customers sent the *coureurs* deep into untravelled territories. Each *coureur* dreamed of breaking through the wall of Indian middlemen and reaching some group of unspoiled primitives whose gratitude for European goods would make his fortune once for all.

The outbursts of enterprise after 1666 inevitably meant new exploration, but new and old were inevitably so closely intermingled that for simplicity's sake it is best to bring out its chief consequence even at the cost of some summary description or outright omission of the shorter strands in the new design. In the process there was one unexpected element, for Lake Superior, like Hudson Bay, gradually ceased to figure greatly in French plans. The first Jesuits, Ménard and Allouez, went out to Chequamegon to work. Yet very soon the upper lake was almost deserted by missionaries, traders and government emissaries in favour of Green Bay and

Lake Michigan. The explanation is quite simple. The western Indians, too, had rebounded once the terror of the Iroquois was lifted. The refugees and the agricultural tribes who had lived along Lake Michigan before 1653 came back from their wanderings in the backcountry to re-establish their villages and farms along the western and southern shores. The canoe-men and carriers among them, no less than the French, found it almost imperative to bring the fur-collection stations closer to the St. Lawrence. In these circumstances the Sea of the North and the Sea of the West faded away before preoccupation with the Sea of the South.

One of the first enterprises was the long-postponed investigation of the Great Lakes system. The French had been in Canada for fifty years without ever having followed the water-way from Lake Ontario to Lake Huron. Now, with the Iroquois cowed, the deed was done quite easily and casually. Talon, keen to develop the copper-mines of Lake Superior, sent out the *métis*, Jean Peré, by the Lake Ontario-Lake Simcoe route in 1668 to investigate them, and Louis Jolliet[1] followed a year later by the Ottawa route to support him. When Jolliet reached the Sault, he discovered that a war involving an Iroquois band on Lake Superior was threatening the hard-won peace. Father Allouez had already gone to the St. Lawrence with some ransomed captive Iroquois in order to save the peace, and Jolliet also set off with the last Iroquois prisoner whom he could obtain. This Indian quite naturally suggested that they travel by the Lakes instead of by the Ottawa river. They went south across Lake Huron to the St. Clair river, down it and across Lake St. Clair to the narrows (*détroit*) of the Detroit river, and thence into Lake Erie. Here they

[1] Sometimes modernised as Joliet.

243

landed on the low, level northern shore and followed a trail which led them across to the western end of Lake Ontario. There, in late September 1669, they unexpectedly met a group of Frenchmen on their way to open up new country for the salvation of souls and the expansion of the fur trade. Two Sulpicians, François Dollier de Casson and René de Bréhant de Galinée, had combined forces with a brilliant student of the fur trade, Robert René Cavelier, later to be Sieur de la Salle, and all three were on the brink of ventures into unknown territory. They eagerly pumped Jolliet for the details of his remarkable new exploration.

The meeting at the end of the lake in 1669 was significant of the plans of the King, Colbert and their servant Talon, and an echo of the projects of the returned Governor d'Avaugour. For the moment France intended that a revived New France should become a mighty North American empire, controlling if possible the land route to the Pacific and reaching down to share with Spain the mines and other riches of the South. North America was revealing itself to be worth fighting for, whether in Acadia, at the mouth of the Hudson, in Hudson Bay, or in the interior. Spain had failed to find either the Strait of Anian or the great inland sea which so many men believed lay between the Great Lakes and Mexico. She had failed also to make any use of the great midland river which Pineda saw in 1519 and whose existence Vaca, Soto and Luna corroborated. France, already measuring her powers with Spain in Europe, was contemplating a test of strength and enterprise in America.

Jolliet was Talon's man and had formerly been associated with the Jesuits, to whom Talon was planning to entrust the development of the North-West. But to

Talon and his Gallican masters in France the Jesuits were too strong in New France and too ultramontane. Their greed for mission territories seemed ominous of another Paraguay. The Sulpicians were chosen as one counter-weight to them and were encouraged to work among the Iroquois along the lower Great Lakes. In 1670 the Récollets were reintroduced still further to break the ecclesiastical monopoly. Casson and Galinée in 1669 were on a pioneering journey to investigate the state of affairs around Lake Erie and to seek out the western and southern tribes.

They had with them a restless spirit in La Salle, brother of one of their order at Montreal. They had granted him a seigneury, mockingly called La Chine because of his dreams of a way to Asia, after his arrival in the colony in 1666, and he had already shewn remarkable skill in dealing with the Iroquois. His brain was alive with schemes to establish a depôt west of the rapids on Lake Ontario itself, to control the Lakes' water-way and to plunge inland south-west from the Iroquois country to find what lay towards New Spain. It was his fate always to exceed present practicality by the novelty and magnitude of his designs, but those designs ultimately proved to be so apt and shrewd that history has been right in elevating him to greatness even though he carried to completion almost nothing of what he essayed.

The Montrealers were on the track of something new. La Salle had entertained two Senecas at his seigneury, and these westernmost Iroquois stimulated him to a journey which he 'had been long premeditating', by their news of a great river 'which had its course towards the west, and at the end of which, after seven or eight months' travelling, these Indians said the land

245

was "cut", that is to say . . . the river fell into the sea'. The Senecas called this river 'Ohio', and by it probably meant the whole Mississippi system, whose north-eastern tributaries, such as the Wabash and the Alleghany, flow west from their sources close to Lake Erie. 'The hope of beaver,' wrote Galinée, 'but especially of finding by this route the passage into the Vermillion Sea [Gulf of California], into which M. de la Salle believed the River Ohio emptied, induced him to undertake this expedition, so as not to leave to another the honor of discovering the passage to the South Sea, and thereby the way to China.'

La Salle shared his information and imaginings with Casson, and both of them in vain did their best to secure an Andaste or Shawnee slave guide from the Iroquois on the south shore of Lake Ontario. Not only could they not get a guide, but the news of the way to the 'Ohio' which they received was discouraging. It was said to be 'six days' journey by land of about twelve leagues each' from the Seneca villages, too great a distance to carry their baggage. 'But at the same time we were told that in going to Lake Erie by canoe we should have only three days' portage to get to that river.' To La Salle, Lake Erie meant a way to furs from the unspoiled Shawnees of the Ohio and possibly a water-route to the Pacific. To the Sulpicians an un-contaminated group of Indian tribes was just as tempting, because it promised to give them an exclusive mission area for the glory of God and of their order. An Indian who had worked with the Dutch assured them that they could secure guides at the end of the lake and he took them there past the mouth of the Niagara river, where the sound of the Falls and the descriptions of its grandeur almost tempted them to pause, late in the season as it was. 'I leave you to imagine if it is not a beautiful cascade, to see all the water of this great river, which at its mouth is three leagues in width, precipitate itself from a height of two hundred feet.'

The meeting with Jolliet produced another change of plan. The Sulpicians were greatly interested to learn that except for a portage round the Niagara river it was possible to proceed by boat from the upper St. Lawrence to Lake Michigan. Moreover, Lake Michigan beckoned strongly when Jolliet told them that near its shores were the Pottawottamis 'amongst whom there never had been any missionaries, and that this tribe bordered on the Mascoutens and the great river that led to the Shawnees'. By a piece of what seemed providential good fortune, they were also able at this moment to reinforce their 'Dutch' guide by securing the services of a veritable Shawnee. La Salle was not so impressed. He clung to his idea of exploring southwards from Lakes Ontario and Erie, and he used the excuse of illness and hints that he must return to Montreal to break with the Sulpicians and become a lone agent again. It is probable that he knew what Jolliet knew and the Sulpicians were still to learn, that the Jesuits were already moving from Lake Superior to Lake Michigan and were powerful enough at least to handicap him in his projects.

The Sulpicians made the portage to Grand river during the first three days of October, worked down its autumn shallows to Lake Erie and turned west to the site of modern Port Dover for a wintering place— 'the most beautiful place I have ever seen in Canada', wrote Galinée on his map. Their two guides went off to secure Jolliet's abandoned canoe, but were never heard of again. Although the winter was a severe one in Canada, they thoroughly enjoyed their enforced delay, for the local climate was temperate, food was abundant and they were able to devote themselves to the quiet practice of their religion. 'Monsieur Dollier often told us that that winter ought to be worth to us, as regards our eternal welfare, more than the ten best years of our life.'

They set off again on 26 March, rather too early in the spring, and after spending Easter (6 April) at the Long Point portage, had the misfortune to lose their altar service and much of their baggage when a storm swept the beach by which they slept at Point Pelée. That meant a return to Montreal before they could set up their mission among the Pottawottamis, Mascoutens or Shawnees, but it seemed to them that the shortest way back would be with the fur brigades from the Sault. After zealously destroying a huge stone idol on the Detroit river near Lake Erie, they followed Jolliet's route to the Sault, which they reached on 25 May. Pausing only long enough to see the Jesuit headquarters there and to reach some critical conclusions concerning the precipitancy of Jesuit procedure in conversion, they set out on 28 May with a hired guide and reached Montreal on 18 June, after a journey which for novelty, distance and speed of travel must always remain notable.

So far as an exclusive mission near Lake Michigan and the Mississippi was concerned, the Sulpicians were both too late and too weak to dispute the region with the enterprising Order of Jesus. The triangle lying between Lakes Superior and Michigan was full of movement. The *coureurs* were trading so carelessly as to provoke Indian assaults. New groups of Indian middlemen were trying to hold back the fur traders. The mighty, if primitive Sioux of the region west and south-west of Lake Superior felt the lightening of pressure from the east and began to drive out the bands of unwelcome Indian guests whose better tools and weapons had lately made them so arrogant. The Jesuits, after courageous enterprise in the footsteps of Radisson on both shores of Lake Superior and even at Lake Nipigon, also moved east to the Sault and looked now towards virgin missionary fields round Green Bay and southern Lake Michigan. They had actually started their Green Bay mission just before the Sulpicians arrived at the Sault.

During the seven years after the curbing of the Iroquois in 1666, the forces which controlled human action in the Mid-West had steadily combined almost to force upon the French the investigation of the Mississippi. Nicolet had told of it in Champlain's day. Radisson and Groseilliers may have seen it, but they deliberately abandoned the south for the north. In their default, it was Jesuit courage and enterprise which found the way. Father Ménard lost his life in 1661 south of Chequamegon Bay near the Mississippi in an effort to minister to some refugee Petun Hurons who lived on one of its tributaries. Father Claude Jean Allouez went out from the trading centre at Three Rivers to Chequamegon in 1665 to tell of the coming French onslaught on the Iroquois. He heard much of the country to the south and of the 'great river named Messipi', but he learned of it in two widely separated places, south of the western end of Lake Superior and south of Lake Michigan. But meanwhile the wise and tactful trader, Nicholas Perrot, had established himself at Green Bay, whence he and Toussaint Baudry had broken through the Pottawottamis along the shores to reach the Menominee on the river of that name and even up the Fox river to the plateau where the Mascoutens and Miamis lived in plenty above the Mississippi valley. Jolliet brought out more traders to Green Bay in 1669 and in the late autumn of that year Allouez went to visit it and establish a mission.

In the spring of 1670 he, too, visited the interior by way of the Fox river as far as the Miamis and Mascoutens. On the upper Fox he was told by the Miamis that 'their river leads by a six days' journey to the great river named Messi-Sipi', but he did not push on, judging it to be wiser to return to the Sault with his news. Father Jacques Marquette, after setting up mission headquarters there in 1668, had gone off for two years' service at Chequamegon, but the ambitious local superior, Father Claude Dablon, was building up a group of missionaries and arranging for mission stations at the Sault, on Green Bay, on Michilimackinac island and on the Fox river. He made a journey with Allouez to Green Bay in the autumn of 1670 and at last they solved the character of the great river, when they were told that it rose in the north, where they had already heard of it, and flowed past a point not far from them to the south. Dablon was uncertain as to whether it flowed to the Gulf of Mexico or to the Gulf of California. Marquette got further information from some Illinois at Chequamegon and wrote that he thought the river had its mouth in California. By the spring of 1673, although Dablon had gone to Quebec to be superior general, there were six Jesuit missionaries at work in the north-eastern part of the Superior-Michigan triangle, and only the occasion was lacking for a journey to the Mississippi. Perhaps some of the *coureurs* had already reached it, but many of them were almost outlaws and most of their journeyings are unrecorded.

The stimulus came from Talon, whose enthusiasm

for territorial expansion found expression as soon as he had laid the foundations for the colony's domestic welfare. His imagination had been fired by the news from the West and he was keen to exploit the situation for France. Between 1668 and 1670 he was in Europe to consult directly with Colbert and to bring out the Récollets, while La Salle and the Sulpicians conducted their explorations. On his return, his plans were upset by La Salle's avoidance of him, but he made his first revealing move by sending the Sieur de St. Lusson as a civil emissary to the Sault to proclaim French sovereignty. Jolliet and the Jesuits gathered the neighbouring Indians for the ceremony, and on 14 June 1671 St. Lusson raised the arms of France. With great pageantry and repeated *seizin* of a bit of sod, he claimed the known lands of western New France and 'all other countries, rivers, lakes and tributaries, contiguous and adjacent thereunto, as well discovered as to be discovered, which are bounded on the one side by the Northern and Western Seas and on the other side by the South Sea, including all its length and breadth'.

La Salle's explorations were to have supplemented this display and to have anticipated the Jesuit thrust towards the south, but Talon could not get into touch with him. Moreover, the matter seemed urgent. The English were reported to be moving west from Virginia. Spain was not much to be feared, but Talon could not calmly allow the English to precede the French in discovering water-ways to the riches of New Spain or to the Pacific. Instead, he proposed 'to confine them within very narrow limits by the annexations that I have made [at the Sault]'. He planned to build a fort at Cataraqui on Lake Ontario to hold in check their trading ventures through the Iroquois. He sent Father

Albanel to James Bay to win back the Indians to trade on the St. Lawrence. It seemed even more important to keep the English close to the Atlantic coast by making the profitable inland discoveries ahead of them.

In Europe, Diego de Peñalosa, lately governor of New Mexico, was smarting from his recent trial for serious offences and his expulsion from the Spanish dominions. He tried to interest the English in an attack from the Gulf of Mexico on the weak eastern frontier of the Spanish mining regions, but Charles II had his hands full at home and used Peñalosa as a pawn in his friendly negotiations with Louis XIV, by sending him to France in 1671. Peñalosa knew of the Mississippi and of its proximity to Spanish North America. Proof of his direct implication in the policies of Colbert at this time is lacking, but when Count Frontenac went out in 1672 to be governor of New France he carried instructions to Talon which declared that 'after the increase of the colony of Canada, nothing is of greater importance for that country and for the service of his Majesty than the discovery of a passage to the South Sea'. It is not surprising, therefore, to find Talon reporting to the king that 'it is by this same river [Mississippi] that we can hope some day to find the opening to Mexico', nor to read the explicit statement by Father Dablon that Frontenac and Talon sent out the expedition in 1673 'either that they might seek a passage from here [Quebec] to the Sea of China by the river that discharges into the Vermillion, or California Sea; or because they desired to verify what has for some time been said concerning the two kingdoms of Theguaio [Tiguex, Coronado's centre, 1540–41] and Quivira, which border on Canada, and in which numerous gold mines are reported to exist'.

In the continued absence of La Salle and in spite of their disinclination to encourage the Jesuits, Talon and Frontenac chose as leader of the expedition Louis Jolliet, 'who has already been quite near this great river', and Father Dablon was able to persuade at least Talon to allow Father Marquette to go along as chaplain and Christian spokesman.[1] Jolliet set out from Quebec in the late autumn of 1672 and succeeded in reaching Marquette's new mission station, St. Ignace, by 8 December. St. Ignace, on the mainland shore of the narrow Mackinac Strait, was to Father Dablon 'the key and the door for all the peoples of the south'. During the winter, the narrative says, 'we obtained all the information that we could from the savages who had frequented those regions; and we even traced out from their reports a map of the whole of that new country'. It can be seen that the expedition was not entirely one of discovery. The great problem to be solved for New France was the direction of the Mississippi. Was it the same stream as the Spanish River of the Holy Spirit? Did it flow to the Gulf of Mexico or to the Pacific?

The Green Bay Indians characteristically did their best to dissuade the small party (two of the *voyageurs* were Pierre Porteret and Jacques Largilliers) from their journey by tales of natives 'who never show mercy to strangers', of 'horrible monsters, which devoured men and canoes together', and of heat 'so excessive that it would inevitably cause our death'. The Frenchmen

[1] A controversy, which has never been settled to general satisfaction, surrounds the Jolliet-Marquette expedition as a whole and the authorship of the so-called narrative of Marquette. The text and citations of L. F. Steck, *The Jolliet-Marquette Expedition*, 1673 (Quincy, 1928), provide the latest guide to the problems. Steck argues that the narrative was written by Dablon from a copy of Jolliet's lost narrative, from Jolliet's written recollections and from the notes of Marquette. His theses have been critically examined, as, for example, by G. J. Garraghan, *Thought*, June 1929, pp. 32-71.

pushed on, however, to the south end of the Bay and up the Fox river to the Mascouten and Miami villages on the height between the Fox and the Wisconsin. The Miamis helped them over the short portage on 10 June 1673, and 'thus we left the waters flowing to Quebeq, four or five hundred leagues from here, to float on those that would thenceforward take us through strange lands'. Current and paddles united on the Wisconsin and 'we safely entered Missisipi on the seventeenth of June, with a joy that I cannot express'. The mingled prairie and river-bottom forest delighted them, as did the abundance of game-birds, fish, deer, bison and fruits of the soil. A huge cat-fish startled them considerably when it darted from the shallows and almost upset one of the canoes, and a wild-cat or lynx brought thoughts of tigers, but in general they felt that they had entered a rich and fruitful land.

The Indians were kindly and prosperous. A group of Illinois, who entertained them, provided them with a peace-calumet (pipe) which they used successfully throughout their voyage to assuage the hostility which the mere strangeness of their appearance might have caused. Their very bark canoes were a novelty, for the river Indians used dug-outs, some of them admirably made and as much as fifty feet long. The current helped them to paddle down the ever-broadening river and valley. They were deeply impressed by some coloured pictographs on a rocky bluff by the river near modern Alton. 'They are as large as a calf; they have horns on their heads like those of deer, a horrible look, red eyes, a beard like a tiger's, a face somewhat like a man's, a body covered with scales, and so long a tail that it winds all around the body, passing above the head and going back between the legs, ending in a fish's tail.'

They were disappointed to find that the Mississippi flowed so directly south, but one June day so mighty a flood swept in from the west that two Mississippis shared the same river-bed. The new river was the Missouri and it at once took its place in the minds of the travellers as the route to the Pacific. They stopped and consulted the Indians. They learned that by ascending it for five or six days they could reach a prairie about 100 miles wide, at the farther side of which there was another river which ran into a lake and thence to the Vermillion Sea. 'I have seen a village', wrote Jolliet to the King, 'which was not more than five days' journey from a nation that trades with those of California.' They decided to go on, however, and settle the problem whose answer they felt was more and more certain, namely, that the Mississippi flowed into the Gulf of Mexico.

They passed the mouth of the Ohio, where they visited the peaceful, abused Shawnees. Then, when they began to pass groups of Indians equipped with guns, they took the first fruitful opportunity to stop for definite information as to what lay ahead and how near they were to the sea. At a point just north of the mouth of the Arkansas (calculated by them as latitude 33° 40′), they had a long conference with the natives. 'They replied that we were only ten days' journey from the sea . . . that, moreover, we exposed ourselves to great dangers by going farther, on account of the continual forays of their enemies along the river, as they had guns and were very warlike.' 'We had obtained all the information that could be desired in regard to this discovery.' 'Beyond a doubt, the Missisipi River discharges into the Florida or Mexican Gulf, and not to the east in Virginia . . . or to the west in California.' 'We could give no information if we proceeded to fling

255

ourselves into the hands of the Spaniards, who, without doubt, would at least have detained us as captives.' They decided to return home.

The journey north against the current was very arduous. At the mouth of the Ohio, Marquette seems to have made the interesting experiment of entrusting a letter in Latin about himself and his mission to natives who said they traded with Europeans. Probably Marquette thought of the Spaniards, but it is possible that he hoped to forward the efforts which were then being made in New France to forge a link with the Jesuits and Franciscans of Maryland. At any rate, the letter fell into the hands of a Virginia trader, who passed it on to William Byrd of Virginia, who gave a copy to William Penn, who finally sent it to Robert Harley in England, among whose papers at Welbeck Abbey it was discovered 220 years later.

Fortunately the Illinois had told the explorers of a short route to Lake Michigan. They turned away from the Mississippi at the mouth of the Illinois, and paddled up that tranquil stream to a short portage which led to the lake. It was now mid-September. Marquette went off to recuperate at Green Bay, but Jolliet, after escorting him there, seems to have used the remaining good weather to explore the shores and possible portage routes near the southern end of the lake. He wintered with his Jesuit friend, making up his report and copies of it to leave with Marquette for safety. In the spring of 1674 he set off for the St. Lawrence, probably by the Great Lakes route and possibly with an interlude of conversation with La Salle at Cataraqui, where Frontenac had put him in command of the fort. Rather than delay his arrival by making the long portage late one July afternoon, he determined to shoot the rapids between Montreal Island and the south shore. His canoe was upset, his two canoe-men and an Indian boy given him by the Illinois were drowned, all his belongings were lost, and he himself was rescued by fishermen after four hours of struggle in the rapids. Warmly welcomed as he was by Frontenac and Dablon, he had neither map nor report to shew until Marquette could forward copies. Nevertheless his oral reports were sufficiently exciting, and these he reinforced with written accounts, drawn from memory, for the King, Colbert and Bishop Laval. The leaders of New France, lay and spiritual, were aflame with the vision of a water-way from Cataraqui to the Gulf of Mexico. Frontenac was so elated that he quite overlooked the Chicago portage in his report to Colbert. He may have salved his conscience by recalling that Jolliet had proposed to make a canal there 'intersecting only half a league of prairie'.

These hopes in New France of a new empire in the Mississippi valley were fated to be disappointed for many years. In 1672 Louis XIV had embarked on the series of wars in Europe which were to add little to his territories, ultimately to wreck almost all his plans, and seriously to damage the French colonial empire. Even the mercantilistic Colbert found arguments to justify him in approving the war policies, but the funds which might have built up French power in the Americas and in India went to equip armies in Europe. In Canada 'the fighting governor', Count Frontenac, had to do his best on meagre budgets, and Colbert refused to let him spread thin his resources by setting up a new colonial empire on the Mississippi. The Jesuits, too, gradually deprived of the broad popular enthusiasm which had made the seventcenth century so notable in missionary annals, entered upon the decline which was to end in their formal extinction. The exploitation of the Middle West fell into the hands of individuals and of small groups who learned how to make their labours pay, relatively unaided by the authorities in Quebec and Paris. Fortunately ten years of vigorous support had given New France the strength necessary for survival.

NARRATIVES

Louise P. Kellogg has collected in English translation narratives relating to Perrot, Allouez, Dollier and Galinée, St. Lusson, Jolliet and Marquette, in *Early Narratives of the North-West, 1634–1699* (New York, 1917). The *Jesuit Relations* (notably vols. xlv *et seq.*) and E. H. Blair's translations (see under Chapter XIV) from Perrot and La Potherie are also illuminating. The best edition of the Galinée narrative, together with the map and inscriptions, is by J. H. Coyne in Ontario Historical Society, *Papers and Records*, vol. iv (Toronto, 1903). L. F. Steck (*op. cit.* p. 253) gives the most recent study of the Jolliet-Marquette records. For the Marquette letter see C. W. Alvord in *American Historical Review*, xxv, July 1920, pp. 676-80.

CHAPTER XVI

PROBINGS FROM THE COASTAL COLONIES

(*Map No. 3, page 482*)

Like as those mountains [Appalachians] do cast from them streams into our north seas; even so the like they do into the South Sea, which is on the back of that continent.   EDWARD HAYES: TREATISE. 1602

Fish and Furres was then our refuge.
JOHN SMITH: DESCRIPTION OF NEW ENGLAND. 1614

WIDELY separated as they were in a largely unoccupied and unexploited continent, the European emigrants to North America gradually became aware that certain implicit rivalries were developing among them during the seventeenth century. At first the clashes were chiefly in claims to territory, accompanied by an occasional sea battle or by such raids as those on Acadia, Quebec or the short-lived Huguenot colony in Florida. Gradually, however, as the potentialities of the interior were realised, a few pioneers began to foresee conflict among those who planned to monopolise it. These men were remote from their home communities, but their eager imaginations ranged over the map as they knew or imagined it, sketching in a skeleton fabric of strategic sites like the Sault, Florida or the Hudson river, linked together by lines of communication like the external seas, the Great Lakes system or the Mississippi. Yet these ambitious designs had to be based on sedentary North American communities seldom able to

259

maintain them unaided, so that the parent communities in Europe had to be called upon for aid. These European states, which had been warring for years, after 1672 became embroiled in a series of wars which were to last with short interruptions until 1815. The succeeding repercussions of European and American rivalries in North America were almost equally continuous, but they concern us here only in so far as they promoted new American exploration.

While Spain and France, during the sixteenth and seventeenth centuries, had been drawn by various considerations to settle Mexico and its outposts, Florida, Acadia and Canada and explore extensively beyond them, the English, the Dutch and the Swedes had made the transition from fish to fur to settlement at various points along the main Atlantic coast, but had been relatively backward in investigating the interior. Superficially, conditions were not greatly unlike those which were met by the French, and settlement began in both regions during the same first decade of the seventeenth century. Fishermen became fur traders, the fur trade led to settlement, and the settlements during their first generation were saved from economic extinction by their exports of furs. 'There was no other means to procure the food which they so much needed and cloaths also,' wrote Governor Bradford of Plymouth.[1]

---

[1] This phase of American colonial history, developed for the St. Lawrence region in 1901 by H. P. Biggar, is only now receiving attention for the coastal colonies and still lacks its general historian. Interesting beginnings may be found in C. K. Bolton, *The Real Founders of New England* (Boston, 1929), and F. X. Moloney, *The Fur Trade in New England, 1620–1676* (Cambridge, Mass., 1931). The pursuit of furs inland has been the subject of a few regional studies, but also lacks its general historian. The narratives are very widely scattered. The late F. J. Turner, in his lectures and essays, frequently drew attention to the subject; see *The Frontier in American History* (New York, 1920).

Just as the St. Lawrence produced the *coureur de bois*, so did the Hudson evoke the *boschloper* and the English colonies the 'Indian trader'. Yet none of the coastal colonies gave birth to a Champlain, to a missionary effort like the Jesuits' or to a combination of practical ability and geographical imagination like Radisson's.

The reasons for this difference are, of course, not to be sought in any theories of relative national skills and adaptabilities. If there was any one controlling influence, it was topography. Except in the south, the coastal colonies were set up on the ocean margin of the relatively short eastern slope of a mountain system (Appalachian) which extended from the Gaspé peninsula almost to the Gulf of Mexico. The rivers which discharged into the Atlantic were only moderately long as compared with the St. Lawrence or Mississippi and they usually flowed south from meagre northern sources which were cut off by difficult country from the St. Lawrence valley or the basins of the Great Lakes and Mississippi. Thus all the colonies were located in good fur regions, so that they could and did provide the European hat-makers with beaver and the garment-makers with other furs. Most of them were extremely dependent on the fur trade to carry them through the period of their greatest dependence on Europe for supplies. Yet none of them ultimately either depended so exclusively upon fur as did New France or Hudson Bay, and none of them explored so vigorously in seeking it out.

Instead of that, each colony gradually built up some local economic enterprise or group of enterprises, first to supplement and then largely to supplant the fisheries and the fur trade. In the poorer agricultural regions, the timber trade and shipbuilding developed and were gradually crowned by an ever-growing maritime trading enterprise which quite overshadowed the inland Indian trade. Elsewhere agriculture was not merely good, but very remunerative, particularly where special crops like wheat, tobacco and rice were developed. While mercantilistic European governments did find it necessary and desirable to assist in the expensive business of trans-Atlantic colonisation, yet the intrinsic economic lure of life in the coastal colonies led to a far more extensive private and corporate immigration than New France ever enjoyed, with the result that when the general populations of the coastal colonies began to be interested in what lay beyond the Appalachians, it was chiefly because pressure of population demanded more land.

The ways through the mountains had been found for them by the Indian traders. These men belonged to a class from which many of the earliest colonial men of wealth were drawn, but a class which had declined in economic importance during the second colonial generation to become a mere adventurous fringe of the sedentary population. The earliest fur traders had to a large degree been sought out by the Indians of the eastern mountain slope, who brought their furs to depots on waters navigable from the coast. The native middleman problem had been relatively simple, although it had involved some wars. Competition among colonial traders themselves brought about most of the early exploration. As the seventeenth century drew towards its close, however, the fur traders, forced to go farther afield for undepleted regions, dropped down into the Mississippi valley just at the time that the French were entering it from the north. Using pack-horses more often than canoes, these men carried better and cheaper commodities than their competitors. There was actually a trade in trade-goods between the Hudson and Montreal. Small wonder, then, that international rivalry sprang up and was accompanied by new exploration.

The movement inland falls roughly into three categories: the probing of the coast and exploration of some of the larger rivers, the advance into the foot-hills or *piedmont*, and the discovery of the mountain passes. The first of these efforts went on at various parts of the coast from 1500 to about 1635 and was overlapped by the second, which began about 1625. The third movement, with the exception of the Hudson-Mohawk-Lake Ontario traverse, overlapped the second, beginning irregularly about 1650 and being pretty well completed before the British in 1755 embarked on the decisive war with France for North America. Geographically and historically the whole movement was less important than the exploratory work of Spain and France. Moreover, it was long-drawn-out and accomplished in piecemeal fashion, with no great integrating recorders like Oñate or Champlain. Its character and chief accomplishments, however, make necessary a somewhat intricate account.

We have already noticed the coastal explorations by the Cabots, the Portuguese, Verrazano and Gómez in the early sixteenth century, which may be said to have culminated in Cartier's investigation of the St. Lawrence.[1] The quest for the North-West Passage accompanied and succeeded that effort.[2] Meanwhile two factors kept drawing attention back to the main Atlantic coast; the sea (Pacific) which Verrazano thought he saw from the Atlantic and recorded on his

---

[1] Chapters VI, VII and VIII. [2] Chapter XIII.

map in the neighbourhood of Virginia, and the inland cities and mines of great richness which were associated with men's thoughts of Vaca, Soto, Marcos and Coronado, and which were believed to be not far inland from the Atlantic coast. The English were much interested, and it was to the most influential English group that David Ingram told his story of a populous, wealthy continent in 1582.[1] His huge inland rivers and lakes aroused images of Verrazano's sea, the Gulf of California and the Pacific.

Sir Walter Ralegh, who preferred colonisation and mining in the Americas to trading expeditions farther afield, had the coast reconnoitred for him in 1584 before sending out a short-lived colony to Roanoke Island (Virginia) the next year. Ralph Lane, one of the leaders, undertook some exploration for the sea and for goldmines, but had to be satisfied with Indian stories of both. Richard Hakluyt, England's Peter Martyr, was meanwhile industriously collecting all the information he could about the sea, the rivers leading towards it, the cities and precious metals, so that in England as well as in France there was a substantial body of men interested in the main Atlantic coast at the end of the sixteenth century. The seventeenth century opened with colonising adventures from both countries and with the Dutch close behind. Champlain spent the years 1604 to 1607 in the Bay of Fundy and in meticulous exploration of the coast. The English settled Jamestown in 1607 and at once explored inland and extended their coastal explorations northward. Henry Hudson happened on his great river in 1609 and the Dutch crowded up it in his wake.

The first phase in Virginia was the work of

[1] See pp. 142-5.

Christopher Newport, who obeyed King James' (or Hakluyt's) instructions by working his way up the James river as far as the present Richmond, and by John Smith, who gave most of his energies in 1607 to searching the seductive bays and estuaries of the neighbouring coast and questioning the Indians. Their actual discoveries were of course slight, for the rivers led to what seemed a continuous chain of mountains and Chesapeake Bay ended at the mouth of the Susquehanna river. That tempting, broad stream was barred by rocks and falls not far from its mouth. Yet the Indians, some of whom on the Susquehanna were already using some French tools, told vaguely of a sea or lake or river far in the interior, and Englishmen at home continued to believe that the sea lay just beyond the Blue Ridge mountains. Newport was equipped with a sectional boat for a vain expedition beyond the fall-line of the James river, and there was so much talk in England about a route to the Pacific and Asia that Spain found it worth while to send out spies to Virginia. Within five years of its founding, however, the rich returns from tobacco culture had begun to supplant exploration and mining in the minds of all save an optimistic minority of adventurers and a little group of fur traders. As time went on, the home geographers continued to make great play in arranging the Gulf of Mexico, Champlain's great lakes and Hudson's bay in appropriate relations to Virginia on their maps. The immediate effect of the Virginian ventures upon further exploration, however, arose from the assurances and maps which Smith sent to Henry Hudson indicating 'a sea leading into the western ocean, by the north of the southern English colony', somewhere about latitude 40°.

After his failure to pass Novaya Zemlya in May 1609

and the disturbances which arose among his mixed English and Dutch crew, Henry Hudson offered his company the choice of two alternatives—an expedition to latitude 40° on the American coast or a 'search through Davis's Straits'. They chose the milder climate. They reached North America from the arctic coast of Russia on 18 July, cut across the open sea from Nova Scotia to the vicinity of Cape Cod, and coasted southwards to the mouth of Chesapeake Bay, that is, Smith's own Virginia. There they turned north again in the second week of August to examine the coast more carefully. Delaware Bay failed to attract them for long, and instead they worked past the confusing sand-dunes and keys of what is now the coast of New Jersey, towards the promise of latitude 40°. On 3 September, at what they calculated to be 40° 30', they found themselves inside Sandy Hook entering upon a fruitful, pleasant region of islands and great river marshes. Indians came to their ship with tobacco and other articles to trade. Suspicion of their motives was justified, however, when they attacked a small boat and killed an English member of its crew. Proceeding cautiously, the *Half Moon's* company entered what is now Upper New York Bay on 11 September, possibly the first white men to do so since Verrazano, almost a century before. The low land and water screen made by the shores of Long Island, Staten Island and Sandy Hook had hitherto hidden the only river of the Atlantic coast which provided an entry to the interior at all comparable to that of the St. Lawrence.

The Hudson river owes its majesty to its great size and to its lofty shores. From the very mouth the west bank is an almost perpendicular high rock escarpment until it joins the Appalachians. Manhattan Island itself rises steadily towards the north and beyond it the east bank also becomes a line of hills which occasionally almost deserve the name of mountains. Between 11 September and 22 September Hudson sailed his small vessel up the noble valley as the leaves were changing to their brilliant autumn colouring. The matter-of-fact accounts of the voyage are full of references to the abounding richness of the country in fish, fur, game-birds and Indian crops. There was, of course, no ques-tion but that they were following a river, but its descent from the depressed interior was so gentle that the tide aided them to navigate for 150 miles before they had to explore farther in small boats. In these they seem to have reached a point close to the mouth of the Mohawk river.

From Sandy Hook to their stopping-place they were almost constantly in touch with Indians, some, like the Manhattans, hostile and intent on thievery or captures, and some 'very loving people' like the tribes in the Catskills, who, when they supposed that Hudson 'was afraid of their bows', 'taking the arrows, they broke them in pieces, and threw them into the fire'. Hudson's rather brutal crew had already had trouble with Indians at their first stopping-place far up the Atlantic coast, and on the river they killed quite a number of natives who alarmed or seemed ready to injure them. Yet these Indians possessed 'Bevers skinnes, and Otters skinnes, which we bought for Beades, Knives, and Hatchets'. Enthusiastic as the commentators were upon the Hud-son valley as a place for agricultural settlement, the actual economic lure which brought men back was the fur trade.

In spite of Hudson's detention in England in 1609, the Dutch returned to the river the next year; indeed

267

they pursued continuously what proved to be an exceedingly lucrative fur trade. Their skilled sea captains made excellent charts of the mid-Atlantic coast from Cape Ann to Virginia, except where, as along Long Island, sand-bars and keys produced a confusion which it was unprofitable to resolve. Meanwhile the *boschlopers* went off among the Indians to trade, particularly along the inviting Mohawk valley which led west from the Hudson. Champlain had earned the enmity of the Mohawks by assisting the Hurons to attack them near Lake Champlain just seven weeks before Hudson came with the coveted European goods to the mouth of their home river. Six years later, while waiting for another Huron war party to collect on the shores of Lake Simcoe, Champlain was glad to have Brulé go off to explain to the Andastes of the Susquehanna valley that the three European prisoners whom they had released the year before were Dutchmen and enemies of the French. It seems probable that those three men were the three who were ransomed near the junction of the Schuylkill and Delaware rivers in 1615 by Cornelis Hendricksen in the course of explorations there. They had gone up the Mohawk valley in the company of Indians and made their way south through the mountains to the Delaware valley, possibly with an interlude as prisoners of the Andastes in the Susquehanna valley. At any rate it would seem that while Brulé was making his way from Lake Huron to the sea, his Dutch competitors were doing the same thing from the Mohawk valley by the south-flowing Delaware river which lay between the Susquehanna and the Hudson.

We have seen how the Jesuits learned, as prisoners of the Iroquois, the two ways between the St. Lawrence and Hudson systems, the Richelieu river–Lake Cham-

268

plain–Lake George route and that from Lake Ontario to Lake Oneida and thence to the Mohawk. The Dutch, although not as enterprising as the French, had naturally known of these beforehand; indeed they, like Champlain and the Virginians, had for a time hoped to reach the Pacific. In his monthly news-letter for February 1624, Nicolaes van Wassenaer recorded the speculation derived from the reports of Indians who came to the Dutch posts more than thirty days' journey from the interior, 'that what many think may be true, that Hudson's Strait runs through to the South Sea, and is navigable'. Yet neither Hudson nor Delaware nor Susquehanna provided an approach except to the St. Lawrence and Lake Ontario, so that further Dutch effort went into the intense trade competition with the French and their Indian allies there.

There was one other long north-and-south river still to be explored—the Connecticut. In 1614, in the course of the early Dutch explorations, Adriaen Block had crossed the awkward bar at its mouth in Long Island Sound and had explored up-stream for about fifty miles. His successors found that they could tap the fur supply of the long, rich valley from its lower reaches and contented themselves with a depot near present Hartford. They had enjoyed almost twenty years of rich returns when, in 1633, an interloper, William Holmes of Plymouth Bay, sailed up the river past their fort and set up his post to intercept the flow. In the same year a group of Massachusetts Bay traders blazed the 'Old Connecticut Path' overland south-west from Boston to almost the same point on the Connecticut. The New England colonies, founded in close succession after 1620, were already reaching out for the furs which were so vitally important to struggling young American communities. Massachusetts Bay won the ensuing conflict among the three rivals for the Connecticut, but farmers pressed close on the heels of the traders and forced them to go up the river. The details of the succeeding years are interesting, but it must be sufficient to say that the valley was thoroughly explored, and that before England conquered the Dutch colonies in 1664, the New Englanders, disappointed to find that the Connecticut had its source in an impasse of inland mountains, had been for a generation suggesting that 'The New English Canaan' was incomplete without the Hudson and its access to the Great Lakes. They had already found a way overland from the Connecticut to the more promising river and had even sailed up it in defiance of the Dutch.

The aggressive New Englanders had also taken part in a Virginian-Dutch-Swedish struggle for the Delaware basin, but that conflict produced little important new exploration. The fur trade of the French in Acadia and Canada also attracted English competition before and after the founding of the New England colonies. Three years after his failure to penetrate Hudson Strait in 1602, George Waymouth was sent out to test the shores of New England for a passage, and his incidental success in the fur trade at the mouths of the rivers attracted numbers of emulators in succeeding years to the Penobscot, Kennebec and other rivers, all of which, they subsequently learned to their sorrow, sprang from the same impassable *massif* between the St. Lawrence and the Atlantic as did the Connecticut. The French managed to retain their hold on the St. John and to learn the very difficult traverse by it to Quebec. The only notable New England achievement was the equally difficult journey by the Kennebec and Chaudière to

Quebec which so interested Father Le Jeune at Quebec in 1640.[1]

Roughly speaking, then, the first and second phases of exploration from the coast were completed by 1650. From Cape Hatteras to the head of the Bay of Fundy the coastal inlets had been explored and the principal rivers had been followed until they dwindled away in the heart of the Appalachian highlands. One river system did provide two passages through the mountains, but both of these debouched in territories long exploited by the French, thus permitting only the bitter commercial and military rivalry whose effects on exploration we have already noticed.

By the time that Jolliet and Marquette had made their journey down the Mississippi in 1673, the third phase of exploration from the coast had begun, that is, the systematic quest for the best passes through the Appalachians and the attempt to control an easy route round their southern limit. This movement did not begin merely because the colonists were obsessed with dreams of cities, mines and the Pacific. Neither was the appetite for new lands as yet urgent, although settlement was killing the fur trade, which had already become a modest one among many economic activities. What seems to have happened is that the frontier Indian traders were working their ways into the mountains and meeting Indians who were on the outer fringes of the Indian distribution of Spanish and French goods, just at a time when North America and Europe were full of rumours as to what the French were planning to do after the curbing of the Iroquois. Jolliet and Marquette, for instance, had found many Mississippi Indians armed with guns, and Marquette's letter found its way

[1] See pp. 190-91.

to Virginia. Thus the interests of the Indian traders, who needed new fur regions and must win them from European competitors, and of the governors of their colonies, who were suddenly fearful of being kept to the east of the Appalachians by the Spanish and French, sharply coincided. It was time to enter the Mississippi basin. North of the head of Chesapeake Bay, the coastal slope afforded no inviting approaches, but southwards from that point there was great activity. The intricate pattern of the Appalachian mountains and valleys, lying for the most part parallel to the coast and across the course of the tide-water rivers, made the whole process of exploration a highly interesting bit of history, but its small scale relative to the whole design of continental exploration makes anything more than a general study of it inappropriate here.

Sir William Berkeley, governor in Virginia from 1642 to 1652 and from 1660 to 1677, was from the beginning of his term deeply interested in the fur trade, both for business and for territorial reasons. In the early 'forties, the Virginian Indian traders, from their lightly protected bases at the fall-line of the principal rivers, were faced by a decrease in the supplies of fur and skins from the *piedmont* and by the characteristic North American problem of obstructive, hostile Indian middlemen. As early as 1641 a group of traders petitioned the Assembly successfully for permission to explore farther, but in 1644 an Indian rising seriously threatened the very existence of the colony. Next year Governor Berkeley and the Assembly began to set up forts at the fall-line of the six principal rivers, and this show of strength provided the foundation upon which new exploration could be based. Chief of these posts was Fort Henry, founded in 1646 near the mouth of the Appomattox river (tributary to the James), partly because of its advantageous position between tide-water and *piedmont*, but largely because its commander was Abraham Wood. This man, once an indentured servant and now a substantial land-owner, was himself Virginia's most vigorous early explorer and as well the instigator and supporter of many others.

By 1648 word reached the governor through the Indians 'that within five days journey to the westward and by South, there is a great high mountaine, and at the foot thereof, great Rivers that run into a great Sea; and that there are men that come thither in ships . . . and have reed Caps on their heads, and ride on Beasts like our Horses, but have much longer eares'. Sir William planned to investigate these tales of the Spaniards, but was prevented. There was, however, a popular revival of all the old dreams of the South Sea ten days' journey away and hopes of mines or loot from New Spain. Just while the French were being driven out of the west by the Iroquois, the Virginians were preparing to break through their Indian warders and enter the Mississippi valley.

On 27 August 1650 Abraham Wood, Edward Bland and two other Virginian gentlemen, with two servants and a guide, left Fort Henry on horseback for the south-west. In spite of repeated discouragement by the favoured Indian middlemen, they travelled about 100 miles through what may well have been previously travelled territory between the James and the Roanoke, and traded a little in furs, although their general attitude was that of land speculators. They heard of other Englishmen trading beyond them, and in later years other known adventurers, of whose itineraries we know nothing, almost certainly broke some new trails in the same direction. For the next decade, however, the colony and its governor were much upset by the existence of the Cromwellian régime in England. Vigorous forward action by home and colonial administrations had to await the restoration of the Stuarts in 1660. Then in rapid succession came the capture of the Dutch colonies, the founding of the Hudson's Bay Company, a renewal of aggressive Virginian exploration and a blunt defiance to Spain in the founding of Carolina in 1670. Sir William Berkeley was the trusted American agent of the acquisitive group at Charles II's court which was involved in all these policies.

Colbert and Talon quickly realised what was involved in English competition from Hudson Bay and the Hudson river, but their own ignorance of the Mississippi valley made Virginian expansion an uncertain quantity. As early as 1668 Berkeley had written to an English court which was full of French agents, seeking permission for a substantial expedition to the West and rehearsing the old arguments about the Pacific and the Spanish mines, but at that time Charles II was secretly mortgaging his foreign policy to Louis XIV in return for financial assistance, and permission did not come. Yet while Berkeley waited, there came to him a German physician named John Lederer, who wanted nothing better than to be allowed to explore. Berkeley let him go out once in 1669 and on two expeditions in 1670. His generally reasonable narratives of these expeditions, which he published in London in 1672 (the year Frontenac went out to New France), were occasionally so highly picturesque and so uncritical in their judgements that his recorded achievements have sometimes been doubted. It is now believed, however, that he and his three separate groups of companions ascended in succession the Pamunkey, James and Rappahannock valleys towards the Blue Ridge mountains, and twice climbed that range to look westward over the Shenandoah valley to the even higher ridges of the Appalachians. The last part of his second journey he made alone, and his prettiest fables (of Amazons, pearls and peacocks) concern his wanderings in the region southwest of that explored by Wood and Bland. There he met some of the recently dispersed Eries, whose story of their wanderings led him to believe them to be from 'the island of New Albion or California'. Lederer's importance in the sequence of exploration, however, is that he tried and failed to find a pass from the *piedmont* through the Appalachians. The Indians told him there were two passes and he himself believed 'that the Indian ocean does stretch an arm or bay from California into the continent as far as the Apalataean mountains, answerable to the Gulfs of Florida and Mexico on this side'.

Before word could be received in England and Virginia of the discoveries of Jolliet and Marquette which dispelled this persistent will-o'-the-wisp, Abraham Wood had renewed his efforts. Indeed it can be argued by a generous geographical technicality that some of Wood's agents or some other Virginians actually preceded the Canadians by at least two years in reaching the lower Mississippi system. On 1 September 1671 Wood, perhaps already acquainted with the route, despatched Thomas Batts, Robert Fallam, Thomas Wood, a servant and an Indian guide 'for the finding out the ebbing and flowing of the Waters on the other side of the Mountains in order to the discovery of the South Sea'. Batts and Fallam crossed from Fort Henry to the valley of the Roanoke and that of its northern branch, the Staunton. Riding up the valley along an Indian trail, they followed the stream through a break in the Blue Ridge to its source close by the main Appalachian range. A passable, if steep, divide faced them on the morning of 13 September and they tackled it on foot. 'When we were got to the Top of the mountain and set down very weary we saw very high mountains lying to the north and south as far as we could discern', reported Fallam to the recently formed Royal Society in London. 'It was a pleasing tho' dreadful sight to see the mountains and Hills as if piled one upon another. After we had travelled about three miles from the mountains, easily descending ground about twelve of the clock we came to two trees marked with a coal MANI. the other cut in with MA and several other scratchments. Hard by a Run just like the swift creek at Mr. Randolph's in Virginia, emptying itself sometimes westerly sometimes northerly.'

Their creek was a remote tributary of the Mississippi, but some nameless Indian traders, whose marks they had already seen on a blazed tree in the Roanoke valley east of the Blue Ridge, had found the way before them. It would be hard to find a more dramatic token of the unknown explorers. All over North America these close-mouthed men, Spanish, French, Dutch and English, found new ways about the continent, yet only seldom have their names or their itineraries come down to us. An unknown Virginian first found the way through the Appalachians to the Mississippi valley.

Batts and Fallam found the stream to which the mountain brooks contributed and followed it until their food ran out on 16 September. They were then at the breach through the western edge of the main range, and their 'New' river flowed off to the north to join with

others and flow as the Kanawha into the Ohio and thence
to the Mississippi. 'We first proclaimed the King in
these words: "Long live Charles the Second, by the
grace of God King of England, Scotland, France, Ireland and Virginia".' They then fired a salute and
branded four conspicuous barked trees with marks for
the King, the Governor, Abraham Wood, themselves
and their heroic Indian guide Perceute. They even tried
to record the 'ebbing' of the New river, 'but found it
ebb very slowly'. As they went homewards, 'when we
were on the top of a Hill we turned about and saw over
against us, westerly, over a certain delightful hill a fog
arise and a glimmering light as from water. We supposed there to be a great Bay.' On 1 October they were
back at Fort Henry, but they brought back, as well as
their own report, Indian news of 'Mr. Byrd and his
great company's discoveries' that same month just beyond the Blue Ridge on their own route. This was
William Byrd, Abraham Wood's chief rival in the
fur trade and later the English recipient of Marquette's
letter. The Virginian penetration of the Appalachians
was obviously no accidental or isolated deed.

The last important contributions to the westward
movement from the coast before Jolliet and Marquette
had established the geographical character of the Mississippi, were to come from England's youngest and
southernmost colony, South Carolina. The very existence of that colony was a defiance of Spain, and its principal subsequent mission was the exertion of a steady
pressure which pushed the Spaniards and their frontier
missions south into the Florida peninsula. In its early
days, like the rest of the American colonies, it found the
fur trade extraordinarily useful as a source of ready
money, a course which its English backers approved

277

because of their interest in the same pursuit from Hudson Bay to Virginia. In fact the Carolinian exploration might well be regarded as a southern extension of the Virginian, for it was known in Virginia after Lederer's reports that the Appalachian barrier finally dwindled away to become *piedmont* about due west of Cape Fear, and it was Abraham Wood who supported, indeed launched from Fort Henry, the Carolinian leader who made the most important new explorations.

Before describing this achievement, one earlier Carolinian explorer deserves a place in the record. When Dr. Henry Woodward joined the colony at Charles Town in 1670, he had already spent four years in Carolina, Florida and the West Indies as friend of the Indians, prisoner of the Spaniards and ship's surgeon on a privateer. At Charles Town, as on the Hudson and the St. Lawrence, policy gradually shaped itself towards using friendly Indians to harass the opposing Europeans by attacking their Indian allies, in the hope ultimately to monopolise the profitable Indian trade of coast and interior. Woodward was the directing agent in this anti-Spanish policy, which entailed many trips of exploration into the interior to make Indian alliances. Before 1673 he seems to have investigated the country between the Santee and Savannah rivers and to have discovered the Indian agents for his purpose in the war-like Westos of the Savannah. Their town at the fall-line became a centre from which Woodward and other traders began to follow the Indian trails due north to the Catawbas in the Carolina Blue Ridge, north-west to the Cherokees at the southern end of the Appalachians, and due west towards the Creeks across the head-waters of the rivers which flowed into the Gulf of Mexico. The Carolinian proprietors had been delighted to learn from Dr. Lederer's narrative that 'the Apalataean Mountains (though like the prodigious Wall that divides China from Tartary, they deny Virginia passage into the West Continent) stoop to' Carolina, 'and lay open a prospect into unlimited Empires'. Woodward and his subordinates were the men chosen to exploit the advantage and they were hard at work at least in the *piedmont* by 1673. Not knowing exactly what they achieved, we must turn again to the recorded explorations from Virginia.

Some time in 1675 John Locke, the philosopher, drew up a memorandum on conditions in Carolina for his patron, Lord Shaftesbury, and to it he appended a laconic, business-like letter from Abraham Wood which described the concluding exploit of early Virginian exploration. On 10 April 1673 Wood sent off from Fort Henry, James Needham of Carolina, his own man Gabriel Arthur, and eight Indians, to follow the Occoneechee Path, an Indian trail which skirted the Blue Ridge as it ran away to the south-west, to see where the mountains ended. All went well until they reached the Roanoke fall-line where Wood and Bland had been in 1650, and where the Occoneechee Indians had since set themselves up as intermediaries between the Indians of the interior and the Europeans on the coast. These well-satisfied middlemen refused to let Needham and Arthur pass and they returned disappointed to Fort Henry.

Wood sent them out again on 17 May, apparently to go round the Occoneechee barrier, but this time they met a band of mountain Indians (Cherokees), and in their company brushed aside the 'unwillingness of the Indians before the mountains, that any should discover beyond them'. They rode down the path beyond the Roanoke for nine days, and then turned west across

279

the lessening heights of the Carolina Blue Ridge and the higher ranges beyond. After fifteen days of difficult travel, during which they lost all their horses but one, they came out on the western slope at the substantial fortified town which was the centre of the Cherokees. This town lay beside one of the head-waters of the Tennessee river, and most of its inhabitants, although they had Spanish goods, had never seen a white man or a horse. They treated the only surviving horse as Cortés' horse was treated in Honduras in 1524. 'A stake was sett up in the middle of the towne to fasten the horse to, and aboundance of corne and all manner of pulse with fish, flesh and beares oyle for the horse to feed upon.' The whites were entertained 'even to addoration' and were placed upon a scaffolding 'that theire people might stand and gaze at them and not offend them by theire throng'.

These Cherokees had been mishandled by the Spaniards and were overjoyed to establish direct contact with the English. It was at once arranged that Needham should take some of them to Wood, while Arthur remained to learn the language. Needham made the journey very quickly and on 20 September started back again. Meanwhile, however, the Occoneechees saw their favoured position cut from under their feet. As Needham's party passed through their town on his return to the Tennessee, an astute Occoneechee, John Hasecoll, who had belonged to the exploring party, plotted with his tribesmen to bring this threat to an end. Several Occoneechees followed the party along the path and, secure in their presence, Hasecoll picked a quarrel with Needham, under cover of which he suddenly murdered him. Then he 'drew out his knife stept acrosse the corpes of Mr. Needham, ript open his body, drew out his hart', and, clutching it, faced towards the English settlements in defiance. The Cherokees were aghast, but he bade them hurry off to kill Gabriel Arthur. He himself loaded Needham's horse with loot and returned to his village. Wood's record suddenly alters its tone. 'Soe died this heroyick English man whose fame shall never die if my penn were able to eternize it which had adventured where never any English man had dared to atempt before and with him died one hundered forty-foure pounds starling of my adventure with him. I wish I could have saved his life with ten times the vallue.'

The frightened Cherokees hurried home, sure that the English would be hostile now, and therefore themselves anxious to retain Occoneechee friendship and services by murdering Arthur. They had tied him to the stake for burning when their chief returned to the town and checked them by shooting the holder of the firebrand. He promised to take Arthur back to Fort Henry, but until that could be done, attached him to the tribe. In this capacity Arthur saw almost as much of the country as Soto had, more than a century before. One raiding party attacked a Spanish post in West Florida. Another looted an Indian village near Port Royal, but studiously spared an English trader among them. Then the chief himself took Arthur to visit some friendly tribes on the Kanawha beyond where Batts and Fallam had been in 1671. The Cherokees thought this visit a good occasion to pester the Shawnees whose eastern members lived where the Kanawha joins the Ohio, but they were thoroughly defeated and Arthur, twice wounded, was captured. The Shawnees, impressed by the oddity of his long hair, 'tooke Gabriell and scowered his skin with water and ashes, and when

281

they perceived his skin to be white they made very much of him and admire att his knife gunn and hatchett'. 'They had not any manner of iron instrument.' When he told them that they could get such a knife for four beavers and a hatchet for eight, they willingly freed him so that he could go back to initiate the trade.

He returned to the Cherokees and found the chief ready to keep his word, although what was possibly a river trip to the Gulf of Mexico intervened. The journey back to Fort Henry was of course interrupted by the Occoneechees, but after difficulties and dangers in which the party was split into fragments, Arthur and an Indian boy reached Abraham Wood's Fort Henry on 18 June and the chief, his two sons and a servant turned up in canoes from the James river on 20 July. The old commander was delighted and 'gave the king a good reward for his high favour in preserveing my mans life'. He also laid the foundations of Virginian trade with the Cherokees of the Tennessee.

Next year, strife arising out of the conflict between the frontier traders and the now aggressive settlers, brought civil war to Virginia and for a time exploration languished. In England Charles II was ruling by dividing his competitors and in consequence support for the colonies dwindled. Yet it is apparent that by 1675 from the Bay of Fundy to Florida the English colonies were at least prepared to make their bids for the interior of the continent. Their efforts had, in general, to wait until after 1688, when William of Orange, Louis XIV's only persistent opponent, supplanted the Stuart kings of England. In the north little new exploration could be expected from a conflict which was to be fought over well-known ground, either directly or through Indian allies. Yet south from the head of the Chesapeake, the struggle was still largely commercial and, as the thin screen of trade skirmishers who conducted it sought to bind the chief Indian groups to their colonial warehouses, the many-rivered eastern valley of the Mississippi was bound to be explored.

NARRATIVES

There is only one specific collection of narratives relating to these explorations: C. W. Alvord and L. Bidgood, *The First Explorations of the Trans-Alleghany Region by the Virginians, 1650–1674* (Cleveland, 1912). Many of the other narratives can be found scattered through the separate regional volumes of J. F. Jameson (general editor), *Original Narratives of Early American History* (18 vols., New York, 1906–1917).

CHAPTER XVII

FROM HUDSON BAY TO THE GULF OF MEXICO

(Maps Nos. 3 and 4, page 482 and end of book)

A very active Lad, Delighting much in Indians Company, being
never better pleased then when he is Travelling amongst them.

HENRY KELSEY, AS DESCRIBED BY THE COMMITTEE OF
THE HUDSON'S BAY COMPANY IN 1688

One of the greatest men of the age. He was a man of wonderful
ability, and capable of undertaking any discovery.

TONTI'S ESTIMATE OF LA SALLE

THE year 1670 might be chosen to mark the beginning of the active rivalry among the European
emigrants to North America which was to open up the
central basin of the continent. Spain, in Mexico and its
outposts, the Caribbean islands and Florida; France, in
the valley of the St. Lawrence and the basin of the
Great Lakes; and England, along the Atlantic coast
and the shores of Hudson Bay, began to reach out
towards each other in efforts to draw to themselves the
peoples and the products of the North American
regions which the Europeans were too few as yet to
occupy. The natives, even thousands of those who had
never seen a white man, were caught up in the uneasy
chain of disturbances and dependences which came
from using European goods. The 'curse of work' was
made worse for them by these new appetites, and they

284

found themselves unconsciously seconding the activities of the white traders in the opening up of untapped regions.

New France was considerably disturbed in 1670 when it heard that English ships had been trading in James Bay. The coveted northern furs had been carried down from that region to the St. Lawrence since before the days of Champlain. Now a competitor was reaping all the advantages of immediate contact with the fur collectors, almost without having to leave the ships which brought his trade-goods from Europe. The Jesuits of the Saguenay river and Lake St. John found that their hitherto annual visitors from the north were well content to trade with the English on the Bay itself instead of making the painful journey to the French posts. In New France it seemed imperative for the sake of trade and of religion that they should be wooed back to their old ways.

Talon decided to act at the Bay just as he planned to act at the Sault, on the Mississippi and in contested Acadia, that is, to send out an emissary who should formally proclaim French sovereignty. To supplement this overland mission, he proposed to allow some adventurers to take a sixty-ton vessel at their own expense into Hudson Bay 'to discover in this region the communication between the Sea of the North and the Sea of the South'. We have no record of an attempt by sea at this time, but on 6 August 1671 there set out from Quebec for Tadoussac and the Saguenay, Paul Denis, Sieur de St. Simon, Father Charles Albanel, the already experienced Jesuit traveller and recorder of the journey, one other Frenchman and an Indian escort. They were instructed to 'push through' to Hudson Bay and investigate the possibility of setting up a wintering place

285

and revictualling station there for ships on their way to the Pacific. Winning back the fur trade was to be their chief concern, and St. Simon was commissioned to take possession of the region by the claim of first discovery 'with orders to raise there the escutcheon of France which he carries with him'. 'Hitherto this journey has been deemed impossible for the French, who had already thrice attempted it', reported Albanel. After he had completed it, he reckoned that there were 200 portages round waterfalls and 400 rapids up which the canoes had to be poled instead of paddled.

Thirteen years before, Radisson had asserted that the Indians of the Saguenay would not let the Jesuits establish direct contacts with the Hudson Bay Indians,[1] and the French party did have the greatest difficulty both in getting away from Tadoussac and later in passing such natural middlemen's stations as Lake St. John and the height of land just south of Lake Mistassini. They had to call upon all their resources of prestige and determination in order to break through. On 17 September they were on or near Lake St. John when they met five canoe-loads of Indians from the deeper interior 'bringing word that 2 vessels had anchored in Hutson's bay and conducted extensive trading with the Savages'. Radisson and Groseilliers, each with a ship, had wintered at Charles Fort at the mouth of the Rupert river in 1670–71. St. Simon and Albanel decided that they had better not run the risk of meeting these English visitors without passports. By the time messengers had gone to Quebec for them and returned, however, it was 10 October and too late in the year to go on. The party wintered near Lake St. John, with reasonable comfort so far as food and shelter went, but

[1] See p. 230.

286

under constant bullying from their Indian escort to retreat.

The party of three Frenchmen and sixteen Indians started north again on 1 June 1672, faced by ten days of the hardest kind of travel up the rivers which tumbled down from the Laurentian height of land. 'Very often we had to land and march through the woods, climbing over rocks, jumping down into hollows, and scrambling up steep cliffs again through clumps of trees whose branches tore our clothes. . . . Even the Savages dread this journey, as one full of fatigues and peril.' They reached the height of land portage on 10 June, and after six days of negotiation with its Indian guardians, crossed it to the 100-mile expanse of Lake Mistassini. 'It is no new thing for the Savages . . . to be extremely cautious in granting strangers a passage, by way of their rivers, to distant Nations. The rivers are to them what fields are to the French, their sole source of subsistence —whether in the form of fish and game, or in that of traffic', wrote Albanel. He saw no anomaly, however, in exhorting the Mistassinis to 'abandon the plan of carrying on commerce with the Europeans who are trading toward the North Sea, among whom prayer is not offered to God; and resume your old route to Lake St. John where you will always find some black gown to instruct and baptize you'.

Near the outlet of Lake Mistassini the shore was low and the water shallow, and Albanel preserved a lively vignette of the northern wilderness for us, when he reported his 'pleasure to see the bears walking on the shores of this piece of water, and, as they go, catching with a paw now one fish and now another, with admirable dexterity'. The French party made all possible speed to the outlet, the Rupert river system which led to the Bay. The natural richness of the valley and the 'sad monuments' of the Iroquois raids which had depopulated it made them recall the blessings of Tracy's curbing of the Iroquois and determine to remind the Bay Indians of what France had done to earn their gratitude. By 28 June the Rupert was becoming a tidal estuary, and almost the first thing that morning 'we encountered, in a small stream on our left, a hoy [sailing vessel] of ten or twelve tons, with its rigging, carrying the English Flag and a lateen sail. A musket-shot's distance thence, we entered two deserted houses.' The journey which Champlain had contemplated in 1603,[1] had at last been made and 'all that evening' the travellers sat on the shore about twenty miles north of the river-mouth, 'amusing ourselves with watching the sea which we had so long sought'. 'There was no night during my visit', said Albanel, but one wonders whether it was enthusiasm and the midnight sun which kept them up or 'the persecution of those little sharp-stinging flies known as mosquitoes and black flies'. Two days before, they had found it impossible to sleep even with the protection of smokes from smudge fires.

They quickly succeeded in establishing relations with their Cree friends on the East Main river and carried out their tasks of proclaiming French sovereignty and of reminding them that it had been the French who cowed the Iroquois. The attempt, at least, had been made to draw the Bay Indians to the Saguenay again for trade-goods and spiritual comfort. Moreover when Radisson and Groseilliers returned to their post from a voyage to the north-west, the emissaries from Canada were able to open the negotiations which were ultimately to win Radisson temporarily and Groseilliers

[1] See pp. 152-3.

permanently back into the service of France. Governor
Bayly of the Company was very angry, but respected
the Frenchmen's passports.

Albanel was a little awed by the vast tidal flats along
the shores of shallow James Bay, but in general he
found the country fruitful and attractive in summer.
'I can assert that on the fifteenth of June there were
wild roses here, as beautiful and fragrant as those at
Quebec.' He knew, however, that summer was short.
The return journey, which began from the East Main
on 5 July, was a swift one, with occasional halts to set
up the arms of France along the route to Mistassini, but
with no hindrance from the Indians. Lake St. John was
reached on 23 July and Chicoutimi on the Saguenay
on 1 August.

In the years which followed this great journey by
St. Simon and Albanel, France and England fought on
land and sea until 1713 for the control of the Bay fur
trade. It was early revealed that the war must be carried
on by vessels in the Bay. The journey overland from the
St. Lawrence was too difficult to compete with the sea
passage except in emergencies. Yet the existence of the
conflict did bring about the exploration of the Saguenay-
Mistassini-Rupert traverse and of the equally difficult
Ottawa-Lake Timiskaming-Abitibi traverse which was
followed by a French war party in 1685–86. This band
of 100 men proceeded from the Ottawa to Lake Abitibi
on snowshoes, built canoes there, and raced down to the
Bay on the spring flood of 1686. The details of these
explorations and re-explorations need not be repeated
here. Perhaps the most convenient way to think of
them is in terms of the rivers which flowed down from
the height of land in opposite directions to the English
and French depots. Thus the East Main and the

19

Rupert can be set over against the Saguenay, the Abitibi over against the Ottawa, the Albany over against Lake Nipigon and Lake Superior, and the Nelson and Hayes over against the maze of rivers and lakes north-west of the western end of Lake Superior. The French well knew that the Indians of the mid-continent found Hudson Bay nearer than Montreal and would go there unless the French themselves set up depots on the upper Great Lakes.

The French were excluded from the Bay by the Treaty of Utrecht in 1713, in spite of having had distinctly the better of the warfare there both by sea and by overland attacks. They had also done most of the exploring from the St. Lawrence system over the height of land to the basin of Hudson Bay. Actually this economic competition, first thought of by Radisson and Groseilliers about 1660, was destined to continue in various forms until 1821 and to have a continuous influence on exploration almost to that date. Its successive steps can be pictured with a good deal of correctness by following the coast of Hudson Bay clockwise from river-mouth to river-mouth, beginning with the Rupert and ending with the Churchill. Alone, the Hudson's Bay Company could have drawn the Indians from the height of land, and beyond, down these rivers to the Bay without going out to find them, but their French and later English competitors from Montreal kept moving along the southern and later the western slopes of the same height of land to cut off the flow of furs to the Bay from the interior. Whenever the Company found that the Indians had stopped coming down to the Bay, they knew that the Montrealers were drawing the furs the other way. It can easily be imagined that this rivalry meant new exploration.

The first notable Company explorations were carried out by 'the Boy Henry Kelsey', who had come out to Port Nelson, a lad of fourteen, in 1684, and had enjoyed acquaintance with the great Radisson, with the son of Groseilliers, Jean Baptiste Chouart, and with Elie Grimard, another able *coureur* in the Company's service. The Company trading-posts, first at Port Nelson at the mouth of the Nelson and then at York Factory at the neighbouring mouth of the Hayes, affected the Indians who lived near the valleys of the two rivers, and even those beyond the height of land in the cluster of lakes and streams near Lake Winnipeg. In 1682 Radisson had made a swift trip of about 100 miles up the Hayes river to invite the Indians down to trade, but the other Company men believed that the Indians would seek them out at the Bay. At the same time the French on Lake Superior and Lake Nipigon were trying to attract the same Indians to come south-east to trade.

It is not clear how immediate the effects of this competition were on York Factory; but all through the 'eighties the Company Committee in London was trying in vain to convert some of its servants at the Bay posts into direct negotiators with the inland Indians. Kelsey seems to have been the only notable exception, 'Delighting much in Indians Company, being never better pleased then when he is Travelling amongst them'. As early as mid-June 1689, having already made the overland journey from the Nelson to the Severn when Indian messengers failed, he was landed with an Indian boy as his only companion on the coast about sixty miles north of the mouth of the Churchill, in order to establish contact with the Indians of the interior. After a difficult circuit of about 200 miles in the barren lands, in which he saw and killed musk oxen and proved to be

a better pioneer than the Indian, he was forced by his
companion's fear of meeting Eskimos to return without
having found the Indian tribes. If the London committee had to be obeyed, Kelsey was obviously the man
to carry out their orders.

'This Summer', reported Governor Geyer in 1690,
'I sent up *Henry Kelsey* (who chearfully undertook the
Journey) up into the Country of the *Assinae Poets*, with
the Captain of that Nation, to call, encourage, and invite, the remoter Indians to a Trade with us.' Unfortunately some whim or self-conceit induced Kelsey to
record the first stages of his journey in atrocious dog-
gerel verse. He had no gift for that form and he was no
geographer. The narrative, therefore, has an inherent
vagueness which is intensified by Kelsey's determination to make his uneven lines rhyme, even by dragging
in inappropriate words. Here are some samples:

> Now Reader Read for I am well assur'd
> Thou dost not know the hardships I endur'd . . .
> Trusting still unto my masters Consideration
> Hoping they will Except of this my small Relation
> Which here I have pend & still will Justifie
> Concerning of those Indians & their Country
> If this wont do farewell to all as I may say
> And for my living i'll seek some other way.

What seems to have happened is that Kelsey set out
from York Factory on 12 June 1690 and made his way
up the Hayes river as Radisson had done in 1682. There
is no indication of his route from the Hayes, but he
probably followed the Indian canoe-route from Oxford
Lake across the broken height of land to the northern ·
end of Lake Winnipeg. From that point he went up the
Saskatchewan river into Cedar Lake and, either on the
portage between that lake and Lake Winnipegosis or

near The Pas farther up the Saskatchewan, on 10 July he chose a site to serve as his base of operations. Mark the vagueness with which he located this point, from which in turn his subsequent travels must be orientated.

> And for my masters I speaking for them all
> This neck of land I deerings point did call
> Distance from hence by Judgement at the lest
> From the house [York Factory] six hundred miles southwest
> Through Rivers which run strong with falls
> thirty three Carriages five lakes in all.

His first task was to make peace between the plains Indians 'which knows, No use of Better than their wooden Bows' and the 'home Indians' who had recourse to the Bay. Although this peace was broken almost at once by the 'home Indians', Kelsey determined to give his whole energies to establishing a general peace among the natives, so that from near and far they would go to the Bay to trade. Before the winter closed in, he accompanied a hunting party which went south-west from the Saskatchewan into the open prairie. He was thus the first European to see the Canadian plains. After the maze of rivers and lakes between Hudson Bay and Lake Winnipegosis it was something of a shock to come on a stretch of prairie forty-six miles wide which 'affords nothing but Beast & grass'. The animals interested him—'a black a Buffilo great' and 'an outgrown Bear which is good meat'. He was relieved to find that occasional woods and water-ways interrupted the prairie, for the Indians would not let him take bearskins because of their reverence for the animal and he had no transportation adequate for buffalo-hides.

> This wood is poplo ridges with small ponds of water
> there is beavour in abundance but no Otter.

He seems to have wintered somewhere in the plains or

at his Deerings Point, but we cannot trace his movements. In midsummer Indians arrived at Deerings Point, bringing the supplies for which he had written to Governor Geyer in the spring. Included in them was a peace-calumet, which, like that carried by Jolliet and Marquette twenty years before, proved to be of great usefulness. Equipped once more, he set off on 15 July 1691, 'through Gods assistance to discover & bring to a Commerce the Naywatame poets'.

Kelsey made a careful, if not very revealing, prose narrative of his journeyings in 1691 and a scanty summary up to the spring of 1692. He was facing the universal middleman problem by trying to break through, make a general peace among the tribes and organise their annual recourse to York Factory. He repeatedly told them 'that they must Imploy their time in Catching of beavour for that will be better liked on then their killing their Enemies when they come to the factory'. He had temporary successes, but the persistent economic bias of the Indians who had formerly gone to the Bay made them break the truces. Moreover, the plains Indians were not canoe-men like the Assiniboines (who lived between the plains and the Laurentian Shield) and could not easily go down to the Bay. The really remarkable thing was that this English youth just attaining his majority, a peacemaker where there was no peace, should have been able to maintain himself for two years alone among the Indians of the interior, aided only by a peace-pipe and by such fire-arms and small presents for the Indians as could be easily carried. Kelsey 'travelled light' and confidently interfered in Indian strife, leaving no trace of fear in his narrative except of occasional near-starvation. He combined, much as Brulé did, the ability to exploit his natural prestige and at the same time to be better at Indian living than the Indians.

Between 15 July and 12 September, when he finally caught up with the fugitive chief of the Naywatame-poets,[1] Kelsey calculated that he had travelled about 585 miles, chiefly on foot. The Indians had no animal transport except dogs and sledges in winter, and, in summer, dogs drawing the same kind of wooden frames (*travois*) as Coronado had seen in 1541 far away in the south-west. Just where he went it is impossible to say. Neither is it apparent what he did between September 1691 and the summer of 1692, when he returned to York Factory. On his journey of 1691 he seems to have gone up the Saskatchewan and the Carrot river (which enters it from the south-west just beyond The Pas). Then, abandoning his canoes, he set out on travels whose direction was determined by news of the Indians he sought and by the prospects for game. It would probably be fair to think of him as having covered a good deal of the territory bounded by the united Saskatchewan, its southern branch, the head-waters of the Assiniboine and the north-west corner of Lake Winnipegosis. The plains Indians were friendly, but had good cause to fear the Assiniboines and Crees, who, by murdering some of their people, frightened them from keeping the promise made to Kelsey to go down to York Factory in 1692. Governor Geyer reported in 1692 that 'Henry Kelsey came down with a good fleet of Indians', but these were the old middleman and canoeman tribes. Kelsey also brought with him in his lively narratives interesting and intelligent accounts of the plains Indians and of such of their customs as the buffalo hunt upon which their lives depended. He even

[1] Probably La Vérendrye's Assiniboines or Mandans. See Chapter XX.

took care to differentiate between buffalo and musk oxen and between the enormous grizzly bears which he encountered and the better-known southern and northern varieties.

In later years Kelsey very much wanted to explore the western shore of Hudson Bay and the interior beyond it. Increasing responsibilities in the Company prevented this, however, and with his return from the interior in 1692 the curtain fell over for half a century on land exploration from the Bay. An isolated figure in the early history of the Company, Kelsey was for long almost unknown outside the Company records and the traces of his knowledge in the reports and maps made by the Frenchmen who fought at Hudson Bay. Now, thanks to the discovery of his papers in 1926, it has been possible to indicate his place in North American exploration.

While French and English rivals for the fur trade had been contributing to the exploration of the northern end of the mid-continent, the linking up of the St. Lawrence and Mississippi systems by Jolliet and Marquette at Talon's instigation had raised the curtain on rivalries among France, England and Spain in the central and southern portions. As Isaac Cox has put it, France began to drive a wedge down the Mississippi, whose pressure was immediately felt by the English and Spanish colonies. In the vigorous enterprises which ensued, the name of La Salle figured prominently, and if he does not seem to play so large a part in these pages, it is because new exploration was not his chief preoccupation. Radisson had had a great idea about using Hudson Bay and had himself put it into execution. La Salle seems to have failed to find the Mississippi between 1669 and 1672, and, after Jolliet and Marquette succeeded in 1673, he was not able to give reality to his similar idea about using the Gulf of Mexico. For one thing, he did not go over to the service of Spain as Radisson had to that of England.

In addition, however, it must be admitted that La Salle's ideas were usually in advance either of his times or at least of the resources available to execute them. In succession, he saw the advantages, first of a French trading-post on Lake Ontario to offset the Iroquois and the English, then of reducing trade costs by building sailing cargo vessels both for Lake Ontario and for the uninterrupted expanses of Erie, Huron and Michigan, and finally of building similar vessels on the Mississippi to carry the poorer southern furs and buffalo hides and buffalo wool down to the ice-free Gulf of Mexico. Yet he cannot be said to have carried any of these shrewd ideas to efficient completion. His business affairs rapidly became a mountainous tangle of debts. He had an incurable way of building superstructures before foundations were set. He made more enemies than friends and lost more servants than he kept. The Jesuits and the fur traders tried hard to defeat him, and even his relations with the Sulpicians and Récollets whom he liked were not free from difficulties. Finally, he developed a proud melancholic stubbornness which brought him so close to insanity as to seem insane to some of his contemporaries and modern recorders.

La Salle's reputation has been very much the victim of the romanticists of his own day and ours and of his opponents in the commercial and religious conflicts in which he was implicated. For instance, the gibe involved in the name 'La Chine' given to his Montreal seigneury, gave him the reputation of a persistent seeker for the Pacific and Asia long after he had given up both the seigneury and his earlier hopes. Actually there is abundant evidence that La Salle (the son of a rich merchant of Rouen) was primarily a fur trader, who hoped to revolutionise the business by large-scale methods and the use of cargo vessels on the Great Lakes, the Ohio and the Mississippi. He foresaw international difficulties with England and Spain and planned to forestall them by swift territorial aggression and by defensive forts at regular intervals from the St. Lawrence to the Gulf of Mexico. Once mistress of the heart of the continent, France must colonise it. She would then dominate the Indian trade and be able to keep the English east of the Alleghanies and hold the Spaniards in the South-West. Then perhaps the West might be explored for a route to the Pacific or whatever else was to be found.

The story of La Salle's life from 1669 to 1687 is a fascinating one, crowded with examples of keen imagination, extraordinary enterprise and the deepening tragedy of accumulating failure which ended in his murder at the hands of his own associates. It involved an immense amount of travel on land and water, most of which was naturally over already explored regions. He did, however, add some important new elements to the geographical knowledge of his day.[1]

When La Salle went west on Lake Ontario with the Sulpicians in 1669,[2] he had been in New France only three years. He had, however, made friendly contacts

[1] The controversial records and comments concerning La Salle began in his own lifetime and have greatly increased since then. It is therefore doubly unfortunate that Pierre Margry, who published the only comprehensive body of the early records, has since been shewn to have been not merely a careless transcriber, but on occasion a perverter of the form and sense of what he printed as original manuscripts. The accounts which follow are an arbitrary interpretation of conflicting evidence.

[2] See pp. 244-5.

fair way to realise his great commercial scheme of a small fleet operating between the posts of Cataraqui and Niagara, a larger vessel operating from above Niagara Falls to a post on Lake Michigan, and another large vessel built on the Illinois river to sail down to the Gulf of Mexico. He had made two journeys to France and had secured royal letters-patent 'to discover the western part of New France . . . through which it would appear that it will be possible to find a way to penetrate to Mexico'. The same grant permitted him to erect forts under his own seigneurial control and authorised his monopoly of the Mississippi valley for five years on the condition of not taking part in the ordinary Montreal trade. He had carefully studied the narratives of the Spanish explorers of the Mississippi valley in preparation for his new field of activity. His ship, named *Le Griffon* 'in honour of the arms of M. de Frontenac', had just made its first trip to Lake Michigan and had been sent back from Green Bay to Niagara in mid-September, loaded with furs to appease his creditors. He had set up one post on the St. Joseph river at the southern end of Lake Michigan and another on the Illinois river, where he was building a boat for the Mississippi journey. Certain special supplies for its completion were to be brought back by *Le Griffon*.[1]

October, November and December of 1679 passed without any signs of *Le Griffon*. Probably it was wrecked in a September storm which had delayed La Salle himself for six days, but there were also Indian rumours in later years that it was destroyed through the agency of

[1] It was during the building of this ship that Father Louis Hennepin, accompanied by Father Gabriel de la Rebourde, visited Niagara Falls and described them in detail for the first time.

the middleman Indians somewhere on Lake Michigan.
The best account attributed the loss to the refusal of the
Danish pilot to be advised by men who knew Lake
Michigan. Father Hennepin described him as one
'whom we could never oblige to pray; and he did
nothing . . . but curse and swear against M. de la Salle,
who had brought him thither to make him perish in a
nasty lake and lose the glory he had acquired by his
long and happy navigations on the ocean'. La Salle
himself was having such great difficulty in breaking
through the Illinois and Miami Indians at the southern
end of Lake Michigan that his men were frightened
into trying to desert to Michilimackinac or even, with
Iroquois guidance, to Albany and New York. The
possible loss of *Le Griffon* was more serious still, and in
February 1680 he decided to walk to Niagara for news,
leaving his resolute and competent Italian lieutenant,
Henri de Tonti, in command at Fort Crèvecœur on the
Illinois.

He set out from Crevecœur with six Frenchmen and
an Indian guide on 1 March 1680, to cross from Lake
Michigan to Lake Erie at the time of year when rivers
and lakes were still icebound, but alternately thawing
and freezing. Until the rivers broke loose and drained
the country-side a little, it was a spongy expanse of soft
snow, slush, treacherous ice and occasional muddy soil.
There were very heavy rains, but also frosts. Snow-shoes
were next to useless. There was not enough water on
top of the river-ice for canoes to travel, nor could the
risk be run of their being cut to pieces by the ice where
it had broken up. At the beginning of the journey the
party went to the trouble of making sleighs for their
canoes, but finally they abandoned one canoe and left
the other with Indian friends who promised to take

maize to Crèvecœur in it. It was now a matter of marching on foot through woods and marshes and streams and carrying along the leather to make a new pair of moccasins or at least moccasin soles every night. Rivers were waded or crossed on rafts. Food, except for a little maize, depended on luck and marksmanship. Worst of all, the whole country was upset by the revival of Iroquois pressure on the Illinois, and the tribal groups were tense and apprehensive of the war which was to come so soon.

La Salle reached his fort on the St. Joseph river on 24 March. His men there had no news of *Le Griffon* although they had left Michilimackinac (where it should have touched) three months after it sailed. In spite of heavy spring rains, he and three Frenchmen and their guide set out again 'through woods so tangled with brambles and thorns that in two and a half days he and his men had their clothing cut to pieces and their faces so scratched and bloody that they were unrecognizable'. When two of the party fell ill, he cast about for a stream flowing to Lake Erie and built a canoe. Logs and trees in the river-bed made the canoe useless, so that they ultimately reached the vicinity of modern Detroit on foot again. Two men were ordered to build a canoe and go back by Lake Huron to Michilimackinac for news of *Le Griffon*, while La Salle and the others, having crossed the mighty Detroit river on a raft, marched along the north shore of Lake Erie. Once again flooded lands and the illness of one Frenchman and the Indian made them take to canoe. They reached Niagara on 21 April, after what seems to have been the most difficult journey yet made by Europeans in New France. La Salle left his French companions at the Niagara fort, and marched on with three fresh men through almost continuous rain to Cataraqui, which he reached on 6 May. Not only had he received no news of *Le Griffon*, but word had reached Niagara of the loss of his new European supplies at sea. His own fortitude deserved a better reward, for it had been an amazing feat to walk from the Illinois to the St. Lawrence in a little over two months.

It was not until two years later that La Salle was able to make his long-deferred journey to, and down, the Mississippi. Among his many intervening misfortunes was the enforced abandonment of the half-completed ship on the Illinois river, so that it was a large canoe party which he assembled at the Chicago portage in January 1682. He had selected his Indian canoe-men from the Acadian, New England and Delaware valley tribes in order to avoid the difficulties and entanglements likely to arise out of the Iroquois-Illinois war. His party amounted to twenty-three Frenchmen, eighteen Indian men, ten Indian women and three children. In the depth of winter they dragged their canoes and supplies across to the Illinois river and down it past the devastated Illinois village centre to the site of Fort Crèvecœur. They were able toe mbark there, although they were held up by ice at the junction with the Mississippi from 6 February to 13 February.

In one sense the journey to the Gulf was not remarkable. Jolliet and Marquette had really established the character of the Mississippi in 1673. Yet in another sense the very nine years which had elapsed without use being made of the discovery indicate the obstacles which had still to be surmounted. Not least of these was the revival of Iroquois ambitions in the west and south and the tribal disturbances which it caused near the Lakes. La Salle had hoped to find and use the central river for thirteen years before he navigated it, and when the time came, he did so with a small armada of canoes. He had hoped to sail south in an imposing, armed sailing-vessel. He did not mean to be intimidated from completing the voyage to the Gulf as his predecessors had been.

In the early spring of 1682 his party paddled swiftly down the river, mightily impressed by its size, by the fertility of the soil and the abundance of game, and by the advanced culture of the Indian tribes which they passed. Their passage down was marked by occasional formal negotiations with these Indians and by the setting up of the French arms and the ceremonial taking of possession, but they met no serious obstacles except shortage of food near the river-mouth where marshes prevented them from landing to hunt for game. Father Zenobius Membré recorded their unpleasant surprise at discovering on this occasion that some dried meat which they obtained was human flesh. 'It was very good and delicate . . . we left the rest to our Indians.' Contrary to all expectations, 'we saw no Indians who used firearms, or even iron or steel articles'. In one village they saw a Spanish sword and three old guns hanging unused on the wall of a hut. The only explanation for this change from the conditions of 1673 is that the trade channels between the Indians and the English and Spaniards had been interrupted by some large dislocations or native wars.

'Advancing on, we discovered the open sea, so that on the ninth of April, with all possible solemnity, we performed the ceremony of planting the cross and raising the arms of France. After we had chanted the hymn of the church, "Vexilla Regis" and the "Te Deum", the Sieur de la Salle, in the name of His Majesty, took possession of that river, of all rivers that enter it and of all the country watered by them.'

That audacious claim made in the spring of 1682 was, after all, a fitting testimonial to the enterprise of the French and to the failure of Spain to link up Florida and Mexico by developing the rich lands which had been so extensively explored by the Spanish city-hunters of the sixteenth century. It may be that it was hardly La Salle's due to have the honour of first travelling from the Great Lakes to the Gulf of Mexico, but New France assuredly deserved the honour. Within eighty years her sons had probed the whole St. Lawrence system to its western limit and had capped their achievement by linking up with it the northern and the southern entries to the continent.

NARRATIVES

Father Albanel's own narrative is in *Jesuit Relations*, vol. lvi. For the 1686 expedition by the Abitibi, see I. Caron, *Journal de l'expédition du Chevalier de Troyes à la Baie d'Hudson, en 1686* (Beauceville, P. Q., 1918). *The Kelsey Papers*, edited by A. G. Doughty and C. Martin (Ottawa, 1929), should be supplemented by the comments of J. F. Kenney, who supervised the transcription and publication, in 'The Career of Henry Kelsey', *Royal Society of Canada Transactions*, Third Series, vol. xxiii, sect. ii (Ottawa, 1929); and by C. N. Bell, *The Journal of Henry Kelsey* (Winnipeg, 1929). Pierre Margry's collection of materials on La Salle is the most comprehensive, but is not entirely dependable—*Découvertes et Établissements des Français, etc.* (6 vols., Paris, 1879–88), vols. i–iii. A useful, but poorly edited, supplementary collection of narratives and extracts in English translation is I. J. Cox, *The Journeys of La Salle* (2 vols., New York, 1905).

CHAPTER XVIII

THE RACE FOR CONTROL OF THE
MISSISSIPPI

(*Map No. 3, page 482*)

DURING the fifty years after La Salle's journey
down the Mississippi the eastern half of the valley
was in an uneasy ferment which was kept up by the
yeasts of rival European policies emanating from many
points on its circumference. The historian can record
the ferment and can even identify some of the human
agents in it, but he faces a baffling situation when he
tries to build up an explicit sequence of the exploration
of the region. All through that rich country, along its
scores of navigable rivers and its scarcely less useful
buffalo trails, through its forests and across its park-
like meadows, dozens of anonymous men were busy in
the Indian trade. Some of them moved from the Atlantic
to the great river, others from the Great Lakes to the
Gulf of Mexico. Some lived most of their lives in
Indian villages or in lonely cabins far beyond the outskirts of settlement, some were carried here and there
as prisoners, and some made vigorous, precise reconnaissances to unify fragmentary knowledge or establish
military and commercial alliances. They were more than
mere fur traders, for by the end of the seventeenth
century the Indian market for European goods had
become an end in itself and the Indians were collecting

sassafras, tanning buck-skins and building up a steady trade in buffalo hides and buffalo wool. In the South-East the demands for cheap labour on Spanish, French and English plantations stimulated an unsavoury traffic in Indian slaves which had much to do with the frequent Indian wars.

In spite of subsequent historical research, it is safe to say that most of the men who found the ways and made the trails and portages in the eastern Mississippi basin are still unknown. Spanish missionaries from Florida made journeys into the south-eastern interior from the Atlantic coast and from the Gulf of Mexico. French *coureurs de bois*, as independent traders or as deserters from other men's posts and expeditions, worked east from the Mississippi as far as the Atlantic. From Anglo-Dutch Albany on the Hudson, from the early eighteenth-century settlements in the gracious Shenandoah valley, and from Pennsylvanian, Virginian and Carolinian frontier outposts, acquisitive, self-reliant traders went out with pack-horse or on foot to make a living in the Indian trade. Many of those who appear in the records do so only as 'an Indian trader', 'a long hunter' or 'a Bushloper', or their successors record having found their marks at the crossroads, passes and portages of the interior. In these circumstances, an account of the various regional activities, illustrated by a few known examples, must serve to indicate the general process by which such a vast region was explored. A glance at the map will shew that the widespread Ohio system forms about half of it and that the rivers which flow south into the Gulf of Mexico and south-east to the Atlantic provide approaches to most of the remainder. Exploration conformed very neatly to these topographical divisions.

Exploring enterprise revealed five approaches to the Ohio from the east. La Salle, who was not immediately interested, thought that the Maumee and the Wabash rivers provided the natural way. In later days, when Anglo-French rivalry became keen, the French would have liked to control the Genesee-Alleghany river route from Lake Ontario, but it was too close to the English and their Iroquois friends, so that, even with the handicap of the intervening Niagara portage, they went west and fortified the portage from Presqu' Isle on Lake Erie to the Alleghany river. Meanwhile the English of New York, Pennsylvania and Virginia were also working west and establishing roads to the Ohio as a by-product of settlement. In the *piedmont* they sought for fertile valleys, and these valleys introduced them to the two easiest paths through the Appalachians to the Ohio.

It may well be that the first or second European to explore the Ohio proper was a Dutch interpreter and *boschloper* named Arnout Cornelius Viele, who, operating from Albany, took advantage of the nerveless French policy towards the Iroquois after Governor Frontenac's departure in 1682. The Iroquois swelled in arrogance for the next eight years, reaching their height in an attack and terrible massacre at La Chine in 1689. In 1690 Frontenac returned to humble them by a winter attack on Schenectady; and the general war of 1689–97 brought both the Iroquois and the Albany traders around to a position closely approaching political neutrality in order to profit by commercial exchange with the French. Between 1682 and 1690, however, Viele and others at Albany, aided by French deserters, had almost succeeded in diverting the Lakes' fur trade from Montreal to the Hudson, and Anglo-

Dutch expeditions had gone up the Lakes as far as Michilimackinac. Then, when Frontenac's strong hand was felt again, a new opportunity was offered by the much-abused victims of the Iroquois, the Shawnees of the Ohio valley, who came east and made successful overtures for commercial contact with Albany.

Viele went out in 1692 to investigate these possibilities and returned in 1694 with a host of Shawnees and large quantities of beaver. His specific route is not known, but it can be inferred that he either crossed from the Mohawk to the Delaware valley and thence crossed to the Susquehanna, or he followed the footsteps of Brulé by crossing directly from the Mohawk to the Susquehanna. Having worked his way up the Susquehanna, either by the Juniata branch or the West branch, he had a short crossing to make to the tributaries of the Alleghany and down that stream to the broad Ohio valley and its Shawnee villages. The length of his absence and the presence of Shawnee escorts presuppose a fairly extensive exploration which may well have taken him to the Mississippi. At any rate Tonti on the Illinois reported in 1694 that an Englishman was 'corrupting' the Indians north-west of the Ohio. New York did nothing to follow up Viele's success except to encourage the Shawnees to come east to trade. When they accepted the invitation they discovered how much more convenient it was to trade in Pennsylvania instead.

The Pennsylvanians, pacifistic and chary as they were in Indian affairs, never neglected commercial opportunity. If Albany men could use Pennsylvanian rivers for the western trade, Pennsylvanians might use them themselves. Moreover, there was a vigorous eighteenth-century immigration into Pennsylvania, whose pressure on the land market sent enterprising English, Ulster, Dutch and German pioneers up the Susquehanna valley. While the farmers settled the broad valley lands, more restless men began to explore the six or eight Appalachian ridges which lay between the Susquehanna and the Ohio. To-day those ridges preserve in the titles of the 'Gaps' too few of the names of the men who found them, and hurrying motorists go unheeding through breaks in the ridges which were found and marked by forgotten Indian traders and *boschlopers* of the seventeenth and eighteenth centuries.

This westward movement was least impeded by natural obstacles if men followed the West branch or the Juniata, but the first was too far north and too distant from the settlements to be much used until a later date, and even the Juniata route was through hilly, rough country. The very alignment of the serried mountain ridges seemed to shepherd the Pennsylvanians south-west and introduce them to the upper valley of the Potomac in north-western Maryland. It is not surprising, therefore, to find that they formed a large proportion of the first settlers in the great valley of its tributary, the Shenandoah.

Early in the eighteenth century settlement was creeping westward up the Potomac and south-westward up the Shenandoah. Ahead of the settlers went the Indian traders. They linked together the various approaches to the mountain barrier and the mid-continental valley beyond. Thus those who went up the Juniata branch of the Susquehanna and those who climbed the steep, erratic valley of the Potomac came naturally to cross the western ridge of the Appalachians by passes which were not far apart and which were later to contain the two northern military and colonisation roads to the

311

West, Forbes' Road and the Cumberland Road. In the same way those who ascended the Shenandoah valley had only low ridges to cross before they met the paths which the Virginians had made to Wood's New river (the Kanawha). Travellers along those routes could not fail to be aware that south-westward from their crossing of the Appalachians there extended several mountain valleys, which in the interior of the great barrier ran parallel to its general course. Buffalo trails led from river-bottom to river-bottom over fairly easy passes. As the traders worked south-west, the mountain streams gradually conducted them to the Tennessee valley which, as we shall see, had been opened up to the Carolinians by the renegade *coureur de bois*, Jean Couture. Out of the upper Tennessee valley the Cumberland Gap, the broadest, easiest pass through the western ridge of the Appalachians, led northward to the rolling uplands of what were later to be Tennessee and Kentucky. At its northern end it met the famous Warriors' Path, the Indian highway from the Ohio to the upper Tennessee.

The Cumberland Gap was 'discovered' in 1750 by Dr. Thomas Walker, a Virginian physician who preferred surveying and land speculation to his profession. Two years earlier he had made a reconnaissance of the north-eastern head-waters of the Tennessee along with other land-seekers, and now he sought to locate a suitable land concession beyond the mountains for a newly formed Virginian company. In the same year Christopher Gist went into the Ohio valley by the traditional Virginian route to do the same thing for another company. Nothing is more striking in the records of these two journeys than the evidence that their leaders were guided by the Indian traders, either personally, or by previous instruction, or by recognition of 'blazes', trails and signs. Walker's principal informant seems to have been one Samuel Stalnaker, an Indian trader who probably had been one of the Germans of the Shenandoah valley. The travellers knew beforehand the names given by the hunters to rivers and other natural features. They found that the passes were marked by blazed trees and by other signs to keep the new-comer on the right path. The chief buffalo roads had obviously attracted traders as well as hunters. In a word, the exploring land-hunter had his way made for him by the Indian trader.

Naturally enough the exploration of the eastern Mississippi basin was an eastward movement from the great river as well as a westward movement towards it. After La Salle's expedition to the Gulf of Mexico in 1682, the valley became the scene of great activity on the part of the French. Tonti had a post near the mouth of the Arkansas, but France was slow to occupy a site on the deserted Gulf shore itself, so that Canada remained the base of operations and it was in the Illinois country and the regions immediately south of Lake Michigan that the traders found it most profitable to work. Among them were many men whose relation to governmental and even local authority was very questionable. There were deserters from the groups of servants so painfully collected by La Salle, eager *coureurs* who had learned scorn of the Canadian licensing system and ways to circumvent it, and men who, like the often suspect coterie at Cataraqui, were not above trading with the English. It was inevitable that some of them should go off alone or in small groups to form profitable understandings with the Indians to the east. We have some details of the achievements of two of these men which must serve to indicate the ways of the larger group.

In the late summer of 1692 the Governor and Council of Maryland were asked to consider and investigate the disturbing news that a group of about 200 strange Indians, accompanied by a Frenchman, had come into the colony by way of the Susquehanna and was settled not far from its mouth. The Council examined the Frenchman in August, kept him in custody until October and allowed him and his Indians to settle in the colony. During the winter, however, the colonials, whose imaginations were already busy with the harrowing tales of Indian border warfare which had come south from New England and New York after 1689, leaped to the conclusion that the Frenchman was no other than a famous, almost legendary, figure, the Baron de St. Castine, who for twenty-five years had been living among the Abenakis of Maine to the great disquiet and occasional peril of New England. Just why and how he should have been expected to come to Maryland may seem somewhat extraordinary to-day, but self-multiplying rumours about him spread rapidly from plantation to plantation on the western shore of Chesapeake Bay. It was not until April 1693, after several meetings, that the Council was able to assure the colonists that the French immigrant was not only harmless, but useful.

From the reports of the Council and from other scattered evidence, the main outlines of the Frenchman's wanderings may be deduced. He was Martin Chartier, a carpenter, who had been one of La Salle's company at Fort Crèvecœur on the Illinois river during the winter of 1679–80, but who had deserted with five others in January 1680. He may have been one of the group concerned in the looting of La Salle's supplies and furs at the depôts along the line of communication with Cataraqui in 1680; there are suggestions that he may have found refuge among the deserted *coureurs* at Albany, or he may at once have gone to live among the Shawnees of the Illinois country and the Ohio valley. At any rate he seems definitely to have cast in his lot with the Shawnees by 1684. His arrival on the Atlantic coast in 1692 was no doubt by way of the Ohio and Susquehanna, for that was the route chosen by other Shawnees in search of new European affiliations. Chartier and his group were actually guided east by Indians of the Delaware and Hudson valleys. We are thus presented with the probability that Viele on his way west from Albany to the Ohio, and Chartier on his way east from it, both in close association with the Shawnees, may have passed each other during the early summer of 1692 somewhere along the Ohio-Susquehanna route. Chartier and his Indian wife and followers found a place to settle in Maryland, from which they quite naturally assisted in the subsequent trans-Alleghany trade with the Ohio.

The second of the notable renegade *coureurs* had the distinction of opening up to his English contemporaries a large new section of the Mississippi basin. This was Jean Couture, known to the Carolinians as 'the Greatest Trader and Traveller amongst the Indians for more than Twenty years'. He was another of the Canadian *coureurs* who were introduced into the Mississippi valley by La Salle and Tonti. After perhaps ten years in French service, he decided to transfer his activities to South Carolina, carrying to that colony his knowledge of the way by the great Tennessee river to the Cherokee towns at the southern end of the Appalachians and thence by the Savannah river to the Atlantic. He probably knew the Warriors' Path from the mid-Ohio through the Cumberland Gap to the Tennessee. He came to enjoy a high reputation among the Indian traders on the Savannah because of his real or pretended knowledge of what the French were doing and of the great valley which they were making their own. He was especially retained in 1699 to guide some English prospectors for gold and silver to regions which he described as abounding in gold and pearls. Nothing came of this proposal, but, when during the same year the Carolinian authorities decided to reach out for the Mississippi trade themselves, it was to Jean Couture that they turned for technical assistance as a guide.

During the winter of 1699–1700, Couture, on behalf of Joseph Blake, deputy-governor of South Carolina, guided a group of traders up the Savannah to the Tennessee and down that river to the Ohio, just above its junction with the Mississippi. The expedition was designed to win the Indians to trade with Carolina, and on this mission it proceeded at least as far south as the mouth of the Arkansas, not hesitating to embroil the Indians in inter-tribal conflicts calculated to embarrass the French and to make at least some of the Mississippi Indians dependent upon the English for supplies. Naturally the French were greatly alarmed over the possibility that their profits from the Mississippi might be lost if English trade-goods should draw the Indians up the Ohio to New York and the Middle Colonies, or up the Tennessee to Carolina.

In fact, Couture's expedition of 1699–1700 might well serve to introduce the cluster of enterprises which brought about the systematic exploration of the southeastern part of North America. Of course, Soto, Pardo, Boyano and Luna had moved across that region a century and a half earlier, but it became *known* as the result of commercial rivalry among Spain, France and England at the end of the seventeenth century.

At first the rivalry was between the Spaniards of Florida and the arrogant English interlopers of Carolina. The English armed the Indians friendly to them and encouraged them to attack the almost unarmed, semi-Christianised Indians of the Spanish outpost missions on the Atlantic coast. The drive and determination behind Carolinian policy put the Floridans on the defensive at once. The Spanish offensive was sporadic and largely military or naval. The Carolinian offensive was continuous in the form of English traders and of cheap trade-goods of better quality than Spain could offer. Spanish influence and control were rapidly pressed back along the coast almost to the base of the Florida peninsula, although they continued to be exerted along the coast of the Gulf of Mexico as far west as the valley of the Chattahoochee river.

These operations had by 1685 freed the Carolinians from serious menace to their southern flank sufficiently to allow them to plunge into the interior for the sake of the Indian trade. They built their commercial structure on the foundations laid for them by the Virginians between 1640 and 1673, and they proceeded to exploit the advantages which Lederer had discovered that Carolina had over Virginia because the Appalachians were no barrier to their westward travel.[1] The valley of the Savannah led directly north-west to the Cherokee towns by a route easier and shorter than the Occonee-chee Path from Fort Henry. A pack-train could travel due west from Charles Town to the Mississippi without encountering any barrier more serious than foot-

[1] See Chapter XVI.

hills. The journey was, in fact, a trip across the *piedmont* of the Atlantic coast into the *piedmont* of the eastern Gulf of Mexico and then across the head-waters of the rivers which flowed south to the Gulf.

As we have already seen, Dr. Henry Woodward was the earliest of the indentifiable explorers of the Carolinian *piedmont*. He had reached the Lower Creeks on the Ocmulgee or the Chattahoochee river as early as 1675, but Indian troubles nearer home kept him out of the West again until about 1685. One of the reasons was that the Carolinians' use of Indians against the Spanish coastal missions had converted their principal allies, the Westo tribe at the fall-line of the Savannah, into a characteristic, obstructive middleman group, whose capacity for resisting westward expeditions was not broken down until between 1680 and 1683. Once they were dealt with, the enterprising Woodward seized his opportunity and made his way west to the Chattahoochee valley. There he busied himself in drawing the Lower Creek Indians into economic dependence on Carolina, in spite of vigorous efforts on the part of the Floridans to keep them tributary to Spanish posts on the Gulf. Woodward was soon followed by other traders, who discovered how short a distance it was from the Chattahoochee and the towns of the Lower Creeks to the richer valley of the Alabama and the towns of the Upper Creeks. The next step was north-westerly to the head-waters of the Tombigbee and the Chickasaw towns, from which the Mississippi itself was a relatively short distance away. In 1698 a famous Carolinian trader, named Thomas Welch, travelled due west from Charles Town to the mouth of the Arkansas, thereby putting the coping-stone on the enterprises initiated by Sir William Berkeley in Virginia fifty years before.

Welch's long journey was part of a flurry of international rivalry which brought about the exploration of the last unknown section of the eastern Mississippi basin. The Treaty of Ryswick in 1697 gave Europe and European colonies in America a breathing-space from the long war in which Spain, France and England had been involved. Five years were to elapse before they joined in conflict again, and during those five years there was feverish activity in the Gulf of Mexico and on the lower Mississippi. Father Hennepin, La Salle's former associate, had fallen out with the French and was in Holland urging on the English to seize the Mississippi valley. Huguenots, lately expelled from France or otherwise victimised by Louis XIV, saw a chance for revenge by assisting the English. King Louis and his advisers at last felt the force of La Salle's ideas and, lest England or Spain effectively forestall France, sent out the Canadian hero, Pierre le Moyne, Sieur d'Iberville, to seize and occupy the mouth of the Mississippi. Spain hastened to occupy and fortify Pensacola as a Gulf outpost for her coastal missions and for Florida. Couture appeared with his Carolinians at the mouth of the Arkansas after having opened up the Savannah-Tennessee route. In August 1699 a Carolinian vessel actually made its way for 100 miles up the Mississippi before it was warned away by d'Iberville. It had been sent out on behalf of a visionary English coloniser, Dr. Daniel Coxe, court physician to Charles II and Queen Anne.

The details of the ensuing struggle do not concern us here. The rivalry speedily became almost purely an Anglo-French one, with the French bases on the Gulf (Biloxi, Mobile, New Orleans) conferring an obvious advantage in the Mississippi basin trade over the remote Charles Town on the Atlantic. The French advantage in transportation more than matched the English advantage in quality and price of trade-goods. Without a base on the Gulf, the English could neither seize nor drain the Mississippi valley, linked as it now was both with the St. Lawrence and the Gulf of Mexico. Yet the English did try to use the Cherokees and the Chickasaws of the Tennessee region to harass the French and interrupt their trade in the Illinois country, along the Mississippi, and in the interior north of the Gulf of Mexico. This effort brought the astute and politic Tonti to the scene. Realising that the Choctaws and Yazoos of the region between the Tombigbee and the Mississippi might form a protective shield for the French on the Mississippi and along the Gulf, he sought them out and made alliances. Then as the French intermingled with their new Indian allies, the last large unknown area of the eastern Mississippi basin became known.

In the broad panorama of North American history as a whole, perhaps the greatest persistent theme is the westward flow of population from the Atlantic to the Pacific, and it has become such a commonplace that there is some danger of its being taken for granted as a feature of the colonial history of the seventeenth century. As a matter of fact, it was not until about 1768 that the expanding populations of the coastal colonies burst through the Appalachians to *occupy* the heart of the continent. When they did so, they found well-beaten trails, skilful, knowledgeable guides, and Indians who had dealt with the white man for a century, for the eastern Mississippi basin had been explored from north and south and east and west by men who, almost anonymously, risked their lives to provide Europe with its furs and buck-skin. It is a matter for regret to us now that their own generations did so little to record and commemorate their achievements.

NARRATIVES

No brief guide to the narratives can be made. They are chiefly to be found in the colonial records of New Spain, New France, New York, Pennsylvania, Maryland, Virginia and Carolina. They have been heavily drawn upon to describe the activities along middle and southern frontiers in C. A. Hanna, *The Wilderness Trail* (2 vols., New York, 1911), in H. E. Bolton's introduction to *Arredondo's Historical Proof of Spain's Title to Georgia* (Berkeley, 1925) and in V. W. Crane, *The Southern Frontier* (Durham, N.C., 1928). The Filson Club has published the narratives of Walker and Gist as *First Explorations of Kentucky*, edited by J. S. Johnston (Louisville, 1898), but W. M. Darlington's edition of *Christopher Gist's Journals* (Pittsburgh, 1893) is far richer in its provision of related materials, French and English. Two very illuminating eighteenth-century American commentaries are Cadwallader Colden, *A History of the Five Indian Nations, etc.*, edited by J. G. Shea (2 vols., New York, 1866), and Peter Wraxall, *An Abridgement of the Indian Affairs, etc.*, edited by C. H. McIlwain (Cambridge, Mass., 1915). Margry's collection (see Chapter XVII) contains scattered materials about the French activities.

CHAPTER XIX

REACHING OUT TOWARDS NEW SPAIN

(*Map No. 3, page 482*)

Il y a de riches marchands qui ont bien des piastres et des lingots.
GOVERNOR DE LAMOTHE-CADILLAC'S REPORT
IN 1716 ON THE SPANISH MINING TOWNS

IT would hardly be fair to say that Spain slumbered
in America while the French, the Dutch and the
English were advancing to the heart of the continent.
In Europe, on the seas and in America those very
rivals kept Spain too worried to sleep. The European
wars of the seventeenth century, the assaults on the
closed Spanish economy made by alien merchants and
smugglers, and the raids and conquests of European
adventurers among the islands of the Caribbean provided
harassing accompaniments to the decline of Spain from
her enviable sixteenth-century position. She began to
withdraw from the West Indian islands; Florida and the
Floridan missions contracted; the gap between Mexico
and Florida was never closed, and the now settled inhabitants of Cortés' empire did little to expand their sway
beyond the lines of occupation drawn in Coronado's day.

Indeed Coronado's country of Zuñi, the upper Río
Grande and the upper Pecos (Oñate's New Mexico),
formed a solitary northward projection from the controlled and partially occupied area of New Spain at
the beginning of the seventeenth century. Westward a

322

vague line ran from the *pueblo* plateau to the Gulf of California, but the utmost eastern boundary was the line of the Pecos to its junction with the Río Grande and thence down it to the Gulf of Mexico. The mining regions of the central plateau were organised as the province of New Biscay. The province of New León, established in 1579, represented a slow advance northward from Pánuco, but in it more attention was given to the left flank and mining prospects in the mountains than to the right flank and scattered agricultural possibilities along the shelf of the Gulf or in the southern half of the Río Grande valley. Until about 1650 no one seems to have made any serious expedition across the lower Río Grande valley in spite of the obvious desirability of a land bridge to Florida and even in spite of the persistent legend that there was a hill all of silver beyond the river.

The chief, and on the whole vain, incentive to further enterprise came from the missionary fervour which was at the same time carrying French missionaries from the Atlantic to Hudson Bay and the Mississippi and Spanish missionaries into the south-eastern corner of the continent. The bait held out to governmental authority by the ambitious missionaries was the richness of the land east of the Pecos-Río Grande line. In 1630 one of the Franciscans, Alonso de Benavides, appealed to Philip IV. Miracle after miracle had made it clear that the Indians were ordained by God for immediate conversion. They 'sent ambassadors to the fathers' asking for baptism and instruction, being bidden to do so by a young and beautiful woman who came to them in the habit of a nun.[1] 'There exists in this Kingdom [Quivira]

---

[1] This legend was seized upon by a mystical nun in a convent at Ágreda in Spain, who told Benavides in 1631 that she had frequently transported herself to North America to win the Indians to Christ.

... very great quantity of gold.' 'The Flemings [Dutch] and English are near them on the side of Florida and barter with them for the gold dust . . . the which they carry off thus to benefit their countries . . . and with it they make war on us.' 'It would be possible easily to have the profit of the hides which could be made from the buffalo herd, and their wool.' Spain should occupy the mouth of the Mississippi and then the trade in peltries from the plains and pearls and amber from the Gulf rivers would belong to Spain, not to the 'hostile Hollanders who roam there'.

Yet the energy was lacking, and in 1680 a revolt of the *pueblo* Indians made it doubtful whether the Spaniards could even hold their own. The Indians of the plains and of the 'high plains' were now mounted and had become mobile, tribal scourges who had converted the eastern slope of the Rocky Mountains into a stronghold not easily to be breached by Europeans. The Spanish-Indian frontier was thought of in military terms, and those who ventured for short distances beyond it were as often slave-raiders and members of punitive expeditions as missionaries. In Spain's default, it was to be France which conducted most of the systematic exploration of the South-West.

The news, in 1678, that Diego de Peñalosa[1] was at the court of Louis XIV urging that monarch to attack the fabulously rich and weakly protected northern mining district from Pánuco on the Gulf of Mexico, roused the Spanish government to disinter Benavides' memorial from the archives; but before lethargy and feebleness could be converted to activity, news began to trickle through of La Salle's journey to the mouth of the Mississippi in 1682. Then, while Spain and New Spain

[1] See p. 252.

still delayed, La Salle succeeded in securing support from the busy statesmen at Versailles and sailed, in 1684, avowedly to establish himself and a colony between Florida and Mexico, at a point 'sixty leagues above the mouth of the River Colbert' (Mississippi), before the English or the Dutch could take advantage of his discovery of the river-mouth.[1]

No one can say for certain what La Salle planned to do on the Gulf or whether what he did was his original intention, or a series of compromises with accident and circumstance, or the result of sheer geographical ignorance. He fell out, perhaps inevitably, with his naval associate; he estranged his brother, the Sulpician Jean Cavelier; and his erratic, uncompromising exercise of authority so frightened and angered his company that it broke up into suspicious factions, one of which finally ambushed and murdered him. Throughout his career he had been unable to keep his followers together, probably because he demanded of them almost as much as he imposed upon himself. His whole life had been a succession of enterprises whose demands had exceeded the capacities of the associates and financial supporters upon whom he depended. His haughty self-assurance was understood by a kindred soul like Frontenac and won almost unconditional loyalty from as competent a fur trader as Tonti, but it drove lesser men into the self-confessed impotence of desertion, slander and, finally, of murder. Probably we should regard his death in a

---

[1] There is no good biography of La Salle, whose reputation has suffered in the past because of uncritical analyses and praise and is now the subject of rather violent reaction. The Gulf expedition should not be taken as a criterion for his whole character and career, but as an example of modern revaluation of La Salle and of his biographers, old and new, see Marc de Villiers, *L'expédition de Cavelier de la Salle dans le golfe du Mexique* (Paris, 1931).

Texan river-thicket, not as the capricious work of villains, but as the natural conclusion of a proud, uncompromising, ill-calculated effort to bend expedient men and stubborn circumstances to his designs. His designs were good, but they had to be carried out by more patient, more 'practical' men a generation after he had first conceived of them at La Chine and twelve years after his death.

La Salle took his colonists and soldiers, not up the Mississippi as he had originally planned and as Tonti expected, but far west to Matagorda Bay. He had passed near the mouth of the great river, and his own private purpose was to exploit its valley directly from the sea, for the hostility of Frontenac's successor in Canada, Antoine Lefebvre de La Barre, had made it useless for him to base his operations on the Illinois and Lake Michigan. He may, however, have been irrevocably committed, voluntarily or involuntarily, to pay the Court's price of superseding Peñalosa by embracing his plan of capturing the silver-mines of northern New Spain, for just at this time France was embarking on a resolute effort to break through the Spanish barrier to mid-American trade. Indeed the attempt to combine his own idea and the one which Peñalosa had made attractive to Louis XIV may well have produced the insoluble confusions which we find in what La Salle wrote and did and in what his companions thought he was trying to do. La Salle seems to have believed, or he pretended to believe, that the Mississippi was so close to New Spain that the Red river would quickly conduct the French, not only to the unprotected Spanish border, but to a region close to the slopes leading down to the Pacific coast. For our purposes it is enough to know that he built his Fort St. Louis and established a weak colony on the rather inhospitable shores of Matagorda Bay.

An almost uninterrupted succession of misfortunes and misunderstandings brought it about that his enfeebled colony was isolated, marooned on the coast between Florida and Mexico, by the spring of 1687. La Salle had made two expeditions overland by that time, the first (October 1685 to March 1686) south and west towards the Spanish settlements, and the second (April to October 1686) north and east across difficult country, seeking the Mississippi or one of its western tributaries. He made no direct contact with the Spaniards, he found no great river, but he made friends with some Texas Indians and secured five horses.

On 7 January 1687 he set out with sixteen companions for the Illinois country to get help for his colony. The Colorado and Brazos valleys were flooded and it took two months for his north-eastern course to bring him to the Trinity. His wearied, despondent party were mutinous and his own melancholic stubbornness seemed to them to hint of madness. They paused to seek some grain hidden the year before and to hunt buffalo along the valley. There were disputes about the division of the meat. One hunting-party aroused La Salle's suspicions by its dilatoriness in rejoining the main group. On 19 March he went off to order its members back, and when he reached their camp they shot him. It was a stupid thing to do, but men of small intelligence like La Salle's murderers do stupid things when fear and bewilderment overcome them. Wiser, less egoistical leaders than La Salle know this and how to counter it. Hudson at one end of the continent and La Salle at the other paid the same price for the same lack in qualities of leadership.

La Salle's stripped body was left lying near where it fell. Three precautionary murders had preceded La Salle's. When the murderers and some deserters whom they met later fell out among themselves, two more murders and two flights left surviving only the least implicated of the conspirators. Abbé Cavelier pardoned him, and the weakened little band prepared to resume its journey to the Illinois country by way of the lands which Moscoso and Soto's men had scoured a century and a half earlier. Henri Joutel, an ex-soldier who had volunteered for the Gulf expedition out of admiration for La Salle, took command. Having recuperated their energies by a seven weeks' stay among the friendly Cenis Indians, they marched north to the Red river, and then turned almost due east to the Mississippi, for they had reached a region whose inhabitants knew about Tonti's post founded in 1686 near the mouth of the Arkansas. On 24 July they had the great satisfaction of reaching that post and of finding there Jean Couture [1] and another *voyageur*. Five days later, five survivors of the party of seventeen which had left the Gulf began to paddle up the Mississippi towards the Illinois country, Canada and France. They did their best to conceal the death of La Salle and the weakness of the Gulf colony, as they made for Europe to salvage what they could of their own reputations and from La Salle's tangled business affairs.

Tragic failure though it was, La Salle's Gulf expedition set in train the activities which were to bridge the gap between the Mississippi and New Spain. Tonti had taken an expedition south from the Illinois country to the Gulf during the winter of 1685–86 to meet La Salle. Not finding him after searching the coast thirty

---

[1] Before his desertion to Carolina.

leagues east and west, he proposed to his men 'that if they would trust me, we should follow the coast as far as Menade [New York], and that by this means we should arrive shortly at Montreal'. This startling proposal failed to commend itself, so that after establishing the Arkansas post, Tonti went back to the Illinois. He housed the little group of refugees from the Gulf during the winter of 1687–88. 'They concealed from me the assassination of M. de la Salle, and upon their assuring me that he had remained at the Gulf of Mexico, in good health, I received them as if they had been M. de la Salle himself and lent them more than 700 francs.' But after their departure for Canada, on 7 September 1688 Jean Couture came in with two Indians from the Arkansas and told of what he and they had learned about La Salle's death and the fate of the colonists on the Gulf. Tonti sent him back at once to get into touch with some French deserters among the Cenis Indians, while he himself made his preparations to rescue the little group on Matagorda Bay.

He set out from Fort St. Louis on the Illinois river for Fort St. Louis in Texas in December 1688.[1] From the Arkansas post he worked south to the Red river valley. All that winter and spring he moved from tribe to tribe in the valley and between it and that of the Trinity. Finally he got word of French deserters who were reported to be away helping the Indians against the Spaniards. 'I told them that they had killed the Frenchman. Directly all the women began to cry, and thus I saw that what I had said was true.' He secured 'four Spanish horses, two of which were marked on the

---

[1] Tonti's own dates are not consistent and this expedition may have taken place in 1689–90, although that seems less likely.

haunch with an R and a crown above it and another
with an N'. He reached a point which he calculated was
within three days' march of where La Salle was murdered, but his supplies were short, his men mutinous,
the Indians sulky and the country almost impassable.
In these circumstances, Tonti reluctantly consented to
turn back to the Mississippi, which he reached on
11 July. 'In short, I never suffered so much in my life
as in this journey.'

Although the French had failed to find the new Fort
St. Louis, the Spaniards slowly succeeded. In his report
of 21 November 1688 Governor Don Juan Isidro de
Pardiñas Villar de Frances of New Biscay reported to
his king that the Indians of the Río Grande had informed him 'that some foreign people are in territory in
that part of this Kingdom'. He sent to Spain Indian
depositions concerning these interlopers—'though they
do not know how to differentiate between them and
other foreigners'—who were trading among the Texas
Indians. There were stories of 'some men wearing
doublets of steel, and that they came up the river [Río
Grande] in canoes', whose leader 'asked them what the
distance was to where silver was being mined'. 'The
declarant replied that it was a journey of twenty-six
days and that it was all full of Indians, whereupon they
told him that they would not venture to go.' There were
three visits of this sort. There were other stories of the
dispersion of these foreigners in Texas, of the destruction of their fort by the Indians and of European loot
passing from hand to hand. It was reported, also, that
one of the tribes had adopted a white man as its chief.
Finally, early in 1689, an Indian chief turned over to
the Spaniards 'some papers and a ship painted on a
parchment written by hand in the French language',

although he assured them 'that the Moors [French] . . . were already dead'.[1]

Governor Pardiñas of New Biscay and Governor Alonso de Leon of Coahuila (a new province north of New León) were roused to positive action by such specific news of Frenchmen on their borders. Some of them seem to have been members of La Salle's expeditions of 1685, 1686 and 1687, others deserters, and still others the children spared by the Indians after their successful attack on the little group of twenty or twenty-five men, women and children left at Fort St. Louis. León made five expeditions in search of the French, on the third of which (in 1688) he picked up the craftily unintelligible Jean Géry or Jarry, the white chief of the Indians, and on the fourth of which he succeeded in finding the abandoned ruins of Fort St. Louis (22 April 1689). Meanwhile Governor Pardiñas sent out General Juan de Retana from the junction of the Río Grande and Conchos rivers (La Junta) to investigate the rumours which had reached him. The Indians were set at work to help the Spanish authorities. As a result of all these activities, the Spaniards seem to have rescued ten of the French colonists under varying circumstances. They also acquainted themselves with inland Texas and learned again of the resources which Benavides had recited forty years before. Several naval flotillas, in searching the coast for the French, had greatly improved Spanish knowledge of it.

---

[1] This parchment, with its picture and its pathetic letters from Jean L'Archevêque and Jacques Groslet, has survived. It is reproduced in facsimile in Hackett, *Historical Documents, etc.*, vol. ii, p. 256, and J. F. Jameson's essay concerning it and the other relics (also reproduced) will be found on pp. 470-81. Spanish and Indian records of the activities and of the dramatic dissolution of the company at Fort St. Louis are in the same volume. See also de Villiers, *op. cit.* chap. xi.

León and his associate, Fray Damián Massanet, in the course of their searches in 1690 crossed the Trinity valley and set up a mission just to the north-east of it where it was closest to the Red river valley. Next year Domingo Terán de los Rios was sent out to establish more missions and explore farther. Under very discouraging conditions he crossed from the Trinity to the Red where Tonti had been two years before. It seemed as if Spain was prepared to keep the French out of Texas. Within two years, however, Indian hostility and adverse climatic conditions brought about the abandonment of the eastern Texas missions. The Spaniards had to be contented with the temporary re-assertion of their military and commercial prestige among the tribes to the east of the Pecos-Río Grande frontier.

Thus, except for part of Texas, the South-West still remained to be explored, and one reason for this relative tardiness was the novel and difficult character of the country. The region contained every possible variety of ground—swamp and desert, sweet springs and poisonous pools, marshy morasses and high mountain ranges, thick forest and open prairie, solid oaks and pulpy cactus, placid navigable streams and debris-cluttered river-beds that could change from a succession of shallow pools to a raging torrent and back again in twenty-four hours. Travel over it had to be varied, with shifts from canoe to foot or horseback. The fact that many of the Indian tribes were mounted made them better raiders and less easy to round up and overawe. Their towns seemed stable, but the tribes actually lived in an uneasy flux of shifting hunting-grounds and precarious alliances. The great, almost the sole basis for Indian life lay in the immense, countless herds of buffalo. Agriculture there was and abundance of the lesser hoofed animals, but the buffalo herds meant sustenance of many kinds and products for trade. The South-West presented the European pioneer with many novel problems.

Once again it was the French who acted, and henceforth, fittingly enough, the initiative in the activities which brought about new exploration of the South-West was largely in their hands. By the establishment in 1699 and the following years of the colony of Louisiana on the lower Mississippi and the Gulf coast to the east of its mouth, France secured a base on the ocean for exploitation of the great valley and for commercial competition with the Spaniards and the English among the Indians west as well as east. Very soon, moreover, following the lead of Tonti, the traders at the French posts near the confluence of the Illinois, the Mississippi and the Missouri ('The Illinois'), found it wise to avoid Montreal hostility and the difficulties of the Great Lakes route by using the Mississippi as their link with the outside world. Thus Spain saw her mainland colonies really separated and realised that her northward expansion from Mexico through the mountains which ever offered new mines, and her potentially profitable trade with the plains Indians must now be flanked, indeed outflanked, along the Mississippi. Both Spaniards and French began to think about the rivers which entered the Mississippi from the west. Unfortunately, from the French *voyageurs'* standpoint, the more southern of these rivers could hardly be classed as navigable, for they seemed always to be either in dangerous flood or too shallow for boats, and were frequently made dangerous by debris.

To Canadian *voyageurs* [1] in and about The Illinois,

---

[1] With the transition from the northern and eastern woods to the central valley, this term is better applicable than *coureur de bois*.

and to the commercial leaders who promoted the colony of Louisiana in order to satisfy a few of the hopes of its stock-holders in France, the Spanish lands in the South-West meant mines and trade. Owing to geographical ignorance, it was generally believed that such rivers as the Red, the Arkansas and the Missouri led very quickly to the mountains and the great silver-lodes which were being worked by the Spaniards. It was more or less known that the frontier Spanish towns, particularly Santa Fé and Taos in New Mexico, were remote from their bases of European supplies. The Indians who crowded to the fairs there traded for goods to whose price enormous transportation costs had been added. To the French along the Mississippi it seemed likely that they could win the trade of the Indians between them and the Spanish settlements with cheaper goods. Moreover, like the English before them, they had discovered that even in Europe and in the West Indies, as smugglers paying no Spanish taxes or customs duties, they could undersell the Spanish merchants if they could escape the attentions of the government. If that had been possible in Europe and the West Indies, it seemed much more possible in the rich mining towns of New Mexico. Picturing the mining towns as being full of men with 'piasters and ingots' to spend, traders from The Illinois and Louisiana planned to take full advantage of the opportunity. They were even anxious to build up a trade in horses, cattle, salt meat and hides. As early as 1703, the flat-boats, canoes and pack-trains of adventurers, some known to us and in all probability still more unknown, began to press west from Louisiana or to make sweeping circuits to the west and south from The Illinois, trading with the Indians where it proved possible, eagerly seeking news of silver- or copper-mines, and searching for the trails over which they might carry smuggled goods to the Spanish settlements. Some men also hoped to find that 'River of the West' leading to the Pacific, which was the eighteenth-century equivalent of the earlier-sought Straits of Anian. It was believed to lie just beyond a neighbouring height of land or to flow from a great lake somewhere near the source of the Missouri or the Mississippi.

While there exist suggestions that Canadian *voyageurs* from The Illinois may have reached New Mexico before the end of the seventeenth century, the greater weight of evidence goes to shew that the French westward movement began in the south about 1700 and involved the north by a progressive advance as one after another of the western tributaries of the Mississippi was explored. The most tempting river was the Red, and from about 1700 on, Louis de St. Denis explored its possibilities for trade with the Indians and Spaniards. From time to time he and his associates had to warn off English interlopers (once '*un mylord anglois, nommé master You*'), coming from east of the Mississippi. A French memorandum of the time lamented that 'Our merchandise is infinitely more expensive than that furnished to the Spaniards by the English and is not of as good quality'. By 1714 St. Denis, backed by Governor de Lamothe-Cadillac of Louisiana, was ready to strike boldly for the Spanish colonies with a reconnoitring expedition organised for trading purposes.[1] He

[1] St. Denis took along as guides Pierre and Jean-Baptiste Talon, who as children had survived the destruction of La Salle's colony and had been purchased from the Indians by the Spaniards. Adopted by the wife of the Mexican viceroy, they were on their way to Spain in 1697 when their ship was captured by the French. Next year they served in Iberville's expedition to the Mississippi, in 1704 they were reported as being imprisoned in Portugal, and they finally cast in their lot with Louisiana. See de Villiers, *op. cit.* pp. 189-91.

made his way up the Red river by boat to Natchitoches and then set out on foot straight across country to San Juan Bautista on the Río Grande. Accompanying him across Texas, were only twelve other Frenchmen and about thirty Indians from near the Spanish missions, but the little party proved able to repel the one serious attack made upon them by Indians from the western Gulf coast. Once arrived, St. Denis became involved in the typical confusions which occurred when a smuggler with tempting goods broke through the barriers of a mercantilistic colony. Officialdom made a great show of correct action, but actually treated him very well. Suffice it to say that he fell in love with the daughter (or niece) of the officer in command at San Juan, was sent to Mexico City, was released, and returned to Louisiana obligingly guiding some Spanish missionaries and soldiers to eastern Texas. He made a second journey in 1717 with a group of traders.

From 1716 to 1719 or 1720 there was a curious sort of half-friendly, half-hostile commerce between Louisiana and the Río Grande, but the authorities in Spain gradually brought it to a stop. The outcome, in so far as new exploration was concerned, was that Spain seemed to block it by 'occupying' Texas with a few scattered missions and military posts between the Río Grande and the old mission region near the Red river. On the other hand, St. Denis and other Frenchmen had spied out the land behind the Spanish frontier and had learned much about its mines, its needs and its organisation. As St. Denis put it in 1715, 'I have no fears of these folk here [at San Juan], my only fears are of Mexico City'.

None the less the Spanish 'front' in east Texas and the difficulties of travelling up the Red river valley beyond its great bend to the west made the Louisianians try their fortunes farther north in order to circumvent the obstacles between them and the mines of New Biscay and New Mexico. An additional incentive was the quest for the height of land between the Mississippi valley and the Pacific coast which was believed to be near the head-waters of the western tributaries of the Mississippi. In the spring of 1719 Bénard de la Harpe, a trader who had received a land grant on the Red river and who was the agent of the Council of Louisiana, made his way in boats up the flooded Red river valley to the westward bend, and then rode north-west to the Canadian river somewhere just above its junction with the Arkansas. He explored carefully and learned all he could about the Indians and about roads to the mines. When he turned back, the loss or theft of his horses compelled him to walk to his post at Natchitoches.

La Harpe later acquired a somewhat questionable reputation with the Louisiana authorities because of the marvels, such as unicorns and mines of precious stones, with which he adorned his reports. Yet he was very proud of the ability of his associate, Sieur du Rivage, 'the famous surveyor whom I brought with me from France', and his journals were most conscientious in their recording of compass directions, corrections for river-windings and so on. He was withdrawn for duties on the Gulf in 1720–21, but in spite of that interruption, between 1719 and 1722 he and Rivage opened up the Indian trade in the territory north of the Red river by exploring the Arkansas and Canadian river valleys perhaps as far west as 100° W. and conciliating the Indians. La Harpe's relations with the Spanish missionaries and soldiers to the south of the Red river were necessarily somewhat confusing and uncertain. He and his men did not succeed in reaching either the Spanish mining towns or the height of land, but they were the first to get around the Spanish left flank to the rich opportunities of the Indian trade. The French thereafter did their best to build up intertribal peace and commercial dependence on French goods among the south-western Indians. The Spaniards had been very loath to sell fire-arms, but the French freely satisfied the demand for them, and whereas the Spaniards had depended chiefly on a trade in horses, the French provided manufactured goods in studied abundance. Competition was keenest for the friendship of the Comanche and Apache tribes, whose military power enabled them to bar the way from the Mississippi to the Spanish settlements.

Nameless Illinois *voyageurs* ventured up the Missouri valley soon after 1700, but they did not contribute specifically to the geographical picture until just after the journeys of La Harpe. It was in 1719 that Claude Charles du Tisné was sent by the commander at Kaskaskia, Pierre Duqué de Boisbriant, westward from near the mouth of the Missouri. He seems to have travelled up the Missouri valley to the Osage river, up that stream about eighty leagues and then south-west out across the prairies for about forty leagues until the Indians stopped him from going on to make contact with their Comanche enemies.

The activities of La Harpe and Tisné worried the Spaniards and roused them to an ill-fated response. In order not to be outflanked on the north, Don Pedro de Villasur, in 1720, led a small military expedition north-west over the mountains from Santa Fé in an effort to extend Spanish prestige along the eastern slope of the Rockies to a position about opposite the mouth of the

338

Missouri, much as it had been extended to the Red river in Texas. After two months of travel which took them to the united Platte river, Villasur's men were practically wiped out by a Pawnee attack. Santa Fé and Taos had thereafter to serve as northern outposts for Spain.

When the Indian allies of the French brought word to The Illinois that a Spanish expedition (whose size they greatly exaggerated) had been as far north as the Kansas and the Platte rivers, the authorities in Paris and at the Gulf were much alarmed and decided to offset the Spanish advance by building a fort on the Missouri. 'The principal object of a post on the Missouri is to get as near as possible to the Spaniards to enter into trade with them,' wrote the authorities in France. The man they chose for the enterprise was a long-established Illinois trader, Etienne Veniard, Sieur de Bourgmond, who used the occasion to strike a very good bargain as to payment, military rank and the promise of consideration for the Cross of St. Louis and letters of nobility if he were successful in establishing an Indian peace from Louisiana to New Mexico. He scored no such startling success in spite of considerable military aid, but he and his men established Fort Orleans about 300 miles up the Missouri and from it, between 1722 and 1728, explored and opened up for French trade a good deal of the region between the Arkansas and Platte river valleys. Their advance towards the Spaniards in the South-West was barred by intertribal Indian wars and by the usual complexities of the universal middleman problem. There exist most interesting records of the laborious diplomacy by which Bourgmond temporarily extended French commercial sway over the Indians as far as the Comanche tribes along the eastern slope of the Rockies. On the other hand, we have only the scantiest records of who the individual French *voyageurs* were, or where they went. They seem, on the whole, to have adapted themselves to relations with the very warlike mounted Indians of the South-West almost as well as they had with the canoe-men of the mid-continent. There were faint echoes, too, of individual Spanish traders among the Indians as far north as the Missouri.

The most spectacular incident in this commercial process and the one which rounded out the pioneer exploration of the South-West was the series of journeys made by the brothers Pierre and Paul Mallet and their followers in 1739 and subsequent years. Their successes may have owed something to the generosity of Bourgmond, in making gifts to the Comanches. He had taken great pains to convince them of the advantages of free movement and trade among the allied tribes and had also warned them 'that when the French shall come to your country to trade and shall wish to pass on to the Spaniards' country, you are not to trouble or obstruct them'. The French, on the whole, had relatively little difficulty with the Indians of the South-West and even made alliances among the most warlike tribes, Comanches, Apaches and Pawnees. Probably, however, the explanation of the contrast between their success and Spanish failure in making Indian alliances lay in the inability of the Spaniards in New Mexico to be at all lavish with presents or trade-goods at a time when both were being poured out from The Illinois and Louisiana in all directions. Some Spanish traders gave up their own affiliations in disgust and made private working agreements with French *voyageurs*.

The Mallet expedition was an Illinois affair which apparently started from the Mississippi some time during the winter of 1738–39. It was composed of the two Mallets, five or six other Canadians and one Frenchman from France. Its leaders, following the example of several predecessors, planned to go to New Mexico by ascending the Missouri, but some Pawnees whom they met in the vicinity of the Platte river convinced them that they would actually be turning their backs on their objective. On 29 May 1739, therefore, the little party cut back southwards from the Missouri, reached the Platte on 2 June and followed it and its southern branch until they reached the high Colorado plains 'where they could find only enough wood to make fires'. Turning south, they crossed three rivers in succession, and on 20 June recognised what seems to have been the Republican river, where they lost almost all their trade-goods with seven horses which were swept away. They determined to go on, however, and on 24 June noted rocks marked by the Spaniards. Somewhere among the northern head-waters of the Arkansas they managed to win the services of an Indian who had been a slave among the Spaniards. They promised him his freedom if he would guide them to the Spanish towns. Between 6 July and 22 July he took them quickly through the mountain passes between the head of the Arkansas valley and that of the Pecos to arrive at Santa Fé.

Almost naked as they were, and with only remnants left of their trade-goods, they were welcomed as heroes by the Spaniards. The commandant at Taos, to whom they had written, sent mutton and wheat bread to meet them. As they approached an outpost mission, the bells rang in welcome. At Santa Fé the religious and the military entertained them cordially for nine months while awaiting from Mexico the answers to Spanish and French proposals for a tempting commercial exchange in which New Mexico would provide silver and either The Illinois or Louisiana manufactured goods. There was real sadness when the viceroy frowned on such schemes. He, too, highly esteemed the Mallet company, and tried in vain to tempt them into the Spanish service by engaging them 'to make the discovery of a country, which, according to the true or false tradition of the local Indians, is three months' journey to the west, where they say are men dressed in silk who live in great cities on the sea-shore'.

The interloping Canadians resisted the temptation to find the Strait of Anian for the Viceroy of Mexico. There seems little doubt but that they had agreed with their hosts at Santa Fé to set up trade with Louisiana in spite of the prohibition of a viceroy far off in Mexico City. Moreover, they were fairly sure (as Pike professed to be sure in following their route in 1807) that they were close to tributaries of the Arkansas or the Red river. They set off to explore the complicated region at the head of the Pecos valley on 1 May 1740, trying one deep stream-bed after another if it promised to lead them east. After two weeks of experiment among the unfamiliar mountain valleys and dramatic 'painted' scenery of New Mexico, three of their party of seven decided that they would go back to The Illinois by the way they had come. The two Mallets and two other Canadian *voyageurs* believed that for the last four days they had been following a stream which would take them to the Mississippi and which seemed to them to be navigable to within a little over 100 miles of Santa Fé. Gambling on that chance, they continued to follow it as closely as they could and were rewarded by meeting Indians of tribes known to them, from whom they secured horses very cheaply. By 14 June their river had become distinctly navigable, indeed so temptingly so that they decided to abandon their eighteen horses and instead build two canoes of elm-bark, although they had only two knives as tools. After five days' work, they were able to embark and run swiftly down the river, in agreeable contrast to the six weeks during which they had climbed up and down the steep banks of the mountain river-beds whenever their narrow canyons had blocked passage at the water-level.

Fittingly enough, their river has since their day been called the Canadian, a name which most appropriately commemorates the enterprises which had at last fulfilled the rather too optimistic anticipations of Jean Alfonse at Lachine almost exactly 200 years before.[1] They found other Canadians hunting just below the junction with the Arkansas. In order to acquire some capital, the four discoverers joined the hunt and set about building up a stock of dried salt meat which they loaded in a boat and took to New Orleans in March 1741. There they soon attracted the attention of the energetic Canadian governor of Louisiana. Jean Baptiste Le Moyne, Sieur de Bienville, was greatly excited by their news. He could not understand how La Harpe had failed when the Mallets seemed to have succeeded so easily, but he did not pause to puzzle it out. Instead he picked out André Fabry, Sieur de la Bruyère, a naval secretary who had shewn some enterprise in exploration, and fitted up an expedition which, under Fabry's command and guided by the Mallets, should establish the water

---

[1] For a dismissal of the only other explanation of the name see J. B. Thoburn in *Chronicles of Oklahoma*, vi, 2 (June 1922), pp. 181-5.

route from the mouth of the Mississippi to the mines of New Mexico. Fabry's commission bespoke exploration, Indian alliances and Spanish trade, but it also contained an echo of old hopes and of the Mexican viceroy's intended employment for his Canadian visitors when it recalled the possibility that the western limits of Louisiana might be joined to China and Grand Tartary.

Fabry's expedition during the winter of 1741–42 failed very dismally, perhaps because of his ineptitude, but chiefly because of the extreme lowness of the upper Canadian following a dry winter. It is not necessary to repeat here how Fabry's boats would not float in waters where bark canoes could have been paddled, tracked and portaged, how the Mallets twice failed to find Indians who would sell horses, and how Fabry went back to the Arkansas and the Red river valleys on the same mission and returned at the end of August only to find that the Mallets had left for Santa Fé on foot. Fabry was helpless without guides. The Mallets were never heard of again.

It might seem that the great work of bridging the gap had been done in vain, but that would involve ignoring the economic forces which had activated the French in Louisiana and The Illinois for a generation. The trade which the Spaniards at Taos and Santa Fé longed for in 1740 was built up in the succeeding years. The Canadian river was travelled by French *voyageurs* and Spanish traders. The route from Santa Fé to The Illinois was gradually established. The commerce was not advertised to Mexico City, and occasionally a zealous official at Santa Fé upset accepted ways by imprisoning an interloping *voyageur* or two. Yet by 1750, French influence among the Indians made New Mexico almost helpless in the commercial rivalry among the tribes and dependent on the French. The French had made the routes across the South-West and, except during the interruptions of Indian wars, the knowledge and use of them was continuous.

Spain had the chance, almost the imperative strategical duty, of exploring and controlling the region which Vaca, Soto, Coronado and the sixteenth-century *conquistadores* had revealed, but she failed. France sent no great military expeditions across it, but Frenchmen and Canadians learned its character and resources and made it support them. Spain bade the Indians come to her settlements, chiefly for the horses which they wore out quickly and which they were for long unable to breed, or invaded their territories on the punitive expeditions which provided labour for the mines and plantations. France learned the ways of the mounted plains Indian, and Canadians lived among them as ably as they had among the canoe Indians. The Spanish settlements were based chiefly on mines in the Sierras. New France and Louisiana had to trade to survive. Thus Spain bowed in enterprise to France. France, in her turn, was soon to bow before the rivalry of a greater manufacturer and trader than she, and finally both France and Spain yielded before the onset of a larger horde of frontiersmen than their own North American colonies had ever been able to nurture.

NARRATIVES

Hackett and Bolton as under Chapter V. Mrs. E. E. Ayer has translated, and F. W. Hodge and C. F. Lummis have annotated, *The Memorial of Fray Alonso de Benavides, 1630* (Chicago, 1916). Margry, vols. i-vi, and Cox as under Chapter XVII. A little-known second-hand account of La Salle's death as given to Tonti by Couture is in Public Archives of Canada, *Supple-*

ment to the Report of 1899 (Ottawa, 1901), pp. 20-23. A number of unpublished records of expeditions westward from The Illinois are heavily drawn upon in M. de Villiers, *La Découverte du Missouri, etc.* (Paris, 1925). La Harpe's Journal for 1719 is translated by Anna Lewis in *Chronicles of Oklahoma* (Oklahoma City), vol. ii, no. 4. The chronicle known as *The Establishment of the French in Louisiana*, attributed to La Harpe, is translated by B. F. French in *Historical Collections of Louisiana* (New York, 1851), vol. iii. A highly original and very helpful discussion of the character of the western Mississippi valley and of its effects on human enterprise will be found in W. P. Webb, *The Great Plains* (New York, 1931).

CHAPTER XX

THE CROSSROADS OF THE CONTINENT

(*Map No. 4, end of book*)

The heights can be reached only in the second year after leaving Montreal.

LOUIS-JOSEPH DE LA VÉRENDRYE'S CONCEP-
TION OF THE DISTANCE TO THE ROCKIES

THE danger of assuming that the search for ways to the Pacific explains at all adequately the continuous exploration of North America by Europeans and Americans after 1492 should be quite obvious. On the other hand, that motive should not be completely dismissed except in enterprises which were clearly political or confined to some profitable local venture. In fact it might be best to think of interest in the Pacific as being a sort of chronic underlying factor in pioneer North American exploration. Most of the time, between 1550 and 1760, it was quiescent, if actual activity is arithmetically balanced against the years, but at almost any time it could be roused by well-chosen or accidental stimulants, that is, by propaganda or by what seemed authentic new information about the West. It is almost always clear, however, that westward exploration, like other exploration, had to pay its way, and that expectation of profit, political or economic, was behind the large capital investments which it required. Even the men who seem most clearly to have been driven along by curiosity and by devotion to the geographer's gods, found that they must either bait their projects with profits in order to secure backing or make money as they went. The explorer, as explorer pure and simple, is largely a product of the nineteenth and twentieth centuries, and even then it must be admitted that he is a rare phenomenon.

It is quite natural that when the explorers had pretty well satisfied themselves about North America as far west as the region lying between Hudson Bay and the Gulf of Mexico, they should be receptive to inducements to go farther west. Unfortunately, the world's knowledge of the Pacific coast of North America was very vague up to the middle of the eighteenth century, so much so that the whole northern Pacific as we know it might be a land bridge from Asia to America for all that the American explorers knew. One has to remember that practically all the men who were in a position to explore were fur traders, and that transportation costs were what determined how far they could profitably go. It would require reassuring new knowledge or some other powerful incentive to take them far westward in the mid-continental basin. Until scarcity raised fur prices high enough to pay for longer expeditions, they were likely to cling to the water transportation provided by Hudson Bay, the Great Lakes and the Mississippi. To be sure, they might find a strait or a lake and river combination from Pacific to Atlantic or to Hudson Bay, but if there were none, a man might march due west from Lake Superior round the world to France, overland all the way, so far as most men knew. No one realised how broad North America was between the fortieth and fiftieth parallels.

The new knowledge and the powerful incentive came

348

together after 1750;[1] but long before the Europeans in North America began to act in response to them, restless individuals had been seeking knowledge and profit from the north-western quarter of the continent. Those of them whose names and records have survived for us deserve an important place in the total design of North American exploration because the later spurts to the Pacific started from the bases which their knowledge provided. Their efforts may seem scattered and fragmentary, yet subsequent exploration revealed that they had significance and a kind of unity in North American exploration as a whole.

The Canadian share in these enterprises developed into circumventing the Foxes and the Sioux, who controlled the triangle formed by Lake Michigan, the Mississippi and Lake Superior, and also circumventing the English of the Hudson's Bay Company by working clockwise around the Bay to cut off the flow of furs down the tributary rivers. Ultimately these two kinds of enterprise were to become merged in one, and Canadian *voyageurs* and Company servants were to clash in the Saskatchewan valley where Kelsey had wandered many years before.

We have already seen how the French explored Lake Superior and became acquainted with the upper Mississippi after the great Indian dispersion of the mid-seventeenth century. Perhaps naturally, more effort was devoted thereafter to La Salle's idea of using the Mississippi and the Gulf of Mexico than to exploring farther west. Many men knew about the Mississippi above its junction with the Wisconsin, and several had approached or actually visited it from the western end of Lake Superior. The first systematic examination of

[1] See pp. 398-401.

349

its upper course, however, was an interesting sort of by-product of French enterprise both on the main Mississippi and in Lake Superior.

The venture began during the winter of 1679–80 when La Salle left Fort Crèvecoeur to walk to Cataraqui for news of the *Griffon*. 'In this extremity', reported Father Hennepin with his usual vanity, 'we both adopted a resolution, as extraordinary as it was difficult to carry out, I to go to unknown countries, where one is at every moment in great danger of his life, and he to proceed on foot to Fort Frontenac.' Tonti's description was more laconic. 'He [La Salle] sent a Récollet father with the Sieur Acau to explore the nation of the Sioux, 400 leagues from the Islinois, towards the north, on the Mississipy river.' Hennepin himself admits that he tried to induce Father Membré to take his place. Be that as it may, Hennepin accompanied Michel Accault and Antoine du Gay Anguel when they set out down the Illinois on 29 February 1680, to find the river-way to the Sioux and trade with them. La Salle chose the two laymen for their bravery and Hennepin to record the expedition.

Fortunately for them, another active Frenchman had decided 'to attempt the exploration of the Nadouecioux [Sioux] and the Assenipoualaks [Assiniboines]' and to do so from Lake Superior. On 1 September 1678 Daniel Greysolon, Sieur Dulhut,[1] set out for the West with seven French companions and some friendly Indians. Count Frontenac was privy to his designs and doubtless hoped to profit from the fur trade which he might open up. Duluth carried with him materials for setting up the arms of France beyond western Lake

[1] His own signature is Dulhut, but the name has been irretrievably Anglicised as Duluth.

Superior; he was, in fact, Frontenac's half-acknow-
ledged emissary towards the Western Sea while La
Salle sought the way to the South. He had been in
Montreal from 1671 to 1673 and again since 1674,
and, sharing in the excitement over the western discoveries of Perrot and Jolliet and the speculations of
the Jesuits,[1] had deliberately cultivated Indian friend-
ships, just as La Salle had done. In 1678 he had three
Indian slaves, presented to him by the western Indians
to assist him in his discoveries. It is clear from his life
and from the scant records which he left that he hoped
to pacify the tribes of the Wisconsin triangle and of
western Lake Superior so that he, on the route to the
Sea of the West, might set up the same kind of commercial empire as La Salle planned in the Mississippi
valley. Unfortunately for him, those Indians were in a
perpetual ferment of economic rivalries generated by
the inequalities which arose from their dependence for
goods on four fronts—The Illinois, Lake Michigan,
Lake Superior and Hudson Bay.

He spent the period from late 1678 to mid-1679 in
re-establishing friendly relations with the Indians of
Lake Superior, whom the French had almost deserted
about 1670 in spite of St. Lusson's bright pageantry at
the Sault in 1671. He then pushed on to the end of the
lake to enter the Sioux country where Radisson and
Groseilliers had been twenty years before, and 'on the
second of July, 1679 . . . had the honor to set up the
arms of his Majesty in the great village of the Nadouecioux called Izatys' on the shore of Lake Mille Lacs,
one of the head-waters of the Mississippi, south-west of
the end of Lake Superior. On 15 September, 'at the
extremity of Lake Superior',[2] he brought the Sioux and

---

[1] See Chapter XV.   [2] Where the city of Duluth now stands.

their northern enemies, Assiniboines, Saulteurs and Crees, together for peace talks, which he fostered during the whole winter. While he was thus busy, he sent three of his men off westward with a Sioux war-party. We do not know how far they went (perhaps as far west as modern Dakota), but they brought back some salt, reporting 'that the savages had told them that it was only twenty days' journey from where they were to the discovery of the great lake whose water is not good to drink'. This reference to what may have been Great Salt Lake of course meant the Western Sea to Duluth, whose main intention it was 'to penetrate to the sea of the west-northwest coast'.

In June 1680 he began to supplement his land exploration by investigating possible water routes. He found a small river (Bois Brulé) on the south shore near the end of the lake and took two canoes up it to a portage over to the St. Croix river. That stream took him to the Mississippi, 'where I learned . . . that the Reverend Father Louis Henpin, Récollet . . . had with two other Frenchmen been seized and taken away as slaves for more than three hundred leagues by the Nadouecioux themselves'. Convinced that French prestige must be promptly restored, he dropped his own plans for western exploration and hurried down the Mississippi to rescue his fellow-countrymen. They had been captured on 11 April, probably not far above the mouth of the Wisconsin, and had been dragged to and fro in the upper Mississippi valley all the summer by their Sioux captors. Hennepin would have us believe that after a few days of risk and indignities his own natural prestige had asserted itself to secure decent treatment, but Duluth's comment was less flattering. 'The want of respect that was being shown to the said Reverend Father provoked

me, and I let them know it.' The Sioux, really perplexed as to what to do with their captives, had vented
their puzzlement in neglect or abuse of them. Unfortunately for western exploration, Duluth decided that
France must be respected along the Green Bay-Wisconsin approach to the Mississippi and, after warning
the Sioux at Mille Lacs, he took his party back to Lake
Michigan by that route. Arrived at St. Ignace in the
autumn, he learned that the intendant at Quebec had
charged him with organising a group of unlicensed
traders. In the spring of 1681, therefore, he went down
to the St. Lawrence to defend himself. For the next
seventeen years it was that able veteran, Nicholas
Perrot,[1] who fought a losing fight to solve the Green
Bay middleman problem and arrest the decline of
French prestige in Wisconsin.

One of the striking features of the last sixty years of
French enterprise in North America (1700–1763) is
the almost negligible control enjoyed by the Canadians
or the Illinoians of the interior of the great block of
territory bounded by the Missouri, the Illinois, Lake
Michigan and a line drawn due west from the Sault.
Much of the region was explored intermittently by
licensed and unlicensed traders, by miners and by
missionary priests, so that there was little mystery about
its general character except north of the mouth of the
Platte river. There was usually some sort of a post or
a mission on the upper Mississippi among the Sioux,
but its position was precarious and its existence interrupted. Many men were sure that the Missouri or the
Minnesota provided a short route to the Pacific, and
two traveller-impostors, Mathieu Sagean and Louis
Armand, Baron de Lahontan, wrote confidently of

[1] See p. 249.

23

exactly how it was done. Their tales seemed amply corroborated by Father Hennepin's vigorous recommendations of himself and of his knowledge of the Mississippi valley. The Mallet brothers were prepared to go on up the Missouri beyond the mouth of the Platte in order to reach Santa Fé, and there are many vague reports after 1700 of groups of *voyageurs* having explored 400 or 500 leagues up the valley. Yet the record of what the French did in a systematic way west of the Mississippi is pretty well summed up in the expeditions to the South-West from Louisiana and The Illinois[1] and in the expeditions to the North-West from Lake Superior. On the face of things it would appear that the Foxes just west of Lake Michigan and the Sioux of the upper Mississippi formed an Indian barrier to real occupation and control which the French could not break.

In many senses, and particularly if the repercussions of Fox and Sioux behaviour on neighbouring tribes are taken into account, that explanation is correct. The Foxes were at war with the Canadians and raided The Illinois intermittently from 1701 to 1738, so successfully that they often closed the Green Bay-Wisconsin route to the Mississippi and seriously threatened the Chicago portage. Duluth's successes among the Sioux could not be continuously maintained between 1684 and 1727, and we shall find that later the French found it wise to skirt the Sioux country through friendlier tribes to the north.

Yet the Foxes and the Sioux were not alone responsible. The truth was that after 1700 the almost continuous water-way from Quebec to New Orleans had become the main artery of a thinly populated French

[1] See Chapter XIX.

colonial empire, threatened from one end to the other by the English. The French in North America, therefore, were forced to face to the east. The two European states, their American colonies and their Indian allies were openly at war from 1689 to 1697, from 1702 to 1713, from 1744 to 1748 and from 1754 to 1763. In order to protect their main line of communication, the Canadians tried to control the Ohio valley as a forward line of defence, meanwhile neglecting the upper Mississippi and Missouri. If the French failed to manage the Fox middlemen, they at least had the excuse of the more immediate problem of the English and the Iroquois. The first half of the eighteenth century in North America was a period of deep-rooted conflicts and of violent fluctuations in the supply and price of furs which involved the Europeans and the Indians in political and economic circumstances to which they could not adjust themselves until some of the rivalries were resolved. In these circumstances it is a cause for real wonder that the French found the energy and resources to make their ways across the South-West to Sante Fé and to push past the Sioux into the North-West.

The position of the Sioux was most peculiar. Roughly speaking, they occupied a triangle whose points were the western end of Lake Superior, a spot about due west from there on the James river and another on the Missouri between the mouths of the Big Sioux and the Platte. On three sides of them, north, east and south, were tribes who served as middlemen for the English of Hudson Bay, for the French of Lake Michigan and The Illinois, and in the matter of horses for the Spaniards in the South-West. Only the French were in a position to break through the middlemen tribes, and Perrot, Duluth and Pierre Le Sueur did so and maintained trading-posts for varying periods. Yet the Canadian position among the Sioux was an uneasy one, particularly when based on Green Bay or Lake Michigan. It was much safer when based on Lake Superior, but there again the situation was complicated by the middlemen Saulteurs (Chippewas) and Crees. The Sioux hated the middlemen, for they were proud and resented dependence. The French, not powerful enough to smash the barriers permanently, had to keep on good terms with the middlemen. The perplexed Sioux, therefore, were very apt to associate the French with their Indian enemies. On the whole, the hand of the Sioux was raised against every man and the Canadians found it wisest in the long run to go around their territory.

An additional incentive for using Lake Superior as a base was the desire to divert the flow of fine western and northern furs from Hudson Bay to the Great Lakes. Duluth had illustrated the process nicely. He and his brother, Claude Greysolon, Sieur de la Tourette, in 1684 turned their attention from the end of the lake to the mouth of the Kaministiquia river and to Lake Nipigon. Their post, La Tourette at the northern end of Lake Nipigon, was the left flank of the French effort to check the Hudson Bay traders. One of their immediate successors or associates, Jacques de Noyon, in 1688 worked up the Kaministiquia river and through the tangle of rivers, beaver meadows and lakes to Rainy Lake, whence in the spring of 1689 he followed Rainy River to Lake of the Woods. His discoveries and Duluth's plans to find the Western Sea had to be pigeon-holed until 1716, however, because of the Indian and general wars between 1684 and 1713, and in particular because the Canadians decided to give up their remarkable overland raids on Hudson Bay[1] in favour of even more successful direct naval expeditions. Unfortunately for them, their North American successes were more than counterbalanced by European defeats and in 1713 France recognised British sovereignty over Hudson Bay.

After the peace of 1713 and the surrender of Hudson Bay to the British, the Canadians had to reconsider their whole situation in the West, and between 1715 and 1730 all the old problems and possibilities were rehearsed. The Illinois was by now closely linked to Louisiana, and after its formal annexation in 1718, its contribution to Canada declined. The furs of the immediate basin of the Great Lakes had been wastefully depleted. Wisconsin had been so rapidly stripped of its furs that the beaver market was badly flooded between 1690 and 1700. Now, therefore, Canada must find a new, dependable source of its principal economic lifeblood. The first step was the gradual reoccupation of the western posts which had been abandoned in 1698. Noyon's report of his trip to Lake of the Woods was brought out, and in 1717 Zacharie Robutel, Sieur de la Noüe, corroborated it as far as Rainy Lake, but the Sioux were roused to active hostility by the resulting cooperation of the French with the Crees. Father Pierre Charlevoix surveyed the French domain from Quebec to New Orleans in 1720–23 and reported on its possibilities, and in particular on reaching the Western Sea.

The years of discussion of that subject, stimulated and perverted by the tales of several impostors, had by now led geographers to believe that somewhere not far north of 43° on the Pacific coast was to be found the entrance (presumably masked by an island) to a huge

1 See p. 289.

gulf or inland sea, not unlike Hudson Bay or the Gulf of
Mexico. The Western Sea of from about 1670 to about
1760 was not the Pacific, therefore, but a sort of North
American Mediterranean with its outlet on the Pacific.
It was expected that into it flowed a river or rivers which
rose along a height of land which divided the Pacific
Slope from the Hudson Bay basin, from that of the
Great Lakes and from the upper Mississippi and Missouri valleys. Such men as Pierre le Moyne d'Iberville, governor of Louisiana, who had studied the question from Hudson Bay Company records captured at
York factory in 1694, and Nicolas Jérémie, who was one
of the French commanders there between 1694 and
1714, assiduously investigated the possibilities of a
route to the sea. Everywhere, from Hudson Bay to the
Gulf of Mexico, the Indians and the traders had been
questioned. One can easily imagine what an amazing
medley of often irreconcilable statements resulted from
their descriptions (and rude maps) of the rivers and
lakes between either Hudson Bay or Lake Superior and
Lake Winnipeg; of the relation of that lake and its
neighbours to the rivers which flowed into them and out
of them in all directions; of the head-waters of the
Mississippi; of the upper Missouri and its tributaries;
and of occasional references to what was probably
Great Salt Lake, but which was taken to be the sea.
And with regrettable, if understandable, frequency the
Indians adorned their scanty accounts of the farthest
West with reports of white men, bearded men, what
seemed to be Chinese inscriptions, gold, silver, copper,
metal utensils, fire-arms and great ships. Doubtless the
practical explorers learned to discount such pheno-
mena as 'men only three and a half to four feet tall
and very thick-set'.

The man who was to resolve the most important of the western mysteries, that is, discover the nature of the continental crossroads at Lake Winnipeg, and thereby establish the routes by which the first two transcontinental journeys were to be made almost two generations later, was Pierre Gaultier de Varennes, Sieur de la Vérendrye, assisted by enterprising members of his family.[1] His great work was to discover and describe the important relation of the three lakes, Winnipeg, Winnipegosis and Manitoba, to the long rivers which came from the south and west and flowed into Hudson Bay, thereby providing important avenues for the further revelation of the continent. He also found the upper Missouri and mapped it reasonably correctly. It is a great pity that a natural interest in whether the La Vérendrye group did or did not reach the Rocky Mountains in their journeyings has tended in the past to obscure the importance of their having placed the Missouri and the great rivers of the North-West in their proper relation.

Canadian policy in the North-West fur trade after 1715 became a blend of the old regional monopoly idea, introduced by La Salle and imitated by Nicolas Perrot and Duluth, and of the principle of establishing separate tribal stations instead of inter-tribal posts in order to solve the middleman problem. At the western

---

[1] There are many controversies concerning La Vérendrye and his sons, as will be readily understandable to any reader of their records or of the maps associated with them. The large literature of the subject is almost completely indicated in L. J. Burpee's edition (with translation) for the Champlain Society of *Journals and Letters of La Vérendrye and his Sons* (Toronto, 1927), which also contains seven of the maps. See also A. S. Morton, 'La Vérendrye', in *Canadian Historical Review*, ix, 4 (December 1928); Burpee's rejoinder, *ibid.* x, 1 (March 1929), pp. 53-5; and N. M. Crouse, 'The Location of Fort Maurepas', *ibid.* ix, 3 (September 1928). My account represents one of several possible interpretations.

end of Lake Superior the Sioux were encouraged to use the posts on the upper Mississippi, but the depots at Kaministiquia and Lake Nipigon did not suffice to keep the Crees (and the Assiniboines to the south-west of them) from going down the Albany or the Hayes river for the cheaper goods at Hudson Bay. It was desirable, therefore, to push posts westward to hold the Crees of the enormous, rich maze of lakes and perhaps to go even farther to set up a post in the Assiniboine country. Such a move would carry the Canadians past the Sioux to the south. It was La Vérendrye who saw the situation and asked for permission to exploit it.

Son of the governor of the Three Rivers district, he had followed a military career in Canada and France from 1697 until he was badly wounded at Malplaquet in 1709. His efforts down to 1724 to continue his European military career were unsuccessful. From about 1715 to 1727, therefore, he carried on the family fur business on the St. Maurice river, but in 1728 he went from that meagre field to control the Northern Posts (Nipigon and Kaministiquia), where he seems to have done very well for himself and his large family. While there he of course faced Hudson Bay competition, and, in the course of questioning his Indian customers about their trips to the Bay, he learned not only of the approaches to Lake of the Woods by the Kaministiquia or the Pigeon river (later known as Grand Portage), but of a great river (the Winnipeg) flowing west from Lake of the Woods to another lake (Winnipeg), which in turn was drained westward by a river flowing into the sea (presumably the Western Sea). Actually he was wrongly informed about the last river, for it was the Nelson, which flowed north-east to Hudson Bay. If the Saskatchewan was meant, the direction of its flow was also incorrect. Armed with this information and with a map embodying it which he attributed to a Cree named Ochagach, La Vérendrye was successful in securing a trading monopoly of the Lake Winnipeg region in 1730. He had baited his proposals with the promise to search for the Western Sea. A syndicate of Montreal merchants agreed to back him in a partnership. The Canadian authorities also counted on him to keep the Crees and Assiniboines from going to Hudson Bay.

Both he and the Canadian governor sought for royal assistance in the new venture by enlarging on hopes of reaching the Western Sea, but the French court was apathetic, probably because of Father Charlevoix's scepticism about his motives and the report that he had served only his own interests at the Northern Posts. It was decided that the monopoly ought to provide him with enough profit to find the Sea at his own expense. In fact the monopoly was made conditional upon a search for the Western Sea. We are here presented with the basic dilemma about the Vérendryes. Throughout their careers in the West, La Vérendrye and his sons never ceased insisting that they were searching for the Western Sea. Among them they made at least two difficult and unprofitable journeys which could properly be described as primarily such searching. Yet there is not the least doubt but that their main occupation was the fur trade and in particular the systematic cutting-off of the flow of furs to Hudson Bay. Was the fur trade the hampering condition of their main object, the Sea, or was the Sea merely the awkward condition of retaining the Winnipeg monopoly? The complex arguments on the point cannot be repeated here. It seems quite clear from their own reports of their own speeches and actions that the Vérendryes were primarily fur traders exploiting a new and very rich monopoly in an elaborate and expensive way, who also knew that they could earn approval at Quebec and Versailles by finding one of the rivers which flowed into the Western Sea. They were either calculating or inquisitive enough to neglect business when they could in order to look for it. 'These people dress themselves in winter in beaver skins and in spring they throw them away, not being able to sell them,' wrote La Vérendrye to the Governor of Canada. Collection of that rich harvest and the fencing of it off from the English were irresistibly the main tasks. 'The English have every interest in getting ahead of us, and if we allow them time they will not lose the chance of doing it.' Luckily for the Canadians, the English on the Bay were laggards.

On 26 August 1731 La Vérendrye arrived at Grand Portage (Pigeon river) with a party of fifty which included three of his sons, Jean-Baptiste, Pierre and François; his nephew, Christophe Dufrost, Sieur de la Jemeraye; and a Jesuit, Father Charles Michel Mesaiger. Learning that the Northern Posts were vacant, he himself moved to Kaministiquia for the winter, but sent La Jemeraye and one of his sons on with three canoes to build Fort St. Pierre on Rainy Lake. The comment of the Minister in Paris is illuminating: 'the stopping of this officer at Kaministigoya would appear susceptible of the suspicion of self-interest'. He asked the Canadian authorities to give him the monopoly of the Northern Posts again for five years as well as that of the new Posts of the Western Sea, and he was allowed to use Kaministiquia. He explained his delay in pushing on to the Sea on the ground of a mutiny among his men, but he spent the winter collecting furs.

Next spring, while Jean-Baptiste went out to Michili-mackinac with the winter's takings, La Vérendrye moved up to the west shore of the Lake of the Woods, where, instead of on Lake Winnipeg, he built his principal fort, an imposing structure 100 feet square and complete with chapel and priest's house, named Fort St. Charles. For the next two years it was the centre of operations designed to hold the Crees and Assiniboines. In the spring of 1733 La Jemeraye and one of La Vérendrye's sons went on down the Winnipeg river, but were held up by ice about fifty miles from its mouth, and it does not appear that either of them pressed on. La Vérendrye had learned by now from the Indians that the outlet of Lake Winnipeg flowed into Hudson Bay, and he was therefore on the whole readier to consolidate his fur-trading position than to seek the Western Sea. Meanwhile, however, the French Court was beginning to shew a more active interest in the Western Sea, and in turn the Canadian governor and La Vérendrye were forced to consider what could be done about it.

Fortunately or unfortunately, La Vérendrye had acquired through the tales of the Crees and Assiniboines a new basis for the search. La Jemeraye was able to tell the Canadian governor in 1733 of a nation on 'the River of the West', 750 miles from Lake of the Woods. They 'have eight villages established there, fields of Indian corn, melons, pumpkins, beans, horses, cats, and dwellings constructed of wood and earth and built like French houses'. 'The Cree . . . have promised the Sieur de la Jemeraye and the son of La Vérendrye to conduct them thither, where they can get information as to how to get down to the Western Sea into which to all appearance that great river discharges.' The 'new nation' we now know to have been Arikaras, Hidatsas or Mandans, whose villages of timber and earthen houses were set among maize-fields between the bend of the Souris and the southward bend of the Missouri. They carried on an annual or semi-annual exchange of goods with the Assiniboines. The 'great river' did not flow west, but, as we shall see, it and the Saskatchewan did come nearest to earning the title of River of the West. The Canadian governor first used the new information to defend La Vérendrye at Versailles and then urged him to get busy on the new clue in order to justify his monopoly. He arranged that La Vérendrye might sub-let his posts to the flood of new traders so as to be free to explore.

While La Vérendrye himself had thus far accomplished little, his sons and La Jemeraye had begun really to explore the Lake Winnipeg basin. The Indians of Lake Winnipeg (Crees and Assiniboines) had promised not to go to Hudson Bay if the French would build a fort among them. Pierre and another Frenchman, after a visit of inspection in March 1734, decided that the best site was about twelve or fifteen miles up the Red river from its mouth, and in the autumn Fort Maurepas was built there, apparently by Jean-Baptiste and Pierre. Soon afterwards the young men discovered a short-cut directly west from Lake of the Woods, by the Roseau river, to the Red river and the new fort. In effect the French had thus made their way through the Crees and beyond the troublesome Sioux almost to the Assiniboines. Unfortunately, and in spite of earnest efforts to divert them, La Vérendrye could not avoid equipping the Cree war parties which warred against the Sioux of the Mississippi. The result was that in 1736 those Sioux fell upon a French party of between twenty

and twenty-five men in Lake of the Woods and massacred them all, including Jean-Baptiste (who had
accompanied a Cree war party against them in 1734)
and the Jesuit Father Jean Aulneau. Inasmuch as La
Jemeraye had died that spring, La Vérendrye might
have been excused for contracting his operations. Instead, he went to Montreal again in 1737 and promised
the governor to seek out the Mandans on the River of
the West and put a report in his hands in time to catch
the autumn sailing for France in 1739. The Assiniboines had brought him word from the Mandan chief
that 'it would give me great pleasure to see him or any
of his people', as doubtless it would to a people whose
only European articles had been purchased dearly from
the Assiniboines.

In 1738 La Vérendrye still believed that the Mandans were white and lived on a great river, but he had
learned from an Indian map that it 'does not run west,
but takes a turn to the south and finally discharges, it
would appear, into the Pacific Ocean, where there are
white men'. He decided to visit the Mandans, but he
felt it wise also to have the Indians record the relation
of Lakes Manitoba and Winnipegosis to the maze of
water-ways because the northern Indians had for some
time been urging him to build a fort near the northern
end of Lake Winnipeg. On the Indian map a new river,
the Blanche, emerged. This we know to be the Saskatchewan, but the Cree account of it mixed it up hopelessly with the Nelson and the Churchill systems. Marvellous to relate, however, it too was a 'River of the
West', and a Cree who said he had travelled it told La
Vérendrye of its warm climate, 'seeds like pepper . . .
a kind of cocoa . . . mines, all kinds of wild beasts in
abundance, and snakes of a prodigious size'. Of course,

365

down the river 'white men dwell who have walled towns and forts'. Missouri and Saskatchewan, the two real river routes to the Pacific, were both offered to La Vérendrye in 1737 and 1738. He felt that he had circumvented the Sioux. He chose the Missouri first because on his way to it he could please the Assiniboines and at the same time cut off another known road to Hudson Bay by building a post at the portage from Assiniboine river to Lake Manitoba (Portage-la-Prairie). Moreover, he was now on trial, for the Minister in France had written to the Canadian governor that the recent information 'confirms the suspicion I have always entertained, and which I have not concealed from you, that the beaver trade had more to do than anything else with the Sieur de la Vérendrye's Western Sea expedition'. The governor had told him that if he did not reach the Mandans he would be recalled. His monopoly was too rich a plum to go to a man under a cloud.

La Vérendrye now moved with great rapidity. He got his stores and his men up to Michilimackinac in time to be able to start west on 20 July 1738. He reached Kaministiquia on 5 August. By the 22nd he was on Rainy Lake and he reached Fort St. Charles on the 31st. He had outstripped his trader associates in their heavily laden canoes, and, after waiting ten days for them in vain, he set off on 11 September for Fort Maurepas, which he reached on the 22nd. The Crees had built a fort at the junction of the Red and the Assiniboine in order to discourage him from visiting the Assiniboines up that river, 'who did not know how to kill beaver, and whose only clothing was buffalo skin, a thing we did not require', but La Vérendrye pushed on westwards on the 26th. The river was low and winding, so he went ahead on foot for six days, while the canoes followed. On 2 October he halted at Portage-la-Prairie to choose a site for his Fort La Reine, 'for that is the road by which the Assiniboines go to the English . . . and, if you wish to go to the Mandans, you are close to the road'. By the 15th the fort and houses were completed, twenty *voyageurs* for the Mandan expedition were chosen on the 16th, and on the 18th the party of fifty-two set off down the Mandan trail on foot, La Vérendrye and two of his sons,[1] François and Louis-Joseph (called the Chevalier), at their head.

Their guide, fearful of the Sioux to the east, made them go cautiously and once drew them away from the trail to visit an Assiniboine village. In spite of La Vérendrye's impatience, it took until 3 December to reach an outlying fortified village of the Mandans. 'Every day they [the Assiniboines] talked to us about the whites we were going to see, Frenchmen like ourselves . . . everything they said gave us hope of making a remarkable discovery.' The expedition made the step from the timbered regions to the prairies and was fortunate enough to do so before the plains Indians of the North had acquired a sufficiency of horses to make them, like the southern and central tribes, a redoubtable barrier to exploration. A group of Mandans came to a rendezvous on 28 November, and then La Vérendrye learned to his disgust 'that there was a large discount to be taken off all that had been told me'. 'They do not differ from the Assiniboines.' He later discovered that some of them did have almost white complexions and 'an abundance of fair hair'.

---

[1] The identity of the sons on this and several other occasions is hard to determine, but can usually be decided by cross-reference. Louis-Joseph was the youngest and a trained geographer. He went to the West in 1735.

Once settled in the Mandan village, La Vérendrye began a systematic investigation of what lay beyond by questioning his hosts. The father was much embarrassed by the loss of his presents, by the desertion of his interpreter and by the unwillingness of the Mandans to entertain the Assiniboines after they had bartered away all the European goods which they had brought, but he and his sons succeeded in collecting a good deal of information. They learned that Europeans lived down the river, but a whole summer's journey away on horseback. The description of these men fitted the Spaniards somewhat better than the French, but the Mandans had been at war with their southern neighbours for four or five years and presumably could not know of the recent enterprises of Bourgmond or the reconnaissances of the Mallet brothers. It was impossible to get exact information without an interpreter, however, and La Vérendrye seemed to lose interest, probably because he had a growing suspicion that his River of the West was the Missouri. He did not entirely give up, and he made arrangements to leave two *voyageurs* and two Assiniboines with the Mandans to learn the language and gather information. After being delayed by three days' illness, he himself set out for Fort La Reine on 13 December.

The best evidence that he was disillusioned about the Mandans' river is that on 10 or 16 April 1739 he sent off his son, Louis-Joseph, the Chevalier, 'to look out for a suitable place in which to build a fort on the Lake of the Prairies [the name given both to Lake Manitoba and to Lake Winnipegosis] in accordance with the request which the Crees of that region made of me, and afterwards to betake himself to the Poskioac River [Saskatchewan] to investigate its lower reaches at the entrance to the end of Lake Winnipeg'. His earlier version of this mission says 'to go and find a site for the fort on Lake Winnipeg and examine the rivers that flow into that lake, especially the Blanche river [Saskatchewan] . . . and to explore the outlet of the lake and make a circuit of it, and try to prevent the savages from going to the English'. Doubtful of the possibilities of the Mandans' river, he was bent on completing his ring of control around the Winnipeg basin, with posts on the Winnipeg river, the Red, the Assiniboine, Lake Manitoba, the Saskatchewan and even the head of Lake Winnipeg.

Before 1744, when an unsympathetic government withdrew the Vérendryes from the region where they had made such fundamental discoveries, they were able to explore beyond the Mandan country sufficiently to satisfy themselves of its impracticability as a field for Canadian enterprise. The two *voyageurs* left behind in 1738 returned next autumn with news of a western tribe of Indians with horses who had visited the Mandans. One of their number had 'been brought up from childhood among whites' who lived 'near the great lake where the water rises and falls and is not good to drink'. They did not understand the language of the white men which he spoke, but he wore a crucifix around his neck and, in the course of several conversations, he drew a convincing picture of what must have been life in the Spanish colonies. He was tremendously interested in the French and promised to guide them to the Spanish settlements if they would take him to the Canadian towns. They could not go without consulting La Vérendrye. He decided that the news warranted an expedition.

After two and a half years of what was perhaps

necessary delay because of Sioux attacks which
threatened their main line of communication, and
during which Pierre made a vain effort to secure guides
to the Sea from the Mandans, the Chevalier and François, accompanied by two *voyageurs*, set out on 29 April
1742 to find the 'Horse Indians' and travel to the Sea.
'They were resolved to perish rather than give up', and
it was not their fault that their efforts availed them and
their successors nothing in the search for the Western
Sea. They waited in vain in the Mandan village from
19 May to 23 July for the arrival of the Horse Indians.
Then, in the blazing summer heat, they set off west-
south-west on foot to find them. It is impossible to be
sure where they went, but one can admire their courage,
for their Mandan guides soon left them, and yet, from
18 September 1742 to mid-March 1743, they moved
about from tribe to tribe. They were soon in possession
of horses and travelled extensively, roughly in the
region between the Little Missouri and Cheyenne
rivers, parts of which are so arid and broken as to have
since earned the American descriptive term, Bad Lands.
'The prairies through which we passed are sparse and
dry; the trail of the horses did not show.' They heard of
the many enmities among the mounted nomads and of
the Serpent tribe (probably Cheyennes or Tetons) who
barred the way to 'the nation living on the coast'. They
even met a chief who described the massacre of Villasur's
expedition on the Platte in 1720. 'All that cooled my
ardour considerably for a sea which was already known,
nevertheless I should have wished greatly to go there,
had it been possible,' wrote the Chevalier. Their
generally southern course brought them in sight of an
odd forested island in the Great Plains, where altitude
caught moisture and moisture fostered trees. These

were the Black Hills, and young La Vérendrye succeeded in getting the Indians to go close to them, but a
panic among them kept him from climbing for the view.
'I had a longing to see the Sea from the mountains.'
Instead they turned east-south-east through deep snow
and slowly made their way to the Missouri again, which
they reached on 19 March 1743.

On 16 February 1913 a party of American school
children found a lead plate in the earth of a hill in
Pierre, South Dakota, which bore an inscription uniting
the names of Louis XV, the Canadian governor and La
Vérendrye *père*, and which had scratched on the other
side the names Louy La Londette and A. Miotte,
30 March 1743. The location of that plate, whose
burial is mentioned in the journal of the expedition, is
the basis for the belief that the Vérendryes saw the
Black Hills rather than the foot-hills of the Rockies.
Their achievement in sustaining themselves for so long
in so troubled an area had been no small one, but their
service to North American exploration was slight. Yet
it might have been greater, for at the Indian village
where the plate was deposited, they learned 'that three
days' journey from where we then were there was a
Frenchman who had been settled there for several
years. I would have gone to see him if our horses had
been in condition.' The Chevalier did make some efforts
to send messages to him and left word that he was going
to the Mandans. 'I should have been gratified to draw
him away from living with the savages.' The chance of
closing the circuit around the Foxes and Sioux was
lost, however, when the Canadian failed to press on to
join hands with the unknown *voyageur* from The Illinois.
It may be that the failure was a calculated one in days of
monopolies. At any rate, the four Frenchmen were back

371

lay tumbling rivers and a filigree of beaver-ponds and lakes. East of it were the harried and predatory agents at Michilimackinac, and beyond them the querulous merchants at Montreal. The mere problem of getting dependable *voyageurs* was never solved.

No doubt La Vérendrye and his sons would have liked to find the Western Sea, and it was not their fault that they did not. There was no Western Sea as the geographers imagined it, and the Pacific was too far away for them to find even when governmental orders forced them to abandon trading for exploration. The Vérendryes did thoroughly explore the crossroads of the continent. They demonstrated by inference from the Missouri and the Saskatchewan how very broad the continent must be. And there is a note of true nobility in a man of sixty-four who died on the eve of a new expedition with his sons to 'the heights which can be reached only in the second year after leaving Montreal'.

NARRATIVES

Margry as above, chiefly vol. vi. Hennepin, though vain and untrustworthy, wrote interestingly. His fairly accurate account of his adventures, *Description de la Louisiane*, of 1683, has been edited and translated by J. D. G. Shea (New York, 1880), and his inflated advertisement of himself to William III of England, *Nouvelle Découverte d'un très grand Pays*, of 1697, by R. G. Thwaites (Chicago, 1903). Shea also included Duluth's memoir of 1678–82. Jérémie's *Relation* has been edited and translated by R. Douglas and J. N. Wallace as *Twenty Years of York Factory* (Ottawa, 1926). There is a considerable amount of original material in the published state collections of Wisconsin, Minnesota and South Dakota. For the Vérendryes see footnote, p. 359. Interesting supplementary material concerning them is to be found in A. E. Jones' edition of *The Aulneau Collection* (Montreal, 1893).

CHAPTER XXI

POLITICAL AND OTHER INTERLUDES, 1750–1803

(*Map No. 4, end of book*)

To the vivacity of a Frenchman, and the sincerity of an Englishman,
he added the gravity and nobleness of a Turk.

FROM SAMUEL HEARNE'S PORTRAIT OF
HIS CHIPEWYAN GUIDE, MATONABBEE

POLITICAL considerations played a remarkably
small part in determining pioneer North American
exploration. Indeed politicians usually found that their
policies were far behind the seekers of loot, souls or
peltry, who, often unauthorised, rushed into the North
American Canaans. Moreover, explorers had an easy
way of ignoring political frontiers. Englishmen, Frenchmen and Spaniards investigated each other's unoccupied
territories whenever their own interests drew them
there and even entered foreign employment. New
Yorkers, for instance, hurried into Canada almost before it had been conquered in 1760 and, along with
other vigorous groups, took control of the French field
force in the western fur trade and worked with them
(and against the Hudson's Bay Company), almost irre-
spective of political events like the cession of Louisiana
to Spain or the American Revolution. Yet between
1754 and 1803 there was such a great deal of political
change in North America, and so much in the way of
re-exploration, change in the direction of human in-

375

terest, and consolidation before new enterprise, that it is convenient to draw together those circumstances before describing the next great steps in the revelation of the continent.

The outstanding event was the great duel between Great Britain and France for colonial empire, whose last episode between 1754 and 1760 began ingloriously for the British, but ended in victory under the resolute direction of Pitt. Actually the French had been outdone by the British in the Indian trade which was the chief support of their colonies many years before Montreal fell. On the Mississippi, in the Ohio valley, on the Lakes and the St. Lawrence, and even in the competition with the unenterprising Hudson's Bay Company, French trade-goods were beaten by British in price and quality. The French went so far as to encourage friendly Indians to trade with the British for such articles as woollen cloth, so that they might in turn purchase it and pass it on in trade with more remote tribes. A Hudson Bay factor described the Indians at York Factory as 'actually turned factors for the French at our settlements for heavy goods'. France was able to conceal her economic defeat and postpone the political by the resolution, skill and co-ordination of her military efforts, alone and through the Indians. Had Great Britain and her American colonies been concerned enough to combine and produce anything even approaching the quality of military intelligence and thrust displayed by the French, the duel would have ended in 1710 instead of in 1760.

The peace treaties of 1763 eliminated French sovereignty from North America except for two small islands in the Gulf of St. Lawrence and some West Indian possessions, but something under 100,000

French North Americans remained. Spain, which had been lured into the war in 1761, had suffered severely in the West Indies and the Philippines. To get back Havana, she surrendered Florida to the British, but France salved the wound a little by ceding to her all Louisiana west of the Mississippi. Unable to hold it herself, France realised that Spain would be a more congenial sovereign for the Frenchmen in the valley than Great Britain, and that Spain and they might be able to keep out the flood of colonial Englishmen who were crossing the Appalachians along the trading paths, until France had enjoyed a breathing-space.

In 1763 Spain was at the beginning of a great revival of strength in Europe and in the Americas, which she owed to the energy of her new Bourbon king, Charles III. In the preceding generation New Spain had suffered severely. The Indians along the whole frontier, Navajos and Utes to the north, Comanches and Apaches to the east, had definitely put the soldiers and the missionaries of the outposts on the defensive. French superiority over Spain in the Indian trade meant that the mounted raiders, now armed with European weapons, became so bold that they were able to set up a regular trade with The Illinois and Louisiana in Spanish cattle and horses. Matters changed after the cession of Louisiana in 1764. After about five years of awkward readjustment, Spaniards and Frenchmen combined in a new and vigorous exploitation. From the Indian standpoint the new situation was highly perplexing, for their former backers had made friends with the very people whom they had once been encouraged to attack. But Spain was wise enough to use French agents and gradually an uneasy equilibrium with the

377

Indians was achieved. The next tasks were to expel the aggressive Englishmen who had crossed the Mississippi and to establish a barrier against their return. Then there were reopened for peaceful commerce all the old trails and routes which France and Spain had established west of the Mississippi. Indian troubles occasionally interrupted their use, for the natives could not understand that prices would fall when the Europeans ceased to compete, but before the end of the century a Franco-Spanish trading company had even succeeded in pushing its operations up the Missouri as far as the Mandans. Then, on La Vérendrye's River of the West, there was the anomalous spectacle of French *voyageurs* working for Englishmen from Montreal competing with French *voyageurs* working for Spaniards from New Orleans!

Meanwhile the old English colonies of the Atlantic coast also had a contribution to make to the mid-continental situation. Many of them had populations ready to burst through the Appalachian passes as soon as France was defeated. They were more interested in farm lands and good transportation routes to the Gulf of Mexico than in fur trade, but ahead of the several groups converging on the passes reached out, like antennae, the 'long hunters' of the fur and skin trade. Getting to the Mississippi proved to be a difficult business. An Indian military genius of the Ottawas, named Pontiac, blocked the advance from Lake Erie to New Orleans from May 1763 to early 1765 by an amazing alliance of the natives which obliterated the frontier outposts. Even after that menace was removed, the Iroquois in the north and the other tribes who stood between the Appalachians and the Franco-Spanish Mississippi were very loath to let in a flood of Europeans who wanted to till their lands and thus spoil their hunting-grounds for ever.

The British government, in its effort to control the situation, tried to hold back the land-seeking flood, to admit traders by licence and to divert the would-be settlers into Canada or the Florida peninsula or the Gulf coast east of the Mississippi. In these measures it had considerable success, particularly in settlement of the South, but the tide was still stronger, and with the French menace removed, the colonists were ready to add exclusion from the West to their other growing grievances against the mother country. The sum of these became impressive enough to weld the scattered agitators into a party. British inability to accept the fact that the colonies had grown up made the party a revolutionary one. Efforts at repression caused overt violence, and between 1775 and 1783 thirteen of the colonies won their independence. Then, as their citizens poured through the Appalachians, there began the extermination or impounding or flight of the American Indians—the most pitiable human cost of Europe's occupation of North America.

France and Spain had both seen an opportunity for revenge on Great Britain by supporting the rebellious colonies. Spain won back Florida, but France's war effort completed the descent to bankruptcy which had been her eighteenth-century history. Her middle class made a revolution to reform their government, and Napoleon took the revolution away from them. As an incident in his career of conquest, he won back Louisiana for France in 1800. Hardly had he secured it again, however, before he realised that he could not defend it against Great Britain in the event of a war and that the United States appeared to want it very badly. In a

379

hastily concluded bargain (1803), the new nation bought
half a continent for 60,000,000 francs about a generation before it had the population to occupy it. Except
for a handful of men interested in the fur trade, the
Americans of the day had little use for what they
thought were prairie deserts in the trans-Mississippi
'West.

While political attention has thus been concentrated
on the eastern and southern parts of the continent, the
North-West was the scene of some variations in the
traditional Hudson Bay-Great Lakes rivalry, which in
an inconspicuous way contributed greatly to the knowledge of the continent. The work of the Vérendryes, for
instance, was not done in vain. The Assiniboine-Souris
route to the plains and the Mandans became an avenue
for the horse trade and thereby transformed the buffalo-
hunt for the tribes on the North-West prairies. The
Saskatchewan, once opened up, proved so astonishingly
rich in furs that even the grave transportation problem,
aggravated as it was by Indian raids and instability between Lake Superior and Lake Winnipeg, was not
allowed to close it. During the decade after La Vérendrye's withdrawal which preceded the British conquest
of Canada, French traders had built several more or less
permanent posts between Cedar Lake and the Forks
and were intercepting the flow of the best furs towards
Hudson Bay.

Before turning to the response of the Hudson's Bay
Company to this drying-up of its supply of furs, one
other French enterprise should be mentioned, questionable and uncorroborated as it is. It is recorded in
a memoir made by Jacques Repentigny Legardeur de
Saint Pierre, an officer of the marines and a practised
manager of Indians, to whom the Vérendrye enterprises

were conceded in 1750. Saint Pierre himself did not get farther west than Fort La Reine, but he sent his subordinate Joseph Boucher, Chevalier de Niverville, up to The Pas during the winter of 1750–51 with instructions to go on up the Saskatchewan another 750 miles in the spring. Both Saint Pierre and Niverville fell ill, but the memoir says of the latter: 'He sent off ten men in two canoes who went up the river of The Pas as far as the Rocky Mountains, where they built a good fort, which I called Fort La Jonquière'.

The memoir goes on to detail the vigorous measures taken by Saint Pierre to control the Indians of the Winnipeg basin and of even farther west. Then it plunges into a most complicated and inexplicable Cree tale of some other Europeans with whom the Brochet or Pike Indians north of the Saskatchewan traded, not English but French, who lived at the end of a road 'towards where the sun sets in June'. The reported corroboration of this tale by Niverville is both weak in substance and suspect on grounds of chronology. In addition there is some indication that Niverville's men may have been guided from The Pas over into the Nelson or into the Churchill system instead of going up the Saskatchewan. Moreover, there is a glibness about the memoir and what seems almost an intent to confuse the ignorant reader. It does not seem safe, therefore, to conclude that the French reached the Rockies before the fall of Canada, and there are many grounds for believing that Saint Pierre was much more concerned with the Winnipeg fur trade than with the Western Sea which he was sent out to find.

The French in the West were often puzzled over the fact that the English of the Hudson's Bay Company seldom seemed to leave the shores of the Bay. It was not until after 1740 that they established outposts on the Missinabi, the Albany, the Hayes and the Nelson, inland from the factories at the river-mouths. One day in May 1734 La Vérendrye asked a Cree chief 'if the English [factor] knew that we were among the Crees and if he was not saying bad things'. The Cree said that he had asked the factor if he was vexed and that he had said 'No, that we [British and French] were brothers and that he would never get angry first and that it was easy for us to get along together'. 'The French', he said, 'want oily beaver and I want dry beaver.'[1] That, of course, was not the whole story. On Hudson Bay, as in India, the British had shewn a habitual disinclination to go inland and become embroiled in native affairs. They used their influence to encourage peace and industry among the natives and were content to depend on the drawing power of their goods at the factories on the coast. In the Canadian North-West the outcome was that they received the heavier and less desirable furs which they could transport cheaply to Europe. The French, with the difficult journey to Montreal to pay for, had to take the smaller, more valuable furs. They could do so because of their controlling position in the Winnipeg basin.

The Company had succeeded in forgetting Henry Kelsey with remarkable completeness, for its thoughts of new enterprise, when it had any, were maritime. Its second adventurous soul of Kelsey's day, Captain James Knight, who founded the fort at Churchill in

---

[1] The English had taken over from the Dutch on the Hudson a preference for the untreated pelts, which still contained the guard-hairs. Their Russian customers depended upon them for these. The *castor gras* was often trimmed and joined to others to make a winter robe ('coat beaver') which was worn with the fur against the skin. In the wearing, the guard-hairs fell out and the downy fur became matted and oily and better for hats.

1717, succumbed to Athapaskan tales of copper and gold to be found along 'a very great river that comes out of the west sea and is in the bottom of a very great bay'. He was a man about seventy years of age and much racked by hardship, but he was so obsessed with the idea that he could sail up the west coast of the Bay to a river, or follow it round to the north and then southwest, and so come to the gold land, that he bullied the Company into letting him have two ships in 1719. 'Knight was so confident of success, that he had strong chests made, bound with iron, to hold the gold and copper-ore which he expected.' He sailed from England early in June 'to find out the Streight of Anian, in order to discover gold', and nothing was heard of his fate until forty-eight years later, when a whaling expedition found relics of his ships where they were driven ashore on Marble Island, and by inference and Eskimo accounts pieced together a most pathetic account of the gradual extinction of the crews from disease and starvation.

The next British enterprises on the Bay were also maritime, and this time arose from the lively efforts of a fiery Anglo-Irish publicist named Arthur Dobbs. About 1730 he grew very interested in the North-West Passage, only to discover the monopolistic position enjoyed by the Company. He then declared that the Company had forfeited its charter, which he said had laid on it the duty of discovering the Passage. He succeeded in creating a great stir in England between 1733 and 1750, out of which emerged three more unsuccessful maritime expeditions and a parliamentary investigation. The end of it was that the Company kept its charter and Dobbs was quieted by being made governor of North Carolina, where he owned a large property. Yet

Dobbs rendered one service to continental exploration by publishing in 1744 an elaborate description of the interior of the continent south and west of the Bay, drawn chiefly from the experience of a renegade half-breed *coureur* from Michilimackinac, named Joseph La France, who had made his way slowly from the Sault to York Factory between the summers of 1739 and 1742.

While this narrative made no great contribution to geographical knowledge and was accompanied by a very confusing map, yet its wide circulation and La France's suggestion that the Company should establish posts inland to cut off the French at the western end of Lake Superior, earn it a place in the sequence of events. His information as to the Far West was alluring also and was derived from Indians who had been among the Flat-heads on the very head-waters of the Missouri. The Flat-heads, he reported, lived on the Pacific coast. In the light, however, of Dobbs' natural unpopularity with the Company and the habitual disinclination of the Company men to go inland, it seems wisest, in explaining the decision to investigate the interior, to attribute it largely to the clearly defined and steady drop in the takings of furs at York Factory between 1738 and 1750, the years when the Vérendryes turned their attention to the North.

On 26 June 1754 Anthony Hendry, six years before an outlawed smuggler in England and now a Company servant at York Factory, set out on a voluntary expedition with a group of Assiniboines, 'to explore the country inland, and to endeavour to increase the Hudson's Bay Company's trade'. They followed the Hayes river to Oxford Lake, from which they turned west through lake country to Cross Lake on the Nelson river. The Indian westward route of the day avoided Lake

Winnipeg in favour of a more direct way through Moose Lake to The Pas, which they reached on 22 July. It had been a hard journey with many portages, 'no provisions to be got but fish', and the mosquitoes 'intolerable', but at The Pas they found 'a French house'. 'Two Frenchmen came to the water-side, and in a very genteel manner, invited me into their house, —which I readily accepted.' They were *voyageurs* who were holding the post while Louis-Luc de la Corne, Niverville's successor,[1] went down to Montreal with the furs. After some polite, but necessarily futile, efforts to detain him, they saw him and his Indians paddle off up the river on the 24th. The Frenchmen were a full season away from their ocean base, Hendry less than a month.

Hendry and his escorts turned up the Carrot river, as Kelsey had done sixty years before, and found the Assiniboines' families almost starving at a point about sixty miles from the mouth. Almost without pausing, they abandoned their canoes on 27 July and took to the prairies to find buffalo or other game. On the 29th they had a feast of wild strawberries and saskatoon berries, and on the 30th the 'Indians killed two Moose'. The tension was over. Now the Assiniboines could travel happily across the grasslands, killing game as they needed it and gently stimulating the more western tribes to do the fur-collecting which they themselves had now almost abandoned. The middleman's autumn and winter was a pleasant one on the buffalo plains.

Hendry did not get back to York Factory until 20 June of the following year, and as his hosts and their customers had no objection to leaving the regular trails when game beckoned, it is impossible to be exact as to

[1] And son-in-law of the Chevalier La Vérendrye.

where he went. It is reasonably clear, however, that their general direction in 1754 was from the Carrot river south and west across the South Saskatchewan to the most southerly point on the North Saskatchewan, and from that point west-south-west to the Blackfeet encampments on the upper Red Deer river in the shadow of the Rockies. The Blackfeet were mounted High Plains Indians and Hendry saw horses ranging wild near their territory. After a little trapping in the hills between the Red Deer and the North Saskatchewan during the winter, he and his Indians built twenty canoes on the latter river or one of its upper tributaries[1] and started for the Bay again on 23 April 1755. The valley was alive with groups of Indians either going down to trade or trading with those who did. At last Hendry understood why the Assiniboines had refused to worry about fur collection during the winter. They now obtained an abundance in exchange for their own worn-out European goods. Hendry found himself conducting a veritable fleet of canoes to the Bay. Then suddenly the picture changed and the worth of Indian promises was revealed. He had to stop his journey to watch the French debauch his Indians with brandy and calmly acquire from them the best of their furs. At The Pas and at its outpost nearer the Forks, he saw the Company's prospective harvest grow smaller and poorer. He had the sense to make the best of it by accepting the hospitality of the French factors, while the Indians dissipated their year's capital. 'I believe many would trade all if they could persuade the French to take their heavy furs.'

Yet Hendry's achievement was a great one. If one can ignore the story of Fort La Jonquière as a piece of

---

[1] Almost as good a case can be made for the South Saskatchewan.

fiction by a Winnipeg monopolist to cover his more profitable activities nearer home, Hendry was the first European to push beyond the Forks of the Saskatchewan and travel among the Indians of the northernmost High Plains and the foot-hills of the Rockies. He was much impressed by the Blackfeet. They were well mounted, used pack-horses and asses to save their women, made pottery and produced fire by flint and nodules of iron ore or bits of steel which they got from the Assiniboines. In later years they became, like the Comanches and Apaches of the High Plains in the South-West, an implacable barrier-group to the advance of the whites, but Hendry was very well treated by them. The reason was that the horse and the buffalo had given them such complete confidence in themselves that they did not even succumb to the allure of European goods. Hendry, for instance, tried to tempt them down to the Bay and their chief's reply was very revealing. 'It was far off, & they could not live without Buffalo flesh; and that they could not leave their horses &c: and many other obstacles, though all might be got over if they were acquainted with a Canoe, and could eat Fish, which they never do.' Hendry then tried fire-arms as a bait. 'The Chief further said they never wanted food, as they followed the Buffalo & killed them with the Bows and Arrows; and he was informed the Natives that frequented the Settlements, were sometimes starved on their journey. Such remarks I thought exceeding true.' One could wish that their happy equilibrium might have been preserved.

It is exasperating to find that Company stupidity and the complacency engendered by the elimination of French competition after 1755 consigned Hendry's work to an oblivion almost as deep as Kelsey's. Andrew

Graham, factor at York Fort, and the man who sent off
Matthew Cocking to follow Hendry's footsteps in 1772,
seems to have been the person who saved Hendry's
journal. Among his annotations to it we find his tribute
and his comment on his Company. 'I knew this man;
he was a bold and good servant. . . . The accounts of
horsemen being inland were not credited. He, Hendey
[*sic*], was misrepresented by those in the Bay who were
not acting a just part to the Company, and he perceiving
not likely to meet with promotion he had so deservedly
merited, quitted the Company's service.' The former
smuggler 'was drove from the Company's service by
the ships gentry because he would not buy slops and
brandy from them.' His tales of the plains horsemen
were too incredible to the conservative directors in
London for them to see and reward his gifts. The Company was earning good dividends. Instead of respond-
ing to southern competition and trying to pre-empt
the forests which lay between the prairies and the
barren lands and which were the richest fur territory in
North America, the Company chose a lazier way. It
would offset the decline in the South by opening up the
North.

It was in 1717 that Churchill, 'Jens Munck's Winter-
Haven' of awful memory, received the first Company
fort north of York, thanks to the energy of Henry
Kelsey and James Knight. The post was designed to
draw down not only the Chipewyans of the Churchill
river system, but also to break through their influence
in order to attract the Yellow-Knives, Slaves and Dog-
Ribs from the interior of the North-West. The
Churchill river had formed a vague dividing-line between the southern Crees and the northern Athapaskan
tribes, who in turn met their mortal enemies, the

Eskimos, along the northern coast or on such fringes of the barren lands as are provided by Chesterfield Inlet and some of the northern rivers. The aggressive Crees soon found that it was easy to cross from the Saskatchewan-Nelson system to the Churchill. They, therefore, pushed the Chipewyans and other Athapaskans farther north.

When French competition began to cut into the takings at the ports on James Bay and even at York, it was quite natural for the Company men to look to Churchill and the North to compensate them for the decline in the South. In fact, Churchill Bay was chosen as the site for the Company's main stronghold in the wars of the eighteenth century, and in 1731 a gang of masons and artisans began there the construction in stone of Fort Prince of Wales. It was henceforth to serve as a base not only for a sustained effort to trade with the Athapaskans, but also for white whale and black whale fisheries in the northern part of the Bay.

It was from this fort in 1769 that Samuel Hearne began over three years of some of the most remarkable exploration in the long North American record. As he himself acknowledged, 'my discoveries are not likely to prove of any material advantage to the Nation at Large'; indeed the result of his efforts was to eliminate a huge area of North America from attention for over a century. Yet the explorer who saves his successors from unprofitable effort is as useful as he who opens up a region for exploitation. Moreover, Hearne was blessed with an odd, judicious literary artistry which enabled him to write what is one of the classics of the literature of exploration, not only because it is an illuminating account of the country, its natural history and its inhabitants, but also because it conveys unconsciously a

389

portrait 'in the round' of a very likeable and inquisitive, if somewhat timorous, man.

Hearne was a volunteer, who was sent out by Moses Norton, the vigorous half-breed governor, who had gone to England in 1768 and secured approval for the expedition. Hearne's main objective was to find the river in the North-West from which the Indians had been bringing pieces of raw copper, and copper ornaments or implements, ever since the Company's return to the Bay in 1714. Jérémie, Kelsey and Knight all knew of its existence somewhere inland. Richard Norton, father of Moses, apparently made a canoe journey in search of it up the Churchill between 1714 and 1718. Captain John Scroggs, who searched for Knight in 1722, learned from two Chipewyans at Churchill 'of a copper mine . . . near the surface of the earth, and they could direct the sloop so near it, as to lay her side to it, and be soon laden with it'. Both the Nortons encouraged the Chipewyans to bring in samples, and by 1768 these had become very tempting. The pamphleteer Alexander Cluny, whose *American Traveller* caused a sensation in London in 1769 and 1770, felt justified in writing: 'In 1744, I myself discovered there several large lumps of the finest Virgin Copper'. He must have picked up the London gossip about Moses Norton's mission, for no such virgin copper occurs on the shores of the Bay.

Hearne was also to investigate the possibilities of a North-West Passage or a River of the West which continued to excite men till the end of the eighteenth century. Alexander Cluny had published a map which in the fashion of the day shewed a passage from the Pacific to Hudson Bay, and Cluny wrote with great assurance. Hearne was to test that claim. He was, of course, to pacify the Indians and encourage them to come to Churchill. Unfortunately the Company and Norton seriously overestimated Hearne's skill as a geographer, perhaps because of his opportunity to associate with two English astronomers who spent the season of 1768–69 at Churchill to observe the transit of Venus for the Royal Society. They sent him portable instruments which he too seldom used, but now the Company was bent on answering the critics who had accused it of being unenterprising.

In order to understand Hearne's achievement, it is necessary to remember that Churchill stood on the dividing margin between the forest belt and the barrens. A line drawn from the mouth of the Churchill north-west to the Mackenzie delta, with slight bulges to the north-east for the basins of Great Slave and Great Bear lakes, indicates approximately the northern limit of the forests. 'And to the Eastward of the woods, on the barren grounds, whether hills or vallies, there is a total want of herbage except moss, on which the deer feed.' The surface is rough and broken, sometimes with rocky hills, and often strewn with boulders. The northern tundra is rather better watered than the slight precipitation would suggest, but the streams, when open, are too shallow and rocky to be navigable for far. The maintenance of human life in its wastes depended on unceasing vigilance and skill in living off the scattered game, notably the herds of caribou and musk oxen. It was much more difficult than living off the buffalo because of the migrations of these animals, but the Chipewyans and other Athapaskans could manage it, as the Eskimos, their successors, do to-day. They had to do so, increasingly, for the Crees were steadily pushing them out of the more bountiful forests. Hearne could never have kept himself alive by his own resources. We must think of

391

him as having been guided and supported by the Indians. It was the resourceful and unusually persistent Chipewyan, Matonabbee, so admirably portrayed by Hearne, who was responsible for the discovery of the Coppermine. He was 'the most sociable, kind, and sensible Indian I had ever met with'.

Hearne's first attempt, undertaken when he was twenty-four years of age, began on 6 November 1769, and ended ingloriously on 11 December. A mixed group of Crees and Chipewyans found that they could bully him and his two white subordinates, so ended up by robbing and deserting him. Two Cree servants managed to get him home. On the second journey he decided not to take any white companions, but Moses Norton made the odd mistake of not sending any Indian women in the party. They set out in the bitterest part of the winter, and their journey, which lasted from 23 February to 26 November 1770, was chiefly remarkable in that, except at the beginning, it was entirely through the barrens to the north-west of the fort. Hearne learned to travel light and how to live on fish or porcupine when large game was not to be had. Because of the absence of firewood, he had to eat his meat raw when rain soaked the moss. He also learned how unenterprising and gluttonous Indians could be when near a food-supply or when one of the party would do the hunting. He was several times close to starvation. 'It may justly be said to have been all feasting, or all famine.' In spite of most exasperating delays, he managed to make a huge figure of eight, going north across the Kazan river along the western shore of Yath-Kyed Lake almost to the lakes on the Thelon river which lie to the west of Chesterfield Inlet and Baker Lake. He then came south-west along the right bank of the Dubawnt river, crossed it near the outlet of Dubawnt Lake and made a great circuit around its desolate, low western shore. The main body of this lake never loses its covering of ice, although the margins of it loosen in the summer. Having crossed south-east to Angikuni Lake, he and his party managed to get to the fort before winter set in in earnest. In effect, exhausting as the experience was, the Chipewyans had merely taken him for one of their own summer circuits in the barrens. He himself, after having broken his quadrant early in August and having been plundered even to his gun by some Chipewyans the next day, had decided that he must return without reaching the Coppermine river. The one great gain from the expedition was that Hearne met Matonabbee, who voluntarily suggested that he conduct him to the 'mines'.

Matonabbee was a skilful hunter who had profited greatly by being retained at the fort for considerable periods. He had great intelligence and could think in white men's terms. His independence of mind can be judged by the fact that he was a complete sceptic in religion. 'Notwithstanding his aversion from religion, I have met with few Christians who possessed more good moral qualities, or fewer bad ones,' wrote the appreciative Hearne. He shewed a complete understanding of the Company's policy of peace among the inland tribes and repeatedly risked his life to effect it. Ultimately he organised many of the Indians of the North-West in an affiliation with Churchill which seems to have been profitable to all concerned. When he heard that the French had captured Fort Prince of Wales and taken away the English in 1782, he committed suicide by hanging, 'the only Northern Indian who, that I ever heard, put an end to his own existence'.

Hearne spent less than two weeks at the fort, after

almost nine months away, before he and Matonabbee set out again on 7 December 1770. They were far enough inland and on short enough rations by Christmas for Hearne to be very doleful about the prodigal waste of good things elsewhere in Christendom on that day. Yet Matonabbee knew exactly what he was doing and planned it all so efficiently that Hearne suffered very little during the year and a half he was away. They took no Crees with them, but always had plenty of women available. 'Women were made for labour,' said Matonabbee, 'one of them can carry, or haul as much as two men can do ... there is no such thing as travelling any considerable distance, or for any length of time, in this country without their assistance.' He himself travelled with from five to eight wives, 'most of whom would for size have made good grenadiers'. Hearne appreciated their usefulness, but was repeatedly appalled by the way in which they were treated.

The journey was exactly organised in terms of the forests and barrens, the long winter and the short summer, and the migratory habits of the caribou. There was great precision also in the provision of wood, sinew and birch-bark for tent-poles, snow-shoes and canoes, of dried meat for swift journeys, and of prepared skins for tents, moccasins and winter clothing. Hearne could not but admire the prescience whereby small, light canoes were made in the woods to be carried by one man hundreds of miles across the barrens for the crossing of rivers and lakes. He was profoundly shocked by much that he saw, and occasionally he was grievously disappointed by Matonabbee's actions or refusals to act, but he did not fail to appreciate that his success was owing to a very remarkable leader.

In spite of Hearne's deficiencies as a surveyor and

the breaking of the only quadrant Norton could let him have, we know reasonably well where they went. Keeping inside the margin of the forests, they went north-west to the lake district at the head-waters of the Kazan and Dubawnt rivers, stopping when game (usually caribou wintering in the woods) was plentiful, and preparing themselves to follow the caribou out into the barrens when the thaws began. They picked up the nucleus of Matonabbee's clan-like group near Neultin Lake, and it was a large party which worked west to an unknown lake (Thelewey-aza-yeth) about due south of Clinton Colden Lake and due west of the southern end of Great Slave Lake. In hot weather and melting snow, they struck straight north on 23 April. They built their canoes at another unknown lake (Clowey), between 3 and 18 May.

They passed out into the barrens on 22 May, just east of Artillery Lake, and, having crossed Clinton Colden at the end of May, decided to leave the main body in good country north-west of that lake, while the fighting men travelled light and fast to the Coppermine. Matonabbee took only his two youngest wives, but some sixty Indians had joined for the pleasure of killing their traditional Eskimo enemies on the river, so that the party totalled 150 at the start. The alternately hot and cold weather, hard going, mosquitoes, snow, sleet, rain and short rations discouraged some of these, who broke away to rest and hunt. The women were not taken on the last dash. The little war-party circled to the east of Contwoyto Lake in late June, and met some Yellow-knives early in June, some of whom joined them. They were now in musk-oxen country, but they hurried along, intent on slaking their unreasoning blood-lust. They reached the Coppermine on 13 July, and scouts

395

found a small party of Eskimos fishing at Bloody Fall near the mouth on the 16th. They put on their war-paint, crept up on the sleeping camp and massacred every Eskimo they could reach. Hearne was of course helpless, but his humiliating attempts at neutrality make disagreeable reading, particularly when an Eskimo girl was none too quickly killed by spears while she clung to his knees for mercy.

The search for copper was cursory. The Indians took him to 'the mine', which was a heap of rock debris in some hills near the river, where fragments of native copper occurred. Four hours' search produced only one piece of appreciable size. It weighed four pounds and ultimately was carried to the Company offices in London. The Eskimo copper implements shewed their dependence on the metal, but there was neither any great supply, nor any way of transporting it had there been. The Arctic Ocean was ice-bound except at its margin.

The raiders were back at Contwoyto Lake on 25 July, and having picked up the women and baggage a little farther on, decided to strike south for the woods. The lakes were frozen again by 30 September, but they moved with the caribou by easy stages across Point Lake and Mackay Lake into the forest and towards Great Slave Lake, which they reached on 24 December. They crossed it at the narrow portion opposite the mouth of the Slave river, and travelled south not far from the river to the bend near the 60th parallel. They liked the country there with its plentiful supply of buffalo and moose, but decided to strike east on 27 January so as to arrive at Churchill before the ship came in from England. Once more there were hunts and meat-drying and canoe-building. The thaws began

in late March and the migrant birds were seen on 12
April. On 29 April they were back again at Thelewey-
aza-yeth. Once more they left the women and baggage
to await Matonabbee's return and on 11 May they
began their dash through thin woods and barrens for
the fort. They reached it on 30 June 1772, after having
been away 'eighteen months and twenty-three days'.

Hearne's graphic account of his adventures must be
read in order to evaluate them, but his own view of his
achievements can be briefly indicated. He had actually
tested the copper-mine legend and demonstrated 'the im-
probability of putting their favourite scheme of mining
into practice'. He had shewn that 'the Continent of
America is much wider than many people imagine . . .
nor have I met with any Indians, either Northern or
Southern, that ever had seen the sea to the Westward'.
His travels had 'put a final end to all disputes concerning a North West Passage through Hudson's Bay', for
if it had existed he would have crossed it. Finally, 'it
will also wipe off, in some measure, the ill-grounded
and unjust aspersions of Dobbs, Ellis, Robson, and the
American Traveller;[1] who have all taken much pains
to condemn the conduct of the Hudson's Bay Company,
as being averse from discoveries, and from enlarging
their trade'.

Hearne's great discoveries were first revealed to the
general public in 1784 when they were incorporated in
a map which accompanied the account of Captain James
Cook's third voyage. That voyage, completed by Captain Charles Clerke after Cook's death, revealed the
character of both shores of the northern Pacific even
beyond Bering Strait. The connection of Hearne's work

[1] Arthur Dobbs, Henry Ellis, Joseph Robson and Alexander Cluny, all
of whom had published books or pamphlets.

with Cook's was not accidental. The same man, John Douglas, Bishop of Salisbury, edited both the Cook narratives and Hearne's for publication. Hearne had demolished the Strait of Anian from Hudson Bay and Cook had sought it in vain from the Pacific. But Cook was not the pioneer of the North Pacific. The last of our interludes, therefore, must be a brief account of how Europe got at the northern Pacific first by the overland route through Russia, and of how Russian discoveries there drew men from all over the world to share in an overwhelmingly rich harvest of furs.

During the first half of the seventeenth century, the Russians, having already secured control of the eastern slope of the Urals, swept across Siberia to the Pacific with a speed unequalled in the record of European expansion. The agents of the advance were chiefly Cossack fur traders, whose brutality, inventiveness in torture, and wanton disregard for human life were almost incredible. They worked east from river system to river system in search of sables and other furs, continually tempted north by the course of the rivers and the greater richness in furs, but drawn south by the hope of rich loot in China. They reached the Sea of Okhotsk in 1638. Some groups worked north to the Arctic, others found the Amur valley route to the Gulf of Tartary. Checked by the Manchus to the south, they worked around the Sea of Okhotsk to the peninsula of Kamchatka, and between 1652 and 1720 they fought their way down the peninsula and even ventured by sea to the neighbouring Kurile Islands.

Meanwhile the passion of Peter the Great to westernise his empire had drawn to St. Petersburg an extraordinary group of foreigners from Prussia, Sweden, Denmark, Holland, Great Britain, France, Italy and

Greece. An academy of sciences was formed. Astronomers and geographers were heaped with favours. Above all, there was boundless opportunity for the inquisitive, the accomplished, and men who were merely adventurous. Naturally one of the great problems was whether there was a land bridge to America or a passage between the continents. Peter had sent two men to solve that problem in 1720, but they sought its solution in the Kuriles. In the last year of his life (1725), Peter selected Vitus Bering, Martin Spanberg and Alexei Chirikof to do this work. The two Danes and one Russian sailed north from Kamchatka in 1728. By 16 August at 67° 18' they had found no bridge, nor did they find America next year when they sailed east. Bering went back to St. Petersburg, and while he was away, a sea expedition incidental to a war against the natives of the North-East, happened on America in the summer of 1732 and mapped part of the coast without being aware of the achievement!

Bering was somewhat under a cloud after his first expeditions, but in St. Petersburg and Moscow the enthusiasts for science and discovery gradually secured backing for even more ambitious efforts in the East. Bering himself was sure that he had been close to America and he convinced others. Approval for another expedition was secured from the Senate in 1733. The French astronomer and geographer, J. N. Delisle, prepared the maps, and his half-brother, Louis Delisle de la Croyère, was detailed to serve as geographer to the expedition.[1] Bering, Spanberg and Chirikof were its

[1] I have learned, too late for investigation of the source materials in France, that Louis had spent some time on the Canadian frontier before 1720. When I have examined the records of his experience there, if any significant connection between his Canadian and Russian enterprises appears, I shall prepare an account of it for publication in one of the historical

commanders. The Academy of Science lent its enthusiastic support. Although the first group left St. Petersburg in February 1733, the ships and supplies could not be got ready at Kamchatka until 1741.

Both the *St. Peter*, under Bering's command, and the *St. Paul*, under Chirikof, reached the north Pacific coast of America in 1741, though they were separated and did so at widely different points. Bering died of scurvy on his expedition, as did Louis Delisle de la Croyère and many others. Their discoveries were very slowly communicated to St. Petersburg and from St. Petersburg to the geographers of the world. They were not very intelligently recorded until after the publication of Cook's last voyage. But among the great kelpbeds of the North Pacific, along the rocky shores of the Aleutian Islands and on Bering Island where the sick survivors from Bering's ships were plagued to death by bold blue foxes, the Russians found an immense supply of two of the world's richest furs, Alaska seal and the sea otter. The Russian traders were out among the islands by 1743, and soon were driving the simple natives to their deaths in scores and hundreds in order to get the otters in clefts of the shore and on the margins of the kelp-beds in those very dangerous waters. They pushed on to the American coasts, had a fur station on Kodiak Island by the late 'eighties and poured such a stream of valuable furs into China after 1750 that the other European fur traders awoke to the situation. The North Pacific and particularly the American coast became a lode-stone for the world. Spain, Holland, France and England sent out expensive maritime expeditions

reviews. Guillaume Delisle, the great French geographer, was full brother to Joseph Nicolas, and they and Louis were sons of Claude Delisle, historian and geographer (1644–1720).

to map the Pacific. English traders from India and China, and adventurous New England traders, on their own behalf or for backers in England or Canada, gathered in the northern waters. The Russians had opened a new treasure-house.

While maritime traders sailed to loot the coast, the North American colonists and inland traders were not unaware of what was going on. In rapid succession Spaniards, Canadians and Americans made vigorous responses to the new situation on the Pacific coast.

NARRATIVES

There is an immense amount of material on Spanish enterprise along the old frontiers and on the reorganisation after 1764, most of which naturally concerns re-exploration. Perhaps the most convenient example of those activities is provided in the excellent selection of documents concerning Anza while he was governor of New Mexico (1777–87), which have been translated and edited by A. B. Thomas under the title *Forgotten Frontiers* (Norman, Oklahoma, 1932). Saint Pierre's memoir in original and translation is in *Public Archives of Canada Report, 1886* (Ottawa, 1887). The report of La France is in Arthur Dobbs, *An Account of the Countries adjoining to Hudson's Bay* (London, 1744), pp. 26, 29-45. The journal of Anthony Hendry, edited by L. J. Burpee, is in *Royal Society of Canada Proceedings and Transactions*, Third Series, vol. i (Ottawa, 1907). J. B. Tyrrell, who (with his associates) was until very recently the only white man who had explored the regions first seen by Samuel Hearne, has edited with excellent maps and photographs the 1795 London edition of Hearne's *A Journey from Prince of Wales's Fort in Hudson's Bay to the Northern Ocean* (Toronto, 1911). The collected information concerning James Knight's fate as known to Hearne is on pp. 44-9. Alexander Cluny's survey of the British American colonies, which contains four letters critical of the Hudson's Bay Company, *The American Traveller* (London, 1769), was an eagerly read pamphlet in the controversy between Great Britain and her colonies. It has been republished as Extra number 162 of *The Magazine of History* (Tarrytown, N.Y., 1930). F. A. Golder, who edited *Bering's Voyages* (2 vols., New York, 1922, 1925), was the author of a valuable monograph in a neglected field, *Russian Expansion on the Pacific, 1641–1850* (Cleveland, 1914).

CHAPTER XXII

FIRST RESPONSE TO THE RUSSIANS: SPANISH CALIFORNIA

(Map No. 3, page 482)

They said that toward the north they had seen an immense arm of the sea, or an estuary, which penetrated into the land as far as the eye could reach.

FAHTER CRESPÍ'S ACCOUNT OF THE DIS-
COVERY OF SAN FRANCISCO BAY IN 1769

FROM almost their earliest days in Mexico, the Spaniards were both curious and apprehensive about the Pacific coast to the north-west of them, curious as to the possibility of there being a strait to the Atlantic, and apprehensive lest some other European power should find and occupy some part of it before them. They had listened to many stories of men having sailed through from Atlantic to Pacific, usually Portuguese or Bretons. We have already seen[1] that before 1550 the shore had been skirted as far as latitude 42° or 43°, but it must be remembered that it was not really well known. For instance, there was a prevalent fear about 1570, and on several other occasions, that the English had found the passage and were maturing a plan to loot Mexico and Peru. During his raid on the Pacific coast in 1578–1579, the astute Drake hinted that his nation knew the way. Frobisher's voyages and the other navigations in the North were reported in Spain and made the authori-

[1] See pp. 93-4.

ties there distinctly more apprehensive than had French efforts on the St. Lawrence.[1] When, at the end of the sixteenth century, the Dutch as well as the English began to round both the southern capes to enter the Pacific, Spain decided that she must resume exploration of the coast, particularly for harbours to conceal and protect the Manila galleons from pirates. One odd result of their subsequent activity was that they thought that they had corroborated the geographical knowledge of the English by demonstrating that Lower California (the peninsula) and Upper California together formed a huge island masking the Strait of Anian and the site of Quivira.[2]

In 1602 Sebastián Vizcaíno, a Basque trader to the Philippines, who had turned pearl-fisher in the Gulf of California, was sent on an expedition up the coast, the reports of which, supplemented by the experience of the Manila galleons, served Spain for the next 165 years. He set off from Acapulco on 5 May with three small ships provisioned for a year. In spite of severe scurvy, two of the vessels sailed north until 19 January 1603. The recorder of the expedition, Fray Antonio de la Ascension, was the man whose geographical deductions converted the combined Californias into 'the largest island known'. Vizcaíno was sent to find the Strait of Anian and to investigate the 'populous and rich city named Quivira' which was said to be on a neighbouring river about latitude 40°. He was forbidden to go into the Gulf of California on the outward journey, and it was this omission which enabled Fray

---

[1] See pp. 129-32.
[2] See Michael Lok's map in R. Hakluyt, *Divers Voyages, etc.* (1582), and the Gilbert map (*c.* 1583), reproduced in *The Geographical Journal,* vol. lxxii, p. 304 (London, Sept. 1928).

Antonio to argue convincingly that the Californias formed an immense coastal island, with the Gulf inside it leading to the Strait and Quivira far to the north.

Father Antonio's conversational narrative, with its good maps and profiles of the coastline, is an interesting report, which was the more important to Spain because of the disappearance of the records of the Cabrillo-Ferrelo expeditions. Vizcaíno covered again the regions seen by his predecessors, but parties from one boat or another landed fairly frequently and they were able to bring back accounts of the natives, of the animals and birds, and of the prospects for agriculture and the whale and pearl fishery which, if much too optimistic, were not entirely out of line with the facts. Most important were the explorations made at Magdalena Bay, at Cerros Island and the bay inside it named after Vizcaíno, at San Diego Bay, at Santa Catalina Island and at Monterey Bay, for these discovered settled native communities. Although two of the ships got as far north as 42° or 43°, San Francisco Bay was missed again. Of course neither the Strait nor Quivira was found, but Father Antonio's theory about the Gulf of California seemed to explain that. The explorers summed up by urging strongly and persuasively that Monterey Bay be chosen for a settlement which could protect a port of refuge for the Manila galleons.

In spite of Father Antonio's enthusiastic descriptions of 'the grandeur, length and width of this Kingdom of the Californias, the many people there and their docility', nothing was done. Indeed, historians are now agreed that both Lower and Upper California offered few temptations to settlement. They were mountainous, arid regions, with very narrow coastal shelves, and from the sea afforded only a few narrow watered strips or enclaves. The gold, upon which ultimately the first broad settlement and exploitation were to depend, lay too far inland for it to affect the coastal adventurers. The Indians had cultures appropriate enough for their circumstances, but held out little temptation to immediate looting or slower exploitation. The coast was stormy and inhospitable, and scurvy took a frightful toll from the ships' crews. Upper California was not neglected for two and a half centuries by accident, particularly when its shores were so frequently visited by the galleons from the Philippines. Spanish determination to occupy it was a direct response to Russian and British activity in the Pacific.

A good deal of exploration and missionary effort and a slight amount of colonisation preceded the decision to jump from the shores of the Gulf of California to the Pacific coast. During the first half of the sixteenth century the region between Culiacan and the mouth of the Colorado had been crossed by several men, and marine expeditions had touched at various points along the shores of the Gulf, but the attractions to adventurers were very meagre. As a result, the slow, painful acquaintance with Lower California and the mainland shore opposite it during the seventeenth and eighteenth centuries was largely the product of missionary enterprise. The advances, halts and retreats cannot be recorded here, but between the days of Guzmán, Marcos and Coronado and about 1685, the missionaries worked north to the Sonora valley and up that valley to the plateau and towards New Mexico. The discovery of some mines in the Sonora valley helped greatly to consolidate this frontier. Meanwhile harsh Lower California had very thoroughly discouraged settlement except as a temporary base (or an excuse) for the pearl fisheries. It was not until the very end of the seventeenth century that the Jesuits began the resolute efforts which were to plant lasting outposts on the peninsula

Yet Lower California and the head of the Gulf were destined to be the bases from which expansion to Upper California was to take place, so that credit must be given to the men who conquered those regions, slight though their hold was. Both achievements belonged to the Jesuits. Although their order was expelled from New Spain in 1767 and other men found the overland ways, yet they did so from Jesuit mission fields. The great pioneer among them, the man who ended Father Antonio's insular myth and not only worked to unite the Gulf shores around the northern end, but had a vision of a road to Monterey, was the Tyrolese Jesuit, Father Eusebio Francisco Kino. He and the other Jesuits whom he fired to emulation laid the foundations for the advance to the North-West.

The annals of the Jesuit pioneers—Kino, Juan Maria Salvatierra, Jacobo Sedelmayr, Wenceslao Link and Fernando Consag—do not lend themselves to any method of brief, typical reproduction. The thing to do is to read the records of Kino's dozens of itinerant missions, along with the map he made of the dry, broken mountain masses and the little fertile, irrigated valleys between the Altar and Gila rivers (Pimería Alta).[1] They recapture the indomitable enthusiasm and courage of the man, and frame his hopes of finding a road around the head of the Gulf to the Lower Californian missions. Almost any land road was preferable to the short

[1] Between 1736 and 1741 it seemed possible that mining might attract a solid Spanish population to this frontier province. In the upper Altar valley nuggets of almost pure silver, weighing up to 4000 lb., were found lying on the surface of the ground. The subsequent rush to secure these nuggets died away when no great lodes were located.

Russian history, published in German in 1758, and speedily translated into other languages. The Seven Years' War absorbed everyone's energy until 1763, but when it was over, Spain, with her vigorous Bourbon king, and with the French menace from Louisiana gone, could turn, felt she must turn, to pre-emption of the Pacific coasts which were attracting so much unwelcome foreign attention. She even feared that the English might push through to the Pacific from Canada and Hudson Bay by the River of the West. The work was put into the hands of an energetic official, José de Gálvez, sent out in 1765 as *visitador general* in New Spain.

Gálvez' plan was to base an expedition to Upper California on the relatively rich Sonora valley, but at the time of his arrival in 1765, Sonora and Pimería Alta were almost slipping out of Spanish control because of Indian uprisings. It took six or seven years to pacify and protect those regions, and, because of this delay, Gálvez decided to use Lower California as a temporary base. In 1769 he launched five expeditions, two by land and three by sea, in order to make sure of Spanish control over San Diego and Monterey, lest the Russian interlopers seize them first. 'The loss would be irreparable.' Members of those and the succeeding California expeditions have left us a truly embarrassing wealth of records of what they did and saw. We need not concern ourselves with the marine expeditions, but the overland journeys were notable revivals of the classic style of Spanish exploration in North America, which can be illustrated by extracts from the records.

First in order of time was the land expedition under the command of Fernando de Rivera y Moncado, which made its way north up the peninsula to Santa María, gathering up cattle and other supplies from the mission stations. It set out from the pastures at Velicatá on 24 March 1769, composed of twenty-five Indian fighters (Leather Jackets) with their bull-hide shields, three muleteers, and forty-two Indian converts. It reached San Diego by a fairly direct route on 14 May. Father Juan Crespí, who accompanied it, recorded the journey vividly. Although as he said, 'the country continues like the rest of California, sterile, arid, lacking grass and water, and abounding in stones and thorns', Rivera managed so well that neither men nor beasts were ever deprived of water. When the prospect was doubtful, they sent out scouts and carried generous supplies with them. It was a rainy season, even cold and frosty, and pastures could usually be found even in dry *arroyos*. The widely scattered Indians of the interior were very timid and often ranged the hills alongside the route until they had seen the strangers out of their territory. Several of their own Indian baggage-men and herders, who bore the brunt of the work, either ran away or broke down under the effort. The Spaniards bore up very well because their progress through this rough country was leisurely and calculated and because they had an emergency food supply with them on the hoof.

After several self-deceptions they at last saw the sea on 20 April, and found that the coastal shelf supported both more Indians and less timorous ones than the interior. Since they could not march along the shore, they had to resort to the arduous business of climbing up and down the shoulders of the hills which ran down to the sea. The Indians heartened them greatly by indicating that two ships had gone by, but from 7 to 13 May they were constantly tantalised by the expectation

That courageous decision brought about the confusing discovery of the enormous harbour which ultimately took its name from St. Francis and which was soon to hold the primacy among the Pacific coast ports. So far as we know, no European had seen it before, although many had passed its entrance (Golden Gate) and had both seen and used Drake's Bay to the north. Indeed Portolá's men, when they sighted the entrance to the bay on 21 October, realised that it was not Monterey, but believed that they had probably happened on Drake's Bay. Ten days were spent in exploring the San Francisco peninsula and parts of the southern and eastern shores of the bay, but it was a disappointed lot of men who turned back to seek again for the elusive Monterey. They had not even thoroughly acquainted themselves with San Francisco Bay, which might, after all, have been the entrance to the Strait of Anian. Only Father Crespí seems to have been favourably impressed by the great harbour. The truth was that they had reached the limit of their endurance and were sceptical as to whether there was a Monterey at all.

They were back at Monterey on 28 November, and when they set out for San Diego on 10 December after a rest, exhaustive explorations had convinced them that they 'had not found the Port of Monterey'. By killing and eating their worn-out mules, they managed to reach San Diego on 21 January 1770, 'giving thanks to God that, notwithstanding the great labours and privations we had undergone, not a single man [Spaniard] had perished'. It was only later in March when they were able to consult with Juan Pérez, captain and pilot of their supply ship, newly arrived from Mexico, that it was realised that the lovely bay, 'magnificent amphitheatre', and fertile region which they had twice visited was, after all, Monterey. Then it was promptly occupied by sea and land in May 1770, and, said Portolá, 'I proceeded to erect a fort to occupy and defend the port from the atrocities of the Russians, who were about to invade us'. San Francisco had to wait.

As Gálvez had to some degree foreseen, the Upper California missions which were founded as a result of the strenuous enterprises of 1769–70 were, and would continue to be, precarious as long as they were based on sterile Lower California and the uncertainties of the long sea voyage from Mexico. They were a legitimate risk in the light of apparently imminent competition from the Russians, but somehow Upper California must be linked with rich Sonora by an overland route. Fortunately systematic efforts had temporarily pacified Pimería Alta by 1771. Advantage must be taken of that breathing-space to establish a good route to the junction of the Colorado and the Gila (Yuma), to discover the best way from Yuma to Upper California, and finally, if possible, to lay down a continuous frontier from San Francisco Bay to Yuma and eastward across the mountains through Zuñi to Santa Fé and Texas. These tasks evoked the last great efforts made by Spain in the exploration of North America. The driving agent behind them was the viceroy who took up the reins in 1771 after Gálvez had broken down, Antonio María de Bucareli y Ursúa.

Pimería Alta contained two men whose predilections made them the natural leaders in the overland trail to Upper California. Fray Francisco Garcés, a Franciscan who had come into the province in 1768 to fill the vacancy left by the expelled Jesuits, was a man upon whose shoulders the mantle of Father Kino might aptly have fallen. Within three years he had learned of the

Their route was through Kino's country, over the mountains to the Altar valley and down it to Caborca, where Anza hoped to get more pack animals, but was disappointed. The mules offered were 'only stacks of bones which the animals torpidly moved'. There was water in the river-bed, however, and fair pastures, so that the commander of the *presidio* at Altar was able to give them some good saddle animals in return for those of their own which were out of condition. Seriously handicapped for carriage, they set out north-west on 22 January. 'All this region is so sterile that neither shade-trees nor roof-timber[1] are seen in it', wrote Anza, but even skirting the dunes on the way to Sonóita, he and his party could usually dig surface wells or find tanks[2] full of January water. Sonóita had been the outpost of the Jesuit missions, but the country-side was almost empty of people following the repression of the Pima revolts. From Sonóita to the Gila water was so scarce that Anza split his party so as not to exhaust the widely separated tanks. By good leadership he was able to conduct his little party and animal train to the Gila just above the junction by 7 February, 1774.

Thanks to the low water and to the friendly relations established with the Yumas at the junction, they were across both rivers on 9 February. They were now faced with the problem of crossing an immense sandy plain, which had once been the bed of the Gulf of California and which still contained one huge salt-water lagoon,[3] and some smaller ones. Upstream Indians knew of

[1] The beams used to support the flat roofs of *adobe* houses.

[2] *Tinaja*, or tank, meaning pot-hole or depression, usually on a mountainside, where the supply exceeds the evaporation.

[3] Lake Maquata. Salton Sea, shewn on modern maps to the north, was dry at the time Anza explored. Irrigation has now converted the desert plain into the marvellously fertile Imperial valley.

Spaniards to the west, but said that the way through the mountains from their country was impassable. From now on there were neither Indian trails nor records of ways used by Father Kino. Neither Tarabal nor Garcés had any exact knowledge. Yet to get to California they had to break away from the populous fruitful delta of the Colorado and find paths and water-holes on the way to the Sierras. Anza's first attempt was too far north and he extricated his party from the dunes only after an eleven-day struggle and the loss of many pack and saddle animals. On 2 March, after resting for a week back on the Colorado and completing arrange-ments to leave his heavy luggage and its pack train among the Yumas, he and his party set off in light order to make a second attempt. His soldiers 'promised their best efforts whatever might happen, saying that in case the horses should all be lost or worn out, they would undertake the march on foot until they achieved their goal'. This time he managed it by going down the Colorado and following *arroyos*, in which there was some thin pasture, west to the middle of the Cocopah Mountains. Then by working north-west along that range until he could make a dash for the Sierra Madre, he reached a good spring on 6 March. He had thus kept north of the worst dunes and had passed between the two great lagoon depressions.

Anza's serious troubles were now over. By sending scouts along the skirts of the Sierras he could make sure of water and pasture. By 8 March they had reached wells at a point from which 'the California Indian has recognized that he is now near a place where he formerly was, and therefore we now promise ourselves that our expedition will not fail'. On 11 March they turned west towards a gap in the mountains and within a few days were refreshed and revived by 'most beautiful green and flower-strewn prairies, and snow-covered mountains with pines, oaks and other trees'. In the high valleys snow mingled with the rain. They travelled along 'a good-sized river, on whose banks are large shady groves'. A lake was 'as full of white geese as water'. Then on 22 March, it would seem quite unexpectedly, they crossed a river and came upon the Mission San Gabriel.

'Even though the friars and the soldiers saw us, they could hardly believe that people could have come from Sonora, and they kept repeatedly asking me if it were true, tears springing to their eyes, caused by the joy and pleasure at seeing this expedition accomplished, and at knowing how close at hand Sonora was and how easy the transit from it.' Anza's idea of ease was somewhat remarkable.

Splendid and useful as was Anza's subsequent career, we shall leave the likeable soldier at San Gabriel, for his later enterprises in Upper California and along the overland routes from Sonora were devoted to establishing the best trails and to taking colonists and supplies from the old provinces to the new. On the other hand, Father Garcés, by his blithe and self-confident plunges into the unknown mountain regions, will serve to introduce the remarkable but vain Spanish efforts to move up the whole northern frontier to a line which could provide a direct route uniting Upper California and Santa Fé. In 1775 Garcés got Anza to leave him behind near Yuma, so that he could satisfy his curiosity about the upper Colorado. Late in May he made the acquaintance of some Indians visiting the Gila valley, who consented to take him with them across the wilderness from near Agua Caliente. In four days they cut across

the angle of the rivers to a point near the modern Bill
Williams Fork, and took him to their villages. While
there he ventured up and down the river and talked to
the Indians about the Moqui *pueblos* of New Mexico
and about the Spaniards in Upper California. Although
he could get no word as to routes, he decided that the
former were about four days away and the latter an
unknown distance. Santa Fé seemed to be about a
week's journey to the east. For the moment, however,
he could do little more than collect vague Indian geographical lore.

He got his chance to do more in 1775. That year the
redoubtable Anza crowned his earlier enterprise by
conducting over 150 colonists from Sonora to San
Francisco. Garcés accompanied the great train of 240
persons and 1000 animals down the Santa Cruz and
Gila valleys, but once again he was allowed to remain
behind at Yuma. With vague approval from Bucareli
and a more explicit understanding with Anza, he intended to 'seek a new road in order to secure this
passage'. He was thinking in terms of a route from the
mouth of the Santa Cruz valley across country to the
Colorado and thence directly to Monterey. Then a
similar plunge eastwards might make a link with Santa
Fé. Anza had played with similar ideas, but decided
they could not be tested on a colonising expedition.
Before the Anza party went on, Father Pedro Font
paused in his diary record to put down his impressions
of Garcés' ability to take on Indian habits in everything,
even in eating. 'Father Garcés is so well fitted to get
along with the Indians and go among them that he
appears to be but an Indian himself. . . . In short, God
has created him, as I see it, solely for the purpose of
seeking out these unhappy, ignorant and rustic people.'

Garcés began by making an expedition to the mouth of the Colorado and back in December 1775. He was very anxious to win the souls of the large groups of Indians who were nurtured by the Colorado delta, and never lost a chance of preparing them for Christianity by what seemed even to another Franciscan rather naïve methods. He was also driven on by a geographical curiosity which made him often break through Indian objections to what seemed to them inexplicable journeyings. He spent about six weeks at Yuma after his return, for ever questioning visiting Indians about the surrounding country. On 14 February 1776 he went off up the Colorado in company with Tarabal and one of the Indians (a Mohave) who lived beyond the villages which he had visited the year before. They did not follow the stream, but worked through the mountains along the right bank, where Garcés hoped to locate a good road to Upper California. They reached the Mohave settlements (near modern Needles) on 28 February, and the friar was warmly welcomed as 'the first Spaniard who has been in their land'. When he asked them to take him westward 'to see the fathers that were living near the sea, they agreed and offered soon to accompany me, saying that already they had information of them and knew the way'.

He set out on 4 March with Tarabal and three Mohaves, travelling almost due west along the Mohave trade trail to the coast and meeting parties of natives returning, some of whom had seen the missionaries. They reached the sink of the Mohave river in five days and began a slow, hard journey across the Mohave desert and up the river valley into the sierras. They had to kill a horse for food and 'not even was the blood thereof wasted'. But they broke through the mountains and on 23 March 'came upon the road of the expedition'. Next day they reached Mission San Gabriel. Garcés paused there for two weeks, during which he failed to secure co-operation from the military in an effort to link his recent traverse with an inland route direct to Monterey. Undismayed by this rebuff, he started off to find the inland route himself. In the Santa Clara valley he met some Indians from the northern interior and, as usual, used them as a means for seeing new country. They took him over two ranges into the great plains of the upper San Joaquin valley, but by 5 May, when he was perhaps twenty-five miles beyond Kern river, he ran out of presents for the Indians and had to turn back. He had been told about the San Joaquin river (which flows into San Francisco Bay) and was sorely disappointed not to learn for himself whether it might provide the western terminus of his 'new road'. Tarabal and the Mohaves had waited for him at the head of the valley, and after crossing the San Marcos Range, they blithely set out on 17 May across the Mohave desert again by a new route. They reached the Mohave villages on the Colorado on 30 May. 'Inexplicable', reported the modest friar, 'are the expressions of delight which the said nation made to see me again.'

Presumably his next step should have been to go down to Yuma. Certainly Anza and the other Franciscans expected him to do so and he found letters from Yuma awaiting him. Indeed on 31 May he started to go down, but was diverted when the Mohaves threatened some visiting Walapais from the east to whom he had talked the day before 'about the distance of Moqui and New Mexico'. Abruptly he decided to protect the Walapais by his company on their way home and thus satisfy his

longing to build his 'new road' eastwards. He started on
this new enterprise on 4 June, although its prospect (or
perhaps their past experiences with the tireless friar) had
been too much for Tarabal and his two Mohave guides.

As nearly as can be made out, he and his new friends
travelled almost straight across country from near
Needles to the Moqui *pueblos*, scrambling up and down
narrow trails along the often almost vertical walls of
the appalling canyons which lay across their path, and
punctuating the journey by stops at the water-holes
known to the Indians, ignorance of which would have
spelled speedy death. Yet the only difficulties which
Garcés stressed in his narrative were the efforts of
various Indians whom he met to discourage him from
risking his life among the Moquis. He allowed himself
once to speak of a 'difficult road' when he had to dis-
mount and climb down a cliff-face on a wooden ladder,
and again he interjected 'they cause horror, these precipices'. The Grand Canyon so impressed him, 'as if the
sierra were cut artificially to give entrance to the Rio
Colorado', that he named after his great viceroy,
Bucareli. Following the crossing of the Little Colorado
on 28 June, he met his first Moquis, and after a two-day
rest, he pushed on to reach their westernmost *pueblo*
(Oraibe) on 2 July.

His guides were frightened by the obvious hostility
of the Moquis (Hopi Indians) and all but an old man
and a boy deserted him. He spent a whole day alone
beside his saddle in a street-corner before three young
converts from Zuñi plucked up courage to address him.
The Moquis 'did not so much as wish to look at me'.
He spent the night alone in the same place, and next
day reluctantly decided that he must turn back instead
of going on to visit the missions at Zuñi. He could not

organise a new expedition or find more presents. He wrote a letter on 3 July 1776, to be carried to the priest at Zuñi by his only friends, and then consented to go back to Needles with his former guides. Four chiefs at the head of the whole population of Oraibe confronted him on 4 July and bade him begone instantly. His trembling boy brought him his mule, and as soon as they thought it safe to do so, his old guides picked him up where he had lost his way among the maize-fields and pastures. He got back to the Mohaves on the Colorado on 25 July, to be welcomed as a beloved one thought dead. In the August and September heat he rode down the river to the Gila and thence up its valley and home to his mission of St. Xavier del Bac in the Santa Cruz valley. His gentle mind was much troubled by the war-like rivalries of the tribes through which he passed, but as yet he had no prescience of the martyr's death which he was to meet five years later at the hands of the Yumas.

The priest at Zuñi to whom he wrote from Moqui was Father Silvestre Vélez de Escalante, but he too was an explorer. On 3 July 1776 another Franciscan was filling his post at Zuñi while he was gathering supplies for a novel expedition. Accompanied by a brother Franciscan, Francisco Domínguez, he set out boldly to the north-west from Santa Fé on 29 July to find a direct road to Monterey. The two friars, a map-maker and two other Spaniards, supported by four half-breeds or Indians and supplied by the governor of New Mexico, were off to test some theories which Escalante had built up from Indian reports to him at Zuñi of an impassable river nine days away which flowed west. If it was impassable it must be large and it seemed as if its mouth must be on the Pacific. If Santa Fé could be connected with it, the direct road, the new frontier, would have been found.

Escalante and his party travelled almost continuously from 29 July 1776 to 2 January 1777, in a great circuit through the mountains and valleys of the modern states of New Mexico, Colorado, Utah and Arizona. Their record and its map have been tested on the ground and found good, but a careful description of their route would involve an intricate catalogue of names applied to a detailed topographical map. Inasmuch as they inevitably failed in their objective, no later enterprise was founded on their discoveries. Yet an indication of their journey is due them, if only to see how magnificently they failed.

They began by crossing the Río Grande and following the canyons roughly towards the north until they came to the junction of the Gunnison and the Uncompahgre rivers. By now they were in a sea of peaks (near the Grand Mesa), many of which were over 10,000 feet high. None of the Indians they met had any knowledge of Spaniards to the west, but two young Indians told them of a great water to the west where they lived. That sounded promising, so westward they went with their new guides, across the Colorado at about 39° 30' and deep into the mountains again. Their guides hurried them along to the great water, only to reveal that it was a mere mountain lake.[1]

They secured new guides to take them westward, and these guided them south-west to avoid the salt desert and to reach the latitude of Monterey. On 5 October, however, when they were just east of Sevier Lake, snow fell and reminded them of the season and of the altitude of the region (about 5000 feet). They travelled south

―――――――
[1] The Lake Utah of to-day.

across a succcession of broad arid mountain terraces, therefore, instead of west. The Grand Canyon of the Colorado lay directly across their path, but two days before they could be confronted with it (16 October), some Indians with whom they traded warned them off. 'There were no water holes, nor could we cross the river there because it had a deep canyon . . . they would show us the way to the plain.' This they did by turning them north-east around dry plateaus to where they could turn south-east to cross the Colorado at about 37°. They were then within the Spanish sphere of influence again and they slowly made their way back to Santa Fé through Oraibe and Zuñi. Their fifteen hundred mile journey had been a splendid, sustained effort, but it had not taken them to the sea.

Spanish enterprise in North America did not end with Escalante and Domínguez, but it did not contribute notably again to new exploration. Short-cuts were discovered, alternative routes were adapted to the seasons, and much re-exploration of the lands which Spain had received from France kept the Spanish record creditable. Anza, as governor of New Mexico, rode north and east and west from Santa Fé to punish the Indians. But the main task was done and only defiant seas of mountains, interspersed with desert, had prevented the Spanish-Americans from drawing their frontier west to the Pacific from the upper Missouri or even from Santa Fé directly to San Francisco. Spanish exploration had rivalled French for extensiveness if not for practicality and permanence. And in picturing it, the cavalry-man, the Leather-Jacket, comes to mind, as he and the missionaries whom he protected ranged for countless miles across what was too often very inhospitable territory.

NARRATIVES

H. R. Wagner has edited, in translation, the narrative materials relating to *Spanish Voyages to the North-West Coast of America in the Sixteenth Century* (San Francisco, 1929), concluding with Vizcaíno and the project of settling Monterey. H. E. Bolton has collected, translated and edited a large body of the narrative materials dealing with the opening up of Pimería Alta and the Californias. These are published as *Kino's Historical Memoir of Pimería Alta* (2 vols., Cleveland, 1919), which includes Jesuit beginnings in Lower California and materials on Salvatierra's work; *Historical Memoirs of New California by Fray Francisco Palóu* (4 vols., Berkeley, 1926), which contains an account of Lower California under the Franciscans and of the Portolá expedition of 1769–70; *Fray Juan Crespi* (Berkeley, 1926), which contains letters and diaries describing the Portolá, Fages and Pérez expeditions; and *Anza's California Expeditions* (5 vols., Berkeley, 1930), which contains thirteen diaries and many other papers concerning Anza's Californian enterprises. Father Andrés Marcos Burriel's *Noticia de la California* (Madrid, 1757) appeared in an abridged English translation as *A Natural and Civil History of California* in London, 1759. It is a history of Lower California and the Gulf regions, designed to foster the advance to the north, and is sometimes listed under the name of Miguel Venegas, whose manuscript history of 1739 was used by Burriel. In the first three volumes of the *Publications* (Berkeley, 1910, 1911, 1913) of the Academy of Pacific Coast History will be found three narratives of the Portolá expedition of 1769–70 (vol. i); Vila's diary of 1769–70, Fages' diary of the expedition to San Francisco Bay in 1770, and Costansó's diary of 1769–70 (vol. ii); Font's diary of the Anza expedition of 1775–76 (vol. iii); translated and edited by F. J. Teggart and others. E. Coues, *On the Trail of a Spanish Pioneer* (2 vols., New York, 1900), contains the narratives of Garcés. This edition is unsatisfactory, and Professor Bolton proposes to replace it in a volume which will also contain the narrative of Escalante and Domínguez, part of which he has published from manuscript in *New Mexico Historical Review*, iii (Santa Fé, 1928). The Spanish edition of these narratives (Mexico, 1856) is faulty.

CHAPTER XXIII

SECOND RESPONSE: MACKENZIE CROSSES
THE CONTINENT

(Map No. 4, end of book)

ALEXANDER MACKENZIE,
from Canada, by land, the twenty-second of July,
one thousand seven hundred and ninety-three

MACKENZIE'S INSCRIPTION ON A ROCK
IN DEAN CHANNEL, BRITISH COLUMBIA

THERE was a saying among the Canadian fur traders of the mid-nineteenth century to the effect that the Hudson's Bay Company never amounted to anything until after it merged with the North-West Company in 1821. Holders of that view had a blind eye to the facts that the old Company had always faced great risks at sea, had managed to survive four wars, and, if tardily, had launched enterprising men far into the interior when Montreal competition seriously threatened. The kernel of the comment was the attention it drew to a group of American, English and Scottish fur traders of conquered Montreal, who introduced such thrust and drive into the North-West trade after 1760 that the older Company finally had to take them in or go to the wall. It was this group which contributed the first transcontinental traveller to North American exploration.

Two of the most typical early members of the group,

Alexander Henry (the elder) of New Jersey and Peter Pond of Connecticut, had both taken part in the last war with France. Pond had served in three campaigns before he arrived at Montreal with Amherst in 1760. Henry was with the same expedition in the less heroic capacity of sutler. Pond took some time to find a new bent after the war, but Henry did not hesitate—'proposing to avail myself of the new market which was thus thrown open to British adventure I hastened to Albany, where my commercial connections were'. He early got hold of a French interpreter and guide, and began his woods career by a snow-shoe journey during January 1761, which also included living with Indians and shooting the icy St. Lawrence rapids in a bark canoe. On that journey Henry was entertained near Montreal by a *seigneur* who 'in the earlier part of his life had been engaged in the fur trade', and who 'gave me to understand that Michilimackinac was richer in this commodity than any other part of the world'. Henry, like other Montreal adventurers, had already thought of the possibilities of the trade as it had been built up by the French, and he promptly decided to enter it. Having secured the assistance of a formerly prominent trader, Etienne Campion, and having extracted a reluctant permission from the authorities, he set off for Michilimackinac in August 1761.

For the next sixteen years Henry was actively engaged in the fur trade and somewhere he found the assistance to make a literate, interesting narrative of his adventures.[1] He and a growing number of his kind gradually took the places of the Montreal merchants of the French régime, but for obvious reasons most of them had to go out to reconnoitre in person. Henry

---

[1] His letters are not those of an educated man.

almost lost his life during Pontiac's rising, others were killed or captured, and it was a slow, uncertain business getting the Indians adjusted to the new relations of Frenchmen and Englishmen in the North-West, just as it was in the changed Franco-Spanish relations in Louisiana. Gradually the work was done. French *coureurs* and *voyageurs* eagerly sought employment from the new masters. At Prairie du Chien on the Mississippi near the Wisconsin, Peter Pond saw traders 'from eavery part of the Misseppey . . . even from Orleans', in the spring of 1774, and at Michilimackinac that summer, there 'was a grate concors of people from all quorters'. When the American Revolution broke out, several groups moved swiftly from Albany to Montreal in order to keep a place in the rapidly expanding North-West trade.

So far as we know at present, James Finlay of Montreal was the first English trader to get as far west as the Saskatchewan after the conquest, apparently in 1767. In 1771 and 1772 another Montrealer, Thomas Curry, was in the vicinity of Cedar Lake, and he may well have headed a fairly large group, for Matthew Cocking of the Hudson's Bay Company reported that he 'intercepted great part of York Fort trade this year'. Andrew Graham, the factor at York Fort, wrote on Matthew Cocking's journal: 'Mr. Currie's encroachment was the reason I sent Mr. Cocking inland'.

Two years later (1774) the old war between Hudson Bay and Montreal for the Saskatchewan was on in earnest again. The Company sent Samuel Hearne and Matthew Cocking to build a post at Cumberland Lake (just west of The Pas). This would serve the double purpose of meeting Montreal competition face to face and of checking a leakage in the flow of furs to

431

Churchill. Hearne had seen the various Athapaskan tribes arduously transporting furs across the barren lands to Fort Prince of Wales. He did not as clearly realise that some Indians of Great Slave Lake and Lake Athabaska preferred to travel south by the Slave and Athabaska rivers and portage across to the Churchill system, so as to have the advantage of canoe-travel to the Bay. Unfortunately for the Hudson's Bay Company, it proved much easier for those Indians to cross over from the Churchill to meet the Montrealers on the Saskatchewan, than to go all the way down the difficult Churchill to the Bay and back. The astute Matonabbee was one of the first to realise this and deeply grieved Samuel Hearne at Churchill in 1776 by threatening to go to the Canadians if Hearne would not yield to his extravagant demands in trade.

Where Indians could go, the Montrealers were prepared to follow. Lake Winnipeg had been the focal point a generation earlier. Now the struggle was transferred to the Saskatchewan, the Churchill, the Athabaska and the Slave. These new regions present a complex geographical picture, but its important elements can easily be isolated. The rich prize was the forest belt between the Saskatchewan and the barrens. The North branch of the Saskatchewan, therefore, loomed far larger than the South. The strategic portages, or bridges from river system to river system, were Frog Portage (or Portage La Traite), reached by going north from Cumberland Lake through convenient rivers and lakes to the Churchill, and Methye Portage (or Portage La Loche), reached by going up the Churchill through Ile-à-la-Crosse Lake and thence north-west by water to Methye Lake, from which the portage ran to the Clearwater river, a tributary of the Athabaska. If those routes and portages are kept in mind, the complexities resolve themselves quite simply into the old Montreal game of going clock-wise around Hudson Bay cutting off the flow of furs down its tributary rivers.

The Company established its Cumberland House on the neck of land between the Saskatchewan and Cumberland Lake just in time to retain a portion of the Saskatchewan and Churchill trade. In 1774 Joseph Frobisher, a Montrealer who had been investigating the Saskatchewan, got over to the Churchill by an unknown route and skimmed the cream of the furs going down to the Bay. He learned about Frog Portage and built a post there to contain the furs he could not carry out with him on his return. In 1775 his brother Thomas, and Charles Patterson of Montreal, joined him. That same year Alexander Henry gave up his trading on the Great Lakes and also set out for the Saskatchewan, probably with his associate, Jean-Baptiste Cadotte. As Henry was proceeding up Lake Winnipeg, he 'was joined by Mr. Pond, a trader of some celebrity in the North-West'. On 7 September all four parties were united, 'composing a fleet of thirty canoes and a hundred and thirty men', as they crossed the northern end of the lake.

The next twenty years of the North-West trade were marked by something closely approaching warfare among the Montrealers and between them and the Company. Careless exploitation of the Indians provoked in 1780 what might have become a systematic extermination of the whites but for a fearful smallpox epidemic which swept the tribes of the west, to use Mackenzie's description, 'as the fire consumes the dry grass of the field'. Gradually a few men emerged to prominence, and among them Peter Pond and Alexander Henry, who looked beyond mere forestalling of he procured twice as many furs as his canoes would carry.'

By 1780 or 1781 Pond, or Henry, or both, had conceived of the next great step in exploration, in spite of the fact that the Athabaska outpost was at least two full seasons of trade-travel from Montreal. In June 1776 Henry had met some Athapaskans at Ile-à-la-Crosse Lake, with whom he travelled down to Frog Portage. They told him that at the far end of Lake Athabaska there was a river 'called Peace River, which descended from the Stony or Rocky Mountains, and from which mountains the distance to the *salt lake*, meaning the Pacific Ocean, was not great'. Lake Athabaska, they said, emptied by a river (the Slave) which flowed northward 'into another lake', also called Slave, 'but whether this lake was or was not the sea, or whether it emptied itself or not into the sea they were unable to say'. Henry bought two of 'several ultramontane prisoners' from the Athapaskans, but it was impossible to question them because these natives from the Pacific slope could not speak any Cree or Chipewyan dialect.

We do not know how much further information Pond had gathered at his 'Old Establishment' near Lake Athabaska, but in October 1781 Henry drew up a memorandum for his admired acquaintance, Sir Joseph Banks, President of the Royal Society, on 'A Proper Rout, by Land, to Cross the Great Contenant of America',[1] and volunteered to command an expedition 'if his Majesty Should . . . think me a Proper Person'. His plan consisted of a quite detailed description of the route. He thought he could get from Montreal to just beyond Cumberland Lake between May and

[1] Printed as an appendix to L. J. Burpee, *The Search for the Western Sea* (New York, 1908).

the end of October of the first year, and to Lake Athabaska for the next winter and the preparation of pemmican.[1] Next spring he would go down the river which flowed out of the lake 'Untill, you come to the Sea—which cant be any very Great Distance'. He thought that at latest it could be reached by July. 'Here an Establishment may be made in Some Convenient Bay . . . where Shipping, may come to. In the mean Time a Small Vessell may be Built, for . . . Exploaring the Coast, which can be no Great Distance from the Streight, which Seperates the two Contenants.' With the Pacific as an ocean base, supplies could be taken in and furs drawn out through Bering Strait in one season and with much smaller effort and expense than from Montreal. For the first journey Henry recommended an exit through Hudson Bay, being as unaware of the absolute impracticability of that route as he was of his own from the Northern Sea to the Pacific.

Pond went out to Montreal in 1784, having secured from the Indians some additional knowledge of the Mackenzie basin and the barrens, and found that the traders were deeply interested in the published accounts of Cook's last voyage. The semi-official English report described the northern Pacific coast through Bering Strait to the Arctic Ocean beyond, and contained a map giving the first public notice of Hearne's travels. Out of the long discussions and comparisons which must have taken place emerged Pond's famous map of 1785, which was submitted to the Canadian governor and to the United States Congress. Because of the capture of Fort Prince of Wales in 1782 and the necessary shift

---

[1] 'Which is dry'd meat, pounded to a powder and mixed up with buffeloes greese'. Pond and Henry seem to have learned of this valuable compressed food from the Athapaskans. Without its use, it is doubtful whether the North-West could have been invaded.

thought it 'a shame for America to let slip such a valuable trade'. 'I make no doubt', he wrote to a friend in New York, 'but Cook's River . . . has a communication with those parts of the North-west I was at, by which a road would be opened across the Continent.'

Although Henry and Pond had reached the same conclusion, neither was to make the attempt to go down what we know as the Mackenzie river to Cook Inlet. Both men were almost too old (nearing fifty), by the standards of their day, for such an endeavour. Moreover, during the winter of 1786–87, the second suspicious death of a rival 'in a scuffle with Mr. Pond's men' made Pond's withdrawal from the North-West desirable to his associates as well as to his opponents.

A young Scotsman from Stornoway, whose apprenticeship for the lonely Athabaska outpost had consisted of five years as a clerk in a Montreal merchant's office and one year at Detroit and two on the Churchill in the active fur trade, was sent in from Grand Portage in 1787 to replace him. Alexander Mackenzie, a newcomer in the North-West trade and only twenty-four years of age, was chosen as the representative in Athabaska of the temporarily united Montreal traders. He spent the winter with Pond at the Old Establishment, where he pumped the veteran adroitly and successfully for the knowledge which he must have as his chief stock-in-trade. Pond was not secretive, but rather alive with his project for reaching the Pacific. Indeed, when he went down to Montreal in 1788, he told a friend that he had arranged for another man (probably Mackenzie) 'to go down the river [Mackenzie] and from thence to Unalaska and so to Kamschatka and thence to England through Russia'. We know nothing of any immediate results of this scheme. Pond remained in

Montreal until 1790 and then retired to Milford, Connecticut, to die in poverty in 1807. Yet he, more than any other man, had taken the first steps on what was to be the first transcontinental path to the Pacific.

Alexander Mackenzie, who made the two great journeys by which the mystery of the North-West was solved, was an ardent, self-confident young man whose courage in his own convictions and capacities had already carried him through several severe tests in the North-West trade. Like most of the thoughtful men actively engaged in the fur trade, he thoroughly hated the life in the field, but he was able to relieve his sense of its deadening qualities by first putting the immediate trading enterprise on a profitable basis, and then entrusting it to subordinates while he himself engaged in exploration. He had unusual qualities of judgement, which enabled him to establish a natural, acceptable authority over his subordinates. A handsome, debonair figure, he could also inspire emotional loyalty and determination in those upon whom he had to rely. When satisfied as to the necessity of a course of action, he could be quite ruthless with his men and with himself in carrying it out. He was a born leader, who happened to work into a position where his curiosity and his ability found instant employment.

There is no doubt but that he was inspired to his exploring efforts by Peter Pond. He wrote of having 'followed the course of the waters which had been reported by Mr. Pond to fall into Cook's River', and it is quite clear that in 1788 he had accepted Pond's idea. He went down to the depot and the partners' meeting at Rainy Lake that summer so as to get his cousin Roderick transferred to his district in order to build Fort Chipewyan on the southern shore of Lake Athabaska and to administer this region during his effort to corroborate Pond's belief. It is not at all clear whether his partners agreed that the prospect of reaching the Pacific justified his leaving the trade in Roderick's hands during the summer of 1789, but Mackenzie knew what he was going to do. The winter of 1788–89 was spent at the new fort[1] in preparation for the summer's adventure.

Mackenzie later found the task of preparing his journals for publication exceedingly arduous. It was not until 1801 that he published the record of his explorations between 1789 and 1793. 'I am not a candidate for literary fame', he wrote; 'the approbation due to simplicity and to truth, is all I presume to claim. . . . I have described whatever I saw with the impressions of the moment which presented it to me.' This extreme diffidence about his published *Voyages*, which seems to have infected his biographers as well in their estimates of them, is not really justified. Mackenzie's writings have sound narrative form and contain an abundance of shrewd observations of man and nature. They are far removed from being mere log-books. Very occasionally they rise to a fine, natural eloquence. One precaution is to be observed in reading them, namely, that Mackenzie persistently underestimated his mileage. That natural precaution of a leader who was rushing on his men to extraordinary efforts became so habitual that he forgot that he had used it when he came to write his record.[2]

'June, 1789 (Wednes. 3). We embarked at nine o'clock in the morning, at Fort Chepewyan . . . in a canoe made of birch bark. The crew consisted of four

---

[1] It was 1850 miles from Grand Portage.

[2] My quotations are from the slightly revised London and Edinburgh edition of 1802.

Canadians,[1] two of whom were attended by their wives, and a German;[2] we were accompanied also by an Indian, who had acquired the title of English Chief, and his two wives in a small canoe, with two young Indians; his followers in another small canoe. These men were employed to serve us in the twofold capacity of interpreters and hunters. This Indian was one of the followers of the chief who conducted Mr. Hearne to the Coppermine river, and has since [Matonabbee's suicide] been a principal leader of his countrymen.' English Chief did not prove to be an unqualified success as an interpreter; he was frequently a thorough nuisance in his efforts to retard Mackenzie and finally to make him turn back, but the Indian hunters did keep the expedition well provided with food. Mackenzie carried pemmican (which got mouldy in mid-July) to fall back upon, and they cached bags of it at various points to relieve them on their return, but the food problem was never a really serious one.

The first day they travelled about thirty-six miles, but the second, between 4 A.M. and 7.30 P.M., they covered eighty-one miles (computed by Mackenzie as sixty-one). They had left the lake, reached the mouth of the Peace river, where the combined streams form in the Slave a swift stream a mile broad, and paused at the beginning of sixteen miles of rapids. Their achievement next day is a good example of what Mackenzie could get out of his men. They began to move at 3 A.M., portaged six times, in all about two and a half miles of often very rough going, and camped at 5.30 P.M., for 'the men and Indians were very much fatigued', having travelled thirty miles. Rain, snow and headwinds now

---

[1] Francois Barrieau, Charles Ducette, Joseph Landry and Pierre Delorme.
[2] John Steinbruick.

evident that these waters emptied themselves into the Hyperborean Sea; and though it was probable that . . . we could not return to Athabaska in the course of the season, I nevertheless, determined to penetrate to the discharge of them.'

In a literal sense he discovered the sea on 12 July, when they reached a 'lake' which was 'covered with ice . . . and no land ahead'. To the west, the Rockies ran from south to north 'further . . . than the edge of the ice'. 'To the Eastward we saw many islands.' The water, of course, was fresh, yet it ebbed and flowed with tide. Mackenzie and his men spent five very hazardous days between the ice-field and the shores of the Arctic Ocean in their bark canoes trying to establish the character of the great semi-circular bay in which they found themselves. They even went whaling in their bark canoes after beluga, 'a very wild and unreflecting enterprise'. They saw many Eskimo camps littered with their possessions, notably whale-bone canoe- and sledge-frames, but could reach no Eskimo to question. Mackenzie knew he was at the sea or a coastal lagoon, but seems to have wanted to get clear of islands and perhaps of the ice-fields in order to get some idea of the way to Bering Strait, for he ran considerable risks in canoeing across the face of the delta. He and his party were very downcast at not having reached the Pacific and being shut in by ice from a seaway to it. On 14 July 1789, while the Paris mob stormed the Bastille, he set up a record post on Whale Island in the Arctic Ocean. He was storm-bound next day, but on the 16th, after a last search for Eskimos among the islands, they 'made for the river, and stemmed the current'.

The journey home during the long hot days after 21 July, when they re-entered the main stream, was a race against winter. They now often had to tow their canoes from the broken stony beaches instead of riding down the current.[1] On their way back they caught echoes of the Europeans on the Pacific—'Bclhoullay Toe, or White Man's Lake'—and even of a river-way to it beyond the mountains (probably the Yukon). One native drew a map for Mackenzie and told him of a 'White Man's Fort'. Mackenzie decided that this was Unalaska and 'made an advantageous proposition to this man to accompany me across the mountains to the other river, but he refused it'. The same Indians told marvellous tales of winged men who 'possessed the extraordinary power of killing with their eyes'.

Just beyond Great Bear river, they investigated the famous burning lignite beds whose smoke is rising to-day. Farther down the river, Mackenzie had picked up a piece of the petroleum wax which has taken modern oil-drillers into the distant arctic river-basin. There was a curious air of tension about the whole return journey almost as far as Great Slave Lake. The English Chief was afraid that Mackenzie would 'obtain such accounts of the other river as would induce me to travel overland to it' and take him along. The reader suspects that the English Chief was right and that, late season or not, Mackenzie would have followed any promising road to the west. He found no such promise, however, so drove hard for home. On 10 September they had their first snow, and 'it froze hard during the night', but they were almost at the mouth of the Peace. On the 12th 'we arrived at Chepewyan fort' and 'concluded this voyage, which had occupied the considerable space of one hundred and two days'. Mackenzie had travelled almost

---

[1] It took fourteen days to go down from Great Slave Lake and thirty-eight days to return.

that he seems to have debated giving up his project, perhaps until as late as the beginning of May. Then he decided to carry it out and sent off his fur brigade and despatches to 'Rory' at Chipewyan with 'a couple of guineas; the rest I take with me to traffic with the Russians'. On 9 May 'the canoe was put into the water; her dimensions were twenty-five feet long within, exclusive of the curves of stem and stern, twenty-six inches hold [depth], and four feet nine inches beam. At the same time she was so light, that two men could carry her on a good road three or four miles without resting. In this slender vessel, we shipped provisions, goods for presents, arms, ammunition, and baggage, to the weight of three thousand pounds, and an equipage of ten people.' These were Mackenzie and his lieu-tenant, Alexander Mackay, six French *voyageurs*, two of whom had been on the trip to the Arctic, and two Indian hunters and interpreters. The canoe of which Mackenzie was so proud proved too light and fragile for the burdens which they tried to press forward against the spring flood of the Peace. It leaked and it was wracked, pierced, patched, re-gummed, flattened out by rapids and almost literally reconstructed before they left it behind them on the Fraser river two months later, after having salvaged from it the many pounds of gum which had kept the wreck water-tight.

The beginning of their journey, through the park-like foothills with their great herds of game, was strenuous, but not impossibly so. On 18 May, however, Mackenzie ignored the warnings of Indian trails and animal tracks and made the mistake of trying to pole, portage and track his canoe and supplies through Peace River Canyon. There the river makes a zigzag of almost continuous falls, cascades and rapids for twenty-two miles, much of the way in a narrow channel between rocky cliffs sometimes 1000 feet high. There ensued six days, first of the imminent danger of losing the canoe and its contents, and then of the extraordinary labour involved in raising the canoe up the wall of the canyon and in cutting a portage path for about ten miles through forest and *bois brûlé* over a high ridge. Mackenzie and the *voyageurs* risked their lives and their goods in the wild river many times on the 19th and 20th, and the 21st, when they climbed the canyon wall carrying the canoe and their goods, was almost as hazardous from falling rocks. It was a very weary and dispirited party which camped beside the quieter upper reaches on the 24th.

After a day's rest from travel, during which they worked on the canoe and cut poles for use where the current was too strong for paddles, they set off through the snowy Rockies for the Forks. Mackenzie had been told about this junction of the Finlay and Parsnip rivers by an old Indian warrior whose information he had come to value so much that he turned up the uninviting Parsnip, although his own judgement (and that of the *voyageurs*) preferred the Finlay. 'The old man . . . had warned me not, on any account, to follow it, as it was soon lost in various branches among the mountains, and that there was no great river that ran in any direction near it, but by following [the Parsnip], he said, we should arrive at a carrying-place to another large river, that did not exceed a day's march, where the inhabitants build houses, and live upon islands.' The old man's information was correct, but at the Forks it had taken twenty-three days to travel 250 miles.

Between 1 June and 4 July, when Mackenzie's party took to the land trails, the expedition almost came

451

to an end. They were in a region of confusing, rapid, shallow rivers, thinly populated by apprehensive, hostile Indians, and with mountains on all sides of them. The forests were thick and tangled and the soil often marshy. There was none of the sense of obvious direction for travel which most North American explorers had had; indeed, Mackenzie soon found that his idea of a river parallel to the Mackenzie emptying into Cook Inlet, could have no reality in the territory where he found himself. To make matters worse, they painfully worked their way in hot weather and amid clouds of mosquitoes and gnats up the Parsnip to the divide and across it to the Fraser, only to learn from the Indians on their way as far south as modern Alexandria, that not only did the river canyon soon become practically impassable, but its southward course to the sea was a very long one. How Mackenzie kept his men together it is difficult to see. After each disaster or disappointment he harangued them and distributed rum, but the impression one receives from his modest account is that his own confidence and determination must have seemed to his subordinates the only certain things in an uncertain world.

Mackenzie decided on 22 June that as 'the distance across the country [is] very short to the Western Ocean', and as the Indians knew of no westward-flowing river, he might have to try it on foot. His great problem was to secure guidance, and he usually used gifts and the promise of his return with an abundance of white man's commodities as a bait. The mountain Indians were somewhat timorous about going to the coast, for the coastal tribes were in the full tide of arrogance and wealth which came from their contact with the Russian and other maritime fur traders. Yet the

452

path was said to be much travelled and 'visible throughout the whole journey', along low passes and often open ground. In his 'distressed and distracted' mood, he knew that 'a retrograde motion could not fail to cool the ardour, slacken the zeal and weaken the confidence of those, who have no greater inducement in the undertaking than to follow the conductor of it', but he finally appealed to his men. To his apparent surprise, they unanimously agreed to go back up the Fraser and take to the overland trail. They faltered somewhat in the face of suspicious behaviour on the part of the natives during the next twelve days, but on 4 July they set out behind their leader with their seventy and ninety pound packs on their backs, having cached the surplus near the junction of the Fraser and the Blackwater. They had also built a new canoe which they left there on a rack in the shade.

The march to the sea took fifteen days, a period which was crowded with novel impressions. They changed guides almost daily, being passed on from one group of Indians to another. The trail was well-beaten, but the warm, moist coastal slope was totally different from anything they had seen before. Its gigantic trees, the scarcity of game, the dependence of the natives' whole pattern of living on fish and particularly on the salmon which once a year almost literally filled the rivers, and the many differences, physical and cultural, between these Indians and those of the interior, kept the Montrealers alert and astonished. Large houses built of half-squared timber, decorated by carvings and paintings, seemed even more remarkable than the huge cedar canoes which were used on the fiords of the sea. There were many evidences of contact with Europeans. Quite near the Fraser, Mackenzie bartered for two children's earrings, halfpence, 'one of his present Majesty, and the other of the State of Massachuset's Bay, coined in 1787'. As they neared the coast, the Indians steadily became more numerous, prosperous and self-assured. Often they were hospitable and friendly, but with such unfamiliar beings as Europeans, their slight fears could quickly excite them to overt hostile acts. The nations on the actual coast proved to be arrogant and quite threatening in their cool independence. Mackenzie had to use all his arts of diplomacy to avoid occasion for attacks, a task the more difficult because, except for sign language, his interpreters had become little more useful to him than his own intelligence and quick ear.

The actual 'discovery' of the Pacific was something of an anticlimax. A misunderstanding with some Indians on 16 July diverted him from the Salmon river which he had just crossed and which would have taken him to the head of Dean Channel. His traverse to the Bella Coola river, however, took him on 17 July to a little group of houses ('Friendly Village') about thirty miles from the sea, whose cordial inhabitants were in some senses the agents of his final success and safe return. They fed the Canadians generously, offered to house them, and next day provided them with canoes in which they proceeded rapidly towards the sea. Mackenzie was amazed at the elaborate fishing weirs and traps which they had constructed in the river, and when his new friends paddled the almost empty canoes over the weirs without shipping any water, he could not contain his admiration. 'I had imagined that the Canadians who accompanied me were the most expert canoe-men in the world, but they are very inferior to these people, as they themselves acknowledged, in conducting those vessels.' They had to pause at another hospitable, impressively substantial 'Great Village', farther down the river, for a feast and a full day's visit, so that it was not until the evening of 19 July, after being regaled at two more villages, that they saw the sea. They had come to an almost empty village and quite casually Mackenzie recorded 'from these houses I could perceive the termination of the river, and its discharge into a narrow arm of the sea'. Had he arrived on 3 June he would have met the ships' boats sent out by Captain George Vancouver in his careful survey of the British Columbia coast! As it was, he met Indians who told of 'Macubah' (Vancouver) and 'Benzins' (Menzies).

Mackenzie's calm was not apathy. The truth was that, until they regained the Friendly Village on 26 July, they went through six days of nerve-racking tension because of the open hostility of the Indians on salt water. Mackenzie shewed remarkable judgement in a long series of explosive situations and only twice had to resort to the seriously meant threat of using his fire-arms. His men were badly frightened and needed repeated reassurances, but he was determined to reach a spot where he could stay long enough to get the necessary day and night observations for latitude and longitude. He finally achieved this on a defendable rock-bluff in Dean Channel, and it was there that with justifiable pride he 'mixed up some vermilion in melted grease, and inscribed, in large characters . . . this brief memorial: "Alexander Mackenzie, from Canada, by land, the twenty-second of July, one thousand seven hundred and ninety-three" '.[1]

We cannot narrate here his exciting experiences on

[1] The inscription is now chiselled in the stone of the same rock.

the shores of the Pacific which he found, nor relate the details of his rapid, well-organised return to the Peace river fort, which he reached on 24 August, with his seven companions alive and uninjured. 'As we rounded a point, and came in view of the Fort, we threw out our flag, and accompanied it with a general discharge of our fire-arms; while the men were in such spirits, and made such an active use of their paddles, that we arrived before the two men whom we left here in the spring, could recover their senses to answer us.' It had taken seventy-five days to reach the rock in Dean Channel and only thirty-three to return.

The great explorer, the first European to have crossed the continent, had finished his work of exploration at thirty. In 1794 he went to Montreal to act as agent for his partners in the field, and there his fame gradually grew. It was not until 1802 that the world really learned of what he had done and the map of North America acquired a superficial completeness. London, Paris, New York and Washington eagerly read the many editions of his travels. Fur traders and geographers followed the trail he had blazed and gradually wove his discoveries, their own and the mariners' charts into a consistent picture of the continent. Alexander Mackenzie and his *voyageurs* were the lineal heirs of two lines of explorers—the sixteenth- and seventeenth-century mariners who tried to sail to the Pacific by the north, and the followers of Champlain who set out in canoes. The North-West Passage had been made, but it was the North-West Passage 'by land'.

NARRATIVES

Alexander Henry's *Travels and Adventures in Canada, etc.* (New York, 1809), has been edited by J. Bain (Toronto, 1901) and M. M. Quaife (Chicago, 1921). Matthew Cocking's *Journal* has been edited by L. J. Burpee in *Royal Society of Canada Proceedings and Transactions*, Third Series, ii (Ottawa, 1908). The remnant of Peter Pond's *Journal*, edited by R. G. Thwaites, is in *Wisconsin Historical Collections*, xviii (Madison, 1908), and H. A. Innis's *Peter Pond* (Toronto, 1930) contains additional material, as does *Public Archives of Canada Report, 1890* (Ottawa, 1891), Note C. Alexander Mackenzie's *Voyages from Montreal through the Continent of North America, etc.* (London, 1801), has been frequently reprinted. A great variety of material is to be found in L. F. R. Masson, *Les Bourgeois de la Compagnie du Nord-Ouest* (2 vols., Quebec, 1889–90). The best guide to the new materials at present being uncovered and published is the review section of the *Canadian Historical Review* (Toronto, 1920 *et seq.*). Useful supplementary narratives and commentaries to what is still rather broken history are H. A. Innis, *The Fur Trade in Canada* (New Haven, 1930); A. S. Morton (ed.), *The Journal of Duncan M'Gillivray* (Toronto, 1929); E. Coues (ed.), *New Light on the Early History of the Greater Northwest* (3 vols., New York, 1897); J. N. Wallace, *The Wintering Partners on Peace River* (Ottawa, 1929); and G. C. Davidson, *The North-West Company* (Berkeley, 1918). The last volume reproduces Pond's maps and the notes which accompanied them (see Appendixes B, F and G).

CHAPTER XXIV

THIRD RESPONSE: LEDYARD, LEWIS AND CLARK

(*Map No. 3, page 482*)

He expects to be kicked around the globe.

JEFFERSON'S REPORT OF HIS NEWS
FROM LEDYARD IN RUSSIA, 1787

His courage was undaunted. His firmness and perseverance yielded to nothing but impossibilities.

JEFFERSON'S ESTIMATE OF MERIWETHER LEWIS

WILLIAM CLARK, December 3rd, 1805
By Land from the U. States in 1804 & 5

CLARK'S RECORD ON A TREE AT TONGUE
POINT NEAR THE MOUTH OF THE COLUMBIA

DURING the first four months of 1783, John Ledyard, an erratic young man of thirty-three from Groton, Connecticut, sat in the home of his uncle at Hartford, writing an account of Captain Cook's third and last voyage, on which he had served as corporal in the marines. Characteristically, he did not finish his story, but his printer was able to fill it out from a hurriedly printed report of the voyage which had been published in London in 1781, and which Ledyard himself had already used to a degree which seriously diminished the originality of his own narrative. While the printer was busy, Ledyard hurried off to New York and Philadelphia to seek financial backing for a voyage to the North-West coast, where he hoped to trade for furs to take to China and then return with Eastern goods. His character and earlier history repay attention.

Thomas Jefferson, who knew Ledyard fairly well, called him, 'a man of genius, of some science, and of fearless courage and enterprise,' but also said: 'unfortunately, he has too much imagination'. The tribute and its qualification do apt justice to a restless, flamboyant enthusiast. As a youth he had first studied law, but had turned from it in the spring of 1772 to train as a missionary to the Indians at lonely Dartmouth College in Hanover, far up the Connecticut river. There he distinguished himself chiefly by his zest for amateur theatricals and by disappearing from college for three and a half months in the summer of 1772, in order to go to travel among the Indians. Next spring he took some college friends to the bank of the Connecticut, where they and he made a dug-out canoe fifty feet long and three feet wide. When the ice broke up in the river, he somehow managed to get his unwieldy craft past falls and rapids down the dangerous spring-freshet to Hartford. He next studied theology with hospitable clergy of Connecticut and Long Island, but when none of them could reward his eloquence with a call to the ministry, he went to sea. After sundry further adventures, he enlisted in the British marines in the first or second year of the American Revolution, and managed to join Captain Cook's expedition before it sailed in July 1776.

Like most of the members of that expedition, he was struck by the wealth of furs on the North Pacific coasts and by the rich traffic which the Russians enjoyed in China. 'We purchased while here [Nootka Sound] about fifteen hundred beaver, besides other skins, but took none but the best, having no thoughts at that time

cooled. Ledyard's position on the outer fringe of the American colony in Paris now became very precarious, but in 1786 a generous and eccentric English acquaintance, Sir James Hall, gave him twenty guineas and secured him a passage in an English vessel lying in the Thames ready to start for the Pacific coast. Ledyard hastily equipped himself with 'two great dogs, an Indian pipe, and a hatchet,' and boarded her. His latest project was to walk overland from Nootka Sound to Virginia. Again his hopes were blasted, for the vessel was 'unfortunately seized by the customhouse'.

London, however, was another capital with another circle of influential men to impress. Ledyard went to work on Sir Joseph Banks and some of his friends, who obligingly raised a small subscription to help him try his last resort, a scheme which Jefferson later claimed that he had suggested to him. This was nothing less than a land journey across northern Europe and Asia to Kamchatka, thence by boat to Nootka Sound and on foot across the continent in 'the latitude of the Missouri' to the United States. Jefferson's share was his application to Catherine the Great for permission for Ledyard to cross Russia, and the Marquis de Lafayette was also pleased to use his influence. Ledyard waited impatiently, but in vain. In December 1786 he left England for Hamburg to start out on foot, permission or no permission. His further adventures, some of which border on the incredible, cannot be detailed here. He got as far east as Yakutsk, passing from one centre of educated foreigners or Russian officials to another, before he was caught by Catherine's order of arrest in February 1788. He was turned loose in Poland (where 'the beautiful daughters of Israel' restored him) after very humiliating treatment, and got to London by drawing on the credit of his English friends. Sir Joseph Banks thereupon offered him employment in crossing Africa from Cairo to the mouth of the Niger for the African Association of London. Ledyard accepted. After visiting friends in Paris, he set out for Egypt. He had engaged a place with a caravan to go out from Cairo, when he was taken ill and died about the end of November 1788.

The versatile Jefferson, who perhaps more than any other American was interested in the expansion of his country to the North-West, seems never to have forgotten Ledyard. He was fond of telling his story, and passed on to his correspondents the news he got in letters from him, as for instance, in Russia 'he says, that having no money, they kick him from place to place, and thus he expects to be kicked around the globe'. In 1788 Ledyard promised him that, if he survived Africa, he would 'go to Kentucky, and endeavour to penetrate westwardly to the South Sea'. After Ledyard's death, Jefferson's interest in the North-West grew rather than diminished, particularly as American maritime trade expanded. The Missouri, recommended repeatedly since Jolliet's day as the best route to the Pacific, had not yet been explored, and the existence of the Columbia seemed to point to a useful combination of the two great rivers. It is probable that Jefferson knew of Peter Pond's representations to Congress, for in 1792 he initiated a subscription by the American Philosophical Society to send M. André Michaux, an accomplished student of American botany, to explore the North-West 'by ascending the Missouri, crossing the Stony Mountains, and descending the nearest river to the Pacific'. Jefferson told him that 'it would seem from the latest maps as if a river called Oregon [Columbia], interlocked with the Missouri for a considerable distance,

463

and entered the Pacific Ocean'. Michaux was recalled from Kentucky by the French government, 'and thus failed the second attempt [after Ledyard] for exploring the region'.

Jefferson became President of the United States in 1801, and as early as January 1803, six months before Washington knew of the Louisiana Purchase, he proposed confidentially to Congress 'the sending an exploring party to trace the Missouri to its source, to cross the highlands and follow the best water communication which offered itself from thence to the Pacific Ocean'. On the grounds of combating British trade and influence with the Indians, he secured approval and a grant of money. He rapidly prepared an expedition to go out under his late private secretary, Captain Meriwether Lewis of Virginia, with Lewis's nominee, William Clark of Kentucky, as second-in-command. While Lewis superintended the preparation of some special equipment, studied surveying and collected the books and maps of his predecessors in the West, Jefferson made two elaborate drafts of instructions for the journey. 'Should you reach the Pacific Ocean,' he wrote, 'inform yourself of the circumstances which may decide whether the furs of those parts may not be collected as advantageously at the head of the Missouri . . . as at Nootka Sound, or any other point of that coast.' Lewis loaded his special equipment on large river-boats at Pittsburg on 30 August, picked up Clark and others at Louisville in mid-September, and the core of the expedition went into winter quarters opposite the mouth of the Missouri before the end of the year.

It is impossible not to feel that the Lewis and Clark expedition opened a new era in North American exploration. It was quite unlike the daring dashes of the French and the Canadians or the grand cavalry marches of the Spaniards. Its success was a triumph of the elaborate co-ordination of geographical and technical knowledge and of the expenditure of public money without interest in immediate material return. It could afford to build great river barges to carry its heavy equipment from Pittsburg down the Ohio and up the Mississippi and Missouri to the Mandans. It soberly spent the full open season of 1804 going from the mouth of the Missouri to its westward bend, and at every serious barrier it paused long enough for complete reconnaissance and careful organisation of the passage. Of course, it did not bring to an end the heroic period of North American exploration. Its own vicissitudes after it reached the Rockies would completely contradict that charge, and individuals or small groups have continued to make hazardous journeys in the wilds of North America down to our own day. Yet since the beginning of the nineteenth century, while some men continued to rival the endurance and courage of their predecessors in almost foolhardy enterprises, a steadily increasing number quite properly drew upon the ever more useful technical devices which human ingenuity provided to make their ventures less hazardous.

Upper Louisiana was transferred from France to the United States at St. Louis on 10 March 1804, and on 14 May the three river vessels used by Lewis and Clark started up the Missouri. The party reached the Mandans[1] on 27 October, after a laborious journey up the river, during which they held councils with the Indians to pave the way for American penetration and

[1] The villages of domed timber and sod huts on the Missouri, discovered by La Vérendrye, see pp. 363-7.

trade. They also met *voyageurs* from The Illinois and Canadian traders who were able to give them useful information. During the long winter at the Mandans, the leaders carefully provided themselves with the lighter equipment necessary for faster travel westwards in 1805. Six dug-out cottonwood canoes were built, but when they proved insufficient, two of the pirogues[1] were put in good repair to supplement them. The supplies were repacked and the iron frame for a buffalo-hide boat[2] was put in such shape as 'will enable us to prepare it in the course of a few hours'. They expected to reach the Rockies about 100 miles west of the Great Falls, and there to meet the Snake or Shoshone Indians, who possessed 'large quantities of horses'. By means of these horses, 'the transportation of our baggage will be rendered easy and expeditious over land, from the Missouri to the Columbia river'. Surplus supplies, specimens, gifts for the President and careful despatches were entrusted to sixteen men who took the keel-boat back down the Missouri, leaving on 7 April 1805.

The easy assurance of Lewis and Clark as to the geography of their further route was built upon what seemed to them good information. Ever since the days of the Vérendryes, there had been contact between the Winnipeg basin and the Missouri, a connection which grew steadily more intimate in the last quarter of the eighteenth century as Spanish, French, American, Canadian and even Hudson Bay traders invaded the upper Mississippi, the Winnipeg basin, the Red river and the upper Missouri. Lewis and Clark talked with Montrealers, both English and French; with *voyageurs*

[1] Flat-bottomed river-boats.
[2] This was finally abandoned after having been carried from the mouth of the Shenandoah to the Great Falls of the Missouri.

and *métis* from The Illinois or the Canadian West, some of whom normally lived among the Missouri Indians;[1] and by a piece of good luck which they were quick to realise and careful to protect, they were able to hire at the Mandans a Montrealer named Toussaint Charbonneau, who had in 1804 bought a Shoshone wife, Sacajawea, from the Minnetarees[2] among whom he lived on the Knife river.

Sacajawea almost deserves the credit of the first Missouri-Columbia-Pacific traverse. A remarkable intelligence and personality in her own right, she happened also to come from, and know the way to, the much-used Lemhi pass in the Rockies between the Missouri and the Columbia. She had accompanied her mountain clan on their annual buffalo-hunt in the Missouri valley five years before and had been captured by the Minnetarees near the Three Forks of the Missouri. Charbonneau, who was himself a somewhat inept fellow, had realised what an excellent recommendation she would be for his own employment. He brought her to Lewis and Clark, and he and she were able to give almost explicit information about the route to be pursued. When the up-river expedition set off on 9 April 1805, it consisted of Lewis and Clark, twenty-six soldiers or river-men (three of whom were Illinois or Canadian *voyageurs*), Clark's 'black servant York' (who was the recipient of much amorous favour from the Indian women), Georges Drouillard (a French hunter from St. Louis), Toussaint Charbonneau, Sacajawea, and on her back, her papoose and the pet of the party, Jean-Baptiste Charbonneau, born 11 February 1805. Clark took a great interest in the child, giving him his

[1] François Antoine Larocque was preparing to make the first recorded exploration of the Yellowstone. [2] Hidatsas.

southern branch ahead of them because they could not 'reasonably hope by going further to the northward to find between this place and the Saskatchewan' a navigable river-road to the Rockies.

Lewis had the honour of discovering the Great Falls on 13 June because he had gone ahead on foot to reconnoitre and to lay up supplies of game for the entry into the mountains. 'His ears were saluted with the agreeable sound of a fall of water, and as he advanced a spray . . . arose above the plain like a column of smoke.' 'Seating himself on some rocks under the centre of the falls, [he] enjoyed the sublime spectacle of this stupendous object which since the creation had been lavishing its magnificence upon the desert unknown to civilization.'[1] While the men hunted and fished and dried meat, Lewis busied himself in investigating the long series of falls, rapids and cascades, in order to plan a portage route. Clark and the men laboriously worked one pirogue and the canoes against the swift current for three days until they reached a landing-place quite close to the last fall. Sacajawea had been so seriously ill for about a week that they were afraid she would die, but 'she now found great relief from the mineral water of the sulphur spring' close by the lowest fall. The Great Falls had heartened them by convincing them that they were on the true Missouri. The sulphur spring now relieved their apprehensions of losing their invaluable guide.

They spent the period from 16 June to 15 July in getting around the ten miles of rapids and in preparing to go on. Their portage was seventeen miles long and they seem still to have had a very large amount of bag-

---

[1] The Falls owed their beauty to their breadth (300 yards) and variety, rather than to their height (80 feet).

gage and equipment, in spite of having made two caches *en route*. They made cart-wheels from cross-sections of 'a cottonwood tree about twenty-two inches in diameter' and used the mast of the pirogue to make two axles. They were seriously embarrassed by grizzlies and rattlesnakes, for these dangerous animals were 'reluctant to yield their dominion over the neighborhood' because of the abundance of game. Buffalo, for instance, in crowding down steep gullies to the water's edge, were so frequently pushed into the rushing river that the travellers saw 'ten or a dozen disappear over the falls in a few minutes'. While the baggage and boats were being taken across the portage, the hunters prepared hundreds of pounds of dried meat, and dressed skins for the clothing and moccasins which were so quickly torn to shreds by the prickly-pear. A great deal of time and effort was spent uselessly on assembling the collapsible boat. As the skins composing it shrank, the needle-holes opened into rents. Their scheme for making tar failed, and the substitute of mixed charcoal, beeswax and buffalo-tallow was quite inadequate. So they cached its frame at the end of the portage, a curious relic of human hopes, and built two dug-outs to replace it.

After passing the Great Falls, they were in Shoshone country, known to Sacajawea and containing the Indians upon whose friendship and horses their further success would depend. A broad Indian trail ran along roughly parallel to the left bank, which Clark and three men followed while Lewis remained with the canoes. Presumably the Indians knew of their presence, for they saw smokes and other signs of their recent presence, but they reached the Three Forks on 25 and 27 July without having seen an Indian in the flesh. Clark saw a

471

horse on the 24th, but could not catch it. They could hardly be mistaken on sight for raiding Blackfeet, for they were not mounted, but the sound of their guns made the Shoshones believe that their old enemies were upon them, and alarm smokes went up ahead of them in the valley. Sacajawea's presence was a kind of peaceful warrant, for 'no woman ever accompanies a war party'. The Three Forks gave them short pause, because the south-west branch[1] (the Jefferson) seemed the correct course to everyone. Indeed on the day after they passed the Forks (28 July), Sacajawea informed them that they were 'encamped on the precise spot where her country-men, the Snake Indians, had their huts five years ago', when she was captured.

Even before they reached the Three Forks, it was be-coming difficult to drive or drag the dug-outs up the river, but it became even more difficult on the shallow, brawling Jefferson, Lewis put Clark (who had been ill) in charge of the river party, while he on land did his best to establish contact with the Shoshones. Trails were lacking, beaver meadows frequent, and the valley twisted confusingly, so that both parties found that most exhausting efforts advanced them very slowly. Lewis reached Shoshone Cove on 10 August, but Clark's boats did not manage it until the 17th, having taken eighteen days to travel about 150 miles. The two leaders became very apprehensive over their slow pro-gress and over the alarming inroads into their food re-serves, as the supply of game decreased.

Lewis had been following some horse-tracks near Shoshone Cove, where the Jefferson divided, and these directed him up the right-hand branch. It was hard to

---

[1] They named the middle one after Madison and the eastern one after Gallatin.

472

locate any trail in such bare country, so that he proceeded up the creek with a scout ahead to right and left to pick up any neighbouring road. This arrangement frightened a Shoshone warrior whom they saw on 11 August, and Lewis feared that his chance of establishing contact was lost. He and his men went on, however, flying the American flag on a long pole, and on the morning of 12 August they 'met a large plain Indian road', which led them by an easy gradient to the Lemhi pass. As they climbed, the creek 'so greatly diminished in width that one of the men in a fit of enthusiasm, with one foot on each side of the river, thanked God that he had lived to bestride the Missouri'. The continental divide was easily recognisable. Having crossed it, they 'reached a handsome bold creek . . . running to the westward' and the hot, dusty little group 'stopped to taste for the first time the waters of the Columbia'.[1]

As they went on next day, they saw more Indians, the second group of whom left an old woman and a girl behind when they fled. Lewis reassured this couple by gifts and by 'stripping up his shirt sleeve to prove that he was a white man', so that they led him towards their camp. A group of sixty mounted warriors rushed to meet them and were in turn conciliated by the women. The three chiefs promptly embraced Lewis, saying in their language 'I am much rejoiced'. Then 'the whole body of warriors came forward, and our men received the caresses, and no small share of the grease and paint of their new friends'. In spite of being in almost desperate straits for food, the Shoshones did their best to entertain the four Americans. One of them gave Lewis a piece of roasted salmon and thus 'perfectly satisfied him that he was now on the waters of the Pacific'.

[1] Their creek was a tributary of the Salmon river in the Columbia system.

473

The next three days were tense and dramatic. The Shoshone chief, Cameahwait, fell under Lewis' influence, but his men were afraid that the whites were inveigling them into an ambush near Shoshone Cove prepared by their great enemies, the Minnetarees or the Blackfeet. Lewis used every possible resource to still their fears, but Clark's slow progress to join him made his position most precarious. Drouillard helped a good deal by his prowess as a hunter and by his generosity with the kill. Lewis held out the prospect of seeing Sacajawea again and of the marvel of 'a man perfectly black, whose hair was short and curled'. Finally, he and his men not only changed garments with the Shoshones, but entrusted their guns to them as well.

On the morning of 17 August, Clark and Charbonneau and Sacajawea went ahead of the boat party on foot, and when the Shoshone scouts saw them, the tension came to an end. Sacajawea, greatly excited, began 'to dance and show every mark of the most extravagant joy . . . suckling her fingers . . . to indicate that they were of her native tribe'. A Shoshone woman, who had escaped from the Minnetarees after capture with Sacajawea, 'made her way through the crowd towards Sacajawea, and recognizing each other, they embraced with the most tender affection'. When the Indians called for a council and a peace-smoke, 'Sacajawea was sent for; she came into the tent, sat down, and was beginning to interpret, when in the person of Cameahwait she recognized her brother: she instantly jumped up, and ran and embraced him, throwing over him her blanket and weeping profusely: the chief himself was moved, though not in the same degree'. No Indian leader could publicly give way to his emotions.

The salmon were leaving the mountain streams at

this season, thus forcing the Shoshones and their neighbours to their annual venture down to the Missouri and
the buffalo-plains below the Three Forks, where, almost
unprovided with fire-arms, they risked the vicious
attacks of Blackfeet and Minnetarees. The arrival of
the large party of whites with their skilful hunters and
tempting goods upset the usual schedule a little, but
Lewis and Clark were as anxious to go west to the Pacific
as the Shoshones to go east to the buffalo herds. Clark
went off on 18 August with eleven men equipped with
tools so as to make canoes on the Columbia if he found
it navigable. Charbonneau and Sacajawea went with
him to bring back more horses from the Shoshone
village. Lewis and the rest of the men remained on
the Jefferson to cache the heavy equipment, sink the
boats in the river, make pack-saddles and bargain for
horses.

Clark was deeply disappointed to learn from his own
laborious investigations in the mountains and from long
conversations with the Shoshones that he had arrived in
a valley whose river (the Salmon) was not only not navigable, but did not provide a way out even for men and
pack-horses. 'The river was so completely hemmed in
by the high rocks, that there was no possibility of
travelling along the shore.' Its canyon was full of sharp
rocks and it descended in a series of precipitous rapids
and falls. He heard of ways to Spanish California which
had been travelled by some Shoshones, but their difficulty seemed prohibitive.[1] Cameahwait had also heard
of the maritime traders at the Columbia, but indicated
that the way to them was impassable. Clark was a very
shrewd questioner and by a process of elimination he

---

[1] They possessed mules, which they did not breed themselves, but traded
for with, or stole from, the Spaniards. These were worth two horses.

gradually brought Cameahwait and an old Shoshone, 'who was said to know more of their geography to the north than any other person', to admit that there was a pass northwards out of the Salmon valley 'to the great river to the north'. Quite obviously, Cameahwait had not wanted his Indian neighbours to the north to make contact with the whites. He had envisaged his own tribe in the future, at the terminus of a road from the east, along which the whites would bring the goods which would deliver the Shoshones from the menace of their plains enemies and raise them to eminence among the mountain tribes.

The two parties were reunited in the Salmon valley on 29 August and started for the northern pass next day, guided by the old Shoshone and equipped with about thirty horses and a mule. The road turned out to be almost non-existent [1] and was very trying to horses and men, but the pass conducted them on 4 September into the Bitter Root valley, through which ran 'the great Indian road to the waters of the Missouri', four days away near the Three Forks. The Indians gathered there for the annual descent to the buffalo plains were friendly and abundantly supplied with horses. The whites therefore traded for more horses and some colts. Game had proved to be exceedingly scarce in the mountains. Horse-meat would be a convenient precaution against starvation. At the foot of the Lolo pass, their hunters brought in three Nez Percé or Flathead Indians,[2] who told them about the way to the Columbia and the traders at the sea. One of them volunteered to guide them, but became worried about his horses and left them to their loyal old Shoshone guide. Fortu-

---

[1] Because the Shoshones used the Lemhi pass.
[2] Heard of by La France two generations earlier, see p. 384.

nately the road up the Lolo pass was 'plain and good', so they set off up it on 12 September. The next ten days were probably their severest test. The Shoshone was not familiar with the Indian trail to the coast, which ran due west through the Bitter Root mountains along the southern slope of a divide between two branches of the Clearwater river. The country was very broken and, once off the trail, progress for men and horses was difficult and hazardous. Once a snow-storm obliterated the road. They could not find or kill sufficient game, so that they had to live on 'portable soup', horse-meat and the last of their bear oil. The men grew thin, some had dysentery and there were signs of scurvy among them. On 17 September Clark and six hunters were sent ahead to scout and collect food. Next day he 'was rejoiced on discovering far off an extensive plain', which he reached on the 20th and found to contain villages of hospitable Nez Percés. Lewis and the rest of the party joined him there on the 22nd.

The whole party remained in the Clearwater valley until 7 October. They were badly run-down and not only found the soft, humid air of the Pacific coast very relaxing, but discovered that the diet of salmon, roots and bulbs, which was customary among the Nez Percés, wrought havoc with their digestions. Gradually they recuperated, but it is recorded that they followed the Indian technique of burning out the interiors of the five long cedar dug-outs which they built instead of expending the effort to hollow them with tools. They made friends with two chiefs, Twisted-Hair and Tetoh, who made excellent maps for them and volunteered to take them to the sea. The size of the Lewis and Clark party, as compared with Mackenzie's for instance, protected them from hostility; indeed, the Indians tried to

477

avert their displeasure by friendliness and by rendering services for very small returns. Lewis and Clark were able to brand their horses and leave them with the Nez Percés until their return from the sea, a contract which was faithfully performed.

The journey down the Clearwater river began on 7 October. Next day the two Nez Percé chiefs joined them, whereupon their old Shoshone and his son ran away. The white leaders wanted to catch him in order to pay for his services, but Twisted-Hair explained 'very frankly, that his nation, the Chopunnish, would take from the old man any presents that he might have on passing their camp', so they let him go. At intervals along the river-banks, the Indians were busy catching and drying the salmon which were their main sustenance. The whites, on the other hand, found fish and roots a poor diet, so 'made an experiment to vary our food by purchasing a few dogs, and having been accustomed to horse-flesh, felt no disrelish to this new dish'. They continued this practice as they went down the river. They entered the Snake river on 10 October, and on the 16th reached the Columbia without remarkable incident except for the rapids which occurred at intervals in their journey and occasionally damaged their dug-outs. Their chieftain guides and the skilful Sacajawea ensured them a good reception from the natives by sending tidings ahead. Lewis and Clark carefully reinforced their welcome by presents and medals, and entertained their new friends with tobacco and tunes on their violins. They found the Columbia filled with salmon and almost continuously bordered by groups of salmon-fishers.

Below the junction of the Snake and Columbia rivers, the combined stream 'widens to the space of from one to three miles, including the islands'. This presage of an easy voyage to the sea was not fulfilled, however, for on 22 October they came to the beginning of the river-pass through the Cascade Mountains. Here volcanic rocks and old lava flows played strange tricks with the great river, sometimes confining it between high walls, sometimes running shelves across its flow and often converting the stream into rapids, cascades and falls. The white party proved to be good river-men, shooting some rapids, portaging around others and sometimes carrying their goods while the dug-outs were carefully let down the rapids at the end of long elk-hide ropes. On one occasion they shot a rapid where the whole Columbia passed through a channel only forty-five yards wide, 'to the astonishment of all the Indians . . . who now collected to see us from the top of the rock'. Near the mountain passage they found Indians wearing European blankets and clothing, and their chieftain guides left them on 25 October, when they were about half-way through the long passage, on the plea that 'they could not understand the language of the people below the falls'. At this point there was a definite suggestion of trouble ahead, but fortunately it did not materialise in spite of the many evidences (notably brass tea-kettles) of abundant contact with the maritime traders. Indeed, Lewis and Clark, like Mackenzie twelve years before, found some natives so hospitable that they too 'gave to the place the name of Friendly Village'.

They reached the last river obstacle, the three miles or so of the Cascades, on 30 October. Here, as they carried and let down their dug-outs during the next two days, they saw their first sea-otters. They were at tidewater at last, but the record of their first voyaging on it on 2 November betrays no great emotion. They had set out to travel by the Missouri and the Columbia to the Pacific, and they had done so, after many vicissitudes, but along the course which Jefferson had projected for them. They were not surprised or excited. Their chief emotion was of gratitude for the abundant timber. All down the Columbia they had suffered from the lack of it and they were tired of making fires from willow twigs. They now enjoyed the opening prospect of the great tidal estuary and followed it contentedly towards the open sea.

But it was November on the North Pacific coast. On the 3rd they were held up 'by a fog so thick that a man could not be discerned at a distance of fifty steps'. A day or two later, cold rains began and they had more fogs. The Indians were not overtly hostile, but they were embarrassingly avaricious and thieving. Perhaps the worst problem was that of the fleas which infested every village and fish-rack, and which the men found it impossible to get rid of. The reader of the narratives has the impression of a company of tired men, ill-clad, monotonously fed, a little apathetic now about their mission and anxious to go into winter quarters of their own. They were almost at the limit of their endurance. They wanted to stop. They wanted the hunters to go out and bring in meat instead of everlasting salmon or tantalisingly small quantities of game-birds. On 7 November 'the fog cleared off' and they thought they saw the sea, 'that ocean, the object of all our labours, the reward of all our anxieties'. It seems almost certain that they were mistaken, although they may have heard, as they thought they did, 'the distant roar of the breakers'. The estuary was now so wide and its waters so salty that to the miseries caused by rain and tide were added the risks from the high waves beaten up by the ocean gales, sea-sickness, hunger, thirst and cold. It was not until 15 November that they made a sheltered camp on the north shore from which they could look across the river-mouth bar at the veritable Pacific. 'Our camp is in full view of the ocean.'

Wisely they did not attempt to spend the winter there, but went back to find a region where their hunters could get some elk. Lewis found such a spot, 'in a thick grove of lofty pines', a short way up a river which flowed into the estuary from the south, and there, on 8 December, they began to make the winter quarters known as Fort Clatsop. Sick and tired as the men were, the mere prospect of timber for building and fires, and of elk to yield juicy meat, crackling fat and rich marrow-bones seemed to revive their energies. They worked hard in the almost constant rain, hail or snow. The hut walls were up by the 14th, and the meat-house was roofed by the 16th. Their stores were wet, their clothes were rotting and their meat began to spoil in spite of 'a constant smoke under it'. On Christmas eve they had to go back to dried, pulverised fish for diet, but 'still continued working and at last moved into our huts'.

We shall leave them with their Christmas celebration. 'We were awaked at daylight by a discharge of firearms, which was followed by a song from the men, as a compliment to us on the return of Christmas.' The leaders could respond only by distributing half of the remaining tobacco to the smokers and handkerchiefs to the others. 'The remainder of the day was passed in good spirits, though there was nothing in our situation to excite much gaiety. The rain confined us to the house, and our only luxuries in honour of the season, were some poor elk, so much spoiled that we eat it through mere necessity, a few roots, and some spoiled, pounded fish.' They had not even salt for seasoning, and they had not got rid of the fleas. But they pulled through that winter, and a year later their woes were to be forgotten when Lewis and Clark led back their party, intact but for one man, after three years' absence, to be the first great heroes of exploration in Louisiana on behalf of the young United States. Their enterprise had revealed the last great natural pathway across the North American continent.

NARRATIVES

John Ledyard's *A Journal of Captain Cook's Last Voyage to the Pacific Ocean* was printed in Hartford in 1783. Thomas Jefferson's comments on Ledyard are scattered through his correspondence and drawn into the ideas of Western exploration in his essay on Meriwether Lewis, which is in the standard editions of his *Writings*. Jared Sparks, *The Life of John Ledyard* (Cambridge, Mass., 1828), consists largely of selections from his journals and correspondence. In 1810 and 1811, Nicholas Biddle, with the assistance of Clark and George Shannon, prepared from the original journals of Lewis, Clark, Ordway, Gass and others what remains the best account of the Missouri-Pacific expedition. Published in 1814, under the supervision of Paul Allen in Philadelphia, the Biddle edition has been many times reprinted, notably with elaborate critical apparatus from the original journals by E. Coues as *History of the Lewis and Clark Expedition* (3 vols. and atlas, New York, 1893). R. G. Thwaites edited meticulously *The Original Journals of Lewis and Clark* (7 vols. and atlas, New York, 1904–5). R. G. Hebard's *Sacajawea* (Glendale, Cal., 1933) contains all the available materials. L. F. R. Masson (see under Chapter XXIII) publishes the accounts of the Canadians in the Missouri country.

EPILOGUE

MANY a small boy in modern North America, appropriately nurtured on stories of the pioneers, when given his first experience of rough, uncultivated country-side, has startled his companion by asking: 'Do you suppose a white man ever trod here before?' The truthful answer must nearly always be a regretful affirmative. Although North America is so large and, in spite of its huge cities, so thinly populated, man's activities during the last century and a quarter have left little of its surface unexplored. Only in the most literal sense of the actual ground covered by small feet could one satisfy the longing of a youngster of to-day to be a pioneer in his own right.

The explorations which have been described in this book were sufficient to indicate only the general character of the North American continent, its coasts and the great gulf entries to the land-mass, its connected water-ways of lakes and rivers, the more obvious passes through its mountain ranges, and the convenient overland routes from place to place across its plains. Enormous areas remained unrevealed. The great Labrador peninsula between Hudson Bay and the Atlantic, the whole region north-east of Hearne's travels in the barrens, the block of mountains and desert between the head-waters of the Missouri and the Platte and the Pacific coast, the Yukon basin and inland Alaska, all still awaited the coming of the white man.

stimulating agent of exploration. The caterpillar tractor, travelling on ice-roads or even through mere clearings in the woods, encouraged lumbermen and miners to establish bases in regions which would otherwise have been forbidding. The lone prospector in the north took cans of gasoline over the winter snow and ice to caches in the lake country so that in the summer he could range farther with the assistance of the little portable motor which he fastened to his canoe. Then, suddenly, these devices were outstripped by the aeroplane. Equipped with pontoons or wheels in summer and with skis and a protective engine-housing in winter, the plane began to take men to all the untravelled sections of the continent. Even in the southwestern mountains there were lakes on which to land, and the water-margins of ice-covered Dubawnt Lake were called upon to provide run-ways for the planes. In the southern deserts and in the mountains the inextinguishable prospector with his *burros* or his packhorses, in the north his brother with dog-team or canoe, looked up at the sound of an engine to see the aeroplane crossing in a moment expanses which would cost him days and perhaps, even nowadays, his life. Sometimes he called the flier lucky and sometimes he cursed him, but he quickly came to depend on him and on the knowledge he so easily acquired. There may still be isolated regions in North America which have not been trodden by the white man, but the last inaccessible acres are yielding up their secrets to the aviator and to his camera's eye.

INDEX

Abenaki Indians, 190, 314
Abitibi, Lake, 289, 306
Acadia, 155-6, 270; conceded to the Jesuits, 183; raids on, 259; returned to France, 184
Accault, Michel, 350
Acla, 30-31
Agua Caliente, 420
Aguilar, Jerónimo de, 27, 48
Alabama, river, 101, 318
Alaminos, Antón de, 35, 36, 48
Alarcón, Hernando de, 89, 93, 95
Alaska, 483
Albanel, Father, 252, 285 *sqq.*, 306
Albany (Hudson), 302, 308 *sqq.*, 314, 430-31
Albany, river, 233, 290, 360, 382
Alfonse, Jean, 134-5, 191, 200, 343
Algonquin tribe, 119, 152, 157, 159, 163-5, 172, 220
Alleghany, river, 246, 300, 309
Allen, Paul, 482
Allouez, Father Claude Jean, 242 *sqq.*, 249; narratives of, 258
Allumette, Lake, 159, 162
Altar Valley, 407, 416 *sqq.*
Alvarado, Luis Moscoso de, 83, 92
Alvarado, Pedro de, 34, 37, 38, 62, 65, 85, 93
Alvord, C. W., 258, 283
America, introduction of horses to, 97; North, *see* North America; sequence of cultures in, 41
Andagoya, Pascual de, 39
Andastes Indians, 173, 175, 178, 179
Angikuni Lake, 393
Anguel, Antoine du Gay, 350
Anian, Strait of, 4, 68, 76, 78, 89-90, 94, 100, 191, 200, 342, 383, 399, 403 *sqq.*, 414
Ann, Cape, 268
Annapolis Royal, 234
Anticosti, 119, 121-2

Antilia, *see* Seven Cities
Anza, Juan Bautista de (Governor of New Mexico), 401, 416 *sqq.*, 427-8
Apaches, 338, 340, 377, 408, 417
Appalache, 71, 74, 75, 80
Appalachian Mountains, 261-2, 271 *sqq.*, 309 *sqq.*, 378-9
Appomattox, river, 273
Argenson, Governor, 230, 234
Arias, Pedro, *see* Avila
Arikaras, 364
Arizona, 98; Escalante's journey through, 426
Arkansas, river, 80, 82, 83, 90, 255, 313, 316-19, 328, 334, 337, 341 *sqq.*
Armada, defeat of the, 103
Arthur, Gabriel, 279 *sqq.*, 281
Artillery Lake, 395
Asher, G. M., 217
Assenipoualaks, 295, 350
Assiniboine Indians, 292, 294-5, 350, 352, 360, 364-7, 384 *sqq.*, 468; river, 295, 366, 380
Athabaska, 434; Lake, 432, 436, 441; river, 432
Athapaskans, 383, 388, 432
Atrato, river, 23-5
Aulneau, Father Jean, 365, 374
Avila, Alonzo de, 37
Ávila, Gil Gonzalez de, 66
Ávila, Pedro Arias de, 29, 30, 35, 39, 65-6
Ayala, Pedro de, 108
Ayer, Mrs. E. E., 345
Ayllón, Lucas Vázquez de, 32, 130
Aztecs, characteristics of, 43-4; conquest of the, 51, 58; culture of the, 41-2; religion of, 46; revolt against Cortés, 61, 63; works of art, 53, 59

Babcock, W. H., 19
Baffin Bay, 199, 203-4; Island, 201

487

32